GREATER ATLANTA

GREATER ATLANTA

Black Satire after Obama

Edited by Derek C. Maus
and James J. Donahue

University Press of Mississippi / Jackson

The University Press of Mississippi is the scholarly publishing agency of
the Mississippi Institutions of Higher Learning: Alcorn State University,
Delta State University, Jackson State University, Mississippi State University,
Mississippi University for Women, Mississippi Valley State University,
University of Mississippi, and University of Southern Mississippi.

www.upress.state.ms.us

The University Press of Mississippi is a member
of the Association of University Presses.

Any discriminatory or derogatory language or hate speech
regarding race, ethnicity, religion, sex, gender, class, national origin,
age, or disability that has been retained or appears in elided form
is in no way an endorsement of the use of such language
outside a scholarly context.

Copyright © 2024 by University Press of Mississippi
All rights reserved
Manufactured in the United States of America

∞

Library of Congress Cataloging-in-Publication Data

Names: Maus, Derek C., editor. | Donahue, James J., 1974– editor.
Title: Greater Atlanta : Black satire after Obama / Derek C. Maus,
James J. Donahue.
Description: Jackson : University Press of Mississippi, 2024. |
Includes bibliographical references and index.
Identifiers: LCCN 2023058434 (print) | LCCN 2023058435 (ebook) |
ISBN 9781496850553 (hardback) | ISBN 9781496850560 (trade paperback) |
ISBN 9781496850577 (epub) | ISBN 9781496850584 (epub) |
ISBN 9781496850591 (pdf) | ISBN 9781496850607 (pdf)
Subjects: LCSH: Atlanta (Television program) | African Americans in mass media. |
African Americans—Race identity. | Satire, American—History and criticism. |
African Americans in literature. | African Americans in motion pictures. |
African Americans in popular culture. | African Americans—Intellectual life.
Classification: LCC P94.5.A372 U567 2024 (print) |
LCC P94.5.A372 (ebook) | DDC 700/.41—dc23/eng/20240201
LC record available at https://lccn.loc.gov/2023058434
LC ebook record available at https://lccn.loc.gov/2023058435

British Library Cataloging-in-Publication Data available

Derek C. Maus: *For Stephanie and Oscar*

James J. Donahue: *For Kristen, Reid, Jacob, and Fletcher*

CONTENTS

"I've Done Told You, These Backhoes Ain't Loyal!":
Atlanta and the State of Black Satire after Obama 3
Derek C. Maus

Downtown Atlanta

On the Perils of Enjoying One's Wound:
Atlanta and Contemporary African American Satire 19
Derek Conrad Murray

Whispering Sexuality: Queer Erasure and Black Satirical Disruption 35
GerShun Avilez

Satirizing Satire Itself: *Atlanta*'s Appropriation Aesthetic
and the Blackening of US Civil Society 49
John Brooks

Awkwardness and Black Millennial Satire in *Insecure* and *Atlanta* 63
Erica-Brittany Horhn and Derek C. Maus

Forsyth County

White (Al)lies: Eating the Other in *Atlanta* and Jordan Peele's *Get Out* 81
Emily Ruth Rutter

Racial Self-Identification in *Atlanta* and Danzy Senna's *New People* 94
Alexandra Glavanakova

"Know Thyself": Education and Identity Fashioning
in *Atlanta* and *Dear White People* 108
Derek DiMatteo

Lake Lanier

Canines and Tricksters in *Atlanta* 125
Matthias Klestil

"That's You": Reflections on Human-Animal Doublings
in *Atlanta*'s Televisual Satire. 139
Sarah O'Brien

DeKalb County

"You Chose Black": *Atlanta*'s Gendered Politics
of Black Respectability and Representation 155
Keyana Parks

Atlanta and the Instability of Racial Performance 171
Tikenya Foster-Singletary

"What the Hell Is Muckin'?": Mistranslation
and Linguistic Pessimism in *Atlanta*. .185
Lola Boorman

Ironic Minstrelsies of Affect in *Atlanta* .199
Phillip James Martinez Cortes

"It's a Simulation, Van": *Atlanta*, *The Twilight Zone*,
and the Uncanniness of Black Womanhood 212
Danielle Fuentes Morgan

East Point/College Park

Becoming Inhuman: Donald Glover, Hiro Murai,
and the Self-Alienation of Celebrity 227
Kinohi Nishikawa

Streets on Locke: The Volition of *Atlanta* 243
Thomas Britt

Hartsfield-Jackson International Airport

Playing on the Border: Racial Ambiguity, Passing, and
Possibility in *Atlanta* and Charles Yu's *Interior Chinatown* 261
Abigail Jinju Lee

Composite Works Cited 277

About the Contributors 291

Index 295

GREATER ATLANTA

"I'VE DONE TOLD YOU, THESE BACKHOES AIN'T LOYAL!"

Atlanta and the State of Black Satire after Obama

DEREK C. MAUS

WHY "AFTER OBAMA"?

A decade has passed since the publication of *Post-Soul Satire: Black Identity after Civil Rights*, and what a ride it has been! Stimulated by a forthright reckoning of the nation's history, the postracial utopia that innumerable commentators predicted after Barack Obama's election as president continued unfolding. Previously esoteric academic concepts like critical race theory inspired nuanced and civil discussions across previously unbridgeable cultural divides, particularly about the effects of race and ethnicity on law enforcement, education, and voting rights. Likewise, the political and social capital obtained through bigoted demagoguery diminished steadily, as compellingly demonstrated by the rational, unified, and wholly equitable response to the COVID-19 pandemic. The nation has never so thoroughly reflected its motto of "*E pluribus unum*"!

I could go on, but this likely suffices to elicit the intended response, namely that the years 2014 to 2024 were in many ways *more* absurd than this fantastical synopsis. Although none of the individual adversities of recent years are unprecedented—lethal pandemics, regional wars, (neo)fascist politicians, emboldened white-supremacist movements, mass migrations, and drug-abuse crises are not new phenomena—their concurrent and interconnected nature this time around makes Shepard Fairey's iconic "Hope" poster from Obama's 2008 presidential campaign seem like an ancient relic. These have been, as the apocryphally "Chinese" curse puts it, *interesting* times, especially for people of color and other marginalized groups.

Of course, this does not transform the Obama presidency into a golden age, the benefits of comparative hindsight notwithstanding. Todd C. Shaw, Robert A. Brown, and Joseph P. McCormick II retroactively observe that "neither the current American racial order nor the nature of Obama's presidency and leadership style have resulted in an American chief executive able and/or willing to freely, as well as more fully, advance the substantive political interests of African American/Black communities" (4). They argue that even though "he had an extraordinary presidency that ushered in a number of progressive reforms and a notable recovery of a postrecession economy . . . , Obama's identification with and connection to Black/African American communities were still delimited by him being president of a center-right, majority-White nation" (Shaw et al. 5). Kimberlé Williams Crenshaw laments Obama's reticence in confronting toxic cultural narratives: "Obama proved to be far more than a political Sphinx to which postracialism became attached. Obama's campaign and subsequent presidency reflected an acute awareness about racial performance. His navigation through and around existing racial scripts came to signify postracialism by virtue of what he affirmed and what he omitted, what he drew attention to and what he obscured" ("How Colorblindness" 132). In his biography of Obama, Burton I. Kaufman asserts:

> [He] sought to reform existing institutions rather than uproot them. This was why so many of those who voted for him in 2008 and even in 2012 were disappointed by the outcome of his administration and turned in 2016, not to someone who was likely to carry on his legacy but to one who gave every sign, even as a candidate, that he was out to destroy it, but campaigning with the same message of hope Obama used in his two runs for the presidency: "Make America Great Again." (267)

Kaufman interprets Donald Trump's election as a sarcastic riposte to Obama's pragmatism by a vacillating subset of American voters.

Despite criticizing Obama's restraint in confronting the nation's racial issues, these scholars would likely agree with comedian and writer Larry Wilmore, who already in 2015 associated Trump's presidential campaign with a reactionary cultural shift, which Janelle Ross summarizes as follows: "The 'unblackening' is Wilmore's pithy way of describing his sense that so many white Americans are eager for more than an end to Obama's presidency; . . . what they sense is the ascendancy of non-white Americans, their concerns, interests and experiences. The 'unblackening' is a political moment, like Reconstruction or the final years of the Cold War." *Greater Atlanta* focuses on this anxious and unresolved "moment" in American cultural history. Although a literal reading of our subtitle suggests an emphasis on works emerging after January 20,

2017—the final day of Obama's presidency—we intend "after Obama" to denote the era in which the optimism surrounding his initial election largely faded. Although the rise of the Tea Party movement in 2009 could reasonably signify that era's outset, such a claim effectively erases the entire Obama presidency, and such a level of cynicism/despair is (hopefully) unjustified. The beginning of the end of the age of Obama seems more fittingly located between 2011 and 2014, a stretch defined by both the Trump-aided mainstreaming of the Birther Movement and increasing societal discontentment and polarization after the killings of Trayvon Martin, Michael Brown, and Eric Garner (among others). By the time Trump descended the escalator of his eponymous Manhattan high-rise on June 16, 2015, to announce his candidacy, the "unblackening" that Wilmore theorized was undoubtedly already happening.

WHY BLACK SATIRE?

Simultaneously underway was the FX network's production of a new television series about a recent Princeton dropout named Earnest "Earn" Marks (Donald Glover); his cousin Alfred, a rapper named Paper Boi (Brian Tyree Henry); Alfred's eccentric roommate Darius (LaKeith Stanfield); and Earn's estranged partner Van (Zazie Beetz). In development since the late summer of 2013, *Atlanta* was primarily the brainchild of the Glover brothers, Donald and Stephen. The former had already garnered acclaim as a writer on NBC's *30 Rock* from 2006 to 2009, as an actor on NBC's *Community* from 2009 to 2014, and as a rapper performing as Childish Gambino from 2008 onwards. With director Hiro Murai, who had previously directed a long-form music video for Childish Gambino, behind the camera, *Atlanta*'s pilot began filming less than a month after Trump's campaign launched.

I did not contemplate these two Donalds in tandem during 2015, but recognizing the roughly contemporaneous inceptions of Trump's presidency and Glover's series five years later set this book's incubation into motion. I rewatched *Atlanta*'s first two seasons in April 2020 to alleviate the anxious tedium of quarantine and endless Zooming. With the darkly satirical vibes of Childish Gambino's 2018 hit "This Is America" (and Murai's accompanying video) still resonating, *Atlanta* felt like the perfect satirical commentary on the moment, despite almost never overtly mentioning contemporary political events or figures (as opposed to its voluminous pop-cultural references). Being housebound for three months also enabled me to read new scholarly contributions to the discussion on contemporary African American satire, including Terrence T. Tucker's *Furiously Funny: Comic Rage from Ralph Ellison to Chris Rock* (2018), Lisa A. Guerrero's *Crazy Funny: Popular Black Satire and the Method of Madness* (2019), and Danielle Fuentes Morgan's *Laughing to Keep from Dying: African American Satire in the Twenty-First Century* (2020).[1] Along with initiating scholarly inquiry into *Atlanta*, Morgan also makes a point that proves vital to our collection. Analyzing Dave Chappelle's uneven performance as host of *Saturday Night Live*'s (*SNL*) first episode after Trump's victory, Morgan concentrates on a sketch in which a pair of Black characters played by Chappelle and Chris Rock sarcastically comment on the increasingly perplexed and horrified reactions of a group of white liberals on election night: "In this moment the critical satirical impulse is at its most acute, as it targets those with the power—in this case the potentially disadvantaged white liberal voting populace—demonstrating perhaps the subtle irony of the communal outrage of a group who has perhaps never before experienced these same feelings of disenchantment with the political system, mediated by a member of a marginalized group who has" (*Laughing* 155).

This sketch's satirical tenor distinguishes it from most of its antecedents, including nearly everything examined in *Post-Soul Satire*—Adam Mansbach's *Angry White Black Boy* (2005) being a notable exception. In that volume's introduction, I posited the "inherently dual-vectored nature" of African American satire produced since the late 1980s, contending that it fused a generally altruistic "satirical commentary on follies and self-destructive habits . . . within the African American community" with a harsher "satire directed at political institutions, social practices, and cultural discourses that arise outside the community and constrain, denigrate, or otherwise harm it in some way" (Maus, "Mommy" xiii). Furthermore, this approach "represents an explicit challenge to the long-standing mandate . . . that African American artists have to use their talents for the 'uplift' and empowerment of the community as a whole, in the process making sure that house business is not revealed to the wider culture" (xvi-xvii). Chappelle's *SNL* performance does not indicate this mandate's reemergence, nor do the works considered in this collection. However, Black satire after Obama notably intensifies the critique directed toward those who claim to be dismantling anti-Black racism without forsaking the privileges afforded them by its continued existence. Thus, a third satirical vector aimed at hypocritical allies—including the fickle "disappointed" voters Kaufman imagines—becomes prevalent in the mid-2010s, buttressing what Morgan defines as an act of existential self-defense: "More recent works . . . push the effort to dismantle to the forefront, seeking justice in the subversion itself rather than in placing a didactic message as the immediate and sole purpose. . . . It is not just the reclamation of tropes but also the reclamation of Blackness itself that is undertaken in these works" (*Laughing* 4). Black satire after Obama largely eschews expectations of reform, instead offering a frustrated self-affirmation that echoes the forthright declaration that Black lives do indeed matter.

As is true of post-soul satire's "dual-vectored" nature, this emergent third vector exists before 2014. James Baldwin basically articulated it in 1964: "People talk to me absolutely bathed in a bubble bath of self-congratulation. I mean, I walk into a room and everyone there is terribly proud of himself because I managed to get to the room. It proves to him that he is getting better. It's funny, but it's terribly sad. It's sad that one needs this kind of corroboration and it's terribly sad that one can be so self-deluded" (74). Darryl Dickson-Carr's invaluable scholarship reveals the satirical "cynicism toward the exploitative white liberal" (*African American* 76) expressed by Rudolph Fisher, Langston Hughes, Wallace Thurman, and George S. Schuyler (among others) during the Harlem Renaissance. Our argument here is not that Black satire after Obama is sui generis, but rather that it reveals a profound shift in the proportion of scorn directed toward self-proclaimed allies in the existential struggle facing African Americans in a rapidly "unblackening" United States.

Kaitlyn Greenidge's debut, *We Love You, Charlie Freeman* (2016), exemplifies this shift. It contains a section presented as a blundering epistolary apology to "You, African American People" (223) by Julia Toneybee-Leroy, an elderly white aristocrat, whose inheritance has funded six decades of dubious research on chimpanzees' language capabilities. Though repeatedly acknowledging shame and guilt, she also denies all responsibility for her institute's profoundly racist work, and Greenidge explains her satire of this nonapology as follows in a subsequent interview:

> Originally, the intention was to explore the use of language that I've heard when talking to white people about race. This language is like: "I want to give you the lip service of identifying with you, but I don't actually want to give up any of my power in this conversation, or show any vulnerability." . . .
>
> Oftentimes it's framed as objectivity: "I am able to recognize where you are coming from and your perspective, but my perspective, which is the objective perspective, is X, Y, and Z. I understand what you're saying, but mine should be the voice that everyone listens to." I wanted to practice what that dance looks like, in language. (Duke)

Following Tucker's lead, I contend that Black satire after Obama redeploys the exasperated outrage that arises from such hypocritical, self-serving discourses.

Given anti-Black racism's long history, the stimuli for outrage have predictably commanded African American satirists' attention through the years; more recently, though, the willful ignorance underlying that history is emphasized, particularly when discussing junctures such as the Emancipation Proclamation, the Civil Rights Act of 1964, and Barack Obama's presidency, which are cited by both sincere and disingenuous commentators as signs of racism's imminent demise. Dickson-Carr echoes Morgan in noting that because such moments failed to stop African Americans' continued social and political marginalization, they motivated a subversively historiographic form of Black self-expression:

> After Civil Rights, after the most obvious forms of de jure segregation had been dismantled, the physical and psychic horrors of Jim Crow were supposed to end. African Americans had been finally liberated, though it was not clear precisely from what, nor from whom. For the American public, that liberation was from symbolic racism easily captured on television: segregated lunch counters; segregated schools; segregated housing; other forms of legal apartheid that could no longer be tolerated in the American majority's moral imagination, the preceding centuries notwithstanding. . . . [T]his narrative has only displaced a reality all too terrifying for African Americans since the 1960s. . . . [C]ontemporary African American literature often rejects old narratives that minimize the full complexity of African American lives and experiences. . . . African Americans cannot live in this state of exception or within narratives written for their erasure and destruction. ("Black Literature" 791, 797)

The tensions resulting from what Salamishah Tillet terms "civic estrangement" (*Sites* 9) provoke contemporary African American satire, particularly when those declaring antiracist kinship are actually perpetuating such estrangement.

Tucker contends that the "need to establish new ways of critiquing white supremacist hegemony has only increased in the second decade of the twenty-first century . . . [making] nontraditional forms of discourse and resistance crucial for black cultural resistance. . . . [Contemporary works of comic rage] achieve a balance that aggressively challenges attempts to simplify or ignore the gulf between the promises of America and its practices" (255). Guerrero adds that disruption of "civic myths" (Tillet, *Sites* 6) and "triumphalist narrative[s]" (Dickson-Carr, "Black Literature" 791) are necessary for Black survival: "Having to diligently hide, redirect, or outright deny a constant state of rage and related trauma in order to maintain social normalcy and equilibrium become a normative, though unnatural, condition of black subjectivity. . . . [C]ontemporary black satire . . . puts on display the material and psychic consequences of the banality of black rage and the normalcy of black trauma" (*Crazy* 4–5). Black satire after Obama exposes performative allyship, virtue signaling, slacktivism, and other duplicitous forms of purported support as empty gestures that ultimately harm African Americans as grievously as overt bigotry. Alfred/

Paper Boi learns this lesson metaphorically—first from a YouTube video and then from first-hand experience—while fixing a machine on the "safe farm" to which he retreats in "Andrew Wyeth: Alfred's World" (s4e9): "These backhoes ain't loyal! They'll roll over you in a second."

Morgan reveals that this approach subtly "open[s] up the power of Black selfhood by pushing back against the status quo, instead reveling in the inherent absurdity of race and racialization . . . while frequently pretending to do *nothing* except make its audience laugh" (*Laughing* 2, emphasis original). She adds that the "laughter inspired by satire opens up space to acknowledge kaleidoscopic Blackness[,] . . . an ethical move that leads to social justice in its revelation of the multiple ways of performing Blackness and being Black, where social justice is the freedom to be, freedom to articulate and perform one's own autonomous identity" (3–4). This acknowledgment parallels the goals of what Guerrero calls "Black satiric epistemology[,] . . . the construction of a particular sociocultural understanding of black subject formation through a lens of exaggeration that specifically highlights how the absurdity of the racial logic of white supremacy determines the very (im)possibilities of an actualized black subjectivity" (*Crazy* 12). In sum, these scholars assert that contemporary Black satire carves out a space for Black existence by subverting ideologies and institutions that prolong white supremacy, whatever their intentions.

WHY *ATLANTA*?

By centering *Atlanta*, we are not pronouncing it this period's best or most influential work of African American satire (although several of us would admit to such sentiments . . .). Debates about the show's legacy and quality permeate the internet, particularly about the polarizing third season.[2] Our choice to make *Atlanta* the hub of this book stems partly from the happy accident of its unusual production and broadcast schedule. The final episode of season 1 aired less than a week before Trump's election in November 2016, while the increasingly surrealistic season 2 (which aired in spring of 2018) mirrored the experience of living in a country governed by what Kellyanne Conway infamously called "alternative facts." Glover had intended to pause until January 2021 before releasing season 3, but delays caused by the pandemic pushed that schedule back by fourteen months. Seasons 3 and 4 were filmed successively between April 2021 and February 2022 and subsequently aired in spring and fall of 2022, respectively. Despite consisting of only forty-one episodes with runtimes between twenty-two and thirty-nine minutes, the series spans nearly the entire "after Obama" period (thus far). Additionally, the chameleonic quality imparted by the steadfast refusal of *Atlanta*'s creators to cater to the demands of either its network or its audiences invites intertextual readings with a broad range of contemporary texts in various media.[3]

As the following essays demonstrate, numerous themes recur across *Atlanta*'s four seasons, and the last three seasons each contain distinct arcs that further unify them. The leitmotif of season 2 is explicitly acknowledged; its title—"Robbin' Season"—refers to "an actual period in Atlanta . . . before Christmas, in which robberies exponentially increase" (Fernandez). For Donald Glover, this title highlights the characters' ethical dilemma as they approach a level of success that escapes them throughout season 1: "Are you gonna eat or are you gonna be eaten? . . . I think that's something people don't realize. Black people have to make a choice. That choice defines who you are. It's hard" (Fernandez). The season premiere's opening sets this tone: two unidentified young Black men are sitting around an apartment talking shit and playing video games—much like the show's principal characters did throughout the first season. Soon thereafter, they initiate a firefight while robbing a fast-food restaurant reputed to be selling drugs along with its chicken and sides. Despite a lengthy exchange of gunfire, the only visibly injured party is a previously unseen young woman, who emerges bloodied and wailing from the robbers' car as it speeds away. The remainder of the season ruminates on the often-Faustian bargains that African Americans must make to endure in a society that sets them against each other like the "crabs in a barrel" in the title of the season finale.

Later seasons' arcs were less overtly signaled, which partially explains the dissatisfaction with the third season's supposed disjointedness. Although season 3 moves the main storyline to Europe, it also includes four "bottle" episodes that diverge from both the central plot and the principal characters. Stephen Glover states that it nevertheless cohered around a primary theme: "When we were in the [writers'] room, we talked about a lot of different things that were going on, a lot of different things that had happened to us—the state that we were in. And we kept coming across these ideas that circled around whiteness, and the idea of whiteness. We just started to break down these feelings that we had. I like the word insidious, or even cursed because on some level . . . it's a curse" (Murphy). He acknowledges that the season's "standalone episodes are really where we got into those big questions," beginning with the grimly comic retelling of a white lesbian couple's 2018 murder of their six adopted African American children in "Three Slaps" (s3e1). However, he insists that subsequent episodes set in Amsterdam, London, Budapest, and Paris reinforce the overarching theme from a different perspective: "Here's this bigger world that we're a part of, but I've learned a lot . . . from Atlanta, already. And the same game is being played here [in Europe], but the rules are different." Season 3 presents white characters eagerly commodifying Blackness in various contexts while simultaneously cannibalizing—as literalized in the season-opening vignette on

Lake Lanier (see below)—the Black bodies and lives to which that commodity necessarily adheres.

The final season returns to Atlanta, albeit now with wealth, fame, and a burden of authenticity and racial unity expressed by repeated variations on the phrase "doing it for the culture." In the season premiere, "The Most Atlanta" (s4e1), Alfred/Paper Boi uses this phrase while talking to the widow of an MF Doom–like rapper named Blueblood, whose work he deeply admired: "I remember he used to talk about the culture. And how he was doing it for the culture." Blueblood's bizarre funeral rites are essentially an elaborate "Easter egg" for devoted fans like Alfred, who strangely receives a plant for successfully interpreting the bizarre clues that lead him to the funeral. As such, they remain true to Blueblood's unconventional artistic sensibility, a stark contrast to the phrase's next utterance in "Work Ethic!" (s4e5) at a studio run by a parodic-satiric amalgam of Tyler Perry and Willy Wonka:

> TOUR GUIDE: Hello, y'all, and welcome to Kirkwood Chocolate's one and only Chocolate Land, a studio for the culture and what . . . ?
> TOUR GROUP: By the culture!

Mr. Chocolate panoptically oversees the slapdash production of dozens of television shows and films featuring grotesque Black characters and scenarios ("I love his rap musical about the Black law professor that kills all her white students!"); he also tries to kidnap Lottie, Van and Earn's daughter, maniacally claiming that he can make her a star.

The phrase returns in "The Goof Who Sat by the Door"[4] (s4e8), a faux documentary about Thomas Washington (Eric Berryman), a Black animator who inadvertently becomes the head of Disney. Washington uses his position subversively to greenlight *The Goofy Movie*, which he intends to be the "Blackest movie of all time" by addressing "segregation, single parenting, low-income career trajectories, fear of gang violence, incarceration, [and] the amount of cheese in African American diets." His concurrent aim is to "carve out his own space and not feel that he was divorced from his own culture." Washington's vision is predictably undermined by the studio, and he dies in frustrated, alcoholic despair.

The series finale, "It Was All a Dream" (s4e10), sums up the season's underlying quandary when Demarcus (Calvin Dutton), the proprietor of a "Black sushi fusion restaurant" located in a strip mall across from a Popeye's fried chicken franchise, chides Alfred, Earn, and Van for insufficient solidarity:

> This entire dinner, you have been staring across the street at a modern-day coon chicken, served to you by an Aunt Jemima, who lies to you

repeatedly, telling you it is her recipe and that she is benefiting from it. It is not her recipe. You know who owns that recipe? An Italian man and his family, none of which have married Black. . . . Look outside. That's the future. That's our future. Salted and battered. Being sold back to us in our own image.

Demarcus's speech alternates between shrewdness and hysteria, but when he attempts to lock the doors and force the trio to eat his potentially poisonous blowfish, they flee in a stolen pink Maserati driven by Darius . . . after getting the Popeye's they have been craving. The self-defining "choice" that Donald Glover mentions in explaining season 2 comes full circle for the viewer—specifically the African American viewer—who must weigh the merits of "doing it for the culture" against the "freedom to articulate and perform one's own autonomous identity" (Morgan, *Laughing* 4). *Greater Atlanta* explores how a range of exemplary satires created "after Obama" have responded to this dilemma.

WHY *GREATER ATLANTA*?

This book's subsections are named after places in the Atlanta metropolitan area, an arrangement suggested by the montage of aerial tracking shots that comprise the pilot episode's title sequence. Flying over neighborhoods exemplifying Atlanta's socioeconomic diversity, this montage also pays subtle homage to OutKast's "Welcome to Atlanta," an interstitial skit from their debut album, *Southernplayalisticadillacmuzik* (1994). As Regina N. Bradley notes, the skit is narrated by the captain of a plane landing in Atlanta:

> The captain gives an impromptu tour of the city, pointing out not only the blackest and poorest neighborhoods in Atlanta at the time but also significant landmarks that symbolize Atlanta lore. . . . The skit's intentional "dirtying" of the South via pairing references to the controversial Red Dog police program's bullying of working-class black communities alongside recognizable white Southern iconography like the Confederate flag grounds Atlanta in contemporaneity as well as in a recognition of the lingering effects of the racial trauma still inflicted on black people in the South. Additionally, the shouting out of multiple communities and subcities that collectively make up Atlanta speaks to its southern urbanity because it references a sprawling urban landscape but also the potential for multiple small communities with urban aesthetics to create a larger urban collective identity. (9–10)

Yvelin Ducotey echoes Bradley in describing how *Atlanta* "intertwines the [city's] territory and its populations, testifying to the daily reality of [its] characters . . . [within] various zones of tension between various social and racial groups" (2).[5] Calling our collection *Greater Atlanta* and organizing it along these geographical lines highlight specific themes related to both the historical and imagined communities of Atlanta and then extend those discussions. Essentially, both *Atlanta* and Atlanta serve as microcosmic exemplars for Black satirists' commentary on life in the United States after Obama.

We start with Downtown Atlanta, the city's central business district and the cultural core of the sprawling metropolis. This section's first three essays lay out foundational critical contexts by addressing the benefits and flaws of satire's rhetoric. Derek Conrad Murray questions whether such contemporary satires as *Atlanta*, Radha Blank's film *The Forty-Year-Old Version* (2020), and the television show *Them* (2021) primarily depart from or reinforce a long tradition of fetishizing Black suffering. Relatedly, GerShun Avilez outlines how *Atlanta* and Paul Beatty's *The Sellout* (2015) largely fail to transcend extant phobias and biases in depicting queer identities. John Brooks examines how and why *Atlanta* must overcome audiences' presumption that the main purpose of satire is to reform existing liberal institutions. Lastly, Erica-Brittany Horhn and Derek C. Maus build upon a generational definition of contemporary satire detailed by Brandon J. Manning, Morgan, and others by situating awkwardness as a primary trait of satire by Black millennials, particularly Donald Glover and Issa Rae.

We next move north-northeast to Forsyth County, a predominantly white suburb/exurb with a notorious history of racial violence, particularly a lynching and subsequent forced expulsion of the county's Black population in 1912 that portends the Black Wall Street Massacre in Tulsa nine years later. These essays focus on aspects of the intertwined and inequitable relationship between whiteness and Blackness. Emily Ruth Rutter illustrates the "third vector" mentioned above by comparing *Atlanta* and Jordan Peele's film *Get Out* (2017) as satirical critiques of destructively hypocritical white allies. Alexandra Glavanakova discusses how racially mixed characters in *Atlanta* and Danzy Senna's novel *New People* (2017) reveal the insubstantiality of racial categories. Finally, Derek DiMatteo considers issues related to formation of Black identities within the predominantly white environment of elite institutions of higher education in *Atlanta* and Justin Simien's film *Dear White People* (2014).

A lengthy section of Forsyth County's eastern border has lain submerged since the mid-1950s beneath Lake Lanier, the same artificial body of water on which two fishermen—one white, one Black—have a conversation in the first scene of season 3 about the lake's haunting as a result of the intentional flooding of a "self-governed Black town." The annihilation of Oscarville and the white fisherman's transformation into a ghoul at the end of the vignette reinforce the season's theme of whiteness as a destructive curse, and Lake Lanier's simulacrum of a natural environment is a perfect setting for two essays considering *Atlanta* from an ecological perspective. Matthias Klestil highlights the series's numerous human-canine relationships to consider its satire of racialized attitudes toward the natural world. Sarah O'Brien follows with an examination of *Atlanta*'s ironic use of a wide range of relationships between Black characters and nonhuman animals to overturn dehumanizing racist stereotypes.

A southwestward drive along Interstates 985 and 85 takes us to DeKalb County, the third-most-populous majority-Black county in the United States as of 2020. The Glover brothers grew up here, and it serves as the setting for the retrospective episode "FUBU" (s2e10). Although the county's socioeconomic profile varies widely, it is in many ways the home of Atlanta's Black middle class, epitomized by the depictions of Earn's family in "The Big Bang" (s1e1), "FUBU," and "Light Skinned-ed" (s4e4). The five essays in this section all speak to the various pressures conveyed by the "do-it-for-the-culture" refrain from season 4. Keyana Parks discusses *Atlanta*'s commentary on the gendered dimensions of Black "respectability" politics. Tikenya Foster-Singletary, in turn, explores how Black identity becomes a performance responding to expectations from both within and outside Black communities. Lola Boorman zeroes in specifically on the linguistic dimension of such performance, pointing out how instances in which Black characters misunderstand one another complicate assertions of shared racial identity. Phillip James Martinez Cortes employs affect theory to discuss how the performances of Alfred, Van, and a Black version of Justin Bieber who appears in season 1 satirically evoke elements of minstrelsy. Danielle Fuentes Morgan concludes the section with the implications for Black women's self-actualization inherent in the blend of comedy and horror found in *Atlanta* and *The Twilight Zone* (1959–1964).

A quarter loop around the Perimeter—i.e., Interstate 285—takes us to College Park, another majority-Black suburb but also the home of Ludacris, 2Chainz, and other notable Atlanta rappers (OutKast hails from neighboring East Point). Although numerous localities claim to be the epicenter of Atlanta hip hop, East Point and College Park get shout-outs in "Welcome to Atlanta"—and Kirkwood Chocolate claims to "own most of College Park" in "Work Ethic!"—so they will frame the two essays in this section. Kinohi Nishikawa looks at the longtime collaboration between Donald Glover and Hiro Murai to theorize how Childish Gambino's album *Because the Internet* (2013) and the two prepandemic seasons of *Atlanta* signify a second phase in Donald Glover's artistic career. Thomas Britt follows up by positioning *Atlanta* as a satirical departure from and commentary on a pair of films—*Hustle & Flow* (2005) and *Snow on the Bluff* (2011)—featuring southern rappers who—like Alfred/Paper Boi—are also involved in the drug trade.

Our tour concludes at the outskirts of College Park at Hartsfield-Jackson International Airport, the bustling international aviation hub at which Out-Kast's imagined plane is landing. Earn is seen here in "The Big Bang," unsuccessfully hawking credit cards to passing travelers, and in "Crabs in a Barrel" (s2e11) as he departs for Europe with Paper Boi, having "stunted on" a white rival in a way that enables his professional success in the latter two seasons (and perhaps presages his spiteful revenge against an airport employee in "The Homeliest Little Horse" [s4e2]). Abigail Jinju Lee's essay suggests some of the other destinations this collection's comparative approach might serve by examining the overlap between African American and Asian American cultures in *Atlanta* and Charles Yu's novel *Interior Chinatown* (2020).

A NOTE ON THE TEXT

We have chosen to follow the lead of the Associated Press, the *New York Times*, and other publications in capitalizing Black, Blackness, etc., but retaining lower case for white, whiteness, etc. in order to signify the different implications of color-based racialization. We have, however, retained the original capitalization in any quoted sources. We have also allowed individual contributors to choose for themselves whether to spell out or use asterisks in writing certain terms that appear within the primary and secondary texts they are considering. We trust that it is self-evident that no endorsement of such terms is implied in this choice.

NOTES

1. For likewise valuable additions, see Edmonds, *Who's Laughing Now? Black Affective Play and Formalist Innovation in Twenty-First Century Black Literary Satire*; Manning, *Played Out: The Race-Man in Twenty-First-Century Satire*.

2. See, for example, Bastién et al.; Charity, "'Atlanta.'"

3. In addition to those discussed in the individual essays herein, other notable instances of Black satire include the television shows *Abbott Elementary* (2021–), *Black-ish* (2014–2022), *A Black Lady Sketch Show* (2019–), *The Carmichael Show* (2015–2017), *The Last O.G.* (2018–2021), *Twenties* (2020–2021), *Ziwe* (2021–); the films *Chi-Raq* (directed by Spike Lee, 2015), *Lemon* (directed by Janicza Bravo, 2017), *BlacKkKlansman* (directed by Spike Lee, 2018), *Sorry to Bother You* (directed by Boots Riley, 2018), and *Zola* (directed by Janicza Bravo, 2021); literary works by Nana Kwame Adjei-Brenyah (*Friday Black*, 2018; *Chain-Gang All-Stars*, 2023), Mateo Askaripour (*Black Buck*, 2021), Danielle Evans (*The Office of Historical Corrections*, 2020), Percival Everett (*The Trees*, 2021; *Dr. No*, 2022), Jeremy O. Harris (*Slave Play*, 2018), Terrance Hayes (*American Sonnet for My Past and Future Assassin*,

2018), Branden Jacobs-Jenkins (*Gloria*, 2015), Mat Johnson (*Loving Day*, 2015; *Invisible Things*, 2022), T. Geronimo Johnson (*Welcome to Braggsville*, 2015), Morgan Parker (*Magical Negro*, 2019), Kiley Reid (*Such a Fun Age*, 2019), Maurice Carlos Ruffin (*We Cast a Shadow*, 2019), Rion Amilcar Scott (*The World Doesn't Require You*, 2019), Brandon Taylor (*Real Life*, 2020), Chris L. Terry (*Black Card*, 2019), Nafissa Thompson-Spires (*Heads of the Colored People*, 2018); and works/performances in various media by W. Kamau Bell, Samantha Irby, Martine Syms, Mickalene Thomas, Baratunde Thurston, Kara Walker, and Carrie Mae Weems.

4. The episode's title parodies the *The Spook Who Sat by the Door* (1969), a satirical novel by Sam Greenlee about a rogue African American CIA agent. Greenlee's novel was adapted as a film directed by Ivan Dixon in 1973.

5. The original quotation is in French: "[*Atlanta*] imbrique le territoire [de la ville] et ses populations, témoignant de la réalité quotidienne de ses personnages . . . [dans] diverses zones de tension, entre différents groupes sociaux et raciaux." Translation by author.

Downtown Atlanta

ON THE PERILS OF ENJOYING ONE'S WOUND

Atlanta and Contemporary African American Satire

DEREK CONRAD MURRAY

The overdetermining of Blackness as pain is the overriding sentiment within contemporary liberalism as it pertains to the Black American visual experience. It is especially toxic within the arts, where the visualization of Black suffering has become the leitmotif of African American existence. From visual art to literature to film and, in many respects, within academia, Black pain is chic and sexy—it's the de rigueur object choice of twenty-first-century wokeness (Charity, "Resist the Impulse"). This visual regime is not only driven by the interests and demands of the so-called dominant culture but is also an often-unspoken mandate of the Black intelligentsia. But at what point does racial and cultural pride merely become self-segregation? Are we just supposed to *love our wounds*? To not simply speak about our pain and historical trauma, but to bathe in it? To romanticize victimhood for the pleasures, reassurances, and validations of dominant institutional liberalism?

We might think of this fixation with Black abjection not as fetishization or exploitation, but as recuperation and celebration, even as a polemical means to compel society to acknowledge its historical and present-day sins. We might regard this tendency as one of pride and dignity, a means to express love, fidelity, and devotion to one's history, culture, and identity. In many respects, our fealty to Blackness is a political choice, a matter of principle. But what happens when Blackness becomes sutured to pain and deprivation? What are the consequences if our representational presence becomes overdetermined as struggle?

In the last decade there has been a rise in Black films and television programming that express a range of challenging themes, including the films *Get*

Out (2017), *Us* (2019), *Antebellum* (2020), *Candyman* (2021), *Master* (2022), and *The Forty-Year-Old Version* (2020), as well as the television serials *Them* (2021), *The Underground Railroad* (2021), and *Atlanta* (2016–2022). Each of these works' emergence in recent years was greeted with measures of both acclaim and controversy. Broadly divergent in narrative, scope, and aesthetics, these works are nevertheless linked by their irreverent, risky, and, in many ways, unexpected approaches to difficult topics. Many of them also employ an edgy brand of satire to engage in a holistic critique of cultural absurdities.

Darryl Dickson-Carr argues that the primary purpose of satire is to lampoon and to "act as an invaluable mode of social and political critique" (*African American* 4, 5). While undoubtedly steeped in satire, Donald Glover's *Atlanta* has also been acclaimed for presenting Black life through a more realistic, introspective, and humanizing lens. Akilah Hughes makes this argument quite compellingly in discussing a pivotal scene from the show's pilot:

> We've seen urban violence depicted on television before, but what makes this scene (and many others throughout the series) fresh is the nuance of each personal interaction. If your only experience with black spaces is via network TV and gritty cable dramas, it is probably the first time you witnessed the repeated attempts at de-escalation, the variety of perspectives and voices present (in a scene with five black people—all of whom speak), the moments of levity and intelligence, all of which add depth and humanize the black experience to those who've only ever glanced in this direction. The true genius, however, is that the show isn't saying it alone is the "black experience." Rather, the genius lies in how specific the circumstances feel to the characters on the show, even if the venues are familiar.

Although Hughes praises *Atlanta*'s storytelling, she also makes a salient point about its formal dimension: "Visually, the series is stunning, with flat realism usually reserved for original programming from Amazon, HBO, or AMC . . . portrayals of black bodies in faded worlds in which their bold personalities and striking dialogue are the focus have rarely reached beyond indie film projects." The show's striking, often overlooked, and elevated filmic quality gives it an air of gravitas and formality that departs from the aesthetic flatness of most TV dramas and sitcoms. The look and texture of *Atlanta* is exquisitely rendered and accurately capture the feeling of the American South: the humidity, the saturated colors, and the sounds. The visual presentation makes the cityscape into a central character, complementing the show's focus on banalities, minimalist storytelling, and quietly introspective moments. In fact, many of *Atlanta*'s satirical moments are purely visual and wholly devoid of explicit narrative. As

Pilot Viruet points out, these moments of contemplative nonaction are usually conveyed through the eyes of the show's protagonist:

> *Atlanta* has a chill vibe largely due to Earn's character, who is more reactive than proactive: He watches things happen, he takes in the scene, he allows himself to be pushed and pulled by the events occurring around him. This gives *Atlanta* the space to breathe and explore deep topics calmly without coming off as preachy or desperate. Rather, it deals with racism matter-of-factly, never pretending that it doesn't exist or claiming to have an explicit solution to fix the world.

Atlanta's approach to addressing racism—or, more accurately, racial folly—is one of its hallmarks. Its absurdism contains an ambivalence that is more observational than judgmental and more introspective than willfully didactic. As Joe Coscarelli opines, "At once trippy and pointedly mundane, 'Atlanta' played in the space where the indignities of being black and poor meet the indignities of striving to get rich." The indignities put on display are arguably where the satirical tension resides, conveying friction through a brazen engagement with stereotypes. In fact, *Atlanta*'s odd mixture of realism and stereotype creates a combustible mixture enabling it to vacillate between seriousness and humor, between tragedy and whimsical absurdity. Many commentators have noted the show's atypical representations of Black subjecthood, as well as its presentations of Black life that focus on boredom and everyday banalities and not the typical "hood" narratives that have permeated Black American cinema from Blaxploitation to the present. Although *Atlanta* is hardly devoid of ghetto stereotypes, it self-consciously holds them up for ridicule while simultaneously debunking them through a more nuanced engagement with Black subjectivity. *Atlanta*'s satire vacillates between the fetishism of stereotype and the humanizing counterimage. It never idealizes, but rather hints at a more intellectual or philosophical approach to thinking about the complexities and challenges of African American life. This quality, largely communicated through Earn's perspective, is contrasted by the intertwined realities of societal racism and Black dysfunction.

How do such stereotypes function within contemporary Black visuality? In *The Location of Culture*, Homi K. Bhabha compellingly argues for reading stereotypes in terms of fetishism, stressing that the policing of stereotypes is key in the maintenance of oppressive social relations (94); this notion seems exceptionally pertinent in considering the consumption of stereotypes in popular visual culture. The interweaving of satire and stereotype is brilliantly calibrated in *Atlanta*, succeeding where other attempts (as discussed below) have been less successful. Its brand of satire wields the stereotype innovatively, not as formulaic representations of well-worn archetypes, but as more whimsical characterizations that evade simple categorization. Satire is difficult to pull off partly because, as Dickson-Carr explains, of two fallacies that can lead to critical misinterpretations of satire: "conflation of different types of humor with satire [and] confusion of the representation of an offensive stereotype with advocacy of that stereotype. The first fallacy, of course, is the result of an assumption that 'satire' and 'humor' are completely synonymous terms" (*African American* 5). In *Atlanta*'s case, the response among critics and scholars has been mostly positive; I tend to view *Atlanta*'s widespread acclamation as both something to celebrate as well as a point of caution and greater consideration. I am not always convinced that *Atlanta* is a satirical show, despite employing biting satire in many of its best moments. It is precisely the show's creative reinvention of stereotypes that is concerning, along with a rapturous reception that starkly contradicts the often-violent realities, social discrimination, and anti-Blackness of American society.

Considering the persistence of anti-Blackness and structural racism in the United States, there is always a great deal of skepticism in the Black community when white America falls in love with popular Black representation. Upon viewing these uncommon visual forms, I almost always find these programs ideologically reductive, demeaning, and violently degrading. Popular programs like HBO's *The Wire* (2002–2008) and others ground into the cultural consciousness exaggerated, ignorant, and false notions of the expansiveness of Black lives in the United States. They suggested unmistakably that the racialized Other is clearly not meant to be known or understood. Anti-Black racism hubristically endeavors to dictate what and who its unwanted and disparaged subjects are and attempts to control their material conditions and everyday realities. But most importantly, anti-Blackness aggressively seeks to determine the cultural narrative that defines African American life. Drug-related crime in Black urban ghettos does not encapsulate the economic, educational, and cultural diversity of African Americans; for a great many Black Americans, the ghetto is as foreign and mysterious as Mars. So, we must ponder why there is such a voyeuristic fascination and obscene desire with the perpetuation of these narratives that define African Americans by such a limited and demeaning script.

This desire for the Other *in representation* may do more harm than good. Although *Atlanta* is largely successful in its aims, it emerged and thrived during a cultural moment defined in many ways by antiracist struggle. The extrajudicial police killings of Black men and women in the United States sparked a global movement against anti-Black racism. Fueled in part by the activism of Black Lives Matter, increased national interest in fighting systemic racism has had an indelible impact on popular representation. In many ways, this is an exciting time for Black representation. Yet there is still concern that Blackness in representation (and Black life in general) is becoming ideologically overdetermined by a set of reductive narratives. This anxiety is compounded by concerns over the presence of disingenuous forms of liberalism that pay lip service to antiracist solidarity while not working toward substantive equitable change.[1]

This tendency reflects a progressive bourgeois cynicism taking the form of cosmetic liberalism. Within the culture industry, disingenuous visualizations of minoritarian victimhood become a means to empathetically engage with the plight of socially defined minorities. These increasingly prevalent forms of supposedly antiracist visual culture engender what Lisa Nakamura characterizes as a "toxic empathy," which enables white viewers to feel that they have experienced authentic empathy for these others (47). She accurately captures a representational contradiction driven by competing motivations. In one respect, there is arguably a sincere desire to create and support empathetic and affective images that are rooted in compassion. At the same time, when such representations dominate the representational landscape, they tend to fix social meanings around a limited set of scripts (48). Beyond their role as entertainment, such representations, Nakamura contends, are designed to immerse viewers in the realities of marginalized and threatened bodies as an ostensible moral education (48). She is primarily concerned with the emergence of socially engaged virtual reality (VR) technologies that enable users to step into the shoes of others as a form of problematic recreation; although cinema and television cannot place viewers within the body of another, they can, as Nakamura argues, "produce spurious feelings of empathy as knowledge. But this kind of embodiment is false, and it is toxic" (54). Her explication of VR technology's troubling characterization as an empathy machine touches on contemporary visual culture's troubling, renewed interest in simultaneously consuming and inhabiting Blackness. This phenomenon's tension between empathetic activism and fetishistic exploitation is driven by the fallacy that empathetic images of suffering will elicit sympathetic responses in viewers.

Another masochistic fantasy that works in tandem with the sadistic pleasure derived from spectacles of suffering helps explain why such images have become ubiquitous. Images of suffering Black bodies are entertainment; in one register, they function as a moral corrective, while, in another, they become a demeaning fantasy. According to Saidiya Hartman, "the desire to don, occupy, or possess blackness or the black body as a sentimental resource and/or locus of excess enjoyment is both founded upon and enabled by the material relations of chattel slavery" (*Scenes* 21). Hartman connects a type of covetous enjoyment of Blackness with the commodifying logic of slavery, echoing a recurring thread in Black cultural criticism. For example, Frank B. Wilderson III argues that "Afropessimism" expresses doubts about the very notion that Black people are *fully* human subjects:

> If, as Afropessimism argues, *Blacks are not Human subjects, but are instead structurally inert props, implements for the execution of White and non-Black fantasies and sadomasochistic pleasures*, then this also means that, at a higher level of abstraction, the claims of universal humanity that the above theories all subscribe to are hobbled by a meta-aporia: a contradiction that manifests itself whenever one looks seriously at the structure of Black suffering in comparison to the presumed universal structure of all sentient beings. Again, Black people *embody* a meta-aporia for political thought and action—Black people are the wrench in the works. (15, emphasis original)

Dominant threads in Afropessimist thought and critical race theory tend to characterize the Black subject as negated and deprived of humanity. This intellectual movement is engaged in a philosophical project concerned with the complexities of Blackness and being, unpacking the forms of terror and control that have shaped Black identity.

Although the aforementioned scholars speak eloquently and forcefully to both historical and present-day conditions, my concern here is explicitly visual. Their work engages with forms of representational troubling that are often unexpected, that quality of semiotic vulnerability or porousness that slips through the tidiness of ideological reduction. There is indeed a stark and disturbing tendency in popular visual cultural today that broadly defines Blackness through the limiting lens of social victimhood. This visual turn toward Black abjection is informed by a history of deprivation, yet it has been impacted by several recent phenomena as well: the apparent rise of extrajudicial violence against unarmed African Americans in the United States; the mass incarceration of Black men and women; the rise of xenophobia and white nationalism (and their attendant forms of violence) in the United States; and the deprived material conditions of Black communities in the wake of the civil rights movement. Afropessimist thought critically and polemically positions Blackness as deficiency and nonbeing—as a debased social condition.

While I understand this characterization of Black subjectivity as a type of lack, I question the notion that Black people are denied humanity representationally insofar as I see humanness as something to be transcended. Perhaps Black people have a surplus of humanity, at least representationally speaking. Perhaps the social role of Blackness visually (and in culture generally) is to fully embody the tragic splendor of humanness. This surplus of Black humanity is contrasted by the ubiquity of whiteness and its utopian promise as an imago, the victory of rising above alterity. Blackness, on the contrary, is so ideologically fixed that everything sticks; it is humanity at its most base level of realness and a subjectivity bogged down by the myriad struggles of human existence. The representational role of Blackness is to suffer brilliantly as a social spectacle, and such representations have become a type of racial pornography, which is gleefully consumed and often institutionally supported and awarded. However, we must be concerned about the types of images that circulate and the reasons such representations gain the financial support to thrive. There is an erotic dimension to racial fetishism that drives a cultural thirst for images of Black deprivation.

Sharon P. Holland has written productively about what she characterizes as a largely unacknowledged erotic dimension of racial fetishism, suggesting that there is a persistent cultural desire for images of Black suffering (41). She comparatively engages with the writings of Emmanuel Levinas and Kwame Anthony Appiah, both of whom consider the inherent hypocrisy of a cultural desire for the Other that is contrasted by the continued and systemic contempt for racial difference. Appiah argues that individualized longing for the Other must be detached from racist desire: "In our private lives, we are morally free to have aesthetic preferences between people, but once our treatment of people raises moral issues, we may not make arbitrary distinctions" (11). At the same time, Levinas explicates his own, more personalized relationship to difference and desire:

> The movement toward the other, instead of completing me and contenting me, implicates me in a conjuncture which in a way did not concern me and should leave me indifferent—what was I looking for here? Whence came this shock when I passed, indifferent, under another's gaze? The relationship with the other puts me into question, empties me of myself and empties me without end, showing me ever new resources. I did not know I was so rich, but I no longer have the right to keep anything for myself. Is the desire for the other an appetite or a generosity? (94)

Holland's interest in these two formulations resides in a need to understand the difference between desire and the reciprocal valuation of the Other's humanity. She concludes that desire, as an appetite for difference, is a drive to consume and to enjoy, which remains disinterested in mutuality and shared human experience: "A personal preference can become morally reprehensible when the private becomes public. . . . In essence, distinctions are okay so long as they remain in the realm of the personal (not always political perhaps), but when members of the group become cognizant of their precarious desires, there is a moral imperative to bring them in line with accepted standards of behavior" (42). Her concern is whether it is possible for an aesthetic preference to simultaneously function as a moral practice: "In reading the words 'appetite' and 'generosity' together, one could surmise that what we need to do is turn an appetite—an 'aesthetic preference'—into an antiracist stance" (41).

Holland's query is central to my own critical interest in the potentialities and pitfalls of Black representation. I do believe Black representational practice can function both as an aesthetic preference *and* as a moral practice containing the potential to disrupt a lengthy and violent history of devaluing Blackness. At the same time, it does not always reimagine the Black subject in a complex, respectful, and empathetic manner. Is it possible for images of Blackness to productively challenge ideological modes of thought that are deeply invested in anti-Blackness when the culture simultaneously demands both suffering Black bodies for visual pleasure and persistent marginalization as a fixed social reality?

Alexander Weheliye rightly points out that, within Black and critical ethnic studies, there is a tendency to think of humanity "from perspectives beyond the liberal humanist subject, Man . . . which offers the means of conceptualizing how the human materializes in the worlds of those subjects habitually not thought to define or belong to this field" (8). He observes that not all subjects "have been granted equal access to Western humanity," a notion which greatly informs not only Black cultural theory, but to a large degree, Black representational politics in the twenty-first century (10). The overlap between Blackness and the human is fraught terrain. The need not just to envision Black bodies but, most importantly, also to do so in humanizing ways has been (and remains) central to Black self-imaging practices throughout the twentieth century to the present.

I argue that aesthetic preference—in this instance, a cultural desire for images of Black subjectivity—more often obscures moral engagement, a position that questions whether *Atlanta*'s popularity makes it a paradigm-shifting moral benchmark or merely an empathetic object of the sort that Nakamura derides. At what point does aesthetic preference ideologically supplant moral engagement? I have written previously about a related conversation among Black scholars in response to the late photographer Robert Mapplethorpe's controversial images of nude Black men (Murray, *Mapplethorpe* 58). David Marriott discusses the paradoxical opposition between racial scopophilia and negrophobia; these are two acts of looking: one desiring and fetishistic, the other phobic and rooted in disavowal. Marriott, like other commentators, places visual emphasis on Mapplethorpe's fixation with imaging the Black male penis—which were often interpreted as playing into stereotypes and myths about sexual prowess, degeneracy, and pathology (58). Several other scholars have written about the perils of racial and ethnic fantasy from a psychoanalytic perspective, from Frantz Fanon and Bhabha to Stuart Hall and Marriott.

All these critical concerns about the perils of visualizing Black suffering coalesce in *Atlanta*. The series centers around the antics and struggles of three central characters, Earnest "Earn" Marks (Donald Glover), Alfred "Paper Boi"

Miles (Brian Tyree Henry), and Darius Epps (LaKeith Stanfield). Earn is a recent Princeton dropout,[2] who has returned to Atlanta to sort out his life. Earn and his cousin Paper Boi, whose nicknames ironically speak to their central predicament, both struggle to navigate the minefield of race, art, and commerce. The fact that *Atlanta*'s protagonists are in desperate need of money is arguably the core theme of the show's first two seasons, which are largely set in the city's lower- and middle-class Black communities. Their quest for success is complicated both by these communities' socioeconomic challenges as well as by their self-defeating behaviors.[3] For these reasons, *Atlanta* has a palpable melancholy about it, a tragic dimension that is often explored visually and satirically. In many respects, the show is an absurdist, whimsical, and unexpected sendup of the foibles of working-class African American life. To that end, it is not *always* (or consistently) satirical, although it does utilize satire brilliantly in particular episodes. Such directly satirical moments include instances in which the show explores the absurdities of race and class and the tensions that emerge between white and Black communities—especially when economic concerns arise. Structural inequality is often a theme, as well the underground economies that offer financial opportunity when more legitimate avenues are either inaccessible or denied entirely.

Earn's quandary is perhaps the most complex. He is highly intelligent, at least by conventional measures, yet also viewed as racially inauthentic (and therefore weak) in just about everyone's eyes. He lacks the markers of authentic Blackness—what Cornel West terms "black cultural distinctiveness" (522)—persistently preventing him from being taken seriously.[4] His nerdiness, intonation, and hipster demeanor—not to mention his admission to and dropping out of an Ivy League university—suggest a more stable upbringing. But Earn's desire is to manage his cousin Alfred's burgeoning rap career and achieve the financial security needed to properly raise the baby daughter (Lottie) he shares with his girlfriend, Vanessa. The comic folly of Earn's apparent lack of authenticity provides some of the more effective and resonant moments of satire in the show. These absurd identity markers are rightly, and accurately, mocked for their ridiculousness, yet their ramifications for Earn's life and ambitions are painfully real.[5]

Atlanta's engagement with race and class is also satirically explored via Earn's mutable relationship with Vanessa, who is biracial and speaks fluent German. Her mixed identity is explored in key instances within some of the show's more satirical episodes, particularly "Helen" (s2e4) and "Tarrare" (s3e10); like Earn, Vanessa is also prone to poor decision-making. Earn spends much of the first two seasons basically homeless, splitting his time between Vanessa's and Alfred's apartments, as well as living in a storage unit. Much of the tension in the show's earlier seasons emanates from Earn's persistent failures: his inability to adequately take care of his family, his failures as a manager, and—perhaps most importantly—his racial inadequacy. Until Paper Boi achieves international stardom at some unseen point between seasons 2 and 3, most doors remain closed to Earn and the other principal characters, whether those doors are in the hood or in the boardroom. In that regard, the class and racial hierarchies of American life take center stage in *Atlanta*.

When race, art, and commerce collide are again among the show's most satirical moments.[6] For instance, "The Big Bang" (s1e1) includes a scene in which Earn tries to convince Dave, a local white radio DJ, to play Paper Boi's self-titled song. Dave asks for a fee to put the song on the daily playlist, but during their conversation and while recounting a funny story to Earn about another DJ, he drops the *n*-word twice, clearly unafraid of Earn's response. Earn is visibly offended but doesn't respond. Later in the episode, Earn, Alfred, and Darius bump into Dave, at which time Earn asks Dave to recount the DJ story to his friends. Dave tells the story, but self-consciously leaves out the *n*-word, which drains the story of its polemical force and humor.

Both Earn and Alfred struggle with persistent structural barriers, so street hustling becomes a viable option to secure financial opportunity. The lingering threat of violence, whether by the community or the police, hovers throughout the first two seasons, as does the potential for incarceration. These tensions are explored through humor, irony, and absurdity—and at times via the irrational (e.g., "Woods" [s2e8]). But there is still a palpable depressiveness that subtends the show. Each of the characters struggles to find motivation and a sense of hopefulness, which at times spills over into nihilism. Although *Atlanta*'s narrative devices and idiosyncrasies generally feel satirical, the show is more concerned with depicting the Black community's complex struggles, as opposed to a more holistic critique of societal folly.

Some episodes are so satirically bizarre and brutally incisive in their observations that they become uncomfortable to view. "Streets on Lock" (s1e2) could certainly be described as a type of *racial absurdity*, a set of bizarrely rendered observations about the cruelty of jail and its explicit structural racism. After an altercation in the previous episode becomes violent—the episode ends with gunshots ringing out, though it remains unclear both who shoots and who is shot at—Earn and Alfred find themselves held in county jail. Facing potential charges yet already processed in the system, Alfred is quickly released. Contending with his first arrest, Earn is kept in the holding cell longer while awaiting his release. The depictions of jail are arguably some of the most intelligent yet generative forms of social criticism on mainstream TV in decades. While Earn waits for his bail to be posted, he witnesses a range of bizarre encounters with other inmates. A mentally disabled man is viciously beaten by guards, when he should be treated in a hospital. In another encounter, a young man reminisces and expresses his love for his ex-girlfriend (another inmate in the holding cell), who is visibly transexual. The other inmates ridicule him for his apparent inability to accept that she is biologically male. When he proclaims, "this is my girl, Lisa," another inmate responds: "Your girl? My nigga, that's a man! Why you think she in jail with the men?" Incredulous, the man rejects his rebuke while other inmates chime in: "Nigga, you gay!" He shouts: "I'm not gay. You niggas fuck guys up in here anyway!" At this point, another inmate responds, "that's not gay; that's just jail." The scene is outrageously funny though also painful in its engagement with both the Black community's struggle to contend with queerness and the resultant antitrans violence.[7]

Atlanta centers on the difficult choices the protagonists face, but these choices generally come with limited options. Paper Boi's brushes with stardom—and his subsequent realization thereof—lack neither absurdities nor perils. Though he struggles to navigate the expectations of realness and authenticity, he must properly channel the dysfunctions and violence of inner-city street life, even while success would allow him to transcend the challenges of that very existence. Earn is forced to contend with the absurdities of race and class, as well as the sense that—having achieved academic success—he should have already moved beyond the socio-economic trials of his youth. Their limited choices are compounded by their foibles and the limits of their imaginations, though there are still societal barriers designed to contain and demoralize them. But among those choices is whether to leave behind the dysfunctions of their environment, arguably not a real choice given that it necessitates abandoning their origins, community, and sense of belongingness (as Alfred finds out the hard way after attempting to escape the negative repercussions of his fame by moving to a rural farm in "Andrew Wyeth: Alfred's World [s4e9]). This conundrum hovers over Earn's decision to leave Princeton and return to Atlanta, which at least reconnects Earn to his family and friends despite the other struggles it brings about. It is within these more fraught negotiations between economic achievement, structural racism, and social pathology that *Atlanta*'s satire is most stingingly effective.

One of the more fascinating dimensions of *Atlanta*'s achievement is the contemporaneous upsurge of other satirical movies and television programs dealing with the Black experience, like Jordan Peele's film *Get Out*, Gerard Bush and Christopher Renz's film *Antebellum*, Radha Blank's film *The Forty-Year-Old Version*, and Little Marvin's anthology series *Them*. There is an increasing interest in programming depicting Black trauma though satire. This turn in Black visual culture has been polarizing, especially among Black critics and commentators, who view these narratives as exploitive, demeaning, and reveling excessively in Black pain. Angelica Jade Bastién has been especially outspoken in criticizing Black-themed films and television programs she feels are detrimental. She expresses particular disdain for the horror film/thriller *Antebellum*'s "noxious tour of historic violence against Black folks," which "implicitly argues that depictions of suffering are the best means of understanding what it means to be Black in America" ("I Am Tired"). She laments:

> I am tired. I am tired of pop-cultural artifacts that render Black people as merely Black bodies onto which the sins of this ragged country are violently mapped. I am tired of suffering being the primary lens through which we understand Black identity. I am tired of being so hungry for Black joy and Black representation that scraps feel like a meal. I am tired of films about slavery refusing to acknowledge the interior lives of Black women even as their being become tools for filmmakers to explore the horrors of the enslaved. I am tired of thin characterization and milquetoast social messaging being the kind of representation Black folks receive. I am tired of films like *Antebellum*.

Much of this criticism was aimed at the depiction of rape, murder, and other forms of violent abuse inflicted upon Black women. And these sensitivities were exacerbated by the casting of the popular performer Janelle Monáe as the central protagonist. Monáe's character in *Antebellum*, Veronica Henley, is a successful sociologist and public intellectual, who is kidnapped and subjected to brutality and sexual abuse. In a similar review of the Amazon series *Them*, Bastién makes an even more aggressive argument that this tendency in Hollywood to produce and distribute films centering on Black struggle is in fact perpetuating white supremacy ("*Them*").

While many of the negative opinions about these controversial representations tend to express concern regarding visualizations of racialized violence, there are also thematic misgivings as well, especially concerning what is perceived as a hyperfixation on histories of slavery and Black degradation. Unlike *Antebellum* and *Them*, there are films that have attempted to address Blackness from different perspectives. *The Forty-Year-Old Version* satirizes the culture industry's demand for representational clichés of Blackness through the eyes of an embattled artist. Writer and comedian Radha Blank stars as Radha, a promising nearly forty-year-old New York playwright, who has floundered for a decade after receiving a "thirty-under-thirty" award. Struggling financially as a part-time teacher, Radha's predicament is a complex interweaving of creative insecurity, white liberal racism, and the often perilous, if not contradictory, parameters of authentic Blackness. *The Forty-Year-Old Version* is a romantic comedy but also a poignant story about personal ambition and a longing for a creative freedom unencumbered by the limits of societal expectation. The film exposes the absurdities of race and capitalism relative to the creative process of Black artists. Blank explicates this predicament with a blunt honesty that is refreshing and hilarious.

The film's satire is skillfully and subtly rendered, especially when it turns its attention to Black complicity with the stereotypical expectations placed on Black artists. Frustrated by her lack of success, Radha turns to successful community playwright and director of YOUmoja Theater Forrest Umoja Petry (campily played by Andre Ward), hoping he will produce her latest play, *Harlem Ave*. Forrest's office is a conglomeration of clichés, including African sculptures, an award honoring a work called "Black Divorcee" as the "Best Play [of] 2003," and posters of previously produced plays with titles like "Hey Honky!" Forrest sits at his meticulously adorned and curated desk, regally fanning himself with an African flywhisk as Radha makes her pitch. Patchouli emanates from an oil diffuser while Radha, distracted by the awkward stillness of Forrest's intense gaze, attempts to persuade him to produce her play . . . for a fee, of course. Forrest's response is to pray to the ancestors that art should prevail over commerce. YOUmoja, which represents the type of underfunded community theaters that operate on the financial scraps of government funding and philanthropic gifts, functions throughout the film as a kind of foil. It's referenced derisively as the place no Black artist wants to wind up, but it's also not entirely ridiculed or dismissed. There is a certain loving familiarity about it and a sense that, despite their flaws and foibles, institutions like YOUmoja ultimately support Black creativity when others refuse.

The Forty-Year-Old Version loses some of its subtlety when it turns its satirical attention to white culture, however. In hopes of generating opportunity for Radha, her agent, Archie (Peter Kim), invites her to a party at a posh society event at which one heavily bejeweled white woman is giddily revealing to another how she and her husband are going to financially invest in a "progressive" multiracial revival of August Wilson's *Fences*. Such scenes are cringeworthy in their awkwardness yet accurately capture a particular brand of toxic white liberalism. While at the event, Archie attempts to persuade Radha to work with the celebrated white queer producer J. Whitman (Reed Birney). The flamboyant Whitman is known for producing plays about African American culture. Archie tells Radha that "black women playwrights are really hot right now," to which Radha replies, "J. Whitman only does black poverty porn plays." Despite her protestations, Radha approaches Whitman, who expresses enthusiasm at the possibility of working with her. Whitman balks, however, at Radha's idea for a play about gentrification, suggesting that she not be afraid of the darkness—i.e., the pain of Black life—and condescendingly dismisses her pitch by saying, "I ask myself, did a Black person really write this?" He then proceeds to invite Radha to serve as writer for his Harriet Tubman musical, at which point she violently and uncontrollably chokes him.

Believing (with good reason) that she has ruined her chance at Broadway success, Radha sulks and begins to formulate a plan to reignite her passion for hip hop and rhyming. She begins to feel that music might allow for the creative freedom and dignified expression foreclosed by a white-controlled culture industry that determines the authenticity of Black expression. In her quest to pursue music, she meets D (Oswin Benjamin), a Brooklyn-based music producer, who spends his days in a tiny, smoky apartment making beats while various aspiring MCs take turns recording their raps. The scene is almost revelatory as Radha delivers her first rhymes in D's makeshift recording booth. In many ways, her lyrics take us deeper into her predicament, as well exposing her repressed anger at the structural and cultural racism that constrain her creativity within a series of reductive stereotypes. The bold directness of her rhymes speaks most potently to what she characterizes as "the white gaze's eroticization of black pain." She explains that success and acknowledgment from the white liberal establishment is dependent on creating stereotypical narratives about Black suffering: "I'll write some poverty porn! / If I'm gonna get on, I'll need to write me some poverty porn. / It's poverty porn, you regular Blacks are just such a yawn. / Yeah, if I'm gonna get on, I'll need to write me some poverty porn." Radha's rhymes are driven by an introspection that is fully aware of the near impossibility of maintaining creative freedom, personal dignity, and self-respect while operating within the mainstream. Radha chooses hip hop as a realm of possibility in which she can forge a more dignified creative space while also expressing her rage against the machine.

The notion of a choice is a recurring theme reflected in *Atlanta*, *The Forty-Year-Old Version*, and numerous other works of recent Black film and television. The darkly satirical TV series *Them* includes a gruesome minstrel named Da Tap Dance Man (Jeremiah Burkett), who terrorizes one of the main characters, a Black patriarch named Henry Emory (Ashley Thomas). Having relocated from North Carolina to southern California in 1953 to take an engineering job, Henry comes to recognize the hostile circumstances of being the only Black family in white suburbia. The minstrel, a Black man in particularly garish blackface, manifests throughout the series as a kind of demonic entity that terrorizes the husband by mocking his complicity and inaction toward the racism that demeans him. While chanting the refrain, "What ya gon dooo?! . . . what ya gon dooo?!" Da Tap Dance Man cajoles Henry into considering retaliatory violence during a scene in which Henry's white boss demeans him. The minstrel functions as both an external evil as well as Henry's conflicted consciousness, but it is his central query that noncomically echoes similar use of satire by contemporary Black cultural producers.

From the perspective of contemporary Black cultural politics, satire is an odd, if also risky, choice. It requires not just the hubris to challenge the dominant society's intolerances but also the courage to indict Black complicity in a societal pathology. Satire is arguably among the most effective means to skewer what otherwise reduces to racial melodrama. "What ya gon dooo?!" becomes a fitting question for—if not also a challenge to—Black cultural producers forced to navigate a series of difficult representational choices. Da Tap Dance Man's question eerily hovers over all these narratives and characterizations because at the heart of their respective predicaments is a kind of reckoning: What will you do in the face of these conditions? Earn, Paper Boi, and Radha are faced with a set of nearly impossible choices, and their fates are directly tied to their ability to make the right decision in such difficult circumstances.

Race and dignity are determining factors that further complicate and muddy these choices. As Jamaica Kincaid suggests, among the choices that Black folks must make is whether or not to abandon their exalted position as the noble suffering Black subject, to let go of an identification that, within certain cultural elite spheres, affords the possibility of professional recognition and success: "Of course, the whole thing is, once you cease to be a master, once you throw off your master's yoke, you are no longer human rubbish, you are just a human being, and all the things that adds up to. So, too, with the slaves. Once they are no longer slaves, once they are free, they are no longer noble and exalted; they are just human beings" (80). Acclaimed filmmaker Melvin Van Peebles once stated that the one thing the white man wants from the Black artist "is to show you're in pain. Show that the system has made you suffer." He was referring to the dismissive American response to his 1968 novel, *A Bear for the FBI* (*Un Ours Pour le FBI*): "When I sent my book to American publishers, they said, 'It's very good, but it's not Black enough.' I said, 'What does it mean, it's not Black enough?' 'Well, we don't feel your anguish of being Black. And furthermore, give us some lynching in there'" (*How to Eat*). As Van Peebles's recollections clearly attest, there is something very sexy about Black suffering, something that satisfies a cultural longing. But at what cost? Judith Butler, in her reflections on Hegel's master-slave dialectic, argues that what is at stake in the philosopher's "life and death struggle" for recognition is the notion that "the body is the ultimate limit to freedom" (52).

Alongside the cultural thirst for such images is arguably also a desire for annihilation and domination, a destructive need that fetishizes racial suffering but is not committed to the vitality of Black life. There is an absurd contradiction in our current cultural landscape between the consumption of Blackness in its myriad forms and the continued wanton destruction of Black bodies. Is it not the social role of Blackness to be visually coveted and consumed yet ultimately destroyed? I should hope not, but this visual regime, in many respects, exerts a type of domination or control: it exerts dominion (as a representational operation), forever fixing Blackness in a condition of irrecoverable debasement. In her explication of Hegel's dialectic, Butler asserts that "domination, the relation that replaces the urge to kill, must be understood as the effort to annihilate within the context of life. The Other must now *live its own death*. Rather than become an indeterminate nothingness through death, the Other must now prove its essential nothingness *in life*" (52, emphasis original).

For some, the excessive humanizing dominating popular representations of Blackness today, these gratuitous representations of Black suffering, are a conduit for greater empathy. But for others, they are an absurd, fake sympathy with the racialized Other. One could characterize this tendency as a political force for change and positioning Black life at the center of the struggle for human rights and justice. *Atlanta* and *The Forty-Year-Old Version* are visual forms that successfully deploy satire against a set of complex social ills. However, there are still dimensions to these representations that are troubling and often painful to view, as they tend to characterize Blackness as deprivation, suffering, and struggle while also holding these experiences up for ridicule. Throughout the nineteenth and twentieth centuries, the folly of Black folks had been held up to mockery, and this is what is vexing about *Atlanta* in particular; it vacillates between ridiculing the Black underclass and satirizing the intolerant and inequitable society that produces it. Be that as it may, I am still concerned that this pornography of Black deprivation—this enjoyment of one's wound—forces the Other, as Butler attests, to merely live its own death as a grand social spectacle.

NOTES

1. See the introduction to this volume.
2. At least, this is what the show suggests until revealing a more complex story about Earn's departure from Princeton in "The Homeliest Little Horse" (s4e2).
3. For more on this subject, see Britt's essay herein.
4. For more on this subject, see the essays by Parks and Foster-Singletary herein.
5. The emphasis in season 4 on the dilemmas surrounding racial authenticity are described at length in the volume introduction.
6. Later episodes featuring this thematic trio include "White Fashion" (s3e6), "New Jazz" (s3e8), "Work Ethic!" (s4e5), and "The Goof Who Sat by the Door" (s4e8).
7. For more on this episode and scene, see Avilez's essay herein.

WHISPERING SEXUALITY

Queer Erasure and Black Satirical Disruption

GERSHUN AVILEZ

"Streets on Lock" (s1e2) finds Earn (Donald Glover) and Alfred/Paper Boi (Brian Tyree Henry) waiting to get processed after having been arrested at the end of *Atlanta*'s premiere episode ("The Big Bang"). "Streets on Lock" showcases problems with the criminal-justice system and the inhumane nature of carceral spaces. Over the course of many hours of waiting to get processed and released, Earn encounters several other people in his situation. A momentary but significant interaction occurs as Earn sits between a man named Johnny (Luke Forbes) and a woman named Lisa (Jason Jamal Ligon). Lisa is Johnny's ex-girlfriend, and the two reminisce about the past, flirting as they sit on either side of Earn. Their playful banter continues until another detainee points out that Lisa must be a man because the processing area is divided by assigned sex, and Lisa has been put in the male intake section. Ostensibly, the scene's humor comes from the fact that Johnny has never known or acknowledged that Lisa was assigned male at birth and only discovers this point through a third party while incarcerated. In some ways, Lisa becomes an unfortunate instrument for this seemingly humorous realization. However, the scene is also a quiet reminder of the prison system's reluctance to think about the needs of queer and trans inmates and the specific kinds of vulnerabilities they might face within detention.[1] Johnny does become agitated, but his frustration is directed toward the other men in the space and not at Lisa.

Like the detention room, *Atlanta* is primarily a male and heterosexual space. Lisa's appearance is a momentary disruption of the gender and sexual dynamics that define the series as a whole. Queerness as a means of sociopolitical inquiry aids in a larger satirical mission of pointing out the cruel absurdity of the criminal-justice system, but the queer body pushes against dominating conceptions of identity and introduces genuine possibilities of radical and inclusive Blackness. This moment offers a way of making sense of the complex employments of queerness in other contemporary Black satiric texts—even those that are not cinematic.

My reading of this brief scene and its framing—which I build on below—sheds light specifically on Paul Beatty's award-winning novel *The Sellout* (2015) and the latter's references to queerness. Both of these twenty-first-century works situate their audience in a nearly all-Black world. However, neither is invested in imagining utopian spaces through such constructions. Both feature devastating and confusing encounters with the state alongside genuine misunderstandings and conflicts among Black people. More importantly, *The Sellout* focuses primarily on male and heterosexual bodies, yet queerness emerges at surprising moments in the novel, as it does in *Atlanta*. Sexual and gender nonconformity serve as vehicles for satirical humor in ways that perpetuate homophobia; however, they also offer opportunities to present more complex expressions of Black identity as well as deft critique of social-identity scripts. Riding the line between progressive representations and more reactionary ones, eruptions of queer sexuality put pressure on the boundaries of Black satire. Turning my focus to Beatty's novel primarily, I pay particular attention to those moments that rupture this ostensibly dominating Black body for other bodies that disrupt and make narrative space for nonnormative actions and bodies. Those moments and those bodies introduce the possibilities of the radicalness gestured toward in the critical humor. After returning to the scene of queer confusion in "Streets on Lock," I shift to an examination of Beatty's use of segregation to support a Black communal ethos and then discuss how this purposeful subversion of racist practices gets connected to queerness. I show how queerness is evoked and erased simultaneously, creating an ironic effect that is in line with the treatment of critique of racism but that silences queer voices for the sake of the joke. Regardless of the medium, queerness may ultimately function as a means for disrupting expectations and conventions to comedic ends, but it is not expressly integrated into the satire's radical social critiques.

Contemporary Black satire foregrounds political exigencies and social-justice concerns, as Brandon J. Manning argues ("Black Millennial Satire"). Accordingly, it is quite appropriate that Glover situates the entirety of "Streets on Lock" inside of the detention area of a prison, evoking the high incarceration rates of Black people and the effects of the criminalization of cannabis in the twenty-first century. The episode opens with Earn and Paper Boi waiting to be processed after being arrested following a public altercation. Earn admits that he has never been arrested before, and Paper Boi insists that Earn should have gotten rid of the half of a blunt he had in his possession. However, the episode summary—very much a component of the show's satirical design—alerts the viewer in a playful way that nonnormative sexuality will be part of the story: "See every rapper think he a thug, well you do the crime, you do the time. *Dont* [sic] *drop the soap haha.* Free my uncle Jay!" (emphasis added).² This framing paratextual material signals that that the attention will turn to spaces of incarceration. The mention of "drop[ping] the soap" refers to anxieties about rape in prison and the fear of becoming someone else's "bitch" or sexual submissive. The "haha" is an explicit reminder that this is a recurring joke throughout US culture that makes light of actual sexual abuse as well as the realities of same-sex desire in *any* space while also allowing same-sex sex acts to oversignify for prison. One apparently cannot tell the story of incarceration without gesturing toward the "joke" of male rape and the humorous nature of same-sex sex acts. The emergence of Lisa on screen becomes inevitable, albeit in problematic ways.

Curiously, the soap-dropping moment foreshadowed in the summary emerges as the joke of same-sex intimacy through Lisa's character. In the holding area scene, men sit complaining about their situation and point out why they should not be there. Earn is never behind bars; therefore, there are no scenes of inappropriate intimacy in a cell or moments in the shower that would facilitate making the "joke" about dropping the soap. It nevertheless still emerges within the context of the detention area. The scene with Lisa and Johnny happens near the end of the episode, and the segment takes up about two and a half minutes. After one of the men points out that Lisa is a man and calls Johnny gay, several others begin to mock him. One points out that same-sex intimacy in prison is understandable (i.e., situational homosexuality) but goes on to explain that Johnny's behavior is aberrant because he chooses to have sex with someone assigned male at birth. The taunts create a social hierarchy in which Johnny is at the bottom, and Lisa's existence is effectively denied. There is no room for thinking about trans identity in the scene. As Johnny is being taunted and forcefully has his and Lisa's identities defined, he becomes angry. In response, Earn quietly chimes in that "sexuality is a spectrum" and that Johnny can do what he wants, but this rejoinder is drowned out by another man's dismissive statement that Johnny is "gay as hell." Incensed, Johnny yells out to the entire room, "I know what y'all think she is, but I ain't on that faggot shit." He attempts to repudiate his declared abjection but is barely able to articulate a defense of Lisa, who quickly tries to pacify Johnny before an uncomfortable silence descends and the scene ends.

Johnny insists on Lisa's womanhood but also registers a deep anxiety and discomfort with the possibility of his own queerness—and that queerness being known. The scene asks important questions about nonnormative sexuality in the space of institutions and public definitions of identity, but it also registers an uncertainty about what to do with Black queerness, as the silencing of Lisa and the scene's general awkwardness indicate. This complicated presentation of queer sexuality—engaging it while also sidestepping it and limiting queer characters—offers us a new way to read Beatty's influential novel, published the year before *Atlanta* premiered. Even though Glover and Beatty are from different generations, queer sexuality remains a challenge in each of their satirical explorations of Blackness and racial conflicts. Queerness is included in but ultimately ancillary to their larger projects. In both *Atlanta* and *The Sellout*,[3] stereotypes about Blackness are "usurped, rebutted, reappropriated, or exploded" (Morgan, "Twenty-First"), but there is often a failure to extend such disruptive attention to the representation of Black queer stereotypes.

Beatty's novel follows the titular "sellout" and protagonist, whose first name is never revealed but whose last name is Me. He lives in a small community within Los Angeles called Dickens, but the signs that define the town's geographical parameters have recently disappeared, and Me understandably feels that Dickens is being erased. The implication is that a gentrifying redefinition of space is behind the signs' disappearance. In a surprising and humorous move, Beatty has his protagonist use mechanisms of historical racial discrimination, particularly segregation, to accomplish the goal of restoring Dickens's official existence. Within conventional American racialization, Blackness can only be visible—i.e., "on the map"—if it agrees to (or appears to agree to, in this case) remain separate and subjugated. The novel is a meditation on the significance and legacy of racial segregation on Black identity. Beatty satirizes the practice of segregation itself to reveal its ongoing impact and how anti-Black racism governs all social interactions. The erasure of the Black enclave of Dickens can be read as a spatial erasure of Black identity in general. Me's work to make Dickens legible once again is a desire to re-present the Black community and the boundaries of Black identity. The question becomes what kind of Black community is made apparent in this emergence of the town.

Just as *Atlanta* is set in and highlights the expansive and distinct Black communities within the eponymous Georgia city, *The Sellout* focuses on a single, though highly unusual, Black community in the urban setting of Los Angeles. The narrator refers to Dickens as the city's "Last Bastion of Blackness" (Beatty, *The Sellout* 150) and later says that everyone there is Black regardless of their actual ethnicity (164). He means that the town has historically been primarily Black but that even the large number of Latinx citizens[4] are still legible primarily through a Black social framework. For example, the high-school principal, Charisma, did not realize that she was of Mexican descent until her mother came to visit her at school years before, and she took note of her mother's difference and began to realize her own: "she took a good look at her own mother in the after-school context of the surrounding black faces and rhythms, and was like 'Oh, fuck, I am Mexican! ¡Hijo de puta!'" (164). Although Me focuses on the people in Dickens of African descent, he also perceives an affective connection to others and place grounded in belonging and mutual concern that he refers to simply as Blacknesss. Me seeks to create or re-create a feeling of community that he fears will be lost along with Dickens's boundaries.

Me's advocacy for his community redeploys the historical means of racial oppression—or at least the appearance thereof. He puts up signs marking the boundaries of Dickens and paints a line on the streets to reinforce them visually and conceptually; he goes further by putting up signs apparently signaling racial segregation within Dickens. Through this plot element, Beatty is playing with and playing on the idea that historical segregated spaces allowed Black people a kind of autonomy and community identity that gets diluted in the pursuit of social equality through integration. Cultural critic bell hooks talks at length about the communal value and support that existed for many when schools were segregated in a pre–*Brown v. Board of Education* world (*Teaching to Transgress*). For hooks, the point is not that different racial groups should be separated, but rather that a lack of concern for Black students' lives and health came to characterize many integrated educational spaces. Beatty essentially takes up this idea, and instead of thinking nostalgically about what was lost by a haphazard rush to integrate, he employs a new form of segregation to show what can be gained by a purposeful focus on Black lived reality that is both literally and figuratively signified by Me's efforts.

The decision to use segregation and enslavement makes Beatty's project align with other Black satirists who explore racial dynamics through subversion. Writer and performance artist Darius James insists, "Nowhere is it written [that] Black people cannot take back the images [or structures] of racism and use them as a weapon against those who oppress them" (5). James himself actively uses racial stereotypes to rethink assumptions about racial identity in his novel *Negrophobia* (1992), but this technique appears in other works, such as Percival Everett's novel *Erasure* (2001), Suzan-Lori Parks's dramatic duology *The Red Letter Plays* (2001), Spike Lee's film *Bamboozled* (2000), Branden Jacobs-Jenkins's adapted drama *An Octoroon* (2014), and Jeremy O. Harris's drama *Slave Play* (2018). In *The Sellout*, Beatty epitomizes James's strategy by taking hold of racist structures for unorthodox and even iconoclastic purposes in ways that go beyond *Atlanta*'s plotlines. He uses the means of oppression to signify differently: "we segregate in an effort to give every tree, every plant, every poor Mexican, every poor nigger, a chance for equal access to sunlight and water; we make sure every living organism has room to breathe" (Beatty, *The Sellout* 214). Such a sardonic approach, of course, comes across as problematic, given that it ostensibly replicates the discriminatory histories that plague the social world of the United States. It is, however, a parodic replication and not a simple mimetic recreation of oppressively limiting ideas. What Beatty actually documents is a move away from concerns about equality toward a focus on equity. Equality presumes that everyone is on an equal footing and should therefore be treated the same, whereas equity acknowledges historical injustice. Equal treatment in the present does not sufficiently recognize the effect of centuries of social inequality. Using a parodic-satiric mode, Beatty evokes racial segregation in his protagonist's social activism to try to imagine an equitable world that serves those who have been disadvantaged and undermined by segregation. He uses the mechanisms of the problem to resolve its consequences. Beatty's playful subversions also imply that the only way to get beyond and to disrupt the social realities of segregation and racism is to embody and enact them—to take them up rather than simply dismissing them as concerns or as irrelevant relics of the past.

But how does queerness relate to this peculiar examination of racism? Queerness is nearly unimaginable within the world of the novel; it is often a tool of the larger critique but granted very little narrative space, just as Lisa gets little screen time and is mostly muted in "Streets on Lock." In some of its earliest mentions in *The Sellout*, homosexuality is presented as having a contradictory social presence that always involves troubling notions of connection, as in the treatment of the Johnny-Lisa relationship. In the novel, homosexuality is first presented as a source of communal distrust: women who have "faggots for best friends" are said to hate men (Beatty, *The Sellout* 60). It is also situated among numerous abject sources of communal connection: "the country needs somebody to throw baseballs at, to fag-bash, to nigger-stomp, to invade, to embargo" (87). The "fag," like the "nigger" here, is oppressed to obscure histories and to offer a sense of solidarity against a commonly held enemy through actual or symbolic violence. These two figures appear to hold similar social positions, but they are presented as being two different and nonintersecting categories of identity that only coincidentally serve comparable social purposes. One need only recall the taunts hurled at Johnny and his own feelings of frustration in the detention scene to sense the anxiety that emerges when Blackness and queerness are in close proximity. Beatty takes up the social conditions that objectified the "nigger" in order to subvert the term's meaning. Unfortunately, he does not do the same for the "fag"; instead, the novel's references to homosexuality are confined to humorously advancing both the trenchant social critique of anti-Black racism and the argument for more capacious understandings of Blackness. This technique mirrors the ways in which queerness works as a supplementary, comedic, and minor component of a deeper consideration of Black incarceration and the protagonist's general vulnerability in "Streets on Lock."

The specific social conditions that Beatty wants to revivify and rethink to expand Blackness are segregation and enslavement. In fact, the novel opens with the protagonist on trial in front of the US Supreme Court for having reinstituted racial segregation and slavery. It is important to note that the narrator does not initially set out to reinstitute either practice. He wants to reestablish Dickens, but he does not immediately turn to racist conventions to accomplish this goal. He lacks a definite strategy and ends up trafficking in the two practices because of Hominy, the most curious character in the novel. Hominy is an elderly former actor who was once associated with the Little Rascals, a group of Black and white child actors featured in a series of comedic short films called *Our Gang* from the early twentieth century.[5] Me rescues Hominy from a suicide attempt near the beginning of the narrative,[6] and to thank him for saving his life, Hominy decides to become the narrator's slave. Hominy explains that he sought to kill himself because, when Dickens disappeared, he disappeared as well. He goes on to explain why he willingly wants to assume the position of a slave for the man who saved his life: "sometimes we just have to accept who we are and act accordingly. I'm a slave. That's who I am. It's the role I was born to play. A slave who just happens to be an actor" (Beatty, *The Sellout* 77). Hominy shows an inability to distinguish between the stereotypical roles he plays and his own lived experience. He acted as a grotesque racial caricature as a child and now willingly embodies a figure of racial objectification. More importantly, though, he feels powerless to move beyond the caricature that defined his life and determined his access to employment. Hominy is making a statement about the circulation of racial stereotypes: if he is only ever legible through stereotypical frameworks that give meaning to racial embodiment, perhaps he should embrace them to gain power over his life. On its face, Hominy's decision to become a slave is reflective of a debt he owes his rescuer, who vehemently refuses the role of slaveowner until Hominy wears him down. However, Hominy's decision is actually a move to self-actualize by using the racial ideologies that have defined his life.

Hominy's transformation into a slave is made possible by a scene of violence common in slave narratives: a whipping. This image intertwines the novel's meditations on same-sex desire, enslavement, and the mission of protecting the Black community of Dickens. The first morning after becoming a slave, a shirtless and barefoot Hominy greets Me by asking to be whipped. After a few moments of arguing, Me acquiesces to Hominy's persistence and proceeds to beat his friend:

> I'll never forget the sounds of my leather belt against the Levi Strauss denim as I unsheathed it from my pants. The whistle of that brown-and-black reversible whip cutting through the air and raining down hard in loud skin-popping thunderclaps on Hominy's back. The teary-eyed joy and the thankfulness he showed me as he crawled, not away from the beating, but into it; seeking closure for centuries of repressed anger and decades of unrequited subservience by hugging me at the knees and

begging me to hit him harder, his black body welcoming the weight and sizzle of my whip with groveling groans of ecstasy. I'll never forget Hominy bleeding in the street. (Beatty, *The Sellout* 79)

This scene of brutal violence that is crucial to both (African) American literary history and (African) American history in general is not presented as either racial objectification or a denial of Hominy's humanity. It is a moment of ecstasy for Hominy and one of bonding for the two Black men. Beatty presents it as a same-sex BDSM scene in which the ostensible dominant provides pleasure for the submissive with his "unsheathed" phallic belt. In addition to emphasizing Hominy's pleasure, the language stresses Me's intense sonic and haptic experiences. The protagonist is not thinking about Hominy's pleasure or pain in the moment but his own embeddedness in the activity and the power connected to his actions. The passage quoted above begins and ends with the phrase "I'll never forget," emphasizing the impact of this sensory experience on him. However, it is not regret or pity that characterizes this act of remembering; instead, the emotional and physical intimacy with Hominy pervades the aftermath of sensual violence.

I am not arguing that Me and Hominy are to be read as homosexual or bisexual, despite the fact that the scene is redolent with same-sex activity and queer energy. Rather, I contend that Beatty uses a moment of same-sex BDSM and the specter of queerness to motivate and define his central character's strategy for saving Dickens.[7] This scene is crucial to the novel as a whole. When Hominy initially asks Me to whip him, of course, the protagonist refuses and asks if there is another way to make him happy. Hominy responds, "Bring back Dickens" (Beatty, *The Sellout* 78). In effect, Hominy says there are two options: prevent the erasure of the Black community or participate in a historical form of anti-Black oppression. In juxtaposing these options, Hominy insists that to allow Dickens to disappear is consonant with the reinstitution of slavery. As Hominy "looked so happy" (84) in the wake of one of their whipping sessions, Me decides to replace one of the missing "Welcome to Dickens" signs. Me's dedication of this act to Hominy is also the first narrative step toward resegregating Dickens, which Me says he likewise does for Hominy (as discussed below). Queer energy is thus linked to race-based activism in the narrative's structure.

Linked closely to Hominy's declaration of enslaved status, the restoration of Dickens quickly gets transmogrified into the erection of signs designating the city's resegregation. As a birthday present for Hominy, the protagonist decides to put up a sign on a local bus that reads: "Priority seating for seniors, disabled, and whites," followed by the Spanish, "Personas mayores, incapacitadas y güeros tienen prioridad de asiento" (Beatty, *The Sellout* 128). Me puts the sign on a bus driven by Marpessa, his love interest, thereby interlacing his heterosexual desire and his attachment to Hominy. The protagonist believes Los Angeles to be a racial vortex, the "spinning epicenter of racism" (129), and the sign registers this understanding in English and Spanish. As opposed to reinstituting segregation, Me's sign alerts us to the fact that it has always been there. His narrative suggests that one cannot reinstitute something that has never gone away; in essence, the signs are descriptive, not proscriptive. Even though the signs stimulate characters in the novel to assume that Me is trying to reinstate racist social conventions, there are very important distinctions between this sign and the familiar Whites Only signs from the Jim Crow era of segregation. Me simply adds the word "whites" (and "*güeros*" in Spanish) to the extant language of a typical bus sign.

The ideas of priority access and exclusionary access to space become interwoven in Beatty's commentary on the social attribution of privilege. As opposed to ignoring and eliding the existence of white privilege, the sign reminds us of actual customs and the ways in which discrimination happens, and it reinforces the semiotic dimensions of white privilege and spatial dominance. To say that whites have priority is a reminder that the insistence on social privilege is a choice that corresponds to a refusal of equity. The sign—along with the others that will follow it—make explicit the racialized social dynamics that already govern everyday encounters. They speak the supposedly unspeakable, but Beatty insists that we all already know them to be true. The pleasure that Hominy gets from the sign comes from the satisfaction of his lived truth being formally acknowledged. The narrator later explains that the sign reminds us that the rights of African Americans "were neither God-given nor constitutional, but immaterial" (Beatty, *The Sellout* 185). They are immaterial because of the possessive investment in whiteness that undergirds all social interactions.[8] This understanding, which Me gains from interacting with Hominy, reinforces the idea that supposed legislative and judicial gains for civil rights have been insufficient in dismantling anti-Black racism.[9] Similarly, Hominy's voluntary self-enslavement is a way of recognizing, through role-playing, how he has been treated his entire life; his actual humanity feels immaterial in the face of constant dehumanization.

Even though the signs take on a life of their own and become an elemental part of the reemergence of Dickens, it is important to remember that Me initially creates the sign on the bus for Hominy's pleasure and peace of mind. Here and elsewhere in the novel, it often seems as if Me works for Hominy. The narrator points out that even though a self-proclaimed slave, Hominy does very little work (Beatty, *The Sellout* 81). Moreover, Me goes out of his way to please him throughout the narrative. His actions motivate the protagonist to save Dickens and to use strategies of racial oppression in a new way. In this sense, Hominy "tops from the bottom," i.e., he acts as a dominant while

Me becomes the submissive being directed. Beatty cleverly inverts the queer dominant-submissive relationship to introduce the idea of ironic subversion in the novel. This move foregrounds the idea of reversal in this novel about the seeming embrace of segregation and enslavement. One character explains: "People grouse at first [at the signs], but the racism takes them back. Makes them humble. Makes them realize how far we've come and, more important, how far we have to go. On that bus [the sign is] like the spectre of segregation has brought Dickens together" (163). Even though the protagonist is focused on the geographical parameters of Dickens and making them clear, he also recognizes that "Dickens exists in our heads" (141), and the evocation of the social forces that created segregation ends up summoning the town on a symbolic level. All of this happens through Hominy's direction, from a position of apparent submission.

I have been arguing that the protagonist's controversial embrace of segregation and enslavement are narratively rooted in a moment of same-sex, violent intimacy and that the shadow of queerness haunts the novel, but the book ultimately finds little space in terms of character development. I see this using and absenting of queerness as related to *Atlanta*'s presentation of Lisa and Johnny in "Streets on Lock." In the scene, Earn mumbles a more expansive understanding of sexuality, but it is a minor element of the scene and finds little purchase among the general chaos and anxiety. Exposing the inhumane nature of the detention center gestures toward queerness but is unable to fully embrace (or speak aloud about) it. Similarly, although Beatty's novel exposes white privilege as an obstacle to equity, it also fails to think about homophobia and the lack of queer life in reconstituting Dickens. Los Angeles, like Atlanta, has a well-known and vibrant queer community, making the near-complete absence of queer characters in *Atlanta* and *The Sellout* all the more striking.[10]

That said, Beatty relies upon more passing allusions to homosexuality than Glover does.[11] Even with the novel's queer erasure, there are recurring references to homosexuality that build upon the same-sex BDSM interactions between Me and Hominy. For example, in a critique of minority representation on television, Me complains, "homosexuals are mythical beings, but you see more ads featuring unicorns and leprechauns than you do gay men and women" (Beatty, *The Sellout* 139). Even as its protagonist complains about the fact that queer people are largely excluded from meaningful representations in the public sphere, the novel effectively participates in precisely this kind of abstraction. One is overwhelmed by the irony of Beatty offering a narrative that regularly depends upon references to same-sex intimacy and queer identity but remains reluctant to present queerness within Dickens or its greater Los Angeles setting. The extent to which queerness is a means to an end compromises the narrative emphasis on equity.

One of the most significant moments that shows this technique of summoning homosexuality while absenting queer individuals occurs when Me visits Career Day at a school in Dickens. After the day's formal events have concluded, the principal asks students what they thought of the visitors. One student responds that she wants to be a veterinarian, to which another students retorts, "That's gay" (Beatty, *The Sellout* 166). The conversation devolves into calling anything that a student wants to dismiss "gay." The principal inquires, "Is there anything you kids don't think is gay?" After a moment, a student responds, "You know what's not gay . . . being gay" (167). This statement seeks to distinguish queer people from the negative epithet employed to express disdain and disempower another person. On one hand, this brief comment rescues queerness from the space of abjection implied by the pejorative use of "gay." It suggests a nuanced understanding of language and lived experience and indicates how language changes with use over time. However, this seemingly progressive way of thinking about queerness occurs in a novel with few storylines about queer people. The discourse surrounding queerness is present in Dickens in a way that lived queerness is not. Additionally, the use of the term "gay" to register negative sentiment carries a history of homophobia and queer bashing that is not completely alleviated by the student's assertion that being gay is "not gay." The moment reminds one of the casual homophobia that circulates throughout the novel and that finds expression in everyday parlance, even when the goal is not to subjugate sexual minorities. The novel's presentation of queerness is simultaneously progressive and a return to familiar derision. More importantly, the conversation shows how Beatty embraces the abstract reality of homosexuality while erasing queer presence. His approach again recalls the moment in which Earn mutters about "sexuality [being] a spectrum" as he seeks to defuse the tension of the moment. *Atlanta* finds very little room for queer characters, making Earn's quiet comment sound even quieter, tangential at most to the show's broader arcs.

Beatty's protagonist insists his troubles began because he has dared to whisper racism "in a post-racial world" (*The Sellout* 262). I have shown that Beatty and Glover each also *whispers* queer sexuality metaphorically in their texts, but neither is able or willing to fully take it on as a major theme in their respective works. There is genuine value in what I will call the "queer moments" in these texts, even though they are sidelined. To be clear, my goal is not to cast aspersions on either work or to dismiss them as homophobic. Instead, I want to point out that neither can tell their stories of contemporary Black identity and community and offer comprehensive critiques of discriminatory practices without thinking about queerness. These artists' projects show how queerness is imagined as disruptive in satirical texts that are themselves about disrupting racial logics. However, queerness becomes a means to that end and not explored fully itself. When queerness briefly appears, there is a largely unrealized potential for productive critique of the wider social context. One might read this absenting of queerness as an ironic indirect commentary on the dismissal of Black queer life in many registers; as noted above, Beatty seems, at times, to be trying to reveal the neglect of queer populations through his own neglect. However, he has gone to great lengths in affirming the diversity *within* Blackness throughout his fiction, dating back to his debut novel, *White Boy Shuffle* (1996). Blackness is not monolithic or homogeneous in Beatty's narrative worlds. His Black communities are comprised of many different and contradictory elements, but its queer elements are underrepresented and undertheorized. His purposeful irony may be an extension of the satiric mode, but it is also a marker of the low threshold of the imagining of the Black community's queerness. In this sense, the appearance of queer figures or language about queerness illustrates the limits around these analyses of anti-Black racism, solidarity, and Black social life.

In addition to making its own groundbreaking contributions to US culture, *Atlanta* sheds light on the choices Beatty makes in *The Sellout*, even as the former is generally more committed to realism and the latter, to more outlandish scenarios.[12] What does it mean to use a scene as both an illustration of an overall approach to sexuality in a serial form and as a lens for analyzing a novel? Satire and parody do not limit themselves to one genre or medium, and one better appreciates the utilization of these strategies toward different goals through comparative and intermedial approaches. However, what is more important here is the recognition that queerness gets taken up (or not taken up) in similar ways across forms and across generations of artists.[13] As I have shown, the dynamics that play out on screen in "Streets on Lock" epitomize *The Sellout*'s quiet attention to queerness over the course of Me's attempt to make Dickens visible again. In the final analysis, one finds that queerness is a lurking presence, a whispered reality, that helps to drive action and social commentary, but its appearance raises a persistent question that goes unanswered: What relationship does queerness have to interrogations of Black community and identity? The answer to this question exceeds the cinematic and narrative boundaries of these particular texts, but it points to the direction that other texts can and hopefully will take as they disrupt stereotypes about Black identity.

NOTES

1. For scholarship on queer life in prison, see Kunzel; R. Robinson. For further consideration, see the chapter on gay men in prison in Avilez.

2. See the digital episode guide for *Atlanta* on Hulu.

3. There is a general absence of explicitly queer characters in *Atlanta*'s four seasons. I focus my discussion on the "Streets on Lock" episode, but my reading of the absenting and muting of queerness in this episode sets the stage for the portrayal of queerness in later seasons as well. For example, in "New Jazz" (s3e8), there is a trans character named Lorraine (Ava Grey) who becomes an insightful emotional guide for Al/Paper Boi. However, it is significant that this important character emerges not in Atlanta but in the European city of Amsterdam and that the character appears after Al has taken a very strong hallucinogenic drug. Lorraine is present, but this trans presence is displaced from Atlanta and is presented as ethereal and perhaps unreal.

4. The narrator later notes that Dickens's population is now predominantly Latinx (Beatty 93).

5. Hominy starts out as the Black character Buckwheat's understudy, which seems to be both a commentary on tokenism and a sign that the show eventually wanted/needed a character even more racially marginalized than Buckwheat. For writing on the history and social meaning of the Little Rascals, see J. Lee; Maltin and Bann.

6. Me, like his father before him, operates as a "nigger whisperer" for the residents of Dickens. This social occupation entails taking people off the proverbial ledge of suicide or violence when racism, social inequality, and a dearth of possibilities have made them feel hopeless. When Me saves Hominy, he is "nigger whispering."

7. Harris uses similar imagery satirically in *Slave Play*, which dedicates more time in thinking through the place of queerness in its examination of the complex psychological dynamics of enslavement.

8. See Lipsitz.

9. For a discussion of the reality of Black civic estrangement, see Tillet, *Sites of Slavery*.

10. See note 3 regarding representations of queerness in *Atlanta*. In regard to *The Sellout*, there is one bisexual white character in the novel who declares himself as such. After the unnamed character identifies as bisexual in a casual conversation (Beatty, *The Sellout* 177), his friend dismisses bisexuality as a real phenomenon, insisting, "You either is or you ain't." Queer sexuality is displaced from the Black body and aligned with whiteness and then effectively dismissed or at least undermined. The humor of the moment derives from the way that the friend tells the bisexual character that he is too dumb to have figured out his sexuality yet. Queer sexuality emerges only to be poked fun at and questioned as a side story to the primary narrative focus.

11. *Atlanta*'s latter two seasons provide a handful of additional references to queer characters and actions, but they remain profoundly muted, appearing as mythic (e.g., Lorraine in "New Jazz") or as vapid stereotypes that supplement the central satire (e.g., Khalil in "White Fashion" [s3e6]). Khalil is a literal apologist for the racist actions of white-owned corporations. In "Crank Dat Killer" (s4e6), Earn and Darius are forced to kiss each other to obtain a pair of sneakers. The consideration of same-sex intimacy has little to do with queer characters or same-sex desire and is more an instrument for the larger satire.

12. Of course, there are seemingly outlandish and surreal events that occur throughout *Atlanta*'s forty-one episodes (including the suggestion in the series finale that the entire show has just been a dream that Darius has been having while in a sensory-deprivation tank). However, I contend that Glover and his fellow writers are still essentially committed to a comedic realism, while Beatty's approach incorporates more purposeful absurdity.

13. B. Manning argues that there are important distinctions between the work of more contemporary Black satirists and that of a previous generation ("Black Millennial Satire"; see also the essay by Horhn and Maus herein). However, I contend that there are certain strategies that connect some younger and older artists, and one of those concerns the representation of queerness. Manning notes that artists such as Justin Simien, who is gay, better attend to Black sexual minorities. I acknowledge the significance of Simien's work, especially in his Netflix series *Dear White People* (2017–), but I do not want a contemporary audience to ignore the limitations of the ways in which queerness is still used across generations.

SATIRIZING SATIRE ITSELF

Atlanta's Appropriation Aesthetic and the Blackening of US Civil Society

JOHN BROOKS

A specter of racial subjugation looms over *Atlanta*'s Black characters, who face a culture of poverty, an unjust legal system, and a neoliberal entertainment industry that treats the Black body like a fungible commodity. The series puts contemporary America's anti-Blackness on display in its depictions of police brutality, such as when a group of corrections officers mock and beat a mentally ill Black man, who is recurrently arrested in "Streets on Lock" (s1e2), or when a white officer kneels on the back of a cartoon wolf—representing a Black man—who craves a cereal that "only kids can have" in "B.A.N." (s1e7). Among such representations of spectacular violence, *Atlanta* also examines such quotidian forms of violence as stereotyping, limited job opportunities, mandatory drug testing, probation, house arrest, and homelessness that collectively delimit Black life and produce the chronic eat-or-be-eaten reality named "Robbin' Season" in "Alligator Man" (s2e1).

At first glance, satire seems well equipped to critique and to mitigate the structures of white supremacy that *Atlanta* chronicles. In "The Nature of Satire," Northrop Frye contends that satire aims to promote civilization's advancement by challenging undesirable social constructs and illicit political activities: "I should define satire, then, as poetry assuming a special function of analysis, that is, of breaking up the lumber of stereotypes, fossilized beliefs, superstitious terrors, crank theories, pedantic dogmatisms, oppressive fashions, and all other things that impede the free movement of society" (79).[1] For Frye, satire is a social corrective that contributes to civil society's ongoing development; he characterizes satire as an instrument of modern liberal thought, an intellectual and moral tradition that aspires to individualist, egalitarian, universalist, and progressive conceptions of equality, liberty, and justice.[2]

Despite ample resistance, revision, and refutation since its articulation, Frye's theory still matters because it became a dominant paradigm for understanding satire, less in terms of contemporary critical scholarship than in terms of the nonacademic perspective about satire's aims and purpose. General audiences tend to assume that satire's goal is to improve social relations, all the while overlooking (or remaining unaware of) the constraints of this perspective. Frye's own examples reveal these limitations:

> If a satirist presents a clergyman, for instance, as a fool or a hypocrite, he is primarily attacking neither the man nor his church. The former is too petty and the latter carries him outside the range of satire. He is attacking an evil man protected by the prestige of an institution. As such, he represents one of the stumbling-blocks in society which it is the satirist's business to clear out. ("The Nature" 79–80)

Here, the object of a proper satirical attack is any deviation from society's established moral principles, the extant and agreed-upon standards of behavior that inform the dominant *forma mentis*. It follows that Frye sees satire as a mode of critique that favors slow, incremental reform, which leaves "outside [its] range" the sort of revolutionary consciousness associated with the deconstruction of institutional knowledge and systemic inequalities.

Like Frye, mainstream audiences frequently assume that liberal institutions are the virtuous standard toward which satire seeks to reorient society. This reflexive faith in liberal ideals matters because, as Charles W. Mills notes, a spirit of white supremacy tacitly (and explicitly) underwrites the long tradition of liberal thought. Mills posits that Enlightenment-era social and moral philosophers sought only to regulate relations between whites, giving rise to a "racial contract" that authorizes formal and informal oppression of nonwhites (1–7, 122). He notes that the liberal tradition preserves this racial contract, denying Blacks any agency to influence the social order. This is not only because the racial logic of chattel slavery and liberalism share a "twin birth" (Losurdo 37) but also because liberalism's historical development unfolds as a dialectic of emancipation and dis-emancipation, a process in which the very idea that liberty has been expanded (for "all") enables the dominant racial group to impose new restrictions on freedom's potential meaning(s) for subordinate racial groups. Put differently, the assumptive logic of liberal thought extols progress but retracts progressive concessions when politically advantageous, thereby preserving and reproducing white hegemony.[3] The "normative" view of satire sees satirists as instruments of liberalism's optimistic teleology, meaning they can influence Western civilization's social contract only by defending its liberal ideals; ergo, they cannot critique the racial contract that upholds that selfsame social contract.

Yet this is precisely what *Atlanta* does; it critiques the status quo by satirically troubling naturalized ideas about equality, progress, and civilization. Steven Weisenburger explains that such a "degenerative" mode of satire departs from Frye's normative presumptions by "interrogating and subverting codified knowledge and revealing it as a dissimulation of violence" (11–12). Consider "Sinterklaas Is Coming to Town" (s3e2), in which white Dutch characters insist that "we tolerate people, nothing like America," even as they celebrate Zwarte Piet, a grotesquely racist "blackface" figure. *Atlanta* attacks—and deconstructs—institutionalized knowledge by parodying received ideas. If, as Linda Hutcheon argues, parody is "a double process of installing and ironizing" (93), an act of re-presenting the overly familiar to reveal the consequences of normalized beliefs and ideologies, then *Atlanta*'s parody of the liberal *mentalité* effectively upends mainstream audiences' assumptions about satire's intentions and purposes. This is to say that *Atlanta* satirizes satire itself. The series does not aspire to rectify any particular social problem or to shift the direction in which civilization unfolds, as viewers might conventionally expect a satire to do, but rather to expose the constituent anti-Blackness of liberal thought and deconstruct conventional satire's meliorative ambitions and faith in incremental reform.[4]

Atlanta explores US civil society's constituent anti-Blackness by dramatizing Black characters' social exclusion and limited agency. For instance, in "Big Bang" (s1e1), Ernest "Earn" Marks (Donald Glover) explains his utter circumscription by the structural realities of race and class: "I just keep losing. I mean, are some people just supposed to lose? For balance in the universe? I mean, like, are there just some people on Earth who supposed to be here just to make it easier for the winners?" Earn's alienation highlights his marginalized positionality and reminds viewers that social belonging cannot be assumed within the civil society modeled in *Atlanta*. His status as an apparent dropout from Princeton University contributes to this reading by suggesting that "winning" is reserved for those with a classical liberal mindset, such as that conferred by an Ivy League education, an ideological project with deep Enlightenment roots. By withholding explanation for Earn's departure from Princeton until "The Homeliest Little Horse" (s4e2), *Atlanta* leaves open the possibility that he is simply "supposed to lose" because US civil society is not built for Black men.

This social-exclusion motif develops further in later seasons. For example, in "Money Bag Shawty" (s2e3), Earn faces discrimination simply for trying to spend a one-hundred-dollar bill. A white cashier at a movie theater assumes his money is counterfeit but then accepts a one-hundred-dollar bill from a white man in line behind Earn. When Earn complains that money does not seem to have empowered him, Earn's cousin matter-of-factly explains that Blackness prohibits economic participation: "There's a reason that a white dude dressed just like you can walk into a bank and get a loan, and you can't even spend a hundred-dollar bill."

Much of the show's exploration of the modern racial contract is conveyed through this same cousin. Although Alfred "Paper Boi" Miles (Brian Tyree Henry) is an up-and-coming rapper within Atlanta's music scene, his bumpy experience of localized fame characterizes the entertainment industry as a space of white cultural hegemony. In "Nobody Beats the Biebs" (s1e5), for example, a white reporter tells Alfred that he will only be successful if he embodies one-dimensional racialized caricatures that reaffirm white preconceptions about rappers. She conveys this message by contrasting Alfred with pop musician Justin Bieber. *Atlanta* racebends Bieber to accentuate the popstar's real-life appropriation of Blackness and his white privilege, which lets him dodge criticism for uncivil behaviors that might end a Black artist's career.[5] *Atlanta*'s Black Bieber performs a song with lyrics alluding to the real-world Bieber's "Sorry" (2015), thereby highlighting the latter's white privilege: "You know what I did, it doesn't matter." The reporter summarizes the racial double standard that Alfred faces and the racial performance that the white entertainment industry will expect: "Listen, I want to give you some advice. Play your part. People don't want Justin to be the asshole. They want you to be the asshole. You're a rapper. That's your job." Alfred takes her advice to some extent, but in "Sportin' Waves" (s2e2), he learns that white tastemakers at an unnamed Spotify-like streaming company at which Earn gets him a meeting still do not find his public image marketable. Instead, they endorse Clark County, an actual "asshole" whose deceitfully mild public-facing persona translates well for television commercials that sell products like Yoo-hoo. Even when Alfred's songs do get radio airplay, the dividends are minimal. As he emphasizes in "The Streisand Effect" (s1e4): "There's no money anywhere near rap. . . . [N]***as die. People are forgotten. Shit is real." The point is not just that the largely white-owned entertainment industry profits from Black performance or that it repeatedly forgives white artists for their transgressions while discarding Black artists once they no longer appear exploitable.[6] It also demands that Alfred continuously sacrifice his self-sovereignty by fulfilling ever-changing white fantasies about Blackness as he chases success,[7] which helps explain why Lorraine—a manifestation of Al's subconscious anxieties in "New Jazz" (s3e8)—suggests that he needs to own his "masters," a term that has a particularly important double meaning in this context.

As vehicles for a normative satirical sensibility, Earn and Alfred are aware of racial injustice but largely powerless to change it. This is clear in "Money Bag Shawty." After having his one-hundred-dollar bill rejected (and seeing the white man's one-hundred-dollar bill accepted), Earn approaches the cashier a second time attempting to reason with him. His reflexive faith in liberal ideals leads Earn to believe that racial injustice can be confronted and corrected through rational debate. The white cashier never looks at or speaks to Earn, though, instead flashing his concealed pistol in a threat of violence that evokes the extrajudicial murders of Black men and reaffirms the fundamentally racial contract's inequitable nature. The white man silences Earn, who can only criticize the racist encounter in private among other Black characters. However, because they also have limited agency, his criticism has no real-world effect.

Alfred experiences similar failure in "White Fashion" (s3e6). When the fictitious fashion house Esco Esco[8] faces backlash for obliviously releasing a "Central Park 5" shirt, Alfred joins their "diversity advisory board." Earn rightly criticizes the brand's performative apology, but he also scolds Alfred for not insisting that they reinvest in Black communities, seemingly convinced that such monetary atonement might offset the injustices wrought by appropriative capitalism. When Alfred proposes a "reinvest-in-your-hood" campaign, Esco Esco whitewashes it with a Benetton-esque display of corporate multiculturalism that echoes the "all-lives-matter" refrain by insisting "we're all from some hood." The fashion house negates Alfred's intentions while also profiting from his idea. Social commentary and critique, in the conventional meaning Frye and others attribute to satire, cannot mitigate the racism that *Atlanta* chronicles.

By representing racial subordination as a pervasive, routine, and systemic reality produced and reinforced (and therefore unresolvable) by Western rationalism, *Atlanta* dramatizes what Saidiya Hartman terms the "afterlife of slavery" (*Lost* passim). Hartman argues that "black lives are still imperiled and devalued by a racial calculus and political arithmetic that were entrenched centuries ago," describing enslavement's continuing effects as "skewed life chances, limited access to health and education, premature death, incarceration, and impoverishment" (6). These conditions reflect the theoretical framework known as "Afropessimism," a mode of Black radical thought that approaches race as a condition of extreme social exclusion and abject ontological negation.[9] Glover has made this theoretical link between racialization and social death tangible in interviews by explaining that Black people cannot substantively alter a society designed by white people for white people: "The system is set up so only white people can change things . . . that's true of *everything* made for white people. I can say there's a problem, you can all laugh at it, but it has to be a group of you guys [white people] who can change it, because it was made by and for you" (Friend, emphasis original). Glover's comment clarifies the depth of Earn and Alfred's social death, the "civic estrangement" (Tillet, *Sites* 3) they endure despite possessing full legal citizenship, rising social status, and increasing financial security. Alfred again discovers that Blackness has no recourse in "The Old Man and the Tree" (s3e3), when he wins $40,000 playing poker but remains powerless to collect when his white billionaire opponent refuses to pay up. This figuration suggests that conventional satirical questions like, "How might civil society be improved?" presume that a separate, more fundamental question—"What does it mean to be a part of civilization?"—has already been asked and answered.

Atlanta revisits the question of "what it means to be a part of civilization" as a metaphysical problem—in a degenerative satirical idiom—through Darius (LaKeith Stanfield). Darius's actions parody the normativity of liberal thought to expose its racist predispositions. As a vehicle for a subversive satirical sensibility, he (re)claims the Black agency that Earn and Alfred are unable—or perhaps, unwilling—to assert. His appropriation and recuration of the Confederate flag serves as a particularly instructive example. The cold open for "Teddy Perkins" (s2e6) shows Darius in line at a convenience store. While waiting, he sees a red trucker hat featuring a Confederate flag and the phrase "SOUTHERN MADE." After he purchases the hat and a red Sharpie, the camera follows him through the parking lot as he blocks out some of the hat's white embroidered letters with the marker, transforming the slogan "SOUTHERN MADE" into the sardonic statement "U MAD."[10]

In Darius's hands, appropriation and recuration are tools for commandeering the devices that legitimize anti-Blackness and reconfiguring the context in which they have been upheld, normalized, and celebrated. Percival Everett's "The Appropriation of Cultures" (1996) is a useful intertext for thinking through Darius's subversion. In the opening of Everett's story, a group of drunk white college students ask a young Black musician named Daniel to play "Dixie." Daniel knows that "Dixie" is a piece of the cultural machinery that reaffirms racial hierarchies: "[It was] a song he had grown up hating, the song the whites had always pulled out to remind themselves and those other people just where they were" (Everett 24). However, being (like Everett) a native of South Carolina, he also recognizes his own blood in southern soil, meaning the song's inversion also rings true: "His was the land of cotton and hell no, it was not forgotten" (25). By "deciding that the song was his" and "resist[ing] the urge to let satire ring through his voice" (24), Daniel defamiliarizes "Dixie" and denaturalizes the hierarchies it would uphold. He repeats this subversive act of appropriation/recuration later by purchasing a pickup truck displaying a Confederate-flag decal on its rear window. Daniel decides the flag is his and begins calling it the "black power flag" (28), subverting its conventional meaning. Daniel's appropriation even prompts officials to remove the Confederate flag from its station above the state house in Columbia, an action that happened in the real world in 2015. As Hutcheon might say, Daniel appropriates "Dixie" and the Confederate flag to "de-doxify" them, a process of parodic unmaking that queries both their discursive meaning and the normative beliefs that sustain them as ideological devices.

When *Atlanta* shows Darius appropriating and recurating the "SOUTHERN MADE" hat, it uses parody as a strategic discursive structure that denaturalizes racial discourse to re-present normative culture to itself as contrived and prejudicial. Like Everett's protagonist, who decides that "the rebel flag is [his] flag" because "[his] blood is southern blood" (27), Darius insists on Black belonging where it is denied. "Dixie," the Confederate flag, and the hat's caption all have complementary functions: to exclude Blacks from US civil society by linking "true" southern identity to whiteness. For this reason, the white convenience-store clerk hesitates when Darius places the hat on the counter; we know that he knows that its usual interpretation debases Black people by recalling their enslavement. In Everett's short story, the white pickup owner similarly hesitates when Daniel tells him not to remove the Confederate-flag decal from the truck's rear window. Daniel explains that he is "not buying the truck" so much as he is "buying the decal" attached to it, an inversion that clarifies Darius's subversive act. He is not buying the hat so much as he is buying its racist message's symbolic capital. Such co-optations subvert the New South's social order by suggesting that Black men like Daniel and Darius represent a constituency with legitimate ownership of southern pride. They are "de-doxifying" the Confederate flag and the idea of southern identity by denaturalizing the malignant anti-Blackness that these symbols' existence upholds, normalizes, and celebrates under the ostensibly benign guise of southern pride.

Atlanta's presentation of the Confederate flag also challenges mainstream audiences' reflexive faith in liberal incremental reform. It collapses the temporal gap seemingly separating the Old South's anti-Blackness from that of the present by signifying on both the "Lost Cause" nationalist ideology and the red "Make America Great Again" hats worn by former president Donald Trump's supporters.[11] This parallel uncovers the historically entrenched and pervasive spirit of anti-Blackness in US civil society, refuting the possibility that America's legacy of racial oppression has been "corrected" or that it ever could be without a wholesale reimagining of civilization and society. Everett's reflections on satire help to clarify how *Atlanta* satirizes satire itself through Darius. As Everett explains in an interview, he does not feel that his fiction is satirical, but rather that it exploits satire: "I'm making fun of satire as well as satirizing social policies. I mean, I shouldn't even say this, but I write about satire" (Shavers 50). What both Everett and *Atlanta* find worthy of mocking laughter is neither social relations nor racial injustice, but rather the assumption that incremental reform can right social wrongs and the related idea that liberal institutions are the virtuous standard that should be defended.

The phrase "U MAD" plays into this process, as it implicates viewers who adhere—consciously or unconsciously—to the assumptive racial logic of liberal thought. It signifies on a popular meme in which rapper Cam'ron taunted conservative broadcaster Bill O'Reilly during a 2003 Fox News segment that aimed to denigrate rap music for its "negative" messages. During the show, O'Reilly became exasperated and tongue-tied, after which Cam'ron mocked him, saying, "You mad, you maaad, you maaad!" ("Is Gangsta Rap"). Cam'ron's response undermined O'Reilly's attempts to pathologize Blackness by insinuating that his paternalizing indictment of rap was a racially coded critique vilifying communities of color while affirming the assumed civility of whiteness. *Atlanta* ridicules white outrage over hip-hop lyrics in "Money Bag Shawty," which begins with a YouTube video posted by a white woman complaining that the vulgarity of Paper Boi's lyrics poses a danger to her ten-year-old daughter. Like O'Reilly, the woman appeals to the veiled racial logic of civility by characterizing Paper Boi's music as "disgusting." Also like O'Reilly, she becomes exasperated, audibly crying as she reads the song's lyrics. In the spirit of Cam'ron's "you mad," Earn, Alfred, and Darius ridicule her criticism by raising a glass and toasting her "white tears." Darius explains that the white woman's viral video has become free advertising that helps Paper Boi market his gangster image. "That white woman crying, that was the best thing that could've happened to us," he tells Earn and Alfred; "Their tears are powerful." As Darius sees it, the new single went gold because the crew appropriated and recurated the "white-outrage" subgenre.

In "Teddy Perkins," Darius's reuse of the phrase "U MAD" signals the "white rage" that Cam'ron ridiculed, but it also contends that normative liberal viewpoints are irrational not to acknowledge modernity's intrinsic anti-Blackness. Terrence T. Tucker describes this kind of militant comic vision as a strategy for defying racist structures, characterizing "comic rage" as a mode of expression that "actively reveals the perpetuation of white supremacist hegemony through its mixture of tones and inversion of traditional discourse" (3). Darius's "U MAD" similarly calls out traditional liberal discourse for upholding the stage of misremembrance on which cultural hegemony posits whiteness's civility while reproducing anti-Blackness as a normative cultural standard. Accordingly, it is significant that Darius's recuration is a statement, instead of a question, since a question would allow hegemonic actors to respond (likely in contrived incredulity), whereas the statement offers no such chance. His "U MAD" calls forth the "mad" realities of the racial contract and thus initiates audiences' descent into madness at Teddy's mansion, where disorienting racial performances become increasingly absurd.

Darius is not the sole embodiment of a degenerative satirical ethos in *Atlanta*, though. The series also satirizes liberalism's engrained racism through Alfred's recently paroled friend Tracy (Khris Davis). Whereas Darius's actions appear as controlled and prudent philosophical inversions of social normativity, the series characterizes Tracy as a chaotic figure whose tendency toward lawlessness marks the limits of gainful societal subversion. The connection between Darius and Tracy as vehicles of subversive satire is clear in "Sportin' Waves," which picks up where "The Streisand Effect" leaves off. In that earlier episode, Earn tries to pawn his cell phone, but Darius tells him that he can get him more money and proceeds to do so through an elaborate process that involves first trading the phone for a samurai sword, then swapping the sword for a full-grown Cane Corso dog, which he in turn delivers to a breeder.[12] Months later, when the puppies sired by the Cane Corso are born, Darius's trade-up hustle turns Earn's $190 phone into a massive (albeit delayed) windfall of $4,000. In "Sportin' Waves," Tracy offers to double Earn's money again by loading it onto a gift card at a local mall. As soon as Earn uses the overloaded gift card, however, mall security flags it, leaving Earn just twenty minutes to spend the remaining balance.

Although both Tracy and Darius appear as subversive figures, *Atlanta* represents Tracy's anarchic hostility toward white hegemony as a riskier and less rewarding version of Darius's deliberate parodic inversions. When at the mall, for example, Tracy steals a pair of dress shoes while explaining to Earn that he is adapting the store's rules for his own benefit: "They got a no-chase policy. They can't stop me.... Even if they see me stealing, they can't chase me... [the salesman] gotta keep giving me great customer service. That's all he can do." Like Darius, Tracy is appropriating a codified social standard and recurating it for his own ends. Through Tracy's recuration, *Atlanta* highlights the salesman's vulnerability to being rendered powerless and, by extension, challenges the authority of the broader capitalist structures represented by the shoe store and the mall, perhaps even the idea of whiteness with which capitalism is historically entangled. Unlike Tracy, though, Darius remains careful not to become a victim of his own parody, even when the stakes are relatively low. For instance, he deliberately removes his "U MAD" hat when approaching Teddy's mansion because he knows that its parodic force might hurt his chances to pick up Benny Hope's rainbow-keyed piano. At the same time, when Tracy co-opts the mall's no-chase policy, he renders himself vulnerable because the clerk could call the police, thereby potentially even precipitating his (or Earn's) extrajudicial murder.

By contrasting Darius's cautious parodies with Tracy's anarchic provocations, *Atlanta* marks subversive satire's limits as a gainful response to anti-Blackness. The series suggests that although both are tenable reactions to white hegemony, the former is a more effectual mode of subversion than the latter. "Nobody Beats the Biebs" again defines these limits when Darius brings a paper target imprinted with the silhouette of a dog to a gun range. After he begins shooting at it, a pair of white patrons confront him:

WHITE GUN-RANGE PATRON: What do you think you're doing?
DARIUS: Who me? Shootin'.
WHITE GUN-RANGE PATRON: You can't shoot dogs. What are you, a psycho?
DARIUS: Why not? Listen, man . . . the dogs in my neighborhood, they're crazy. They bite babies and they—
WHITE GUN-RANGE PATRON: I don't give a damn . . . my kid could be in here. You can't shoot a dog.
DARIUS: Well, why would I shoot at a human target? I mean, that's weird, right? I mean, look at that one [points at target labeled "Dad"], I mean that's just way too specific, man.
WHITE GUN-RANGE PATRON: I don't care . . . I'm not going to let you shoot a fucking dog in here.

Through this interaction, *Atlanta* asks its audience to consider why it is "normal" to shoot at targets featuring a human but unthinkable to shoot at targets with dogs on them.

Another character enters the scene and highlights the racial undertones of this question by telling one of the white men: "He can shoot at whatever he wants. You shoot at your racist targets with no problem. I saw you shoot at that one with a Mexican holding a knife." Darius's violation exposes the illogic that dictates which bodies normally matter and which bodies are normally targets, revealing the normativity of the everyday to be a dissimulation of racial violence. Darius nevertheless also knows the limits of advisable social subversion. When the character who comes to Darius's defense threatens that "a revolution will rise from within" and that "blood will spill," Darius backs down because such hostility is outside the range of his judicious satirical worldview. Darius's disavowal of the other character's threat rejects the anarchic opposition that Tracy embodies. In this case, however, the threshold has already been crossed, and the white proprietor expels Darius from the range at gunpoint, an action that negates the parodic work Darius accomplished with the dog target—for the range's patrons, though not *Atlanta*'s audience—by reaffirming the racial contract's fundamental inequity.

Although *Atlanta* does not valorize Tracy, it represents him as a character who still knows better than Earn how social norms might be appropriated and recurated. Consider this conversation about job interviews, which contrasts Tracy (as a vehicle of subversive satire) from Earn (as a vehicle of normative satire):

TRACY: Yo, you went to Princeton, right?
EARN: Yeah.
TRACY: Man, how should I talk to these white folks?

EARN: Um, I don't know. Probably don't call them "white folks," and . . . talk confidently.
TRACY: A'ight. A'ight, cool, cool. 'Cause you know, I'm a talker [laughs].

Earn tells Tracy to treat his white interviewer respectfully and to avoid drawing attention to race, advice that invokes verbal code-switching and the potential benefits of abiding by established behavioral norms. But Earn misunderstands Tracy, who is interested less in civility and more in how he might take control by subverting the white interviewer's power. Tracy has already begun preparing a racial performance that he believes will do this, although his performance relies on physical appearance rather than speech and demeanor. He has "picked up" (read, "stolen") a pair of "preppy" (read, "white") loafers, telling Earn: "these white folk people gonna love me. I'ma get hired on the spot." Additionally, he has chemically relaxed his hair into a wavy conk. Malcolm X associated this hairstyle with self-hating Black men whose imitation of European beauty standards signaled a desire to assimilate into whiteness, but Tracy thinks it might also be appropriated and recurated to trouble the Black-white power differential. For Tracy, the conk completes a racial performance that strategically feigns a sartorial civility he associates with whiteness, which he therefore believes will appeal to the interviewer.

Atlanta depicts this racial performance as absurd, though, and Tracy is predictably denied the job, at which point he verbally attacks his interviewer. He yells "Y'all racist as hell up in here, man!" as he exits the room, continuing, "Get some Black people up in here. . . . Ameri-KKK, n***a!" Tracy's aggressive provocation verges on buffoonery, but it also creates a rich satirical moment that queries the virtue of civility and exposes behavioral norms as tools of racial hegemony. As one who values civility and does not fully recognize his own social death, Earn might have thanked the interviewer for his time and then calmly left the room, only criticizing the interviewer's racism privately with other Black characters. Tracy, though, upbraids the interviewer and the racial gatekeeping he oversees, then denounces US civil society by refiguring "America" as explicitly and the fundamentally racist "Ameri-KKK." Nothing in the scene ever suggests that Tracy thinks he can change the outcome of the interview; rather, his outburst confirms that he can do what Earn cannot. By rejecting the terms of white-defined civility and by pushing against the racist structures that reinforce his civic estrangement, Tracy recovers—in a symbolic sense—some of the self-sovereignty that white hegemony denies him.[13] *Atlanta* suggests that it is through incivility, not civility, that Tracy contests Blackness's abject ontological negation.

As engines of satirical "counter memory" (Roach 5–6, 26), Darius and Tracy reflect normative culture back upon itself as a contrived and prejudicial construct, effecting a Blackening of US civil society in which audiences can encounter the inequality, regression, and incivility that are obscured by liberal discourses of equality, progress, and civilization. Their degenerative satirical sensibilities create an interstice in which Black agency becomes intelligible. *Atlanta* shows viewers how Western social organization imagines civil society as a definitively white space, effectively excluding Blacks from civilization. Instead of appealing to reason to combat racism, as Earn futilely tries to do, Darius and Tracy reject rationalism's imperializing authority. Their responses to racial inequality are significant not only because they constitute an unruly and irruptive refusal of white civility, but also because their actions inherently claim the authority to refuse. By mocking the notion of their social death and divesting civility of its assumed virtue, *Atlanta* paradoxically (re)claims the agency that white hegemony tries to deny Darius and Tracy.

The series further juxtaposes these normative and subversive satirical sensibilities in "North of the Border" (s2e9).[14] This episode follows Earn, Alfred, Darius, and Tracy to Statesboro, Georgia, where Paper Boi is scheduled to perform at a Black Greek life event called Pajama Jam. The night sours when a female student splashes her drink on Alfred, and it goes completely off the rails when Tracy mistakenly confronts and assaults the woman. To avoid an all-out brawl, the crew makes a quick exit, leaving behind Alfred's weed. Things get surreal as Darius leads everyone to a fraternity house with an all-white membership that invites them inside to smoke marijuana. *Atlanta* underscores the campus's racial segregation when one of the young men on the house's porch asks why Alfred and his friends are wearing silk pajamas; by asking, he reveals his unawareness of Pajama Jam, even though several of the fraternity's members are hopelessly starstruck at meeting Paper Boi, whose music they revere along with southern hip hop in general.

The doubly Georgian fraternity house itself acts as a symbol of liberal thought. With its stately Greek columns, French doors, expansive porch, and balcony, its exterior resembles an ornate plantation house. The house's address plate reads 1863, alluding to the year Abraham Lincoln issued the Emancipation Proclamation. For some viewers, these surface details might evoke decorated, hoop-skirted gowns and other lineaments of southern romanticism or perhaps even the ideals associated with Lincoln as the Great Emancipator. Once the action moves inside, though, *Atlanta* scuttles such possibilities by revealing a giant Confederate flag hanging on the living-room wall. Displayed out of public view, the flag represents the racial subconscious of liberalism, which is quick to forget plantations' entanglement with chattel slavery[15] and also fails to acknowledge the emancipation/disemancipation dialectic of the Emancipation Proclamation, a document that granted Blacks freedom while imposing new restrictions on what freedom meant for them, effectively preserving the white supremacy of US civil society in legal and material terms.

Earn and Alfred are noticeably—and unsurprisingly—uncomfortable in this setting. When one of the fraternity brothers talks about southern rap and the philosophy of the Texas hip-hop duo UGK, Alfred guards his responses while Earn stares ahead silently. Their discomfort increases when, in a hazing ritual visually reminiscent of "dancing the slaves," the fraternity brother prompts two rows of naked, white pledges with burlap sacks over their heads to perform a synchronized snap dance to D4L's 2005 song "Laffy Taffy." Because the pledges' humiliation signifies the torture of enslaved Africans, it complicates the racial hierarchy that the scene's Confederate undertones and iconography evoke; however, viewers are assured that the pledges' embarrassment is temporary and that it will be rewarded. The fraternity brother explains, "Newbies gotta pay the price," characterizing their momentary discomfiture as an entryway into a social arrangement of authority and power. In this arrangement, the white pledges will soon have full citizenship and full civic belonging, both of which are predicated on Black peoples' exclusion—de facto, if not de jure—from both the all-white fraternity and, in a broader sense, US civil society. Although there is never any explicit threat to Earn and Alfred, they cannot relax until after the white characters have left the room. For them, it is only in the absence of whiteness that Black life—represented here by their restrained and uneasy laughter—can resume.

Alternatively, Darius and Tracy are relaxed, even laughing, throughout the scene. "Man, this shit is bugged the fuck out," Tracy exclaims, then compliments the fraternity's concealed irrationality, which aligns with his own worldview: "I like what y'all doing here, bruh. You don't give no fucks." Darius then comments on an elephant rifle hanging on the wall, and when a white character brags about their gun room, Darius and Tracy accept an invitation to see it for themselves, unafraid of descending deeper into the house. Viewers later learn that Tracy is even comfortable enough to steal one of the fraternity's eighteenth-century pistols. This is yet another subversively anarchic act that disrupts the white-Black power structure on which the scene plays, given that the flintlock has no utility. For Tracy, it is a souvenir that represents agency, a symbol of the power that the fraternity assumes he lacks.

The feelings of racial subjugation and civil estrangement that *Atlanta* dramatizes are not incidental features of the modern world, but rather base elements in the inceptive logic of Western social organization. Through depictions of Earn and Alfred's social death, we see how liberal notions of equality, progress, and civilization preserve—while obscuring—the racist ideas we are told the United States has overcome, reproducing racial subordination as a structural reality that predisposes them to "losing." With a more radical, degenerative sensibility, however, Darius and Tracy trouble the social normativity that governs this losing. Doing so challenges rationalism's imperial racial logic, in effect subverting white hegemony and (re)claiming the agency that modernity denies Black people. The series thus satirizes reason and civility—the grounds of conventional satire—as ineffectual responses to racialization. Indeed, for *Atlanta*'s Black characters, it is fugitivity, not rationality, that upends racial politics and creates an opening for Black life.

NOTES

1. Frye builds on David Worcester's *The Art of Satire* (1940) and Ian Jack's *Augustan Satire* (1942) and, in turn, influences Gilbert Highet's *Anatomy of Satire* (1962), Frederick Kiley and Jack M. Shuttleworth's *Satire: from Aesop to Buchwald* (1971), Leon Guilhamet's *Satire and the Transformation of Genre* (1989), and John Clark's *The Modern Satiric Grotesque and Its Traditions* (1991).

2. See J. Gray xi–xii.

3. For historical examples of racial retrenchment, see Du Bois, *Black Reconstruction* 700; Bunche 297–326; and Crenshaw, "Race to the Bottom."

4. The invitation—itself a parody of a television cliché—in the final episode ("It Was All a Dream" [s4e10]) to see the entire series as nothing more than Darius's dream contributes to this sense.

5. For further discussion of this episode, see Cortes's essay herein.

6. This aspect of the music business is developed further with the concept of "young white avatars" in "Born 2 Die" (s4e3).

7. For further discussion of this topic, see the essays by Foster-Singletary and Rutter herein.

8. A possible allusion to the hip hop designer and brand Willie Esco.

9. See Patterson; and Wilderson.

10. For further discussion of this episode and scene, see Foster-Singletary's essay herein.

11. It also anticipates the Confederate flags prevalent among the mob that stormed the US Capitol on January 6, 2021.

12. For further discussion of this episode, see the essays by Lee and Klestil herein.

13. Tracy's participation in Earn's elaborate revenge on a rude white airport employee in "The Homeliest Little Horse" perhaps suggests that Earn has absorbed some of Tracy's approach over the years.

14. For further discussion of this episode and scene, see the essays by Foster-Singletary and Rutter herein.

15. This strategic forgetting is evident in the many antebellum homes that have been remodeled into wedding venues, some of which trade on the "romance" of the plantation in their advertising.

AWKWARDNESS AND BLACK MILLENNIAL SATIRE IN *INSECURE* AND *ATLANTA*

ERICA-BRITTANY HORHN AND DEREK C. MAUS

The coinage and application of generational categories within the scholarship on contemporary African American culture show little sign of abating as of the new millennium's third decade. Even while such inherently generational terminology as "the post-soul aesthetic," "post-Blackness," and "Black post-Blackness" still enjoy various degrees of relevance and/or acceptance, scholars of contemporary Black satire have introduced additional wrinkles that offer both complications and clarifications. In her *Laughing to Keep from Dying: African American Satire in the Twenty-First Century* (2020), Danielle Fuentes Morgan theorizes the development of a "kaleidoscopic Blackness," the recognition of which she calls "an ethical move that leads to social justice in its revelation of the multiple ways of performing Blackness and being Black, where social justice is the freedom to be, freedom to articulate and perform one's own autonomous identity" (4). In a brief essay published a year after Morgan's book, Brandon J. Manning insightfully surveys the state of "Black Millennial Satire" (the title of his work) by juxtaposing the "current cohort of Black satirists against the Baby Boomers and Gen Xers who dominated the end of the last century and the beginning of this one." Manning posits that more recent satire is notable for its rejection of what he calls the "Cosby Effect," which for decades contributed "to a focus on upper- and middle-class Black America and to centering blackness without naming race and racism: the cultural wing of respectability politics." Manning contends that much Black satire from "the 90s and 00s . . . diverged from *The Cosby Show* in its displays of ambivalence about politics . . . but often laughed at the inevitability of anti-blackness," whereas "today's Millennial Black satirists" transcend such "fatalism" by "insist[ing] on moving beyond ambivalence, toward action. They name injustice toward its eradication."

Although both Morgan and Manning valuably augment the discourse surrounding contemporary Black satire, we assert that further distinction is necessary to fully comprehend the changing relationships between Black identity and satire from Trey Ellis's "New Black Aesthetic" of the late 1980s to the era of Black Lives Matter. As of the early 2020s, artists from the younger end of the millennial age range are only beginning to find wider audiences for their work, which inherently makes Manning's discussion heavily reliant on an older subset within the general (if somewhat hazy) conception of his chosen generational terminology.[1] Although Manning singles out the "trajectory of [Dave] Chappelle's career" from *Chappelle's Show* (2003–2006) through his 2020 Netflix special *8:46* as evidence of "a necessary passing of the baton for a comedic genius who realized that he might not have the tools to capture the voice of this new younger generation," we believe that close examination of Donald Glover's *Atlanta* (2016–2022) and Issa Rae's *Insecure* (2016–2021) actually demonstrates this transition more effectively. Manning rightly notes that Chappelle has demonstrated, in numerous ways, that he is still "not fully ready for his moment to pass," an assertion that seems still more astute after the controversy that Chappelle has courted and embraced through his jokes about transgender people—among others—since *The Age of Spin* (2017) and *Deep in the Heart of Texas* (2017). At the same time, both *Atlanta* and *Insecure* indicate that Glover and Rae have transcended the influence of various post-soul/Gen X forerunners, including Chappelle, Chris Rock, Spike Lee, and Wanda Sykes, in becoming significant members of a kaleidoscopically and millennially Black "post-Obama scene" (Manning, "Black Millennial Satire") that "eschews the respectability that delimits behavior and instead acknowledges *all ways of being black as valid forms of identity*" (Morgan, *Laughing* 8, emphasis original). *Atlanta* and *Insecure* signal an intergenerational "passing of the baton," which attests to the artistic maturation of two Black satirists too young to be among Mark Anthony Neal's "children of soul" (3) but also old enough to have experienced the racialized highs and lows of the Barack Obama and Donald Trump presidencies as adults.[2]

Neal outlines the temporal parameters of the "post-soul" generation of African Americans, as well as its relationship to various political and cultural shifts:

> I locate the beginnings of the post-soul era in the *Regents of the University of California v. Bakke* challenge to affirmative action in 1978. I'm most concerned about those folks, artists, and critical thinkers, who live in the fissures of two radically different social paradigms; folks born between the 1963 March on Washington and the *Bakke* case . . . who came to maturity in the age of Reaganomics, and experienced the change from urban industrialism to deindustrialism, from segregation

to desegregation, from existential notions of blackness to metanarratives on blackness. (3)

Although many of the processes Neal ascribes to the post-soul sensibility are clearly still underway, his timeframe serves as a reminder that the first Black millennials were themselves barely departing adolescence as Neal was writing this definition; *their* cultural-historical touchstones are neither Reaganomics nor the end of the Cold War, but rather the events and conditions that Reniqua Allen catalogues:

> [Millennials are] a generation profoundly shaped by the events of its time—9/11, the Iraq War, the Great Recession, climate change—and baleful socioeconomic trends: growing income inequality, staggering levels of student debt, stagnant wages. . . . Black millennials came of age in the so-called post-race era, their worldview defined by Barack Obama's historic rise to the presidency, Beyonce's dominance of the entertainment industry, and Ta-Nehisi Coates's emergence as one of the premier public intellectuals in this country. But they also witnessed tragedies like the Rodney King beating, Hurricane Katrina, and the police shootings of Mike Brown and so many other young black men and women. They saw the horrific and racist treatment of our first black president and his wife. And then they saw the alleged "post-race" period give way to the election of the most openly racist president in modern American history.

Allen concludes by asserting: "To comprehend the black millennial experience in America is to comprehend what it means to hope. Not in a feel-good way, not in a naive way, but in a desperate way, as a way of life, because the alternative is unacceptable." Allen's claim strongly echoes both the title of Morgan's book and her argument that contemporary Black satire is a form of "revolutionary laughter that keeps us alive in the twenty-first century" (Morgan, *Laughing* 23).

Both *Atlanta* and *Insecure* are influenced by a wide assortment of comedic ancestors in expressing an emergent Black millennial satirical sensibility deeply reliant on a pervasive sense of awkwardness. Awkwardness is hardly a recent development in either television comedy generally or African American television comedy more specifically. Such wildly popular shows as *Seinfeld* (1989–1998) and *Curb Your Enthusiasm* (2000–) to *The Office* (US version, 2005–2013) and *New Girl* (2011–2018) showcase awkward characters fumbling through everyday circumstances. As Gaylene Gould notes about Rae in regard to *The Misadventures of Awkward Black Girl* (the web series that preceded *Insecure*): "She encroaches on territory usually occupied by older Jewish men—existential comedy. Rae has said she was inspired to write the series after studying Jerry Seinfeld and Larry David—comedians who amble through the musing mind, revealing frailties most of us are too cool to admit to" (28–29). Gould finds *Insecure* to be a "gentrified version of . . . *Misadventures*" (29) and specifically claims that "*Atlanta* is full of the problematic tropes that Rae consciously wants to move away from . . . [as she] has seemed to drift to a more centrist view, while Glover has continued to travel way past leftfield" (30). We strongly disagree with Gould's dichotomy[3] and contend that *both* Glover and Rae "humorously blend . . . the historical weight of black abjection with other kinds of abjection" so that their characters' particular situations are no longer primarily "determined by the history of white supremacy. The term awkward becomes a synonym for abjection and also a modification of it, lessening its power to wound" (Wanzo 30). As Keyana Parks succinctly puts it, within this contemporary version of awkwardness, "Blackness becomes one source of abjection and not the sole defining one" (n.p.).

Tyrone Simpson has produced one of the most sustained surveys of awkwardness as a trope in contemporary Black self-expression, starting with the observation:

> [Awkwardness conventionally] involved a change in station, conspicuous yet perilous movement within the social hierarchy, wherein a subject finds itself having to exercise privileges and responsibilities with which it is uncomfortable. Both body and mind comport themselves strangely, moving the person to gesture, if at all, in ways inappropriate to the moment or the scene. . . . [A]wkwardness is so out of sorts with social graces that it leaves its subject vulnerable to a wide range of mistreatments, violence being not the least among them. (229)

Arguing that Black awkwardness is "an affect suggestive of a new racial category" (230), Simpson largely interprets it "as a strategic response to the racial terms of society's new economic preferences, because of the decided racial ambivalence with which they are laced" (233). This is particularly relevant to the ways that many of the principal characters of *Atlanta* and *Insecure* struggle to live and to make a living.[4] These characters embody Simpson's assertion that "awkwardness no longer solely denotes a discrete moment or period of sensation, or even a number of them. Instead, it appears that the term 'awkward' has accrued the broader power of being an ontological descriptor. One can now use 'awkward' to speak of a way of being and by tricks of narrative [to] suggest the condition's infinity" (233).

Simpson's theorization also speaks to how and why Glover and Rae project their own unconventional expressions of Black identity onto fictional characters who bear some resemblance to them without *being* them: "Awkward blackness is an enduring or recurring condition that becomes manifest when issues of race, class, identity, and narrative self-production collide as they do in autobiographical writing. . . . I find it hard to imagine a more awkward gesture than for a black writer within the context of a racist culture to agree to documenting one's personal experiences for readers who are generally unlike oneself" (234). Both Glover and Rae have, in other contexts, created works that more directly document their "personal experiences." Much of Glover's standup comedy and many of the lyrics of his early Childish Gambino songs document aspects of his youth, as evident in these lines from "Outside" off his debut album, *Camp* (2011): "Mrs. Glover ma' am, your son is so advanced / But he's acting up in class and keeps peeing in his pants. / And I just wanna fit in, but nobody was helping me out. / They talking hood shit and I ain't know what that was about." Rae also published a book with the same title as her web series; explicitly marketed as an autobiography, it drew clear parallels between her fictional protagonist J and herself by identifying them both as examples of the archetypal "Awkward Black Girl."

Thus, although Glover and Rae both use autobiographical Black awkwardness in their earlier work, its repurposing in *Atlanta* and *Insecure* indicates the maturation of their Black millennial satirical perspectives. Writing specifically about contemporary Black women's satire, Jessyka Finley identifies the strategic nature of such a choice: "Representational discourse is a structure in which ideas about social identities cohere and maintain traction. Popular culture is a significant site where black womanhood has been maligned and misunderstood with dire consequences" (262). By parodying and then satirizing various elements of the "representational discourse" surrounding awkward Black characters, Glover and Rae extend their respective processes of liberating self-expression by subverting the limitations placed on Blackness in both real life and on television.

The specific "undercut[ting]" of Manning's "Cosby Effect" began somewhat haltingly as selected sitcoms from the late 1980s and 1990s[5] began including nuanced portrayals of awkward Black people. Rae singles out the influence these shows had on the awkwardness she embodied in *Misadventures*: "That felt like an identity that I had not seen reflected in television or film before or at least in a very long time, not since the '90s with side characters" (Gross). Such "side characters" include Winifred "Freddie" Brooks (Cree Summer) of *A Different World* (1987–1993) and Synclaire James (Kim Coles) of *Living Single* (1993–1998). The former arrives at the fictional Hillman College as an eager but socially inept mixed-race student, and the latter is an aspiring actress with a conspicuous love of Troll dolls, who moves in with her gregarious and ambitious cousin Khadijah (Queen Latifah), who is also her boss at the publishing office in which she works as a receptionist. Freddie and Synclaire are initially portrayed as naïve and comparatively unsophisticated; despite frequently becoming the butt of relatively benign jokes among their peers, they are never ostracized for their awkwardness. As their characters develop throughout their respective series, though, Freddie and Synclaire offer audiences clear alternatives to the predominant tropes of Black womanhood found on television, including on the very shows in which they appeared.

Carlton Banks (Alfonso Ribeiro) from *The Fresh Prince of Bel-Air* (1990–1996) is a prime example of Black male awkwardness on television in this same timeframe.[6] On the surface, audiences are encouraged to juxtapose Carlton's awkwardness against his effortlessly cool cousin Will (Will Smith), whose persona feeds into many of the traditional stereotypes of Black masculinity. Because of his suburban, upper-class, private-school education and closer proximity—both physically and socially—to whiteness, Carlton is superficially positioned in diametrical opposition to the "West Philadelphia–born-and-raised" Will and his more stereotypically "authentic" lived experience of Blackness. As much as his famously uptight dancing, stilted diction, and assimilationist tendencies open him up to mild derision from Will, though, Carlton remains unashamed of his background and his experiences throughout the series and performs a version of Black awkwardness that was rarely seen—at least without being maligned—in film and television of the time.

Freddie, Synclaire, and Carlton are undoubtedly quirky compared to their respective shows' leads, and their lack of awareness about racialized social expectations often lead them into uncomfortable and even embarrassing situations. Nevertheless, they are ultimately not pushed to the margins, but rather embraced by their communities. The characters themselves became iconic and commodified figures for the generations of young Black men and women who grew up with them, a process perhaps best exemplified by the "nerd-chic" aesthetic embraced publicly by such professional basketball superstars as Kevin Durant, Russell Westbrook, and LeBron James in the early 2010s. Freddie, Synclaire, and Carlton are not awkward *because* they are Black, they are awkward largely because of how their Blackness is externally circumscribed. This fact becomes clear within the shows whenever they move between predominantly white social spaces and predominantly Black ones.

Glover and Rae expand and critique such performances of awkward Blackness from an uninhibited in-group perspective. Whereas Freddie, Synclaire, and Carlton are occasionally the targets of comparatively mild jesting, they only rarely become the vehicles by which satirical commentaries are transmitted, whether directed intramurally or extramurally. However, by working primarily within Black locales and with almost entirely Black casts of characters, *Atlanta* and *Insecure* create a "space for Black culture to reveal itself to itself, to come to know itself in the process of doing" (E. Johnson 449). Both shows accelerate the subversion of the "Cosby Effect" through their loving but also unflinching depiction of the full kaleidoscopic nature of Black communities within the larger cities in which they are set (and where each of their creators grew up).[7]

Atlanta avoids iconic associations with the city's Black culture—whether Morehouse College, the Ebenezer Baptist Church, or the Cascade roller rink that was immortalized in the film *ATL* (2006)—in favor of a wide range of comparatively mundane settings throughout metropolitan Atlanta and, especially in season 2, in Georgia more generally; season 3 diverts the principal characters to Europe before bringing them back to Atlanta and its environs in the final season. The lengthy aerial tracking shots over socioeconomically varied neighborhoods that accompany the title sequence in "The Big Bang" (s1e1) signal both the show's awareness of the city's history of segregation and its unwillingness to reproduce that "redlining" of Atlanta's Black citizenry in its own storytelling.[8] *Atlanta* primarily revolves around the relationship between Earnest "Earn" Marks (Glover) and his cousin Alfred Miles (Brian Tyree Henry), who is an aspiring rapper using the stage name Paper Boi. The show follows Earn, Alfred, Earn's on-again, off-again partner Van, and their friends Darius (LaKeith Stanfield) and Tracy (Khris Davis) as they try to survive and/or to thrive in both the hip-hop industry and their hometown. From its inception, Glover sought to create a show that gave him the creative space to talk about Black life differently: "I knew what FX wanted from me.... They were thinking it'd be me and Craig Robinson ... horse-tailing around, and it'll be kind of like 'Community,' and it'll be on for a long time. I was Trojan-horsing FX. If I told them what I really wanted to do, it wouldn't have gotten made" (Friend). The resulting show accomplishes Glover's stated goal of "fuck[ing] up television" by exploring the nuances of Black life through Earn, "an antihero ... [who] wasn't an expert in anything. He wasn't a great manager or a great part-time boyfriend or, for that matter, a particularly promising human being. Curiously boyish in shorts and a backpack, he wasn't even active, the minimal standard for television characters" (Friend).

Rae similarly uses *Insecure* as a love letter—though far from an uncritical one—to South LA, particularly the city of Inglewood. Echoing *Atlanta*, the establishing shot of "Insecure as Fuck" (s1e1) is a video montage that includes not only the de rigueur tall palm trees but also locations such as Randy's Donuts, the Forum (being overflown by a plane landing at nearby LAX), Louisiana Fried Chicken, and an array of visibly "ethnic" businesses. Reminiscent of Paul Beatty's novels *The White Boy Shuffle* (1996) and *The Sellout* (2015),[9] these rapidly interspersed shots introduce non-Black audiences to a multicultural Los Angeles, which moves beyond the stereotypically racialized spaces of "the hood" or "*el barrio*" while also largely eschewing such conventionally glamorous (and predominantly white, at least in the popular imagination) spaces as Hollywood and Beverly Hills. Rae articulates her intent in this regard explicitly:

"I never get to see [South LA] not displayed as the 'scary hood' and that's not the experience that I know.... I just wanted to make it feel sexy in a way that other places in L.A. are allowed that. Black and Latino places are not afforded that same luxury" (Jennings).

By locating their characters' awkwardness in primarily nonwhite physical environments, Glover and Rae decenter and critique the constraining influence of the white gaze on the performance of Blackness. This is in itself a "defiance of the status quo [that] manifests in an opening up of Black interior space[,] ... the hidden, private realm of Black thought and feeling beyond any expected performance of Blackness" (Morgan, *Laughing* 2). Rebecca Wanzo's assertion that *The Misadventures of Awkward Black Girl* "makes abjection safe for post-civil rights generations" (51) is even more true for *Atlanta* and *Insecure* as examples of their creators' fully matured Black millennial satirical sensibilities. What these shows depict is "an abjection that is not governed by traditional stereotypes but rather reflects millennials' hybrid status as individuals who are part of multiracial communities. It is an abjection rooted both in the black community ... and yet not limited to it" (51–52).

Insecure debuted one month after *Atlanta* and chronicles the lives of two longtime friends, Issa Dee (Rae) and Molly Carter (Yvonne Orji), as they experience love, friendship, and the daily trials of adulthood in their late twenties and early thirties. As is the case with *Atlanta*, the primary pairing of characters on *Insecure* is supplemented by a pair of additional companions, a feisty and sexually confident accountant named Kelli (Natasha Rothwell) and the happily married and thoroughly bougie Tiffany (Amanda Seales). Leading up to the show's final season, Rae insists that her intentions with *Insecure* were largely about including awkwardness within a kaleidoscopic vision of Blackness: "True representation is the ability to show your vulnerability and be able to say, 'I don't have it all together, just like the next white person doesn't have it all together.' ... I think the show gave Black people permission to also be like, 'You're right: We are insecure'" (Tillet, "'Insecure' Broke Ground"). Although *Insecure* is perhaps less explicitly satirical than *The Misadventures of Awkward Black Girl*, it still engages in a substantive critique of both individual behaviors and social conditions that relies on satirical representation.

For example, Rae engages in her own version of "Trojan-horsing" the television industry by embedding parodic television shows with satirical undertones into *Insecure*. In season 2, the embedded show is a salacious Civil War melodrama called *Due North* that evokes both *Underground* (2016–2017) and *Scandal* (2012–2018) in depicting the charged trope of a romantic relationship between a slaveowner and an enslaved person.[10] In season 3, it is a contemporary reboot of a quintessential 1990s-style Black situation comedy called *Kev'yn*. Showrunner Prentice Penny calls it "our homage to all the shows of color" and adds that he was inspired to write it after seeing networks resuscitate *Roseanne, Will & Grace*, and *Full House* (Montrose). Finally, in season 4, it is a fake reality show about the search for a missing Black woman called *Looking for LaToya*. In addition to showing snippets of these fake shows within *Insecure*'s diegetic frame, we also see promotional materials, such as billboards and bus placards, for them and frequently hear Issa and other characters discussing particular scenes or episodes. This nesting creates a metatextual discourse about television—both its products and its audience(s)—against which *Insecure*'s representations of Blackness can be compared critically.[11] Although there are, at times, some mild critiques of clichés and played-out formulas in these elaborate parodies of televisual conventions, they also convey more externally focused satirical criticisms as well (e.g., the white policemen who are searching for the missing LaToya repeatedly refer to her as "Toyota," suggesting a lack of interest in finding nonwhite missing women).

Given their multitude of such personal foibles as indecisiveness, impulsivity, idleness, and a tendency toward self-sabotage, both Earn and Issa are occasionally criticized for their actions and decision-making processes. Earn's status as a former Princeton student—which is mentioned but not elaborated upon at length in "The Big Bang"[12]—provisionally establishes him as an awkward "blerd." As "FUBU" (s2e10) later reveals, Earn has been recognized for being "book smart" long before his incomplete Ivy League education, but that trait has seemingly not helped him navigate the uncompromising city of Atlanta either before or after his possibly involuntary return: "He didn't seem to do or want anything. He just watched and flinched and got yelled at to grow up" (Friend). Issa is a perpetually self-conscious twenty-nine-year-old Stanford graduate and the only Black employee at a nonprofit aiming to improve the lives of inner-city kids. As awkward as she often is when speaking or acting, Issa has also learned to suppress her thoughts, which emerge both through her first-person voice-over narration (which largely subsides after the first season) and through rap monologues (and, later in the series, conversations with an alter ego she calls "mirror bitch") performed in her bathroom.[13]

Although neither show spares its protagonists from some partial measure of blame for the often-shambolic state of their respective lives, both Earn and Issa are also regularly used to direct satire toward external targets that exacerbate, manipulate, or unduly magnify the effects of their awkwardness, *especially* when they do so in ways that suggest their awkwardness is intrinsic to their Blackness. Because their respective jobs frequently require an ethically complicated engagement with representatives of various white power structures, Earn and Issa occasionally become conduits through which both shows critique ways in which ostensible white allies constrain them as individuals and as Black people.[14]

In his efforts at managing his cousin's career, Earn regularly interacts with white members of the music industry in ways that reveal both the exploitation of Blackness that goes on within the "rap game" and the systemic racism expressed by seemingly benevolent individuals, like Dave, the radio-station employee to whom Earn gives Paper Boi's mixtape to play on the air in "The Big Bang." As Earn and Dave interact affably, Dave casually drops the *n*-word into their conversation:

> DAVE: I didn't know you were in town.
> EARN: Uh, yeah, I've been low key, man.
> DAVE: Yo, obviously . . . Oh, dude, if I knew you was in town, I would've hit you up with this party last night. Yo, we needed a real DJ. This dude . . . well, he can't spin worth a shit, but then he goes and he plays Flo Rida.
> EARN: No!
> DAVE: Back-to-back. So, I calmly pull him aside, I was just like, "Really, nigga?"
> EARN: You actually said that?
> DAVE: Yeah, man, I had to.

Earn's skeptical facial expression makes clear that he disapproves of Dave's presumption that Earn will not be bothered by his language, but he does nothing to push back until he again encounters Dave, this time in a car with Alfred and Darius.

> EARN: [To Alfred] Hey, man, this is Dave. He works at 106.5. He likes your stuff, so he's got good taste. Actually, to a fault. [To Dave] Yo, tell them that Flo Rida story. It's so funny. Yo, tell them.
> DAVE: [Sheepishly] Oh, uh . . . yeah, so I was at a station party. And, uh, the DJ . . . a friend of a friend, was awful, and, uh . . . you know, it's a big event for the station, and the party's going and going, and he's ruining it, and so then he goes and he plays Flo Rida back-to-back. I had to go into the booth, calmly take him aside, and look him right in the eyes and just said, "Really?"
> DARIUS: I don't know, man, I like Flo Rida. I mean, moms need to enjoy rap, too.
> DAVE: Yeah, I mean, that was a wack-ass story, man. I don't know why he made me tell that.

Earn, of course, knows *exactly* why he's making Dave tell the story; in this context, Dave is highly unlikely to audaciously assert his white privilege as he previously did when only he and Earn were present. It is perhaps a minor victory for Earn to revel in Dave's obvious discomfort as he walks away, but it is also a marked contrast between Earn's own struggles with club owners, promoters, event planners, social-media influencers, and countless others throughout the series. Curiously, Earn seems to have his few scattered moments of success as a manager or empowerment as an individual when he can reorient a situation to force a white person—e.g., foisting a forgotten gun off on a rival rapper's white manager at an airport security checkpoint in "Crabs in a Barrel" (s2e11) or the elaborate revenge he exacts on an officious airline employee in "The Homeliest Little Horse" (s4e2)—to experience the awkwardness and discomfort of not being privileged; especially during the third season set in Europe, this dynamic reinforces the idea that Earn's awkwardness is situational at least as much as it is essentialized.

Issa similarly has fleeting moments of agency that arise from initially awkward encounters with privileged white characters. As audiences get their first glimpses of Issa's job at We Got Y'all in "Insecure as Fuck," she notes in a voice-over, "My boss [Joanne] founded a nonprofit to help kids in the hood, but she didn't hire anybody from the hood." Joanne's (Catherine Curtin) office is every bit as much an appropriative shrine to Blackness as the inner sanctum into which Craig (Rick Holmes) invites Earn to retreat in "Juneteenth" (s1e9).[15] During a conversation in which Joanne seems to be as much demonstrating her "cred" as seeking Issa's input, she is dressed in a dashiki and sitting in an office surrounded by signifiers of Blackness, including a photo of her with Barack Obama, a black-and-white picture of Dr. Martin Luther King Jr., traditional African artifacts, and even a poster from Beyoncé's Mrs. Carter tour.[16] Joanne also invokes the names of numerous Black intellectuals to signal to Issa that she understands Blackness and the plight of Black people:

> JOANNE: I'm torn between the Booker T. method and the Du Bois method. What would James Baldwin say is the most beneficial for people of color?
> ISSA: In 2016? That's what you're talking about?

The fact that Joanne mispronounces Du Bois's name as "Du-*boy*" rather than "Du-*boys*" and familiarly refers to Washington as "Booker T." is telling, as is her reduction of the longstanding debate over racial uplift to a choice of two "methods." Issa's quizzical nonresponse to her boss's superficial invitation to interpret James Baldwin's intent decenters Joanne's perspective and signals to an audience equally removed from the "white gaze" that she, not Issa, is the awkward party here. In doing so, Issa conveys an impression of Joanne's allyship as largely *per*formative instead of *trans*formative, a sense visually encapsulated by the We Got Y'all logo, which features a white hand holding up three black silhouettes of children and becomes an explicit source of conflict in season 3.

The show's first season also engages at length with obvious tokenism that marks the staff of We Got Y'all. Although Issa is the only Black employee, she is not the only visible minority; there is also a Latina and a South Asian woman. Nevertheless, the voices of Joanne and the white employees still dominate in decision-making situations, despite the lip service paid to seeking input from Issa and the other employees of color. The organization is superficially diverse and inclusive, but their actions, for the most part, are not, even when undertaken by the relentlessly earnest and bubbly Frieda (Lisa Joyce) with whom Issa is frequently paired on projects. Issa's response to one comparably mild incident of tokenizing at work reveals how feigned ignorance becomes her default response to such discomforting moments:

> Issa: [In voice-over] I've been here five years, and they think I'm the token with all the answers.
> Kitty [Veronica Mannion]: Let's just ask Issa. Issa, what's "on fleek" mean?
> Issa: [Deadpan] I don't know what that means? [In voice-over] I know what that shit means, but being aggressively passive is what I do best.

Issa herself only explicitly derides such microaggressive moments in the inherently Black spaces defined by her interactions with her friends or in her performances for her mirror. The multilayered narrative structure of these scenes and elements of their visual composition combine to convey a subtle satirical message that Rae outlined in an interview:

> I really wanted to just depict my nightmare nonprofit organization.... [Y]ou see that people are so altruistic and they're so benevolent and they're pretty selfless.... [But s]ometimes they don't listen to the people they're trying to help. And for me, this white guilt is so prevalent at this nonprofit.... I would hate to work in an environment like this, but it's ripe for comedy. (Gross)

Despite their initial juxtaposition, Issa and Frieda do occasionally strike up a rapport that transcends the inherent tension of this "nightmare" environment. As Frieda solemnly recounts the struggles Issa faced in connecting with the room full of nonwhite students at the ironically named school at which they've been working together, Issa's thoughts—i.e., her "Black interior space"—begins to influence the audience's perception of Frieda's words, a technique that recurs throughout the series:

FRIEDA: And these poor, poor children need our guidance more than
    anything. They were so intent on not acknowledging the burdens that
    face them every day that they focused mostly on Issa's love life . . .
    which, I must say, served as a great icebreaker. [Everyone except Issa
    chuckles.] Thomas Jefferson Middle School's statistics state that
    40 percent will not graduate high school, [audio begins fading out as
    camera shifts to Issa's face] and 20 percent will be teen parents, and
    45 percent will be involved with gang activity. We absolutely have to
    intervene. . . . [Camera focuses on close-up of Frieda, who seems to be
    addressing Issa directly.] Educated Black women are highly unlikely to
    get married the more education they have. On the bright side, many
    Black women are work focused and find happiness in their careers. But
    then there is a small percentage of pathetic women who have neither.
    They are purposeless.
ISSA: [Shouting] You're wrong!

Although Issa's awkward outburst to her projection onto Frieda results initially in an uncomfortable moment for everyone in the conference room, it also opens a space for her to recover and propose an alternate strategy:

> I know our jobs are to bring extracurricular programs to the school, but I think we're doing it wrong. The environment is the problem. Nothing is going to change for them if they're stuck in the same, shitty place. They need to know that there's more out there, so at least they know they have options. As youth liaison, I want to take the lead on building a program for kids outside of the school.

Joanne nods approvingly and assigns Issa and Frieda to work together on this project, the implementation of which the series depicts over the remainder of season 1.

In addition to wanting to get the students out of the "same, shitty place" of their neglected schools, Issa also works—in keeping with Rae's stated goals about counteracting the negative mediated image of South LA—to revise their perception that their whole community falls into the same category. During a We Got Y'all meeting in "Guilty as Fuck" (s1e6) about a fundraising event to which the program's nonwhite students are invited, the organization's blind spot about its own racism is again revealed in the initial choice of where to hold this event:

JOANNE: And have we secured a location in Malibu?
KEN [Mason McCulley]: Oh, we have several options that I can show
    you, but most places are saying that we can't bring kids because they're

worried about damage. But a lot of them are saying that they'll provide chairs and tables at no additional cost.
FRIEDA: I thought the whole point was to invite kids this year.
ISSA: Yeah. Why are we pressed to do it in Malibu?
KITTY: Did you hear the part about the tables *and* chairs?
ISSA: I did, but can't we do it somewhere near, like Inglewood or Baldwin Hills? I mean, Malibu's nice, it's just We Got Y'all is in this community. It would just be great to show the kids that there's beauty in their own backyard.

The fundraiser ultimately is held in Baldwin Hills, showcasing a part of Black Los Angeles—albeit a gentrified one—that is clearly outside the usual consciousness of the We Got Y'all staff and presumably most viewers unfamiliar with the city. When she does not simply fall back on being "aggressively passive," Issa can make small inroads into changing the culture of We Got Y'all from the inside, though the show also repeatedly suggests how emotionally exhausting being required to do so is for her. This tenuous dynamic begins collapsing in season 2, though, largely over a disagreement between Issa and Frieda about how to handle a Black principal who demonstrates unmistakable bias against his Latinx students. The repercussions of this incident—in short, Frieda is promoted while Issa is reprimanded—eventually contribute to Issa's long-overdue departure from We Got Y'all in the middle of season 3, after which Issa turns her efforts, in season 4, to organizing a block party that will showcase Inglewood's Black businesses and culture as a barrier against encroaching gentrification's "unblackening" (to use a phrase coined by *Insecure*'s cocreator Larry Wilmore).

In discussing Glover, Jordan Peele, Keegan-Michael Key, and other contemporary Black comedians "at the forefront of a new trend in contemporary African American humor," David Gillota asserts that their work "ultimately challenges the rigid and essentialized visions of blackness that are often perpetuated by mainstream media, including most African American humor" (18). He adds that "the humor of these 'black nerds' . . . points to a small yet increasing diversification of the ways in which blackness can be represented and explored in mass culture." His qualification that their "approach to race" is only "*seemingly* idiosyncratic and apolitical" (18, emphasis added) is justified by Finley's aforementioned observation about the power of televisual representation and the need for under- or misrepresented groups to push back against their depiction in pop-culture media. *Atlanta* and *Insecure* use their awkward protagonists in a variety of ways to produce "an embittered, disgusted satirical humor" that is intended "to undercut ideologies in pop cultural media that are the brick and mortar holding structural inequalities in place" (Finley 262).

NOTES

1. Ziwe Fumodoh is the only satirist mentioned in Manning's piece who was born later than 1985. Most definitions of the millennial generation begin with those born in the early 1980s and end with those born in the late 1990s.

2. Glover (b. 1983) and Rae (b. 1985) are both significantly younger than Lee (b. 1957), Sykes (b. 1964), Rock (b. 1965), and Chappelle (b. 1973).

3. In fairness, only the first season of both shows had aired when Gould made these assertions.

4. Primarily because of space limitations, we focus solely on Earn and Issa as the awkward protagonists. Nevertheless, considerably more could be said about the ways in which Alfred and Molly still embody Black awkwardness despite being successful compared to Earn and Issa. Furthermore, the fact that the most eccentric characters in each show's primary dramatis personae—Darius and Kelli, respectively—are also the ones who seem to thrive the most is worth further inquiry.

5. Awkward Black characters sporadically appear before the 1990s in sitcoms such as *Good Times* (1974–1979), *The Jeffersons* (1975–1985), *Diff'rent Strokes* (1978–1985), *What's Happening!!* (1976–1979), *227* (1985–1990), and *Amen* (1986–1991), but Black millennials largely did not come of age with these shows, except perhaps in syndication.

6. Steven Urkel (Jaleel White) from *Family Matters* (1989–1997) and Dwayne Wayne (Kadeem Hardison) from *A Different World* are two other exemplary "blerds" from the early to mid-1990s.

7. Born in California, Donald Glover grew up in the majority-Black suburb of Stone Mountain, east of Downtown Atlanta. Born in Los Angeles, Rae moved back there when she was in sixth grade after living in her father's native Senegal and in suburban Maryland.

8. See this volume's introduction for more on this montage.

9. For more on *The Sellout*, see Avilez's essay herein.

10. Jeremy O. Harris's *Slave Play* (2018) satirically addresses this same theme at roughly the same time, albeit in a considerably more graphic manner.

11. In *Atlanta*, the bottle episode "B.A.N." (s1e7) features a fictional talk show, *Montague*, serving a somewhat similar purpose, although only Alfred appears on it directly. For more on this episode, see the essays by Glavanakova and Lee herein.

12. For more on this, see DiMatteo's essay herein.

13. This trope is repeated in Radha Blank's *The Forty-Year-Old Version* (2020). For more on that film, see Murray's essay herein.

14. For more on this theme, see the introduction and Rutter's essay herein.

15. For more on this episode and on Craig in particular, see the essays by Parks and Rutter herein.

16. The organizational website that the show's writers produced as a parodic-satiric paratext lists the "fun fact" that Joanne's favorite musicians are "Bruce Springsteen, Melissa Eth[e]ridge, [and] NWA" and that she's "seen The Boss in concert over 200 times" (*We Got Y'all*). These details only amplify viewers' doubts that Joanne went to see Beyoncé perform in person, as Issa and her friends do during a multiepisode arc in season 3.

Forsyth County

WHITE (AL)LIES

Eating the Other in *Atlanta* and Jordan Peele's *Get Out*

EMILY RUTH RUTTER

In "Woods" (s2e8), a hauntingly brilliant episode of *Atlanta*, Alfred Miles (Brian Tyree Henry) finds himself in a dense forest after fighting off and fleeing from three young Black men who recognize him as the rapper Paper Boi and try to rob him at gunpoint. In the woods, Alfred encounters an older man who berates him about his life choices before holding a knife to his throat and then abruptly dropping it, allowing Alfred to escape his second near-death experience in approximately twenty minutes of viewing time. Emerging from the woods behind a convenience store, Alfred's sweatshirt is covered in blood, his face bruised and bleeding. The camera then cuts to him standing in front of a drink cooler, the fluorescent light beaming down on him as he holds a cold bottle to his injured face. Alfred turns to see a smiling young white man approaching him to ask if he is Paper Boi, echoing the earlier encounter that ended in Alfred's narrow escape. With the camera following the white fan's voyeuristic gaze, Alfred reluctantly turns and confirms that he is Paper Boi and, knowing what is coming next, asks, "You want a picture?" The fan nods and smiles eagerly, not asking Alfred/Paper Boi if he needs medical assistance for his injuries and seeming to presume that this is how all rappers might appear outside of the studio. A beleaguered Alfred/Paper Boi dutifully plays along with the exoticized and criminalized role into which he has been cast, posing for the fan photograph with his bloodied grin. The camera's close-up shot of the two of them paints a richly satirical portrait of white hip-hop fans who idolize figures like Paper Boi not because of their artistry but for the vicarious thrill of feeling and appearing dangerous. Whereas the first group of young men robbed him for his fame, this fan similarly capitalizes on Alfred's celebrity while disregarding his humanity. As the fan leaves the store, Alfred/Paper Boi tells him to "be safe out here," a message clearly driven more by the need to reassure himself than to prepare the young white man (an embodiment of institutional power and privilege) for a dangerous world.

As bell hooks observes, "Encounters with Otherness are clearly marked as more exciting, more intense, and more threatening" (*Black Looks* 26). Within this racial schema, "the suffering imposed by structures of domination on those designated Other is deflected by an emphasis on seduction and longing where the desire is not to make the Other over in one's image but to become the Other" (25). This simultaneous fetishization and denial of agency is on display in contemporary American culture practically wherever one looks, a fact lost on neither the ever-astute Glover nor the acclaimed writer-director Jordan Peele, to whom his work is sometimes compared.[1] Glover's *Atlanta* and Peele's tour-de-force horror film *Get Out* (2017) are especially poignant examples of the recent use of satire to expose patterns of white hypocrisy and treachery masquerading as sincerity and even allyship. As Danielle Fuentes Morgan notes, "many contemporary satires force our disavowal of the conventional silence surrounding race by imagining what racial essentialism might look like if whiteness were made observable" (*Laughing* 70). Combining tropes of satire with the burgeoning Black comic-horror genre,[2] *Get Out* and *Atlanta* employ an "oppositional black gaze" (hooks, *Black Looks* 117) to make white threats to Black safety and autonomy legible. As with "Woods," Peele's and Glover's white characters are not Ku Klux Klan members or even those donning Make American Great Again (MAGA) hats but instead those professing their love for Black culture while simultaneously participating in vampiric acts of appropriation.[3]

Relying primarily on point-of-view shots in which the camera adopts the perspectives of their Black male protagonists, Peele and Glover debunk the dominant fantasy that renders "whiteness synonymous with goodness" (hooks, *Black Looks* 169). Drawing on the tropes of horror while using a satirical mode of expression, Peele portrays Rose Armitage (Allison Williams), the girlfriend of *Get Out*'s protagonist Chris Washington (Daniel Kaluuya), as an embodiment of performative racial allyship; her antiracist rhetoric is designed to conceal (as in the "lies" embedded in this essay's title) her family's elaborate plot to preserve white lives by destroying Black ones. Glover's comedic representation of white male fans of hip hop and Black culture similarly, if also more generally, satirizes the ways in which habits of consumption and admiration remain tethered to white-supremacist beliefs and behaviors. Holding a mirror to white viewers—a sizeable slice of the audience for both *Get Out* and *Atlanta*[4]—Peele and Glover dramatize the consequences of their "love and theft," as Eric Lott felicitously phrased it, of Black people and culture (passim).[5]

Guiding viewers through *Get Out*'s horrific plot from Chris's perspective, Peele illuminates the myriad feelings associated with trusting white women as confidants, lovers, friends, and allies in the struggle to dismantle white supremacy only to discover that the wolf—in this case, Rose Armitage—arrives in sheep's clothing. We need only consult the history of lynching for evidence of white women's involvement in the scapegoating and criminalizing of Black men. Reversing this race and gender logic that has long governed audience expectations of dominance and vulnerability,[6] the satirically named Rose is not a delicate flower but a thorny, sadistic figure whose every action has been calculated to manipulate Chris into willingly sacrificing his fetishized body to rich white men seeking immortality.

Peele introduces Rose as a figure striving to be "woke," poking implicit fun at innumerable contemporary white people who brandish their "knowledge about the facts of racism" but fail to put that "knowledge to use in order to eradicate the problems of racial injustice" (Bunyasi and Smith 12). When Chris asks if she has told her parents that he is Black, she assures him with a wide grin and says: "Baby, it's fine. My dad would legit vote for Obama a third time if he could. Yes, he will want to talk to you about it, and that will be embarrassing, but they're gonna love you. I promise." As we later discover, telling Rose's parents that Chris is Black is unnecessary; after all, she has selected him precisely because of his skin color to be quite literally auctioned off to the highest bidder among the Armitages' wealthy white friends. Not yet privy to Rose's machinations, viewers are drawn into Chris's understandable trepidation about meeting his white girlfriend's family. Moreover, Peele suggests both the affordances and limitations of white allies who purport to understand their Black counterparts' legitimate fears of racial marginalization and persecution. On the one hand, Rose can joke with Chris about the white invocation of an Obama vote to deflect accusations of anti-Black racism; on the other hand, she dismisses the potential threat that Chris faces by suggesting that her father's endorsement of Obama forecloses the possibility of other forms of anti-Black sentiment. As Tehama Lopez Bunyasi and Candis Watts Smith contend, "'I voted for Obama' is the twenty-first-century version of 'I marched with Dr. King' or 'My friend/neighbor/cousin-in-law is Black.' Here's the thing: none of these things means that you are antiracist" (150). In this early scene, Peele exposes this fallacious line of reasoning, evincing the failures of white liberals to confront their own and their family members' perpetuation of white-supremacist behavior.

Perhaps no scene more clearly elucidates interlaced patterns of exoticizing and dominating Black people than the party Rose's parents throw on the day after Chris and Rose arrive at the Armitage estate. As the couple makes their way through the crowd of guests gathered on the lawn and deck, Rose has her arm linked with Chris's, physically indicating that she is commiserating with him regarding the demonstrable ignorance of her parents' friends. One former professional golfer boasts that he once met Tiger Woods and asks Chris about his own golfing abilities, assuming that he is athletically gifted because he is Black. A woman squeezes Chris's bicep and asks Rose pointedly: "So, is it true? The lovemaking. Is it better?" Yet another asks Chris if Blackness is in vogue, simultaneous fetishizing tanned or dark skin and disregarding the feelings of a person who actually has it: "Fairer skin has been in favor the last couple of thousands of years, but the pendulum has swung back again hasn't it?" Throughout these encounters, Rose exchanges appalled glances with Chris and strives to distinguish herself from the party guests' casual racism, feigning solidarity to gain his trust only to utterly violate it later. In fact, the scene culminates with Rose absconding with Chris to a secluded lakeside spot for a heart-to-heart while her father, Dean Armitage (Bradley Whitford), auctions off his body to be lobotomized and utilized by the highest bidder, who turns out to be a blind art dealer named Jim Hudson (Stephen Root).

Consonant with both horror films' characteristic goriness and the absurdity manifest in satire, the so-called "Coagula method" pioneered by the Armitage patriarch Roman (Richard Herd) entails implanting the brains of aging white people into the bodies of healthy young Black people, like Chris. Both through his own name and that of his gruesome method of ensuring white immortality, Roman Armitage recalls the despotism of the Roman emperor Caligula; moreover, the coagulation alluded to in the transplantation method, the color and thorns associated with Rose's name, and the dual martyrdoms—those of Christ and St. Christopher—suggested by Chris's name all emphasize the bloody violence at the heart of Anglo-European history. Indeed, these allusions remind viewers that wielding tyrannical power and trafficking in flesh are part of white people's *heritage* (echoes of which adhere to the surname Armitage), even when the patina of antiracist rhetoric initially suggests otherwise. Hooks observes that white people "think they are seen by black folks only as they want to appear" (*Black Looks* 169), and as the camera follows Chris throughout the party and during the subsequent preparation for the Coagula surgery, Peele demonstrates her point that "whiteness in the black imagination is often a representation of terror" (172).

Moreover, Peele particularly encourages white viewers to imagine how it would *feel* to be treated as a commodified object ripe for plunder. Once it becomes clear that Rose has betrayed him, Chris is unable to fend off her family. His defenses are especially imperiled by Rose's mother, Missy (Catherine Keener), who hypnotizes him by stirring a spoon against the side of a teacup, a seemingly benign gesture symbolic of bourgeois life that Peele utilizes to suggest the sinister aims underlying performances of white women's goodwill. The camera then jumps to Chris strapped to a leather armchair as Dean and Jeremy Armitage (Caleb Landry Jones) prepare to implant Jim Hudson's brain into Chris's body in the next room. In order to avoid Missy's hypnotism,

Chris ingeniously makes use of the chair's cotton stuffing—an unambiguous reference to one of the cash crops that enslaved Blacks were forced to harvest in America—to plug his ears against the sound of the teacup (and the corresponding siren song of white women's feigned gestures of empathy and care toward him and other Black people). Once unbound, Chris kills nearly the entire Armitage clan in self-defense against their murderous intentions.

In *Get Out*'s original ending, Chris is arrested and jailed, despite being the victim of the Armitages' ghastly crimes, thereby demonstrating the anti-Black racism governing the criminal-justice system. Deciding that viewers instead needed a "hero" and a "positive feeling," Peele opted for a new ending in which a traumatized Chris ultimately prevails (Nigatu and Clayton). As Chris's best friend, Rod Williams (Lil Rel Howery), appears on the gruesome scene with the lights on his Transportation Security Administration car flashing, Chris raises his hands in expectation of the film's original ending playing out. After getting in the vehicle with Rod, Chris realizes he is finally safe, but the beleaguered, despairing look on his face conveys his traumatized state in the aftermath of being maniacally brutalized by whiteness via the trap set by the white woman he loved and trusted. Through this series of horrific and satiric events, Peele alerts audiences to the connection between the racist comments that white people excuse away as slips of the tongue or unintentional misunderstandings and the whole-scale devaluation of Black life. Furthermore, in portraying Rose as a treacherous villain masquerading as a trusted loved one and confidante, Peele enjoins viewers to consider the contemporary white usage of antiracist rhetoric as a cover for concealing the perpetuation of anti-Black ideologies and terrorism well after their purported end in the wake of the civil rights era.

Not long after the show premiered, Peele noted that "for black people, 'Atlanta' provides the catharsis of *Finally*, some elevated black shit" (Friend, emphasis original). Not unlike *Get Out*, *Atlanta* is both innovative and unapologetic in its choice of satirical targets, including white people who effuse about their love of Black culture but fail to confront the ways in which they perpetuate anti-Black oppression. As Imani Perry reminds us: "The love of black culture with the simultaneous suspicion and punishment of black bodies is not unusual. Nor is the public fascination with the perceived depravity or dangerousness of black artists, who are simultaneously loved" (28). Since *Atlanta* is more readily classifiable as dramedy rather than horror, its use of satire is more deliberately comic than in *Get Out*. It is, however, no less poignant in prompting its white viewers to reflect on their own infatuation with Black culture and their complicity in the systemic degradation of Black people. Like Peele, Glover also makes use of an oppositional Black gaze in which the camera selectively adopts the perspective of the series' Black protagonists and thereby destabilizes dominant narratives of whiteness as either benign or the default norm.

"Juneteenth" (s1e9) deftly exemplifies these strategies, satirically rendering the proprietary relationship that whites who conceive of themselves as allies often have with Blackness. The episode pivots around a Juneteenth party at the lavish Atlanta home of Craig (Rick Holmes), a white self-anointed expert on Black culture, and his wife, Monique (Cassandra Freeman), a Black woman who tolerates her husband's missteps because he provides her with wealth and privilege. Van Keefer (Zazie Beetz), the mother of Earn's child, Lottie, has been invited to attend a party at this couple's house; with Earn in tow, Van hopes to network with the guests and learn about the fine art of socioeconomic mobility from Monique. During the gathering, Earn wanders into Craig's study, and the two engage in a conversation that illuminates white desires to claim Black experiences as their own in a manner parallel to the conversations Chris is forced into during the Armitages' party in *Get Out*. When Craig finds Earn staring at his bizarre painting of a Black man spearing a gigantic gryphon, he proudly broadcasts the Malcolm X quote that inspired his artwork: "Nobody can give you freedom. Nobody can give you equality, or justice, or anything. If you're a man, you take it." When Earn replies politely but skeptically that Craig's visual interpretation is "interesting," Craig asserts sole and rightful ownership of Malcolm X's message of Black liberation: "It's the only interpretation. It accurately depicts the plight of the contemporary Black man. That is why I painted it." This amusing but stunning example of appropriation evinces Craig's desire not to work in solidarity with Black people to dismantle white hegemonic power structures but instead to assert control over the narratives of Black life, even Black nationalist ones.

Moreover, when Earn tells Craig that he is in "music management," Craig tells him that "it's nice to see a brother on the business side of music." Earn quips, "Why's that?" to which Craig responds: "Music is such an integral part of the African American culture, its expression, and it's been stripped from you. Black music artists are products for white American consumption and appropriation." Not only does Craig seem unaware of the long—if also disproportionately small—tradition of Black executives in the music industry, he is also precisely the kind of white appropriator that he describes. A short catalogue of his own offenses in this regard includes his claim to be *the* visual interpreter of Malcolm X, the Black slam poetry about racism that he performs for the party's attendees, his ardent reminiscences about making a "pilgrimage" to Africa with Monique, his choice of Hennessy as his social drink, the Juneteenth party he and Monique are throwing, and even quite possibly his marriage. As Monique tells Van in a moment of candor: "You don't think I know how crazy my husband is? This whole 'Black people as a hobby'. . . . I get this big-ass house, and he gets the Black wife he always wanted." With his comical but scathing portrait of elite white men for whom "ethnicity becomes spice" (hooks, *Black Looks* 21), Glover critiques the proprietary attitude that white people often impose onto Black culture.

At the same time, "Juneteenth" demonstrates "the potential of satire to expose and empower" (Finley 248). When Monique and Craig discover that Earn is not managing "respectable" Black artists but rather is both Paper Boi's manager and his cousin, Craig responds by fawning over Earn while Monique calls Paper Boi a "thug." Earn has finally had enough of the couple's highfalutin hypocrisy, and he and Van leave the party, with Earn telling Craig to "stop stunting on me about my culture." On the drive home, Van tells Earn to pull over, and she climbs on top of him to have sex, suggesting that this confrontation with Monique and Craig, however disastrous it has been for Van's attempts at networking, has ultimately made them feel both self-possessed and closer to one another.

Whereas "Juneteenth" resembles *Get Out* in training its gaze on white liberal hypocrisy, "North of the Border" (s2e9) demonstrates the ways in which anti-Black politics of the nineteenth century remain deeply engrained in southern landscapes. The episode begins with Earn having arranged for Paper Boi to perform at an event called Pajama Jam in Statesboro, the home of Georgia Southern University; Earn, Alfred, and two of Alfred's friends, Tracy (Khris Davis) and Darius (LaKeith Stanfield), head out of town for the gig. The trip proves disastrous on a number of levels. Violet (Jerusha Cavazos), the woman who has invited them to perform at Pajama Jam and to spend the night at her apartment, becomes jealous when she sees Alfred talking with two other women and spills a drink down onto him from a balcony. Tracy, who has decided to play bodyguard, subsequently pushes Violet down a flight of stairs, with Earn catching her just before she hits the ground. A fight and chase ensue, and the four men tear through campus trying to escape the wrath of Violet's brother and his entourage. They are shown walking down a dark campus road as flashing lights appear behind them, and they dart quickly to the shrouded darkness of a nearby tree,[7] with the camera zooming in on their trepidatious faces. As the flashing lights pass, they see that the vehicle is not a police cruiser after all but instead a campus golf-cart-sized vehicle with an injured white woman (presumably a student) riding in the back seat. Despite the comic relief of its resolution, this scene demonstrates a pervasive fear of anti-Black police harassment and violence that echoes both Peele's original ending for *Get Out* and its revised ending, in which Chris instinctively raises his hands at the approach of the flashing lights that turn out to be from Rod's car.

Moreover, the scene that follows immediately thereafter satirizes how young white men idolize hip-hop artists without questioning their own adherence to white-supremacist social codes. Darius follows the scent of marijuana smoke to a fraternity house, and the four men gingerly greet the stoned residents clustered on the columned front porch of a building unmistakably reminiscent of a plantation house. Two of the fraternity brothers, Prescott (Tim Johnson) and Duncan (James Rackley), immediately recognize Alfred as Paper Boi and stare in wonder as he asks them if they have any weed. They eagerly pass him a blunt and tell him "we'll smoke you out!" Tragicomically collapsing the years between the Civil War and the episode's temporal setting, the camera's subsequent moves juxtapose the two grinning white men mesmerized by Paper Boi's presence with the backdrop of a banner reading "1863" hanging on the house and the tiki torches (reminiscent of those carried by white supremacists at their infamous 2017 Unite the Right rally in Charlottesville, Virginia) framing the doorway. After showing Alfred and Darius smiling at the improvement in their prospects (while Earn and Tracy stand behind them with skeptical expressions), the camera moves again quickly to show Alfred's point of view at the foot of the porch. Through the visual obstacles of the columns and porch rails, we see a brown-shirted man forcefully pushing a hooded and seemingly naked figure into a side door, causing Alfred to exclaim, "Yo, what the *fuck* was that?" Prescott explains, "It's all good. . . . It's just some pledges here. Newbies gotta pay the price, eh?" which clearly flusters Alfred, though not enough to turn down the invitation to come inside. The scene's architectural allusions to the antebellum South, conspicuous use of imagery tied to recent events trumpeting white nationalism, implications of hierarchical violence, and slightly surreal dialogue combine to suggest that the racial inequities that have always shaped white consumption of Black culture persist, even if they have been sublimated somewhat by the white men's adoration of Paper Boi.

Once inside, Alfred, Earn, Darius, and Tracy find themselves in a toxic atmosphere in which the fraternity brothers' fetishistic attraction to Black culture but disregard for Black people—at least those who are not beloved celebrities—becomes even clearer. Alfred, Earn, and Darius are seated beneath an enormous Confederate flag as they smoke marijuana with the fraternity brothers; the camera moves between it and their grim facial expressions, which reveal more loathing than fear. Two rows of hooded, naked white men—pledges to the fraternity—kneel silently in the foreground. Behind the pledges is a tall rack of antique guns; when Darius inquires whether one of them is an elephant rifle, Duncan affirms that it is, noting also that many of the house's alumni are in the NRA (National Rifle Association). When Darius unexpectedly replies that he has "been thinking about joining the NRA," Prescott smiles broadly and says, "Y'all are crazy," implying that, even while the organization does not explicitly bar Black members, it is still widely perceived as advancing an anti-Black agenda.[8] Meanwhile, Duncan begins showing off the weapons and boasting further of the house's "gun room," with an invitation to view it, which Tracy and Darius enthusiastically accept. Although the general demeanor of the fraternity brothers is affable and even solicitous, its dissonance with the surrounding physical environment looms throughout the scene.

Similar to Peele's dramatization of the horrific dangers manifest not within the racially diverse environment of New York City but instead in a supposedly idyllic upstate landscape, Glover suggests that Atlanta is the episode's titular "north," offering relative freedom from the centuries-old racism endemic to the South and its white inhabitants, including hip-hop fans. Prescott finds nothing incongruous about telling Paper Boi that he is "one of my two favorite rappers, you and Post Malone." He waxes nostalgic about southern hip-hop music—even sounding momentarily like a five-percenter in referring to Pimp C as "one of the last real prophets, man"—while one of the most iconic symbols of anti-Blackness serves as the backdrop for his stoned encomium. Prescott even plays a few bars of D4L's 2006 hit "Laffy Taffy," commanding the pledges to "do this dance for our new friends" and snap along; his infatuation with "Laffy Taffy" symbolizes his greedy consumption of Black culture as if it were like the eponymous candy, simply packaged for his delight and amusement. Moreover, the pledges' subjection to this ritualized, humiliating abuse in proximity to the Stars and Bars restages the master-slave dynamic in a manner that surely resonates with Alfred and Earn—and presumably the episode's viewers—even if Prescott remains oblivious. Taken together, the entirely white fraternity, the hazing of pledges, the Confederate flag, and the arsenal of guns on display indicate that racial time has essentially stood still in this space, despite its inhabitants' words.

Alfred's facial affect is pained throughout this scene, as though he is calculating the costs of having white fans and determining that the potential payday is not adequate compensation. Such a calculus is further complicated by the fact that Pajama Jam was an unpaid gig that Earn pragmatically insists is a gateway to a subsequent massive payday that comes along with getting a piece of "this college fanbase." Given that Paper Boi's reputation seems to have been stronger at the white fraternity house than at Pajama Jam even before the events that unfold in the episode, the reliability of Earn's claim is dubious at best. Being grouped with Post Malone, a figure many view as "taking on the attributes of black music with none of the burden" (Iandoli), and D4L, who proved to be a one-hit wonder with "Laffy Taffy," cannot sit well with Alfred's ambitions as an artist. The sustained close-ups of Alfred's wary face as he puffs on a blunt and reluctantly listens to Prescott's unexamined musings about his love of hip hop similarly indicate his mounting frustration with the hypocrisy engulfing him. Not unlike the potent symbolism of the cotton Chris is forced to use to mute the sound of Missy's malevolent spoon stirring, Alfred and Earn find themselves enveloped by (neo-)Confederate iconography. When the oblivious Prescott suddenly remembers, "I gotta go give these pledges a mud bath," he asks, "Y'all need anything from the fridge?" Alfred and Earn decline, uninterested in receiving any more favors from their host,[9] a juvenile embodiment of white-supremacist patriarchy.

The final shot in "North of the Border" captures Alfred's grim expression as he drives back to Atlanta, with the Band-Aid across his nose from his aforementioned struggle in "Woods." Earn, who now has a welt on his forehead and a bloody nose after rashly provoking the much stronger Tracy during the episode's climax, is seated directly behind him. The chorus to Them Two's song "Am I a Good Man?"—"Am I a good man? / Am I a fool? Am I weak? / Or am I just playing it cool?"—plays as the episode ends and the credits roll, posing questions about all four men, especially the dejected Earn and the aggravated Alfred. Reminiscent of *Get Out*'s theatrical version, Alfred is finally headed home, where he is free from the toxicity of both white fraternity houses and Violet's jealousy. Nonetheless, the events that have transpired have bitterly reminded him of the challenges he faces while struggling to cultivate a profitable fanbase without compromising his artistic integrity. As hooks observes, "The over-riding fear is that cultural, ethnic, and racial differences will be continually commodified and offered up as new dishes to enhance the white palate—that the Other will be eaten, consumed, and forgotten" (*Black Looks* 39). Both "North of the Border" and "Woods" show Alfred/Paper Boi facing this fear through encounters with vampiric fans who relish opportunities to "eat the Other," consuming his music and even his image without considering his humanity.

Atlanta's third season expands on this theme, satirizing and rendering surreal and grotesque white liberals who exploit Black people in particular and a racist system more generally under the guise of white innocence or even allyship. While this season dramatizes Paper Boi and his entourage on a tour across the United Kingdom and mainland Europe, the specters of white-supremacist ideologies and structures are everywhere, including in Amsterdam, London, and Budapest, cities that, at first blush, seem far removed from the imprint of chattel slavery. Drawing on surrealism and politically conscious horror tropes à la *Get Out*, the season's inaugural episode, "Three Slaps," unfolds as a series of concatenated dreamscapes, culminating in Earn's awakening in the final scene. The episode begins with a white man and a Black man night fishing near a bridge over an arm of Georgia's Lake Lanier, the darkness engulfing their small skiff as it rocks back and forth to the slow rhythm of a Porter Wagoner song. The two men ruminate on the pernicious costs of investing in the idea of whiteness—"It's easy to see the Black man as cursed because you've separated yourself from him. But you don't know you're enslaved just like him. Cold whiteness"—and the horrific tale of a Black town's residents being drowned by the state to construct the lake. At the end of the scene, the white man's facial features suddenly dissolve into an opaque mask, and he turns to his Black counterpart, hissing, "We're cursed, too!" A host of Black arms then reach out of the water toward the Black fisherman and begin to drag him under.

The camera then jumps to the episode's central character, the young Loquareeous (Christopher Farrar), who is sleeping on his classroom desk; this cut suggests that the story about Lake Lanier's has been his dream, though the episode's final scene consequently figures Loquareeous as an element of Earn's reverie. Not long after Loquareeous awakens, he defies a white teacher's admonishment, and his mother and grandfather are called to the school for an intervention. After leaving the principal's office, Loquareeous's grandfather casually delivers the episode's titular three slaps, and his mother warns him, "If you don't start using your common sense and acting right, these white people are going to kill you." This threat is almost immediately tested as a white school counselor reports his grandfather's actions, and Loquareeous is removed from his home by Family and Children's Services (FCS) and placed with a maniacal white lesbian couple, Amber (Laura Dreyfuss) and Gayle (Jamie Neumann).

Forcing their four Black foster children into quasislavery, Amber and Gayle make Loquareeous—renamed "Larry" because they cannot pronounce his name properly—and his counterparts tend their garden and sell kombucha at the local farmer's market; moreover, they malnourish and verbally abuse the children, all the while masquerading as social-justice allies.[10] Loquareeous tries unsuccessfully to get help from both a white police officer patrolling the farmer's market and a Black Family and Children's Services official following up on a neighbor's complaint about Amber and Gayle. The policeman thinks Loquareeous is lying because his foster-mothers are too strict about video games, and although the FCS official deduces the couple's crimes, Gayle kills her before she can report them. Amber and Gayle decide to escape with the children and commit murder-suicide by driving their minivan off the same bridge near which the men were fishing in the episode's opening. Shortly before enacting their heinous plan, Amber recounts to Gayle the ways in which the entire economic and social structure encouraged their exploitation and abuse of Black children: "When we adopted Fatimah, I knew we were doing the right thing. The agency even said so. I mean, we got that big loan from the bank. I thought that meant we were solid. Everyone was so supportive. Every single person. And I just kept thinking, Why isn't anyone stopping us? Why didn't anyone stop us, Gayle?" Coupled with the prophetic warning by Loquareeous's mother that "these white people are going to kill you," Amber's question implicates institutions and people who allow these patterns of "eating the Other" to continue not only with impunity but also with financial incentives. Fortunately, Loquareeous and the other children escape, and Loquareeous returns home with a renewed appreciation for the comparative security he had taken for granted. When Earn wakes from this nightmare, the camera pans out to reveal that he is in bed with a naked white woman, who remains asleep and thus both literally and metaphorically unaffected by his disturbing dream's implications.

While the suggestion is that this series of events has been conjured within Earn's dream (which the series finale somewhat jestingly suggests may itself only be part of a dream Darius is having inside a sensory-deprivation tank), the danger white would-be allies pose sets the stage for a range of threats to Black solidarity and autonomy that unfold across *Atlanta*'s third and fourth seasons. In addition to "Three Slaps," the third season features the duplicitous machinations of Socks (Hugh Coles), who poses as an antiracist crusader in "The Old Man and the Tree" (s3e3) and "Cancer Attack" (s3e5); white Americans paying reparations for their familial ties to chattel slavery in "The Big Payback" (s3e4); Dutch blackface traditions in "Sinterklaas Is Coming to Town" (s3e2); Black people used as props to mitigate the misdeeds of white capitalists in "White Fashion" (s3e6); white families' exploitation of Black nannies in "Trini 2 De Bone" (s3e7); and the benefits and drawbacks of racial passing in "Rich Wigga, Poor Wigga" (s3e9). Season 4 highlights the psychological fallout from white women's microaggressive undercutting of Black men's social mobility in "The Homeliest Little Horse" (s4e2), as well as depicting the challenge for Black rappers to remain relevant in a music industry that consistently lionizes white artists—even in genres pioneered by Black people—in "Born 2 Die" (s4e3). *Atlanta* repeatedly demonstrates ways that white liberals reinforce hegemonic power structures while hiding behind the rhetorical guise of social-justice advocacy, on the one hand, and adoration of Black culture, on the other.

"Refus[ing] the anticipated privileging of the white gaze" (Morgan, *Laughing* 123), *Atlanta* and *Get Out* satirize contemporary manifestations of white fetishization and objectification of Blackness in both distinct and overlapping ways. Reflecting recent interests in comic horror and uncovering covert investments in anti-Black violence, Peele spotlights the grotesque consequences of white liberal hypocrisy, while episodes from all four seasons of *Atlanta* demonstrate a pervasive white obsession with the Black body as one "to be watched, imitated, desired, possessed" (hooks, *Black Looks* 34). Through their expertly rendered satires, Peele and Glover urge white audiences in particular to acknowledge that, as Wesley Morris puts it, "Loving black culture has never meant loving black people, too. Loving black culture risks loving the life out of it."

NOTES

1. For example, commentary on "Teddy Perkins" (s2e6) often compares the episode to *Get Out*. See, e.g., Nguyen.

2. For other examples of contemporary Black comic-horror film and television, see Justin Simien's film *Bad Hair* (2020) and Misha Green's HBO series *Lovecraft Country* (2020).

3. See this volume's introduction for more on this theme.

4. As Michael Ryan and Melissa Lenos note, *Get Out* "achieved both box office success and near universal critical acclaim" (240). Moreover, *Atlanta* "is the most watched comedy in the network's [FX's] history" (Friend).

5. Lott's oft-cited *Love and Theft* shows how racialized cultural dissonances, whereby white men are both intensely attracted to Black culture yet actively propagate the myth of Black inferiority, were enacted through nineteenth-century minstrelsy.

6. While I do not address it here, Rose's mother, Missy, uses hypnotism to plunge Chris into the "sunken place," where he is forced to re-endure the trauma of his mother's death and to otherwise cede control over his physical and psychological faculties to Missy, providing another example of anti-Black oppression remaining intact but manifesting in new guises.

7. This is a possible callback to Alfred's escape into the woods in the previous episode.

8. Darius's possibly joking, possibly serious comment here is consistent with other moments in the series in which he enters spaces that are culturally encoded not only as white but also as anti-Black. For example, he goes target shooting at a gun range in "Nobody Beats the Biebs" (s1e5), and in "Teddy Perkins" (s2e6), he buys a red baseball cap featuring both a Confederate flag and the motto "SOUTHERN MADE" (which he modifies into "U MAD" with a red pen). Darius's seeming comfort with such transgressions of the expected racialization of social spaces starkly contrasts the discomfort that Earn and Alfred feel in such situations. See Brooks's essay herein for additional discussion of the two aforementioned episodes.

9. Prescott's mention of a "mud bath" as a hazing ritual also recalls white fraternities' well-documented penchant for blackface.

10. The plotline of "Three Slaps" strongly alludes to the story of Jennifer and Sarah Hart, a white lesbian couple who killed themselves and their six adopted children of color by driving over a cliff in Mendocino County, California, in 2018. Loquareeous appears to be based on the Harts' adopted son Devonte, whose image went viral in 2014 after he was photographed at a Portland, Oregon, Black Lives Matter rally hugging a police officer. The episode parodies these events as Gayle and Amber force Loquareeous to wear a "Free Hugs" sign at the farmer's market, at which he rushes toward a white police officer, wrapping his arms around his waist and pleading for him to rescue him from Gayle and Amber's abuse.

RACIAL SELF-IDENTIFICATION IN *ATLANTA* AND DANZY SENNA'S *NEW PEOPLE*

ALEXANDRA GLAVANAKOVA

Despite their generic differences, the television series *Atlanta* (2016–2022) and Danzy Senna's novel *New People* (2017) offer important thoughts on racial self-identification in an ostensibly postracial context. Their respective explorations are particularly relevant for critiquing the idea of a "postracial" society in which race is perceived as "no longer a significant or important discriminator" (Gillespie xiv). While the "postracial" remains for some an "American ideal of great rhetorical force" (Stephens and Stewart 9), it also functions as another "way of burying the persistence of slavery under the veneer of progress, inclusion and the acceptance of diversity" (Gillespie xiv). *Atlanta* and *New People* explore how racial categories are influenced by the interplay between phenotypical characteristics, socially constructed expectations, prevailing stereotypes, and subjective self-identification. Both debunk fixed racial categories and implode postracial fantasies through the representation of contemporary racialized experiences that involve a discrepancy between a performed and/or claimed racial identity and a phenotypical and/or perceived one in either mixed-race or transracial characters.

As Nell Irwin Painter notes, the criteria for racial classification constantly "shift according to individual taste and political need" (396). Since the line dividing racial categories is neither well defined nor stable, it often takes someone trying to cross that line from white to Black, from Black to white, or embracing one single grounding identity in the case of mixed-race people to expose the fluidity and uncertainty of race. It is within this larger framework that *New People* and *Atlanta* can be read for they repeatedly question, through a satirical lens, whether racial categories are regulated, policed, appropriated, and internalized and who superintends such defining. These works' portrayal of racial self-identification by mixed-race and transracial characters undermines any notion of a definitively dichotomous color line.

A salient preliminary question to address is whether racial identity is an innate reality, a construct donned by the self, or one imposed by external perceptions. Depending on the answer, race is often still reductively perceived as either "authentic" or "achieved." Both perspectives on race entail performativity, though clearly not in equal measure. Supposedly "authentic" race is gauged by known (or presumed) ancestry and phenotypical features and is therefore perceived as reducible to an innate quality, whereas racial self-identification that aims for a specific racial category involves appropriation of exterior markers (fashion, hairstyle, etc.) and cultural practices, mastery of behavioral and linguistic codes, and striving for group inclusion. Therefore, it is constructed and manipulable. "Achieved" race, in contrast, is an outcome of a process whereby "identities are chosen, rather than assigned, voluntarily rather than involuntarily" (Harrison-Kahan 35). This process is observable in mixed-race individuals' conscious choice to self-identify with one particular race. The masquerade of race in transracial self-identification implies a more rigid underlying racial categorization and likewise involves a conscious choice to identify with one particular race.

In their exploration of racial self-identification, *Atlanta* and *New People* both utilize two major forms of incongruity. The incongruity of the body as a signifier of race functions on a thematic level and is foregrounded through the satirical strategy of "perspective by incongruity," which is predicated on the idea that "people laugh at what surprises them, is unexpected, or is odd in a nonthreatening way. An accepted pattern is violated, or a difference is noted— close enough to the norm to be nonthreatening, but different enough from the norm to be remarkable" (Meyer 313). The reason this perspective is useful for discussing satire stems from the fact that it "emphasizes cognition. Individuals must have rationally come to understand normal patterns of reality before they can notice differences" (313). Satire frequently subjects its targets to moral and/or ethical critique by first drawing its audiences' attention (and, thus, their cognition) to particular incongruities that inhere in those targets. Embodied notions of race are a ripe target in this regard. The social requirements and public expectations for categorical definitions of race have historically centered on the body especially since genetic ancestry has dominated phenotypical definitions of race. However, as the markers of race are not always legible on the body, they frequently fail to signify, thus confirming that "the category of race does not lend itself to definitions" (Charles 155–56).

The satirical perspectives of *Atlanta* and *New People* are instrumental in exposing this incongruity through their portrayals of mixed race or transracial characters. Satire generally "enact[s] some judgement or attack" (Greenberg 7), and African American satire is characterized in particular by an "unremitting iconoclasm, criticism of the current status of African American political and cultural trends, and indictment of specifically American forms of racism" (Dickson-Carr, *African American* 16). Their satirical approach toward racial categorization and identification is inscribed through the "perspective by incongruity" because it involves the suspension of normativity, according to Glenda R. Carpio (*Laughing* 6). The images of race discussed here are purposefully rendered ambiguous and provocative, destabilizing established expectations and prevailing discourses in order to invite diverse interpretations. The goal is to reconfigure readers'/viewers' entrenched habits of mind and language to facilitate critique of racialized presumptions (6). As Black satirists, Senna and *Atlanta*'s principal creator Donald Glover have each taken on yet another important task: to "make blackness a visible and viable subject position that can have meaning beyond systems of racial signs" (Guerrero, "Can I Live?" 269). In this manner, any essentialist notions of race are destabilized and the notions of "authentic" and "achieved" race are exposed as bogus categories while, at the same time, the authors seek to trace Blackness in "postracial" America. These points offer a critical framework for exploring select episodes of *Atlanta* that satirize characters whose transracial crossovers reveal the fundamental illogicality of essentialist notions of racial authenticity alongside the mixed-race characters in *New People* who negotiate the minefield of racial performativity from a liminal social position.

Atlanta presents disturbing visions of the experience of being racialized; Glover specifically states: "The thesis with this show was to show people what it's like to be black, and you can't write that down. You have to feel it" (Miller). Several episodes in the show's earlier seasons depict acts of transracial self-identification that attempt to leave Blackness behind. In general, "transraciality" is "the adoption of physical traits of difference for the purpose of impersonating a racial other" (Awkward 9). The use of the term here is to be distinguished from another usage describing the identities of minority children adopted into white families. As Elizabeth Raleigh points out, "an increasing number of white parents have been adopting nonwhite children via international, domestic, and foster-care adoptions," which has led to the fact that "over the course of a decade, almost a quarter million children were born abroad and adopted by families in the United States" (US Department of State qtd. in Raleigh 86). She indicates that "84 percent of these placements are transracial" (86).[1]

Transraciality in *Atlanta* evokes the real-life white-to-Black passing of Rachel Dolezal by simultaneously calling into question such interracial desires and mocking the heated debate surrounding such cases. Dolezal was born (in 1977) in rural Montana to white parents. They eventually adopted four Black children. It seems reasonable to infer that growing up in a transracial environment (in the sense Raleigh describes) induced her later attempts at racial crossing. Self-identifying as "trans-Black," Dolezal seems to have taken advantage of her "achieved" identity for professional advancement and, in this way, exploited the long history of Black suffering while, at the same time, she engaged in the struggle for racial equality for Black people ("Rachel Dolezal"). At the same time, she admitted to having identified as white at certain points in her adult life, including when she sued Howard University for racial discrimination in 2002.[2] The Dolezal case fueled a national debate in the United States about racial self-identification. Parallels to the transgender experience have been drawn, especially regarding the great disparity in the social reaction in 2015 to Caitlyn Jenner's coming out as a trans woman and to Dolezal's transracial exposure. This problematic analogy was further foregrounded in what came to be known as the "transracialism controversy" played out on the pages of the academic journal *Hypatia* and beyond.[3]

For many African Americans, Dolezal is a fraud who got exposed as such; for others, her self-identification is genuine. Even though Julia Charles condemns Dolezal's transracial act as yet another expression of the privilege that comes with being born white (165), she also finds Dolezal's case to be valuable for several reasons: first, for attempting to overcome the racial binary; second, for revealing "the unreliability of the body as the sole signifier of race" (159); and third, for questioning the arbitrariness of the boundaries of racial identity. Dolezal's racial impersonation points to some of the systemic effects of a racialized society by questioning racial privilege and the right to racial self-identification.

Many aspects of the transracial phenomenon and the debate it gave rise to are brought to the fore in the *Atlanta* episode "B.A.N." (s1e7) by being rendered through a deliberately incongruous perspective. "B.A.N." purports to be an episode of a talk show called *Montague* that airs on the fictional Black America Network. The episode raises a series of questions regarding the formulations of race, gender, freedom of speech, liberal tolerance, and political correctness as well as their gatekeepers. Moreover, transgender and transracial identifications are satirically paralleled throughout. Paper Boi's (Brian Tyree Henry) appearance as a guest on the show largely seems to offer a chance for both the host (Alano Miller) and the other guest on the show, a white academic woman named Dr. Deborah Holt (Mary Kraft), who is introduced as the head of the Center of Trans-America Issues, to chide him for the ostensible lack of sympathy with trans people in his rap lyrics. Paper Boi admits that he is "afraid" to speak about issues like these, adding, "It's hard for me to care about this when nobody cares about me as a Black human man." He provides the standard definition of tolerance, while railing against the double standard in its implementation: "I don't have a problem with gay people, trans people, because that's tolerance. But where's tolerance for people like me?"

This episode's key moment comes later, though, when it shifts from the issue of transgender to transraciality through the character of Antoine Smalls

(Niles Stewart), a Black teenager from Atlanta who self-identifies as Harrison Booth, a thirty-five-year-old white man from Denver. Antoine reverses the direction of Dolezal's racial crossing and even hopes for an eventual surgical procedure that will help him transition to whiteness more smoothly. The episode seems to expose the artificiality of racial categorization by implying that race is defined not just by skin tone but by an entire range of affective and behavioral cues. At the same time, it also mocks this notion of "achieved" race by indexing his whiteness through such stereotypical actions as playing golf, visiting the farmer's market, dressing and talking as he believes a white man would, and rehearsing the presumably white codes of affect in front of a mirror.

"B.A.N" exposes the absurdity of Antoine's transracial desire. Presented as an act of folly, it calls attention to the fact that regardless of self-identification, societal perception of racial identity is inextricably linked to skin color; unlike light-skinned mixed-race individuals, no dark-enough-skinned person has ever been (mis)identified as white or successfully passed for white. Paper Boi considers Antoine's act of appropriating whiteness farcical, as does Smalls's/Booth's own mother. Antoine later appears in the episode wearing an ill-fitting blond wig, which recalls both Eddie Murphy's transracial experiment in a 1984 sketch entitled "White like Me" on *Saturday Night Live* and Chris Rock's satirical 2012 campaign ad that soothes white voters' fears by insisting that "Barry" Obama (featured with a blond wig) "is the white president you can trust" (Rock). His performance of whiteness challenges widespread views of the genetic and phenotypical boundaries of race and lampoons the ostensibly fluid lines of "achieved" race that he invokes by insisting that "race is a made-up thing."

There is a latent paradox in Antoine's choice: "[He] can only reject his racialized identity because he accepts it as valid and aims to attain a more privileged one" (Morgan, *Laughing* 69). Danielle Fuentes Morgan's claim is supported by the episode's ultimate ironic twist, which takes the form of Harrison's admission that, despite the discrimination he has faced as a transracial person, he opposes both transgender identity and same-sex marriage. His impersonation of a white man seemingly entails appropriating a set of bigoted sociopolitical views, including presuming the criminality of Black people (as he does when injecting himself into a conversation between a Black man and a pair of police officers in order to flatly state that "he [the Black man] did it").

By simultaneously giving voice to the desire for transracial identity and parodying it, "B.A.N." succeeds in representing both sides of the argument without defending either of them. The already much-abused notion of tolerance is destabilized further by being shown as a wholly contingent personal judgment. Paper Boi, who previously protested the intolerance he was continuously subjected to as a Black man, laughs at Antoine in his blond wig, saying, "You look like a fake Ellen DeGeneres." Paper Boi's intolerance toward Antoine's race change is subjected to a minor form of satire. He seems to be "keeping it real" and guarding the presumed boundaries of "authentic" Blackness by performing a culturally expected identity as a rapper. Paper Boi is often presented as playing his role hypocritically since he clearly resents the ancillary implications of the stereotype he must embody to get ahead.

Another aspect of the various manifestations of racial code-switching is presented in "No One Beats the Biebs" (s1e5). Here a Black performer (Austin Crute) plays the show's version of Justin Bieber. The writers create an intentional incongruity regarding his racial identification as Bieber's phenotypical race is "swapped" for the one that Bieber blatantly appropriates in real life. The fact that the episode never comments on this transformation forces viewers to come to their own conclusions about seeing a "authentically" Black Bieber instead of just one who performs an at-times offensively "achieved" performance of Blackness. On the one hand, it can be seen as a commentary on Bieber's continuous and largely unchallenged adoption of Black culture for personal gain. On the other, it could serve to highlight the double standard in society's perception of Black people who misbehave publicly as opposed to white ones.

A phenotypically white person's cultural appropriation of Blackness is lampooned in "Juneteenth" (s1e9) through the character of Craig Allen (Rick Holmes), who thinks he knows what the Black experience is all about and even refers to Africa as "the motherland" in his conversation with the show's protagonist, Earn (Donald Glover). His performative empathy ironically prevents him from comprehending any actual Black person's experience. More significantly, it seemingly inspires him to believe that he is better equipped to determine what constitutes "authentic" Blackness. Craig's wife flabbergastingly confesses that he "told my ninety-five-year-old grandmother that she was cooking her collard greens wrong," thereby reaching a level of presumption that eludes even Antoine in "B.A.N."[4]

Racial code-switching that highlights the connections among racial categorization, performance, and social privilege is also present in "The Streisand Effect" (s1e4). This episode features a racially ambiguous peripheral character, a blogger named Zan (Freddie Kuguru), who addresses Paper Boi as "my nigga." Unclear about how offended he should feel, Alfred responds, "Are you even Black?" to which Zan retorts, "Of course I am." Throughout the rest of this episode, Zan is assigned different identities—e.g., Indian, Dominican, half-Chinese—by the other characters but remains racially nebulous. The satire here cuts in multiple ways. On the one hand, it is directed at Zan's code-switching and playacting as Black to make money, which grates against Paper Boi's own misgivings at profiting from the stereotype of the violent, drug-dealing rapper who *is* also phenotypically Black. On the other, the motives and methods of those who try to "assign" (or deny) Zan a definitive identity are also mocked. For example, Paper Boi's rejection of Zan's claims to Blackness ultimately backfires (hence the Streisand effect mentioned in the title) when Zan deprecates him on social media.

Performative Blackness is again juxtaposed against embodied authentic Blackness in "Value" (s1e6). At the predominantly Black school where she works as a teacher, Van (Zazie Beetz) sits in a room with a young boy wearing whiteface and smiling insolently at her. Recalling the convoluted history of "the white Negro" in a single shot, this image again raises the issue of racial impersonation in order to complicate easy categorizations for the viewer. As with Black Bieber's racial change, no explanation is provided for the schoolboy's incongruous appearance, and the scene is unsettling for both Van and the viewer.[5] This "produces shades of meaning and ambiguity" as satire's "indirect methods can be contradictory, confusing, and inconclusive" (Greenberg 33).

The exploration of transraciality takes perhaps its most radical form in "Teddy Perkins" (s2e6). Transracial whiteness is rendered not only through the white masklike face of the titular character (Donald Glover, in heavy makeup and prosthesis) but also through the choice of setting: Teddy's luxurious and old-fashioned, colonial-style mansion. Teddy's unnaturally lightened skin, surgically altered face, and curious choices in hairstyle and clothing conflate aspects of Michael Jackson, Little Richard, James Brown, and others, thereby conjuring an impersonation of race that is almost impossible to resolve in terms of a binary color line. Teddy's white face is foregrounded in most shots, deliberately shot to make it seem as though it is "floating" in the darkness that envelops the background. The glow of his masked face, his distant gaze, his ambiguous lines of dialogue, the strange tenor of his voice, and his inexplicable behavior all compound the effect of Teddy's fundamental inauthenticity.

He remains a disconcerting and enigmatic figure right up to the episode's violent end. Although the viewer may anticipate the conclusion, due to the episode's visual reference to copious horror-film tropes, none of the mysteries enveloping Teddy are resolved. Is he—like Michael Jackson—a victimized child prodigy who takes revenge on his emotionally and physically violent father? Why is Benny being held hostage in Teddy's house, and why is his body entirely covered up? Is he a victim of ongoing physical abuse by Teddy, or is his condition an outcome of a skin-lightening procedure gone terribly wrong? The trauma of Teddy's past is revealed not only by the video of a young Teddy and Benny being hectored by his father onto which Darius (LaKeith Stanfield) stumbles inadvertently but also by Teddy's recitation of the names of actual children who were relentlessly pushed into stardom by their abusive fathers.

It is implied that all these tyrannical fathers justified their methods because of their children's skin color as all the celebrities mentioned are Black. Perhaps revealing the depths of the damage inflicted upon him, Teddy defends their actions: "Great things come from great pain," he tells Darius, emphasizing once again the suffering he has gone through. Darius refuses this formulation, though, replying: "You know . . . not all great things come from great pain. Sometimes it's love. Not everything's a sacrifice."

The dominant motif in Teddy's characterization and visualization is his incongruous skin color, thereby emphasizing an attempted transracial crossover through phenotypical change. The episode suggests that all aspects of the Black subject's life have become "invisible, unimaginable, or wholly impossible" (Guerrero, "Can I Live?" 276). It does so in a satirical tone that initially contains the show's signature incongruous humor but evolves into tragedy as the animosity within the erstwhile Black family escalates. The conflict between Teddy and Benny ends in madness, violence, and death: one brother is murdered; the other commits suicide.

Atlanta continues its satirical exploration of racial self-identification to a somewhat lesser extent in seasons 3 and 4. The stand-alone episode "Rich Wigga, Poor Wigga" (s3e9) is a grotesque commentary on racial role-playing based on simplistic categorizations, which leads to further confusion about who is actually Black and how one determines that. The episode centers on a scene in which students of all races and ethnic backgrounds—including the episode's multiracial but previously passing-as-white protagonist—audition for Black racial identity before a panel led by a Black philanthropist looking to fund college scholarships for Black students. The litmus tests this panel uses are variously arbitrary, ambiguous, and stereotypical: "Name me six things that mix with Hennessy? . . . Where's the first place you take your cousin after he get out of prison? Why did The Five Heartbeats break up? 'Your mama' or 'your mother'? . . . What color are Wendy's napkins?" These tests result in a wildly idiosyncratic classification that excludes not only the episode's protagonist but also a Nigerian student for "not really [being] Black." Other instances of reversals of racialized privilege occur in "The Big Payback" (s3e4) and in "Light-Skinned-ed" (s4e4). In addition, "The Goof Who Sat by the Door" (s4e8)—a faux documentary reminiscent of "B.A.N."—offers both a scathing commentary on racist and discriminatory practices in Hollywood as well as a sly Gates-esque reminder that Black audiences may perceive a text—in this case, the seemingly mundane Disney film *A Goofy Movie* (1995)—very differently because of signifying practices within Black culture.

All the episodes of *Atlanta* analyzed above undermine the view that race is "something to be performed *accurately* and *authentically*" (Morgan, *Laughing* 71, emphasis original). In doing so, they both acknowledge "the significance of strategic racial performance" (Charles 34) and expose the rigidity of racial stereotypes.

Senna elaborates on the theme of self-identification not in terms of transracialism but in regard to how and why it matters for mixed-race characters, that "interracial realm of 'neither, nor, both, and in-between'" (Sollors 10). As "a connoisseur of the liminal," to use Henry Louis Gates Jr.'s words (*Thirteen Ways* 208), Senna embodies a multiracial identity herself as the daughter of an Irish American mother (the poet and novelist Fanny Howe) and an African American and Mexican father (the writer Carl Senna). She identified as Black in her youth and childhood, but her writings attest to her gradual embrace of multiracial identity. First, she has learned to flaunt it: "I've found it's not so bad being a fetishized object, an exotic bird soaring above the racial landscape" (Senna, "Mulatto Millennium"). However, she also felt fear of disappearing, "of being swallowed whole by the great white whale" ("Mulatto Millennium"). She writes, "I have come to understand that my multiplicity is inherent in my Blackness, not opposed to it, and that none of my 'identities' are distinct from one another" (Senna, "To Be Real" 18). Few of her characters can boast a similar awareness, though; even fewer feel comfortable with their mixedness, a reminder that nearly all forms of racial identification are problematic.

Mixed-race characters seem to offer less incongruity—in the sense of incompatibility between body and race—than the transracial characters discussed previously. Senna reveals that racial identity is constructed and performed by the self, although such a process is influenced or even counteracted by various kinds of social pressure related to phenotypical traits. Her characters repeatedly experience the incongruity of the body to signify their racial identity. Senna's focus falls on the biracial individual, a product of "miscegenation" that has traditionally been portrayed as a tragically liminal character.[6] Recently, however, the "mulatto" has come to "represent assimilation, the end of blackness, the end of the discussion on racism" (Arias and Senna 448). This has led to a dramatic change of perspective, which is demonstrated by the growing wave of mixed-race advocacy, exemplified by the articulation of "A Bill of Rights for Racially Mixed People" (originally published in 1993) by Maria P. P. Root, who hailed mixed race as "the new frontier" (3–14, passim).

Extending the ideas found in two of Senna's earlier texts—the essay "Mulatto Millennium" (1998) and the novel *Caucasia* (1998)—*New People* lampoons the fascination with "mixedness," stating, "Every sentence is funnier with the word *mulatto* in it" (185). Senna's "Mulatto Millennium" satirizes the fetishization of the "mulatto" by imagining a mixed-race-supremacist dictatorship in the year 2000, refashioning the reversal of white supremacism found in George Schuyler's satirical dystopia *Black No More* (1931). *Caucasia* offers a range of divergent perspectives on race, none of which is ultimately endorsed. For example, the Black father of two mixed-race girls teaches them: "There is no such thing as passing. We're all just pretending. *Race is a complete illusion, make-believe. It's a costume. We all wear one.* You just switched yours at some point. That's just the absurdity of the whole race game" (Senna, *Caucasia* 334, emphasis added). Yet he paints a postracial fantasy in a book entitled *The Petrified Monkey: Race, Blood, and the Origins of Hypocrisy*, arguing that the "mulatto in America functions as a canary in the coal mine" whose fate "will manifest the symptoms that will eventually infect the rest of the nation" (335). He interprets the fact that his daughters are "a little injured, perhaps, but alive" as a development that he interprets as a sign of improved racial relations in the United States (336), but Birdie rejects this thesis vociferously. The final dialogue in *Caucasia* is telling in this regard, as Birdie, the "invisible" biracial girl who has been forced to pass for white, laments: "They say you don't have to choose [race]. But the thing is, you do. Because there are consequences if you don't" (349). Her nonpassing sister demonstrates the mixed-race individual's social liminality by replying, "Yeah, and there are consequences if you do" (349).

Maria, the female protagonist of *New People*, experiences biracial identity as a similar conundrum; she is expected to but fails to partake in the triumph of "the 'new' multiracial population [that] has repeatedly been portrayed as a very special community with real transformative power to call a racism-free America into being" (Morning 114). Essentialist racial classifications are challenged through the cool and trendy category of "new people," that is, those of mixed-race identity. The irony is obvious in the very choice of the title and the label for this racial category for there is nothing "new" about the presence of people of mixed race in the United States. What is new is the tentative willingness not to perceive them as either Black or white.

Beige-colored Maria is a Columbia University doctoral student struggling to finish her dissertation on modes of resistance in the hymns and songs recorded by the Peoples Temple of the Disciples of Christ, the religious cult led by Jim Jones, who ordered nearly one thousand of his followers to drink cyanide-laced Kool-Aid in 1978. Thwarting the reader's reasonable expectation that she will become the epitome of the titular "new people," Maria is eventually crushed under "the unbearable whiteness of being" (Senna, *New People* 50) and by her own attempts at strictly Black self-identification. Senna utilizes the tragic "mulatto" stereotype, moving away from *Caucasia*'s central theme of racial passing to examine whether resisting racial boundaries makes it possible to avoid being categorized by them.

Senna lampoons the fallacy of self-racialization by foregrounding the racial performativity demonstrated by the "new people." Maria is phenotypically biracial and was adopted at birth by a single Black mother. Biracialism could be described as a straddling of the perceived boundary between Black and white.

Others' unwillingness to accept Maria's racial ambiguity makes her feel pressure to choose a single racial category to define herself. The pervasive external judgment surrounding her choice precipitates a crisis within her. Realizing that her mother had hoped Maria would be darker skinned (and thus easier to categorize as Black), she feels that "being black and looking white was enough of a freak show" (Senna, *New People* 43). She vacillates among numerous (and occasionally contradictory) representations of Blackness in American culture, complicating her self-perception in the process. James Baldwin's *Giovanni's Room* is a favorite of hers, as is Whitney Houston. Maria is first introduced to images of Blackness by seeing *Roots* on television, but she is also pacified by *The Cosby Show*'s efforts to quiet white fears by portraying Blacks in a somewhat deracinated and "assimilated" manner. She resorts to superficially remodeling her Blackness through such shallow gestures as changing her hairstyle. Though she feels contempt for her whiteness, Maria never becomes resolutely Black, never truly identifies as such. Henry Louis Gates Jr.'s observations about Anatole Broyard's efforts to conceal his African American ancestry shed light on Maria's behaviors: "When those of mixed ancestry—and the majority of blacks are of mixed ancestry—disappear into the white majority, they are traditionally accused of running from their 'blackness.' Yet why isn't the alternative a matter of running from their 'whiteness'? To emphasize these perversities, however, is a distraction from a larger perversity. You can't get race 'right' by refining the boundary conditions" (*Thirteen Ways* 207). Maria's attempt at dissociating from her phenotypical whiteness leads to her being perceived in college as "an odd, twisted girl" (Senna, *New People* 71) by her white boyfriend, Greg, whom she despises for his whiteness despite the strong sexual attraction she feels for him. She is also nicknamed "Sacagawea," a further mismatching of identities that recalls the scattershot attribution of ethnicity to Zan in *Atlanta*. After Maria and Greg break up, her white boyfriend purposefully undertakes a transformation in reaction to Maria's loathing for his race (which also is *her* race, at least superficially). He changes his name, religion, sexual orientation, and ethnicity to become Goya the Chicano. By reinventing himself, he aims to become part of the "tangle of mud-colored New People who have come to carry the nation—blood-soaked, guilty of everything of which it has been accused—into the future" (80).

Eventually Maria becomes engaged to an ex-boyfriend who predates Greg, a mixed-race man named Khalil, whose skin is the exact same "shade of beige" (Senna, *New People* 4) as hers. Raised by mixed parents in upper-middle-class, bourgeois, bohemian luxury, he was brought up to think of himself as a citizen of the world. Khalil gradually undergoes a transformation in his racial self-identification, though, and starts publishing a column in the Stanford school newspaper, in which he denounces the "colorblind humanism of his upbringing, which left him unaware of the racism in the world" (45). He "discovered he was black" (43) but only after being the victim of racialized abuse inflicted on him by his then-girlfriend Maria in a moment of drunken impulsivity. She made a prank call in which she directed a racist threat at Khalil, momentarily self-identifying with the whiteness she despises in herself. It is precisely this cruel prank that propelled him in the direction of Black self-identification: "he had seen the dark and he wasn't going back" (177).

As a trendy and attractive couple, Maria and Khalil are central to a forthcoming documentary about the "new people" who will bring forth "a new race" (Senna, *New People* 188). Khalil boasts in front of the camera, "We're like a Woody Allen movie, with melanin" (15). He chooses to celebrate mixedness by flaunting his Blackness in a chic way, as does his sister Lisa. She espouses her racial identification through the superficial markers of fashion and appearance, purposefully modeling herself as an "African objet d'art" (13) that is exotic and therefore (sexually) attractive to the white men she dates. She aims to gain access to white social capital by validating the racial value of Blackness as a desirable commodity, and her efforts to do so are uncompromisingly satirized. The couple styles their faux-bohemian lifestyle as that of the "new Niggerati" (14)—a historically fraught term from the Harlem Renaissance period—but it comes off as an affected farce. Once again, essentialized Black identity is satirized—in this case, a mixed identity that tries to meld white privilege onto a commodified and fetishized Black exoticism—by undermining the belief that it is reducible to certain behavioral and material patterns.

Maria entertains the notion that "maybe she and Khalil are some kind of solution" to all the racial issues, but she remains unconvinced (Senna, *New People* 178). She perceives their life as an act: "the pantomime of their newly discovered blackness" by a group of "born-again black people," who "have taken on their duties as Negroes with aplomb" (124). Unlike Maria, Khalil seems more content with his self-identification; she perceives him as "entirely black and entirely white" at the same time, as if "both parts were held together in balance" (76). Both are eventually drawn to an anonymous poet, whose readings they attend precisely for his indisputable performance of Blackness. Maria becomes pathologically obsessed with him, while Lisa becomes his girlfriend. The poet functions as the embodiment of an unconflicted Blackness that stands in opposition to Maria's troubled and deceitful self and Lisa's self-identification, which "was not always [as] a Negro" (115).

The expectation that the "new people" will ultimately subvert racism is quickly revealed as utopian. Racist stereotypical perceptions of people of color are reinstalled with a little shift in context and circumstances. Nevertheless, the text does not focus so much on overtly racist cultural practices, but rather on the more insidious forms of racialization that come out in self-contradictory notions. Senna makes a direct reference to Juvenal's *Satires* in the context of Maria's academic research on the mass suicide in Jonestown by citing the following line from the *Satires*: "*Nobody becomes depraved overnight*" (Senna, *New People* 6, emphasis original). Senna's satirical approach includes the excessive use of a variety of fancifully racialized labels. For example, Maria is described as having "high Cotton Club yellow" skin (89); Maria and Khalil are the "King and Queen of the Racially Nebulous Prom" (76), who were born after the "Era of the Mulatto Martyrs" in "the Dark Ages of Mestizo Abandonment" (165). Maria thinks of her future children with Khalil as "second-generation mutts" (98) and as the "culturally elite mulatto spawn" (99). The simultaneous specificity and inescapable self-referentiality of these labels satirize the rise of the "new people," revealing the failure of society and the individual to grasp the complexities of self-identification by resorting reductively to fixed categories.

Maria's failure to define herself through a suppression of whiteness in search of an "authentic" Black self leads to self-destructive behavior. The novel's ambiguous ending leaves her in a space of hiding and confinement, alone with the realization of her failure at self-identification. Senna leaves Maria with no compensatory self-discovery. Senna thus lampoons the search for any valid criteria for determining racial authenticity by invalidating the notion of its innateness, as the characters flaunt their Blackness in studied gestures of "achieved" racial identification.

It seems logical that acknowledging a self-articulated racial identity would counter essentialist notions. However, *Atlanta* and *New People* reveal the incongruity of this idea by affirming the opposing view: racial self-identification involves individual internalization of socially constructed conceptualizations of race. Senna reveals, though her mixed-race characters, an awareness that race is not innate but is constituted through a series of performative acts. Transracial characters in *Atlanta* follow a similar path in playing the part they appropriate but, at the same time, assuming, paradoxically, a less fluid and deeply essentialist perception of race.

Through this ostentatious playacting, both *Atlanta* and *New People* reveal that "race becomes not only something that is performed but something that is performed so thoroughly convincingly that its essentialized characteristics become adopted, internalized, experienced, and believed" (Leverette, "Revisions" 117). The transracial and biracial characters in both texts become so "thoroughly convinced" of their own performances that they lose sight of their inherent unreality. What is more, the practices of racial self-identification in *New People* and the *Atlanta* episodes discussed here arise from frustration and rage at the assumed irrelevance of race in the postracial era and the realization that the perpetuation of the color line does not allow for any freedom of choice in racial self-identification.

NOTES

1. Though the phenomenon of transracial adoption falls outside the scope of the current discussion, it should be noted that appropriating the term "transracial" to describe race change constitutes, for some social critics, an erasure of transracial adoptees' identities with many complex implications. The episode "Three Slaps" (s3e1) touches on such issues.
2. For more on this side of her identity, see "NAACP Imposter."
3. See Charles 156–78.
4. For more on this episode, see the essays by Rutter and Parks herein.
5. For further discussion of this episode, see Parks's essay herein.
6. See Elam.

"KNOW THYSELF"

Education and Identity Fashioning in *Atlanta* and *Dear White People*

DEREK DIMATTEO

The TV show *Atlanta* (2016–2022) and the film *Dear White People* (2014)[1] contribute to Black popular culture's pantheon of stories engaging higher education "as a means of upward mobility and assimilation" for African Americans (Cousins 247), as well as education's effect on Black identity fashioning. If, as Trey Ellis argues, the new Black aesthetic is a mode of expression particular to "cultural mulattos" who can "navigate easily" both the Black and white worlds without needing to "deny or suppress any part of our complicated and sometimes contradictory cultural baggage to please either white people or black" (235), then *Atlanta* and *Dear White People* show that ideal is still not so easily realized. Both satirize social forces (especially education) that circumscribe Black individuality and collective advancement by employing a "dual-vectored" approach of Horatian satire aimed at the Black community and Juvenalian satire aimed at institutional and societal structures of racism (Maus, "Mommy" xiii–xiv). As "intragroup satire," which seeks to "destabilize and ultimately to undermine morally or ethically suspect behaviors and/or beliefs" (xix), *Atlanta* and *Dear White People* satirize the ways that stereotypical conceptions of Blackness continue to affect autonomous Black identity construction, especially among the college educated.

Atlanta and *Dear White People* present collegiate Black characters struggling to craft identities liberated from what Stuart Hall calls an "essentialized black subject" (443). They exhibit what Danielle Fuentes Morgan might agree is a "defiance of prescriptive identity" in their characters' attempts to fashion "autonomous selves" beyond racial stereotypes (*Laughing* 6). I argue that the satire in both *Atlanta* and *Dear White People* ridicules lingering beliefs about essentialized Blackness both within and outside the Black community, the pursuit of racial uplift through assimilation to so-called white middle-class values at predominantly white institutions (PWI), and the relatively unquestioned belief in higher education as the path to upward social mobility. Simultaneously, they imply that meaningful uplift can be achieved through racial solidarity and a reinvestment in Black communities.

Through their satire of prescriptive Black identity as signified by respectability politics, *Atlanta* and *Dear White People* affirm their creators as post-soul artists championing the new Black aesthetic's insistence on the legitimacy of what Morgan terms "kaleidoscopic Blackness—the multiple autonomous ways of being Black" (*Laughing* 3). According to her, most people gauge the "authenticity" of Black experience by its "adherence to expectations. African American satire rejects this limited scope by framing it as laughable." She suggests that if you fail to "decode the authorial intent of the [satirical] speaker or performer," then you are also failing to understand that Blackness is "kaleidoscopic," and you will inevitably also fail to achieve "awareness of the limitlessness of Black identity in the face of its denial" (7). In other words, you cannot recognize kaleidoscopic Blackness and its concurrent "ethical move that leads to social justice in its revelation of the multiple ways of performing blackness" (7) by adhering to expectations conveyed by stereotypes. *Atlanta* and *Dear White People* participate in the quintessentially post-soul project of exploding essentialized notions of Blackness while also drawing attention to the ways that education at elite, predominantly white institutions affects Black students' identities.

How education is represented in *Atlanta* and *Dear White People* and how it affects characters' identities interest me for two reasons: first, because *Dear White People* is among the first college films to feature protagonists who are Black students at an Ivy league school (albeit a fictional one); second, because *Atlanta*'s main character, Earn, is a Princeton University dropout whose college years are not depicted in the show and whose departure from the university remains shrouded in mystery until "The Homeliest Little Horse" (s4e2), even though satirical references to his time at Princeton and representations of education in general recur throughout the series. Because *Atlanta* reveals precious little about Earn's collegiate experience, I analyze education and its effects on Earn's identity in *Atlanta* through comparison to its immediate precursor, *Dear White People*, which depicts the black collegiate experience at a predominantly white, elite educational institution that is much like Princeton. These satires help reveal how the relationship between higher education and Black identity has become more complicated in the twenty-first century. I approach this analysis by elaborating the relationships among racial uplift ideology, respectability politics, and education, then discussing their representation in *Dear White People*, which I will consequently use as a framework to analyze representations of education and its effects on Black identity in *Atlanta*.

Schooling, particularly higher education, is widely acknowledged to have a significant effect on an individual's identify formation, including in terms of race and class. For example, a college education is now commonly perceived as a prerequisite to getting a job that provides entry into the American middle class; correspondingly, the college degree itself has become symbolic of middle-class identity. For African Americans, education has been a pillar of racial-uplift ideology since at least the 1900s. W. E. B. Du Bois and Booker T. Washington called on the educated Black elite—the "Talented Tenth"—to lead the race to greater prosperity and social status "through an ethos of service to the masses" (Gaines xiv), uplifting the entire race while disproving negative stereotypes. Kevin Gaines explains, in *Uplifting the Race* (1995), that the desire to negate stereotypes gave rise to respectability politics, through which Black elites disciplined the attitudes and behavior of the less privileged, thus creating intraracial tensions that are inherently rooted in social class and educational status.[2]

Although it was once true that most prospective Black elites attended historically Black colleges and universities (HBCUs), both the number and proportion of Black students educated at historically white institutions, including Ivy League colleges, has gradually increased over time. Despite their own histories of anti-Black racism, Ivy League institutions have long offered Black students power and prestige upon graduation. That they confer "the highest levels of access regarding American decision making, policy, and industry" is exemplified by the Ivy League degrees held by 70 percent of Barack Obama's Black cabinet members, according to Stefan M. Bradley in *Upending the Ivory Tower* (1). Access to higher education is supposedly meritocratic, yet Black students remain underrepresented outside of HBCUs. As Bradley and others observe, the challenge for Black students entering PWIs is not just to gain admission but also to overcome both the casual and the systemic racism that lingers on PWI campuses. Black students encounter such racism early in their college careers, such as when others question the merit of their admission through assumptions about affirmative action or athletic scholarships, undermining Black students' sense of belonging and making them feel unwelcome.

Not all Black students feel unwelcome at PWIs—take for example Mellody Hobson, for whom Princeton's Woodrow Wilson residential college was renamed in 2020. Quoted in the university's name-change announcement, Hobson recalls feeling "at home" at Princeton in the late 1980s and early 1990s; she expresses hope that, when future students of color see her name on the building, they will feel "that they too belong" (Spike). Hobson implicitly acknowledges that many students of color feel ambivalent, uneasy, or alienated when attending a PWI. This feeling is discussed by fellow Princeton alumna (class of 1985) Michelle Obama—then still Michelle Robinson—in her senior sociology thesis, in which she observes: "no matter how liberal and open-minded some of my White professors and classmates try to be toward me, I sometimes feel like a visitor on campus; as if I really don't belong. Regardless of the circumstances under which I interact with Whites at Princeton, it often seems as if, to them, I will always be Black first and a student second" (2). She reveals a degree of alienation not uncommon for Black, Indigenous, and people-of-color (BIPOC) students at PWIs, who regularly feel marginalized, stereotyped, and profiled while in overwhelmingly white campus spaces.[3]

As a senior at Princeton, the future lawyer, university administrator, and First Lady (among other things) not only worried about alienation from the academic community, but she also openly wondered whether her education might alienate her from the Black working class (M. Robinson 2). The phenomenon of working-class students in higher education feeling marginalized from both their university community and from their socioeconomic roots was described decades earlier by Richard Hoggart in *The Uses of Literacy* (1957). Hoggart writes specifically of white working-class British males and gives them the label "scholarship boys" because of the way that they were plucked from their local grammar schools, educated on scholarships at elite institutions, and raised into the social ranks of middle- and upper-class white-collar professionals (passim). Hoggart's study usefully describes the identity struggles experienced by white students who undergo this process, but he does not consider the impact of gender and race.[4] Michelle Robinson's thesis attests to a fundamental similarity in the experience of some Black students whose educational paths paralleled that of Hoggart's "scholarship boy." Such students likewise experience alienation that clearly arises from class differences, but her words also reveal a corresponding preoccupation with race when she considers how her Princeton education may have affected her feelings of membership in and "obligation" to give back to the Black community because, she says, "the path I have chosen to follow by attending Princeton will likely lead to my further integration and/or assimilation into a White cultural and social structure that will only allow me to remain on the periphery of society; never becoming a full participant" (M. Robinson, 2–3). Here she reflects on how her Princeton education affects her identity and her relationship to the Black community, threatening to cast her as a liminal figure caught between two worlds, never fully at home in either, a situation that echoes characters in both *Dear White People* and *Atlanta*.

Upon its release in 2014, Justin Simien's *Dear White People* was one of only a handful of films to offer a representation of the Black collegiate experience at a predominantly white institution.[5] Unlike its predecessors, *Dear White People* focuses on the core characters' struggle to maintain autonomous identities despite social pressure to conform to the conflicting demands of essentialist stereotypes and respectability politics. Elite higher education is implicated in such characters' struggle through *Dear White People*'s setting at a fictional Ivy

League school named Winchester University. The institution's name signifies on the Winchester rifle, which Ida B. Wells-Barnett famously advocates as a weapon for Black self-protection against lynch mobs[6] and which I read as a reminder of the promise of education as a tool for Black liberation and equality. Although elite colleges like those of the Ivy League might be expected to offer Black students greater advantages and professional success than other PWIs and HBCUs, studies consistently show that it is actually HBCUs that grant Black students the greatest benefits after graduation (Tatum 169–70). Schools are also widely understood as important locations for adolescents' individual and group identity construction.[7] Winchester University promotes this through its motto *"Nosce te ipsum"* (know thyself) and its marketing slogan "Where You Belong." However, the film satirizes this understanding by suggesting that it is difficult to know yourself when you are suffocated by pressure to conform to imposed stereotypes, and it is impossible to feel like you belong if you are ostracized when you defy such stereotypes.

Characters such as Samantha "Sam" White (Tessa Thompson), Troy Fairbanks (Brandon Bell), and Lionel Higgins (Tyler James Williams) attempt to develop autonomous identities at Winchester, yet they struggle not simply because it is a PWI but also because both its white and Black leaders appear to embrace the colorblind, postracial ideology that reached its zenith during Barack Obama's presidency. The ideology of colorblindness refers to the belief that past racial wrongs have been righted, that equality of opportunity is sufficient for equality of results, and that race is no longer a factor in a society built on meritocratic principles. Since higher education supposedly epitomizes the colorblind meritocracy, many conservatives began openly opposing the continuation of affirmative action. The ideological successor to colorblindness is postracialism, which Ian F. Haney-López argues "constitutes a liberal embrace of colorblindness" (808). The notions that the United States was realizing a postracial society and that the nation's higher-education institutions were leading the way were based on the belief in higher education as a vehicle for the "assimilationist-integrationist success" of minority groups (Napper 29). Faith in higher education's power to create racial equity on college campuses and to transfer that into our broader political system (S. Bradley xv) has proven premature if not entirely misplaced. Simien's film roundly mocks the rush to declare the country's racial problems obsolete.

Dear White People satirizes postracial ideology by showing how minority students and faculty continue to experience racism on college campuses. The film demonstrates how efforts to use higher education as a means of social integration failed partly because institutions, such as Winchester, clung to the belief in their status as utopian enclaves rather than recognizing themselves as microcosms of a mainstream society that includes those opposed to integration and pluralism. Winchester's postracial ideology is exemplified by its white president, Dr. Fletcher (Peter Syvertsen), who, when faced with Black-student unrest over racist behavior by white students (including his son), claims that "we don't have an intolerance problem here" and that "racism is over in America," to which the Black dean of students, Dr. Walter Fairbanks (Dennis Haysbert), merely raises his eyebrows. President Fletcher's claims are belied by the words and actions of his son Kurt (Kyle Gallner) and other residents of Garmin House who host a Halloween party at which attendees are explicitly encouraged to "liberate their inner Negro" by dressing and behaving in overtly racist stereotypes of Black culture, including (of course) blackface. The party, vehemently protested by Black students, results in a "race war" at the university, according to the news media. *Dear White People* satirizes liberal America's idyllic image of college campuses as places where multiculturalism and meritocracy fuse to create an environment of academic *humanité* by showing that racism is just as alive in the hallowed Ivy League as in the rest of society. The insufficiency of colorblindness and postracialism has become ever more apparent with the growing frequency of highly publicized racial incidents on college campuses since Henry Louis Gates's arrest on his own front porch—and his subsequent "beer summit" with Barack Obama and the arresting officer—in July 2009.

Dean Fairbanks is ultimately just as culpable as President Fletcher for Winchester's uneasy campus climate, and the film uses his character to satirize the bankruptcy of the campus's idealistic racial rhetoric, particularly through his treatment of his son Troy. Troy's autonomous identity construction is stifled by his father's heavy-handed emphasis on respectability and uplift. Pressured to mold himself into a law-school candidate and future politician, like Barack Obama, Troy hides both his love of *Star Trek*[8] and his use of marijuana, dumps his Black girlfriend to start dating Fletcher's daughter Sophia (Brittany Curran), and sacrifices his dream of writing satire for *Pastiche*, Winchester's version of the *Harvard Lampoon* or the *Princeton Tiger*. Dean Fairbanks criticizes Troy for smoking weed and asks him if he wants to be numbered among the "Black men wast[ing] their lives trying to be on TV, be rappers or ballplayers." Troy is caught in a false dichotomy that pits the stereotypes of essentialized Blackness against an overly narrow definition of Black excellence, which prevents him from constructing an identity that encompasses all his interests.

The source of Troy's conflict resides in his father's own identity formation, which he seeks to impose upon Troy (and, by extension, other Black students). Dean Fairbanks's insistence on respectability politics is made most explicit when he commands Troy to correct his behavior: "The men who really run this world . . . , oh, you've got no idea what they see when they see you. You are *not* going to be what they all *think* you are. You are *not* going to give them that satisfaction. *Do you hear me?*" The dean later implicitly reveals that he resolved his own identity conflict by choosing assimilation in a conversation with Sam, an outspoken young Black student (and the girlfriend that Troy dumped in favor of the president's daughter) whose clever campus-radio rants about white students' racial blind spots give the film its title. He suggests that she had a difficult time growing up biracial, "wondering which side you fit into, feeling like you have to overcompensate, perhaps."[9] After Dean Fairbanks refers to Sam feeling forced to choose a racial allegiance, Sam astutely makes the analogy to academia when she replies, "If that's true, Dean, then I'm not the only one," intuiting that the dean faces a similar dilemma as a Black intellectual working in higher education. The satirical implication is that by constructing his academic identity on a foundation of respectability politics, the dean is akin to an Uncle Tom who, in Sam's words, "would rather please his massa [President Fletcher and wealthy donors] than stand up for his own." The ideology of respectability politics also plays out at the institutional level as both Fletcher and Fairbanks worry about both Sam's radio show and the protests about the Halloween party causing bad press for the university, damaging its reputation, and deterring donors. That either Sam or the protesters could have valid complaints remains a nonstarter.

Rather than conform to an identity that models itself after white middle-class values, Sam attempts to blaze a path that allows her to be both an intellectual and a fierce advocate of Black racial uplift unconstrained by respectability politics. She achieves this when she resolves to no longer be the mouthpiece of the university's militant Black students after accepting that she is not a revolutionary but rather an "anarchist" who has always been "independent, even as a child." These designations seem entirely in step with Morgan's conception of a freewheeling kaleidoscopic Blackness "that includes racial specificity but isn't predicated on racial essentialism as necessary for selfhood" (*Laughing* 150).

In addition to the positive example of her character arc, one of Sam's most important contributions to the film's intragroup satire of Black essentialism is her role as a pro-affinity housing activist. In an effort to maintain Armstrong-Parker House as a residence exclusively for Black students, Sam agitates against the university's randomization of campus housing. While higher education has generally recognized race- and ethnicity-based affinity housing as beneficial sites of unity, mutual support, and uplift, such residences can also promote ideologies that discipline occupants for being either insufficiently respectable or "not Black enough," neither of which is a kaleidoscopic view of Blackness.

Lionel Higgins is a prime example of such disciplining in *Dear White People*. Lionel doesn't fit any of the race-focused categories in Sam's booklet *Ebony & Ivy: A Survival Guide to Keep from Drowning in a Sea of White*[10] and accordingly struggles to belong at Winchester. He is not a "boofta" who "modulates his Blackness" based on social context nor a "nose job" who "smooths their Black edges" to blend in nor a "one-hundred-percenter" who keeps it "Black as hell all the time." As a gay Black man who "listen[s] to Mumford & Sons and watch[es] Robert Altman movies," Lionel feels alienated from every group on campus, including other Black students, as he appears neither "Black enough for the Black kids [nor] Black enough for the white ones." In many ways, he exemplifies Ellis's notion of the "cultural mulatto" but without the corollary benefit of "navigat[ing] easily" across racial boundaries. Lionel's ostracism from Armstrong-Parker House belies its pretense of racial solidarity and communal racial uplift. At the start of the film, Lionel actually lives in the same dorm where the racist party occurs and has to endure Kurt's homophobic practical jokes until Dean Fairbanks proposes to move him into Troy's room, to which Lionel responds, "The worst thing about high school and believe me, it's a long list, were the Black kids." The film uses Lionel's mistreatment to satirize a wide range of constraining conceptions of socially acceptable Blackness.

Dear White People's satire of affinity housing's complicated racial dynamics does not entirely negate the significant systems of support that such arrangements can provide to students of color at PWIs (Tatum 168–70). Affinity housing has been shown to help students cope with environmental stressors such as racial profiling, stereotype threat, microaggressions, and accusations about unmerited admission, as well as other institutional factors, such as disproportionately low numbers of faculty of color, insufficient diversity training, poorly funded cultural centers, and low student-body diversity (Libresco). The cumulative effect of such conditions undermines BIPOC students' feeling of belonging and can cause a "disidentification with academics" (Verschelden 44) that negatively affects performance.[11] All of these issues may tacitly pertain to Earn's departure from Princeton in *Atlanta*.

That education is central to understanding the identity formation of Earn (Donald Glover), *Atlanta*'s main character, is evident by his name's connotative meaning and the depiction of his high-school experience in "FUBU" (s2e10). His full name, Earnest Marks, suggests someone who strives to receive good grades, and "FUBU" shows that Earn's family emphasizes education and respectability as paths for upward mobility.[12] The Marks family is solidly working class yet also aspirational and upwardly mobile; Earn's mother (Myra Lucretia Taylor) shops at thrift stores but also insists that he wear a suit to his piano lessons. Through this insistence, she teaches him about race and respectability, justifying the suit by reminding Earn that, as "a Black man in America," he will be judged by his appearance and should therefore strive to make a good first impression through his clothes, a factor he can control. "FUBU" also depicts Earn's academic habits in several scenes in which Earn appears ready to learn while some classmates are more interested in clowning; his lab partner

(A'Nya Schofield) in a science class directly states, "You're pretty smart, Earn" as he readily discerns the differences between various kinds of cells. Of course, his later matriculation to Princeton also implies that he excelled academically.

Unfortunately, Earn never graduates from Princeton, a fact that hangs mysteriously over him for the first three seasons, and the reason for which his family members and the audience alike are left to speculate about. Finally, in "The Homeliest Little Horse" (s4e2), we learn that Earn is expelled for entering his friend and fellow resident assistant (RA) Sasha's room to retrieve his suit (which she had been safekeeping for him) so he could wear it to a job interview. Sasha had abruptly left town, and in desperation, Earn uses his RA master key to enter her room. Earn tells us that Sasha "was furious and told the dean." Earn reports that Sasha (a young, white female) and the university administration (implicitly white and male) describe Earn's actions by using "rapist language," such as "intruder, personal assault, attack on privacy." Earn speculates that these white university officials saw him not as a young, panicked job candidate retrieving the suit he needs for an interview from a friend's room but rather as "this big Black gorilla [who] came into this white girl's room and just destroyed it." Princeton's white administrators stereotyped Earn with the broad paintbrush of Black male criminality. Earn tells his therapist that nobody listened to his explanation, which made him feel "hurt" by Sasha's betrayal, "powerless" by his inability to get a fair hearing, and "angry" and more "alone" than he already felt being only "like one of twelve Black kids [on campus]." This feeling of alienation and isolation echoes Lionel's experience in *Dear White People*.

However, none of this is known during *Atlanta*'s first three seasons. The series begins three years after Earnest returns home from college to the Black middle-class neighborhood in which he grew up. "The Big Bang" (s1e1) reveals only that Earn attended but never graduated from Princeton, and it does so through a conversation with his cousin Alfred Miles (Bryan Tyree Henry), who quips, "Three years is a long year off." Alfred presumes to know why Earn first took a break from and then dropped out of Princeton, but we never hear his theory because Earn swiftly interrupts: "I really think you *don't* [know]." Earn declines to explain the reason to Alfred (or the audience). Seeking answers, Alfred asks Earn's parents:

> ALFRED: Like, what happened at Princeton?
> EARN'S FATHER [Isiah Whitlock Jr.]: I never asked. He'd tell you before me.
> ALFRED: No, Earn is good at keeping his mouth shut.

Knowing his family's values were an important factor in his K–12 success and admission to Princeton, the fact that Earn refuses to explain what happened is understandable. Having spent his life adhering to his parents' respectability politics, the circumstances of his expulsion would have been too shameful and embarrassing to reveal, regardless of his innocence. But for viewers just getting to know his character, the lack of explanation makes his dropping out even more mysterious.

The silence about this significant plot detail invites audiences to fill in the blank. One plausible reason is the birth of Earn's daughter, Lottie (Mia Atehortua), and the responsibility he may feel as a father, an experience to which he might not expect Alfred to be able to relate. Viewers attuned to contemporary academia might also recall events from the mid-2010s that negatively impacted BIPOC students' mental health and wellbeing, such as incidents of racial profiling across the nation's campuses, blackface parties (e.g., at University of California, San Diego, and Penn State), student protests over lack of inclusion (e.g., at Missouri and Oberlin), and increased activity by white nationalist groups. That Earn could simply have run out of "bandwidth" (Verschelden x) in the face of such challenges would hardly seem farfetched as the first season aired in 2016.

Although Earn's time at Princeton University is neither shown nor discussed to any great extent in *Atlanta*'s first two seasons, *Dear White People* offers a window into some likely aspects of Earn's experience even before the incident that led to his expulsion. Like Troy, Earn may have felt caught between the stereotypes of essentialized Blackness and the pressure to be an exemplar of Black excellence and assimilation given the emphasis his mother seems to have placed on respectability politics. And like Lionel, Earn is shown as illegible to mainstream culture because he does not perform an essentialized and stereotypical Blackness (unlike Alfred's rapper persona, Paper Boi), which makes the context of his expulsion from Princeton all the more ironic and tragic. Earn does not even code-switch when others use Black vernacular English with him. This contrasts with *Dear White People* when Lionel watches a fellow Black student code-switch while moving between groups of friends from different races. Like Sam, conforming to expectations is antithetical to Earn's independent spirit, as his father notes in the series premiere: "When [Earn] wants to do something, he does it. On *his* terms." Earn's departure from Princeton theoretically removes him from the situation of feeling forced into a false choice between assimilation and essentialism. Moreover, by not conforming to stereotypical portrayals of Blackness, Earn resists external expectations about who and what he should be, albeit with mixed results.

Back in his old neighborhood, Earn finds that his illegible Blackness *and* his education—interrupted and incomplete though it is—set him apart. The failure to perform a stereotypical Black masculinity results in Earn repeatedly being disrespected and "stunted on" in "Money Bag Shawty" (s2e3). By not acting

Black enough, Earn is read as a "Don Lemon type" by Darius (LaKeith Stanfield) in "The Big Bang," a reference to Earn's educated diction, preppy clothes, and nonthreatening demeanor. All these traits can be read as assimilationist, but Earn—echoing Ellis—instead frames them as being able to "play both sides if needed." Alfred emphasizes Darius's point by telling Earn that being a "man" is "not your lane" and that he is "too Martin" in a situation when Alfred needs someone "more Malcolm." Given that Malcolm X never completed high school while MLK earned a PhD, this could also be a dig at Earn's education.[13] A less subtle dig comes in "Sportin' Waves" (s2e2), which satirizes Earn's education when Alfred's friend Tracy (Khris Davis) asks him for advice before going to a job interview; however, that advice is limited to "how to talk to white folks" and what shoes to wear, indicating an overemphasis on race, diction, and other superficial aspects of identity while ignoring factors such as education, skills, and experience. Tracy's request for Earn's advice satirically reduces his Princeton education to the equivalent of an expensive finishing school.

Earn's perceived assimilation into white middle-class values and his Ivy League education alienate him from the communal Blackness of his working-class neighborhood even while his continued identification with that working-class community inhibits him from feeling comfortable moving in bourgeois circles, especially when they are predominantly white. This discomfort with the bourgeois is exemplified in "Juneteenth" (s1e9) when Earn and his on-again, off-again partner Van (Zazie Beetz) attend a dinner party at the luxurious home of Monique (Cassandra Freeman) and her white husband, Craig (Rick Holmes). Neither Van nor Earn fit into this milieu, but Van wants to attend because of the career-networking opportunities it offers her. Van implores Earn to help her blend in: "Can you pretend for once that we aren't who we are?" They conceal their fulfillment of common stereotypes about poor and working-class Black people, including being recreational drug users, unemployed, a single mom, a largely absentee father, and a college dropout while also failing to fulfill other stereotypes by being disinterested in jazz, African art, and slam poetry (three of the passions that define Craig's thoroughly appropriative personality). Stressed by their charade, Earn and Van cope by drinking heavily. This episode confirms that Earn has little interest in living inauthentically in a place he doesn't belong—perhaps an echo of what it might have been like for him at the similarly well-heeled and predominantly white Princeton.[14]

Earn is alienated not only from the bourgeois world but also from communal Blackness. This alienation inhibits Earn's ability to give back to the community in fulfilment of racial-uplift ideology. By virtue of his access to elite higher education, Earn is theoretically a member of the "Talented Tenth" and thus ostensibly obligated to spread middle-class assimilationist values to the rest of the Black community. At the same time, Earn's failure to gain respect for his education is because, in a world that is "all about that paper, boi" (as Alfred raps in his breakthrough single), he conspicuously lacks the cultural capital conferred by that all-important paper: the college diploma. In this way, *Atlanta* satirizes uplift ideology and the intraracial suspicion with which the Black elite is sometimes received. Alfred echoes this in "Crabs in a Barrel" (s2e11) when he refuses to hire a "janky" Black entertainment lawyer and instead instructs Earn to find a "high-level Jewish dude, not somebody gonna rob me like Don King or some shit." Alfred rehearses racist stereotypes about both Black criminality and Jewish influence in the entertainment industry while dismissing the attorney's education—degrees from Howard University and Georgetown Law School, where he finished in the top ten in his class. This moment satirizes how the "Talented Tenth" are sometimes rejected by members of their own community, ironically undermining uplift ideology and suggesting that Earn may have become disillusioned by Princeton's potential to improve his lot in life.

K–12 education plays an important role in communal racial uplift, so we might expect the decision to send gifted Black students to the best school available to be obvious. However, this decision is fraught with consequences for both the individual students and their communities, as implicated in "Crabs in a Barrel" (s2e11). The episode's title refers to an ostensible behavior among crabs trapped in a small container, such as a barrel; when one crab reaches the top of the barrel, the others try to pull it back down, thereby dooming all the crabs. This is analogous to the situation confronting Earn and Van regarding their daughter Lottie's education. Lottie's preschool teacher (Greta Glenn) tells them that Lottie is "gifted" and encourages them to enroll her in the pre-K program at a prestigious private school. Although happy that Lottie is "gifted," they are concerned about the tuition given their precarious financial situation and ask about keeping Lottie at her current school for the time being. The teacher tells them bluntly that the school is "awful," that it "lacks resources and teachers," and is "stunting her education." Giving Lottie the best education possible will come at more than just a financial cost. As previously discussed, academically gifted Black students at predominantly white educational institutions often struggle with environmental stressors and identity development. Van reminds Earn of this when she notes: "The school will be mostly white. All the private schools are. But you know that. You chose Princeton." Metaphorically, letting one of the crabs escape the barrel paradoxically means removing the best students from the public schools (either by sending them to charter schools or to private schools), weakening the local school system not only in terms of funding but also by impoverishing the classroom through a kind of brain drain. Thus, one of the traditional strategies of racial-uplift ideology—plucking out the brightest students and giving them an elite education—paradoxically damages the community, a situation satirically referenced by the episode's title.

Given Earn's upbringing in a Black neighborhood and school system, his education at a predominantly white university, and his eclectic interests, we might expect him to fall into the Ellis's category of the "cultural mulatto" who fits comfortably into both Black and white cultural milieus. However, Earn finds himself in a liminal space between the world promised by his education and the world circumscribed by his old neighborhood, neither of which feels comfortable. Earn embraces communal Black identity, but he rejects essentialized Blackness, searching instead for an authentic self. Ironically, Earn, Van, and Alfred are regularly encouraged to behave out of character if they want to get ahead or be treated with respect by others. To the extent that these three characters are torn between rejecting the rules of different social groups or succumbing to those groups' social expectations (which they sometimes do), the series questions the very notion that an authentic self can be achieved.

Atlanta and *Dear White People* would be comedies if it were not for their characters' sincerity and their frequent serious turns, and they would be tragedies if it were not for their satirical attitude toward essentialism, education, and identity fashioning. They encourage audiences to recognize the characters' battles against life's injustices—even if those battles are frequently lost through their own flaws—and to sympathize with their struggle to forge authentic selves in environments that often refuse to acknowledge Morgan's "kaleidoscopic" view of Blackness. Rather than "projecting stereotypes and biases as essential 'truths'" (Russell 268), *Atlanta* and *Dear White People* challenge preconceptions of education and race long embedded in the social imaginary by critiquing the continued adherence to limited forms of authentic Blackness, whether that is through intragroup satire or by targeting institutional and societal structures. These two satirical works illuminate how the complicated intersection of education and respectability politics impacts Black identity fashioning in the twenty-first century.

NOTES

1. I limit my discussion to the film because the subsequent TV series feels like a separate text and, more importantly, because the film being released in 2014 would have greater potential influence on the creation of *Atlanta* and its characters.

2. For further discussion of respectability, see Parks's essay herein.

3. See Jenkins et al.; Nelson; Takei.

4. To some extent, this is, of course, likely a reflection of the comparatively small numbers of nonwhites and women who attended elite British institutions of learning in Hoggart's time.

5. Prior to *Dear White People*, a handful of films have featured Black college students as main characters and were thereby able to portray Black collegians' experiences; however, the majority of these were set at HBCUs, not PWIs. John Singleton's *Higher Learning* (1995) and Jesse Dylan's *How High* (2001) are two of the few exceptions to this rule. Thanks to Laura J. Vollmer for mentioning *How High*.

6. Thanks to Derek C. Maus for reminding me of Wells-Barnett's quote in *Southern Horrors* (23).

7. See Nakkula; Tatum; Verhoeven et al.

8. Presumably, Avery Brooks's *Deep Space Nine* character Benjamin Sisko—a Black space-station commander and a moral/ethical exemplar—would not satisfy his father's requirements as a role model.

9. For further discussion of this theme, see Glavanakova's essay herein.

10. Sam's book title signifies on Craig Steven Wilder's *Ebony and Ivy: Race, Slavery, and the Troubled History of America's Universities* (2013).

11. See Hausmann et al.

12. For further discussion of this episode, see Foster-Singletary's essay herein.

13. Thanks to James J. Donahue for suggesting this reading.

14. For further discussion of this episode, see the essays by Rutter and Parks herein.

Lake Lanier

CANINES AND TRICKSTERS IN *ATLANTA*

MATTHIAS KLESTIL

Atlanta introduces Darius (LaKeith Stanfield) in a way that hints at two of the character's key facets when, in a parking lot in front of a nightclub, Darius claims to feel a sense of "crazy déjà vu" while looking at a stray dog. His first lines in "The Big Bang" (s1e1) thereby function as a metacommentary on the episode's circular narrative structure, presaging Darius's predilection for the philosophical and mythical, as well as possibly foreshadowing the possibility—winkingly raised in the series's final shot—that the entire show is just a hallucination he experiences while inside a sensory-deprivation tank. Moreover, the moment establishes a verbal and visual link between Darius and the stray that foreshadows his subtly meaningful and ambivalent relations to canine animals, which I explore here as part of *Atlanta*'s satirical play with environmental and biopolitical discourses. Turning to two episodes from the first season that feature, respectively, a cane corso as a commodity and a poster of a dog as a shooting target, I examine how *Atlanta*'s representations of canines and of Darius as a trickster satirically negotiate environmental values, stereotypes, and affects.[1]

I take up the notion of contemporary African American satire as a "multi-vectored" discourse (Maus, "Mommy" xvi). That is, while understanding satire generally as a way "to entertain us *and* give us food for thought" (Bergenholtz 90, emphasis original), my argument builds on the idea that African American satire "simultaneously transmits its ethical critique at two distinct frequencies," aiming at both African American in-group audiences and American culture at large (Maus, "Mommy" xiii). A concurrent focus on such satire's "comedic self-critical tenor" (xv) as well as its often more scornful attacks on systemic forms of oppression and racism can greatly enhance an interpretive lens based on ecocriticism and/or animal studies. The "Horatian" ridicule that aims at "follies and self-destructive habits . . .]within the African American community" (xiii–xiv) involves environmentally relevant points of critique by ironizing African American environmental stereotypes or histories. At the same time, a

"Juvenalian" mode of satire "directed at political institutions, social practices, and cultural discourses that arise outside the community" (xiv) decries racialized environmental or biopolitical practices that are linked to a longstanding association of Blackness with animality in which canine anti-Black violence plays a significant role. Against this backdrop, this essay listens in to *Atlanta*'s environmentally resonating frequencies as part of its "multivectored" satire, especially when the messages on such frequencies are broadcast in indirect and subtle ways.

Recent decades have witnessed the development of a considerable ecocritical discourse on African American perspectives that also draws from animal studies. In this regard, note that I am not suggesting a reading of *Atlanta* that uses the term "environmentalism" in its mainstream sense. What a diverse and growing body of environmental work on African American literature and culture has proposed over the past two decades, namely the necessity of using concepts related to the "environment/al" more inclusively,[2] is arguably even more critical when turning to African American satire. Here, both a traditional view of African American cultural production as primarily engaging in social protest and a tendency to perceive environmentalism as a "serious issue" play into the subtlety of *Atlanta*'s environmental dimensions and testify for the necessity of a broader lens that an ecocriticism focused on African American perspectives provides. In accordance with the dual focus of this field on environmental and/as social issues, my readings are not intended to draw attention away from the social criticisms articulated in *Atlanta*, but rather to highlight their centrality while suggesting intersections with environmentally relevant points of critique that arise specifically from the show's human-canine encounters.

Two means—one a general mode of operation, the other a specific concept—are especially productive in the present context. First, I believe genealogical contextualization of specific environmentally relevant allusions essential, particularly the interrelated meanings of canines, "tricksterism," and African American cultural relationships to the pastoral. Satire is often an "attack on clear and specific historical material" (Knight 13), and although I am not suggesting that African American satire is fundamentally different in this respect, the subtlety, metaphoricity, and misdirections prominent in *Atlanta*'s satire featuring canines require a careful disentangling of references to determine the potential environmental targets of its multivectored critique. Insights from scholarship on the history of African American cultural relationships to dogs (for example, Boisseron; Parry and Yingling) are particularly useful in this respect. Second, I employ Nicole Seymour's notion of "bad environmentalism," which she defines as "environmental thought that employs dissident, often-denigrated affects and sensibilities to reflect critically on both our current moment and mainstream environmental art, activism, and discourse" (6). Although not exclusively pertaining to satirical modes, this concept's emphasis on stereotyping and "racialized environmental affect" is useful for describing the environmental dimensions of *Atlanta*'s satirical play with tricksters and canines, whether the latter figure is in the form of enigmatic symbols, commodities for breeding, or targets for shooting practice.

Although Darius's initial appearance foreshadows his aloofness, his metacritical function, and his ambivalent relations to canines, such traits also hint at the character's links to tricksterism. Tricksters have a long and complex legacy in African American culture. Related to precolonial traditions and cultural heroes such as Anansi (Ashanti) and Esu (Yoruba), the trickster has also been

> filtered through the particular conditions African Americans have had to endure to reflect a material existence that is at once similar to that found in sub-Saharan Africa and yet altered considerably for the social situations found under slavery and other oppressive conditions. For this reason, the trickster may range from the selfish/self-centered to the altruistic, but she or he consistently reifies the potential for the witty and idealistic to effect an alteration of material conditions. (Dickson-Carr, *African American* 35)

Darius is notable not only for his wits and his ambivalent ethics but also for a verbal playfulness that frequently marks African American trickster figures. Throughout *Atlanta*, his characterization allusively evokes the African American–trickster tradition, turning him into a twenty-first-century trickster in two significant ways. First, Darius is frequently portrayed in relation to nonhuman animals (not only dogs), whether through his clothing or his choices of entertainment—for example, the *Zoo Tycoon* video game. Various demonstrations of his arcane knowledge about animals—for example, the difference between caimans and alligators—further align Darius with a tradition of African American animal tricksters.[3] Second, as the "weird dude" of his group of friends, Darius often figures as an outsider and mediator who draws his power from an ability to express alternative perspectives that expose and subvert social and cultural norms. He transgresses spatially, temporally, and discursively, repeatedly appearing in unexpected places—for example, at a very NRA-friendly shooting range, at an orthodox Jewish passport agency, and at an eccentric musician's mansion—but also introducing "weird" language and ideas. His rewriting of white-supremacist slogans on hats, philosophizing beside Drake's pool, and invoking of quasi-mythical elements—for example, "Florida Man" and Marcus Miles's invisible car—complicate the conception of *Atlanta*'s storyworld as a strictly mimetic one, most emphatically in the time-loop narrative of "It Was All a Dream" (s4e10). As Darius strategically employs discourse for his own morally ambivalent purposes, he embodies the role of economic and cultural mediator, endowed with a trickster's ability to "effect an alteration of material conditions" and with empowering forms of knowledge that resemble a trickster's expansive temporal play and perspective (Dickson-Carr, *African American* 35).

Darius's status as trickster-mediator is particularly prominent as both a means and a target of *Atlanta*'s satire in "The Streisand Effect" (s1e4). In one of the episode's dual and intertwining plots, Darius sets out with Earn (Donald Glover) to go to a pawnshop at which Earn hopes to get some much-needed cash in exchange for his cell phone. In this context, Darius takes the lead and utilizes all his abilities as a trickster, a contemporary "interpreter, storyteller, and transformer" and "master of borders and exchange" (J. Smith xiii). From the start, he claims an outsider position that comes with a strangely specific knowledge, implying that, although "most Black people don't know who Steve McQueen is," his own "Nigerian" perspective affords him this insight (and, by implication, others). Rather than confirming his nationality or linking him directly to West African–trickster traditions, Darius's out-of-the-blue self-identification as Nigerian (which is only explained more fully in seasons 3 and 4) exemplifies his character's "weird" discourse and initiates his tricksterism. Even the specific indications of his Nigerian heritage—for example, his taste for "Naija jollof" and his origins in the "river state" of "Ijaw"—later in the series ultimately remain relatively vague. As such, they intertwine with the dream logics associated with Darius's character and usually also serve additional purposes such as conveying a critique of cultural appropriative business practices in "White Fashion" (s3e6). In "The Streisand Effect," Darius's claim neither establishes a direct link with a precolonial past nor adequately explains the origins of his knowledge about Steve McQueen (or such trivial knowledge's potency); moreover, it can hardly be taken at face value in the moment given the surprised reaction of his closest friend, Alfred (Bryan Tyree Henry), upon learning of Darius's nationality in "The Club" (s1e8):

> ALFRED: Make sure you keep an eye on that promoter. I don't trust his kind, man. He gonna try and play us.
> EARN: His kind?
> ALFRED: Yeah.
> EARN: What is this, *The Hobbit*? "We're from two different worlds."
> ALFRED: Man, he . . . he Nigerian, man. I don't trust Nigerians.
> EARN: Darius is Nigerian.
> ALFRED: He is?
> DARIUS: Yeah.

The way in which Darius smoothly expresses a somewhat idiosyncratically Nigerian identity both verbally and symbolically—for example, by wearing a wooden amulet reminiscent of a West African tribal charm—to claim an outsider and mediator status is itself a trickster move. The chain of events in the episode seemingly confirms this status as Darius acts as cultural "interpreter" and material "transformer" of Earn's cell phone into first a sword, then a cane corso, and finally (months later) cash. All the transactions within this chain are enabled by his wits, his (trans)cultural wisdom, and seemingly his knowledge about dog breeding—or at least his personal connection to a knowledgeable breeder—eventually netting Earn $4000 in "Sportin' Waves" (s2e2).

Upon closer consideration, though, the sequence also uses aspects of Darius's strategy to acquire and to monetize the dog to satirize both his tricksterism and wider environmental and biopolitical discourses. Although some of Darius's trickster-like "wisdom"—for example, his claim that "Chinese people are short because of Genghis Khan"—is questionable, at best, and possibly racist (as Earn suggests), at worst, the episode's primary means of mocking tricksterism consists in exposing the stark discrepancy between the extensive effort required to complete Darius's scheme and its short-term fruitlessness for Earn. The promised monetary gains will come, but for the time being, all Earn receives is the minimal satisfaction of teaching Darius and viewers the reproachful lesson that "poor people don't have time for investments." Besides ridiculing the practicality of the trickster's vision of time, this line also pronounces a broader and considerably harsher social critique. The scene's second satirical frequency draws attention to systemic problems of a society in which neither resourceful (if semilegal) trading skills nor deeper cultural knowledge have much immediate value. Importantly, the two targets are not hit with the same intensity. Lampooning Darius's approach from Earn's perspective is a comparatively mild criticism, especially since the trickster's efforts are still rewarded with an important and reciprocally genuine emotional bond as Darius offers Earn his own phone to pawn for immediate revenue and then smilingly intones, "We're friends now."

A more systemic critique persists into the second season via the subplot initiated by the belated windfall from the breeding of the cane corso. The money Earn eventually receives, after all, gets him involved in another hustle in "Sportin' Waves." Tracy's (Khris Davis) comically rationalized scheme to double Earn's money points indirectly toward inequitable socioeconomic conditions and their entanglement with marginalized individuals' flawed decision-making:

EARN: Yo, Darius. Thank you so much.
ALFRED: Yo, how much is it, man?
EARN: There's like 4K here. I did not know people liked dogs this much.

ALFRED: Hell yeah.
TRACY: Yo, I could double that for you.
EARN: Uh . . . no, I'm good, man.
TRACY: Man, you better tell your little cousin to ask about me, man.
ALFRED: Yeah, man. Tracy ain't lying. He be on them damn gift cards, man.
TRACY: Man, you give me the cash, and I'll double it on any card you want.
EARN: Oh, yeah?
TRACY: Yeah. You know how Al got that TV? Let's just say it was a steal.

Not surprisingly, this scheme fails spectacularly; Earn loses nearly all his money because of being associated with Tracy as he openly steals some dress shoes to wear to an ultimately unsuccessful job interview. Tracy's brand of tricksterism is satirized along with Earn's eventual failure to learn from his past financial rashness, but this plot arc also suggests that Darius's tactics are effective in the long term in addressing the poverty that Earn invokes in the earlier episode.

This plot arc also engages in another vector of satire in negotiating both historical associations with dog violence and African American relations to the pastoral. It is significant to note that we are not dealing with just any canine, but with a cane corso, a breed whose appearance and physique is reminiscent of those types of dogs historically involved in anti-Black violence. As Tyler D. Parry and Charlton W. Yingling note, dogs were an integral part of a "socially conditioned, culturally weighted interspecies violence [that] permeated the management of slave societies in the Americas" (71), and such oppressive deployment of canines continued during Jim Crow, the civil rights era, and beyond.[4] Despite these inherently negative associations, though, dogs were also potential allies in resistance;[5] as a result, their depictions carry ambivalent meanings in Black culture along the lines of what Kimberly N. Ruffin calls an African American "ecological burden-and-beauty paradox," which simultaneously involves an "ecological burden . . . placed on those who are racialized negatively" and "the experience of ecological beauty [that] results from individual and collective attitudes toward nature" (2, 3). As domesticated elements of nature, dogs evoke contradictory feelings for African Americans; they are companions and allies readily experienced as forms of "ecological beauty," but they can nonetheless also be an "ecological burden" in their instrumentalization as tools of anti-Black violence and icons of racialized dehumanization.

Thus, having two young Black men—one of whom is facing a dire financial situation—take a cane corso to a white dog breeder is far from a neutral image. By foregrounding the animal, if only briefly, the episode activates a canine iconography that calls to mind a history of anti-Black violence to play satirically with biopolitical practices of (dog) breeding and training, aiming its critique both at in-group audiences and at American society more generally.

The latter is the more obvious target through the sequence's iconic quality, linking the plot's systemic critique to the deeper roots of today's socioeconomic hierarchies in historically racialized social strata; after all, "the dog attacking the black is the ultimate simulacrum" and has become so iconic that "one no longer needs to see the black man next to the dog's fangs or the white man holding the leash in order to know that the attack dog *means* racism" (Boisseron 78, 79, emphasis original). The scene, thus semiotically (over)determined, turns the cane corso into a symbolic reminder of white supremacy's systemic continuation and suggests how overt racisms of the past have covert effects on contemporary socioeconomic relations. The fact that the barter involving the dog comes last—after interactions in spaces that are almost entirely devoid of white people—also implies that the success of the entire operation depends on the ultimate sanction of the white dog breeder, thereby reinforcing the scene's critique of the foundational racial hierarchies of American society.[6]

Crucially, though, *Atlanta*'s critique is not one-dimensional, especially considering how the sequence moves beyond the dog's iconographic quality to engage questions of economic access, breeding, and training more broadly. Thanks to Darius's tricksterism, the dog signifies not just as an icon of anti-Black violence but also emerges in its capacities both as a pet and as a commodity. As Earn warily keeps both his physical and conceptual distance from the dog, Darius strategically embraces both its quality as an object of bartering and its capacity for companionship; he smoothly and lovingly handles the animal, addressing him as "Buddy" and "Barfight." While the latter name once more hints at the possibly questionable ethics of Darius's business,[7] the scene purposefully transcends the various negative forms of iconicity conveyed by the dog's appearance. It figures also as semiotic resistance to the "ultimate simulacrum" (Boisseron 78) and spotlights practices of dog breeding and dog training, thereby becoming part of a broader satirical negotiation of African American involvement in historical and present-day biopolitical practices in relation to both the nonhuman and the human.

Aligning Darius as a representative of tricksterism with the breeding of attack dogs hints at historical interdependencies between African American cultural forms and biopolitical practices in the United States that have perpetuated inequality. Darius's tricksterism in "Teddy Perkins" (s2e6) gives way to an empathy with the pain inflicted on those—like the titular Teddy and his brother Benny—who are bred and trained as cultural commodities. This development retrospectively complicates his earlier participation in the breeding of the cane corso and becomes part of a comprehensive warning about the destructiveness of biopolitical schemes. Similarly, the second plotline in "The Streisand Effect" involving Alfred and Zan (Freddie Kuguru) contributes to this warning gesture by depicting Zan's reprehensible coaching of a young boy as part of his online brand building. Zan teaches the boy to utter profanity that even astonishes Alfred and possibly sets him up to be robbed on camera while delivering a pizza. *Atlanta*'s critique of biopolitical breeding and training practices is therefore not restricted to broadly attacking the mainstream American society but implicates various people of color engaged in commodification and disciplining of "living assets." While criticizing a deeply unequal socioeconomic reality through the cane corso as a racialized icon, "The Streisand Effect" also exposes the complexities of in-group responses and (un)ethical attitudes toward both human and nonhuman life.

Apart from first employing and then extending the iconic meanings of the dog, the sequence at the breeder's home in "The Streisand Effect" conveys environmental implications in ways that satirically comment on stereotypes concerning African Americans' relationship to nature and the pastoral. The scene's aesthetics contradict an antipastoral impulse frequently attributed to African Americans. The pastoral—particularly in its nineteenth- and twentieth-century forms—was commonly tied to romanticized images of the plantation that misrepresented slavery and dehumanized Blacks so that "the nature of slavery in the United States created the link between anti-pastoralism and African American culture" (M. Bennett 195). The subplot involving Darius and Earn, by contrast, builds up to its climax from an ostensibly pastoral movement, emphasized through the top-down camera shots showing their car leaving the city—a movement repeated in episodes from the fourth season that play with white-coded environmental traditions of camping ("Snipe Hunt" [s4e6]) and farming ("Andrew Wyeth: Alfred's World" [s4e9]). "The Streisand Effect" concludes with an almost clichéd pastoral image at the breeder's picturesque farm. The shot is bathed in yellow sunlight and the reflected greens of grass and plants; a tree on the left and a barn on the right frame the characters in the foreground against the partially and gently tamed images of nature in the background. Crickets and songbirds chirping completes an idyllic tableau reminiscent of antebellum Georgia.

This scene ultimately mocks mainstream pastoral modes and expectations, though, using a tripartite strategy to imply the presence of a distinctly African American environmental knowledge concerning the dog. First, the scene's visual and aural coding suggests that Darius and Earn are indulging in the pastoral, and the evocation of pastoral renewal in the countryside is supported through the episode's closing song, Michael Kiwanuka's "Home Again." Second and simultaneously, the exaggerated bliss of this pastoral imagery grotesquely contrasts with Earn's situation; he is not "home again" at this moment but quite literally homeless, a status confirmed in the final shot of season 1—that is, before he gets the money from the breeding of the cane corso—as Earn goes to sleep in a storage unit. The tension between an overtly pastoral aesthetic and Earn's seeming exclusion from the pastoral due to his dire financial straits reminds readers of the discriminatory socioeconomic roots of the stereotypes that disassociate African Americans from the restorative aspects of rural nature. Third, the scene's ironic mockery of such stereotypes arises from Darius's far-reaching wisdom concerning dogs. The cane corso's arrival at the breeder's rural home is a direct result of the trickster's bartering and becomes implicit evidence not only of Darius's cultural and economic wisdom but also of his environmental knowledge. The relative docility and even companionability of an animal once potentially bred and trained to attack African Americans suggests at once the willful construction of such historical violence between species and Darius's expertise in handling dogs, both as creatures of the natural world and as tools to transcend Earn's impoverishment. Without his implied environmental knowledge, after all, the scene at the dog breeder's home would never take place.

"Nobody Beats the Biebs" (s1e5) echoes some of the environmental themes introduced in "The Streisand Effect" but also departs from them in significant ways. On the one hand, Darius's characterization veers away from its pastoral overtones in showing him as a gun enthusiast who brings a sheet of paper with the silhouette of a dog on it to use as a target at a shooting range frequented primarily by white customers.[8] On the other hand, both his link to canines and his potential as a trickster figure are carried forward as we watch Darius prepare for this adventure early in the episode. As Darius listens to dogs barking in the neighborhood, a mask in the background attests to the continuity of his tricksterism. Although this mask does not evoke any particular trickster tradition, it symbolically reminds viewers of Darius's ability to smoothly appropriate and move between identities while also alluding to the concealment of his knowledge about dogs. "The Streisand Effect" makes it clear that he possesses such knowledge, but its masking becomes central to the shooting-range subplot in "Nobody Beats the Biebs" and facilitates the episode's satire of racialized environmental stereotypes and affects.

In this context, it is vital to note how *Atlanta* subtly takes on mainstream tendencies to ignore African American environmental engagement, tendencies that also manifest in stereotypical views concerning African Americans' alleged disinterest in environmental issues.[9] While it is true that African Americans are demographically underrepresented within mainstream environmental organizations, the inaccurate belief that African Americans "don't care about the environment" has been thoroughly debunked (Dorceta Taylor qtd. in Mock). Having more to do with a traditionally narrow environmentalist focus on issues such as "wilderness protection, recreation, [or] a strictly aesthetic appreciation of nature" (Ray 121) than with actual environmental knowledge and activism among African Americans, such a prejudicial notion falls apart in light of such developments as environmental justice, urban gardening, and Black veganism. Nonetheless, an unwarranted disregard of Black environmental thought persists in the mainstream and becomes crucial in the consideration of contemporary African American satire, often upholding rather than undermining such environmental stereotypes (Seymour 183).

In the shooting-range subplot of "Nobody Beats the Biebs," *Atlanta*, too, chooses to mask Darius's environmental knowledge, employing what Seymour terms "the trope of the Urban African American" (183–86) in order to comment on racialized environmental stereotypes and affects. The sequence depicting the quarrel over Darius's canine targets and his eventual forcible dismissal from the range with a shotgun pointed at his back qualify as a satirical form of "bad"—that is, "inappropriate" or "improper"—environmentalism (242), considering that there are few things, from many environmentalists' perspectives, that are more "inappropriate" than shooting at animals. These scenes deploy a twofold "bad-environmentalist" strategy: they humorously expose intersecting environmental and racial inflections of stereotyping sign systems in order to criticize such systems' harmful effects and mainstream society's moral inconsistencies, and they also present various instances of racialized environmental affect to draw attention to social injustices and to the paralyzing effects of affective suppression.

The episode's satirical critique of racialized environmental stereotypes revolves around the semiotic relations between shooters and their targets and the specific meanings of the canine target Darius has brought with him. The targets play their simulating character as they involve signifiers in relation to shooters but no real lives—no heart, neither human nor canine, stops beating. The gun-range setting thus serves to isolate the meanings of various signifiers and allows for considering the implications of semiotic qualities and relations among the assembled shooters, their weapons, and targets. Besides Darius's dog poster, various shooters take aim at shapes vaguely reminiscent of human torsos; others shoot at more specific images of humans, one of which suggests a hostage situation, while another features a male figure marked "Dad," and still others include overtly "racist targets" like "a Mexican holding a knife," as an apparently Middle Eastern shooter points out. The shooters, in contrast, include Darius and two white men in camouflage hats, though an African American woman and the aforementioned Middle Eastern man are also present. Before objecting to Darius's targets, the other patrons exemplify the default relation of shooters to targets at a gun range as they target representations of human images "with no problem" since no one would assume that this implies shooting at what their images signify: actual human beings. Embedded as the scene is in the iconographies of sport shooting and (racialized) self-defense, the simulation of violence works seamlessly until Darius arrives.

Darius is, of course, a young African American man wearing not a camouflage hat but a cap emblazoned with the word "Art." Moreover, he is shooting at an image that clearly is not human, but canine. While his poster's simulation of a living being parallels the other shooters' targets, it also reflects the metaphorical quality of canine figures in *Atlanta* more generally—for example, the use of Disney's iconic Goofy character both in "New Jazz" (s3e8) and in the mockumentary in "The Goof Who Sat by the Door" (s4e8). Both Darius as a shooter and his target are significant as signs endowed with additional meanings, and the sequence toys with Darius's simultaneous environmental and racial stereotyping in a "bad-environmentalist" strategy through which "the violence of and against animals becomes a source of humor" (Seymour 180). While Seymour refers to cases of "treating regal, powerful, or beautiful animals as stupid victims" (180), *Atlanta*'s shooting-range scenes bear specific meanings because they deploy a domesticated animal. Dogs, after all, are "companion animals" (Waldau 26–27) and have a longstanding status in American mainstream culture as "best friends" and loving family members whose lives are valued highly. If both human and canine lives are regarded as valuable, however, why is it more appropriate, as Darius pointedly asks, to "shoot a human target . . . that's weird"? The reply he receives is as disconcerting as it is revealing: "I'm not gonna let you shoot a fucking dog in here." This infantile response signals the underlying power dynamic, hinting at a particular relation between Darius and his canine target in comparison to the offended shooters' relations to their human targets. The unspoken premise is not simply a racist assumption that a Black man is more likely to shoot not only at the signifier but also the signified. The confrontation is also implicitly fueled by a racialized stereotype that gives moral high ground to the white shooters by positing Darius as environmentally disinterested and destructive "urban African American."

The sequence satirizes two contradictions in the offended shooter's logic. The underlying conflation necessary for mobilizing the racialized environmental stereotype lies in the ability of dogs to stand in for nonhuman animals and nature more generally. The shooter's claims are exposed as contradictory, first, because the innate connection between sport shooting and killing animals (a notion visually underpinned by the hunting rifles being used by some of the shooters) muddles his insistence that dogs cannot be shot at. This contradiction supports Paul Waldau's contention that "the human-animal bond . . . is often subordinated to . . . attitudes that shut down, even betray, a full range of animal protection" (30). Second, the image of the dog satirizes a contradiction in (predominantly white) self-defense discourses, which pervade the depiction of the range and are one of the nominal raisons d'être for such institutions in general. Self-defense requires justification; it demands a credible threat. For the offended white shooters, racialized or otherwise marginalized humans can serve as such targets, but a dog—a creature categorized as a companion, as "man's best friend"—cannot. The sequence thus ironically points to contradictory simultaneous processes of dehumanizing racialized humans and humanizing companion animals and the corresponding idea of sacrificing the life of the former while sparing that of the latter, which *Atlanta* picks up in "Three Slaps" (s3e1) when the white lesbian couple sets their dog Cornpop free—albeit with questionable prospects for survival—while preparing themselves for the murder of their Black foster children. "Nobody Beats the Biebs" thereby highlights the social power that emerges at the intersection of the environmental and the racial, exposing its discriminatory (and potentially life-threatening) effects on Darius, the only person who, held at gunpoint, gets expelled from the facility because of the conflict. The episode reveals how stereotyping semiotic systems and their underlying conflations, contradictions, and (biopolitical) norms fuel social violence and discriminatory practices.

Additional effects become visible by considering how the scenes comment on racialized environmental affect, that is, "the emotions and dispositions expected of certain racial groups in terms of their relationships to environment" (Seymour 151). In this respect, the subplot at the gun range employs potential but masked affective dimensions to draw attention to deeply unequal socioeconomic realities. Here, Darius's attempt at justifying his choice of target by claiming "the dogs from my neighborhood, they're crazy. They bite babies . . ." is revealing. The line not only obscures Darius's previously demonstrated affection for nonhuman animals but also other emotions (rage, sadness, frustration) that would presumably be related to his explanation. The aloofness of the utterance fits a general strategy of upholding the urban-African-American stereotype. Darius's comment counteracts the offended shooter's objection that "my kid could be in here," which reinforces the dog's sacrosanct status as a companion animal. Darius implicitly suggests in return that his own theoretical kids could be killed by dogs, thus highlighting the precarity of Darius's community and indirectly invoking a history of anti-Black violence. Since the dog's bite "not only dehumanizes but also, and more importantly, commodifies the human victim by making her fit for animal consumption" (Boisseron 71), Darius's explanation moreover exposes the ongoing commodification of the African American population by suggesting its disposability and literal edibility. His claim in this regard becomes powerful precisely because of its vagueness (we do not know who the biting dogs in the neighborhood belong to, if anyone). It hints at a more fundamental animalization of Black bodies within America's biopolitical landscape, a status symbolically confirmed when Darius suddenly finds the range owner's shotgun pointed at him. Here, the strategy of maintaining the urban-African-American stereotype conveys humor while also serving to reveal social injustices and continuing forms of dehumanization suffered by African Americans.

Darius's attempted justification for his canine target is also meaningful as an example of (environmental) affective suppression. If, as bell hooks reminds us, "to perpetuate and maintain white supremacy, white folks have colonized black Americans, and a part of that colonizing process has been teaching us to repress our rage, to never make them the targets of any anger we feel about racism" (*Killing Rage* 14), the shooting-range subplot demonstrates how environmental effects are implicated in such processes. The contemporary effects of denying environmental affects along racial lines are visible in racialized environmental stereotypes and in the ways in which mainstream environmentalism often characterizes African Americans as "insufficiently affective" (Seymour 156), which has sometimes fueled its unethical mobilizations of Black history (for example, in an infamous 2005 People for the Ethical Treatment of Animals campaign).[10] By portraying how Darius suppresses both his possible rage and benevolence toward dogs, *Atlanta* also comments on African Americans' affective economies. Darius, after all, would appear to be justified in expressing rage, sadness, or frustration regarding his community's infestation by "crazy" killer dogs or for being banned from the shooting range; his aloofness therefore figures not only as an innate feature of his character but also as a paralyzing consequence of affective suppression that manifests in defensiveness. His subdued response—"I didn't say all that"—is perhaps meant to distance himself self-protectively from the Middle Eastern shooter's calls for "revolution," but it is also symptomatic of his inability to respond fully and genuinely to the emotional violence pervading these scenes. The sequence thus also criticizes an emotional "colonizing" of African Americans that has environmental implications as well.

Both of the episodes discussed herein show the subtlety and sincerity characteristic of *Atlanta*'s environmental satire involving Darius as a trickster in relation to dogs. Both extend the aura of ambivalence that marks Darius's relation to canines in his encounter with the stray dog in the pilot's opening scene. Whereas "The Streisand Effect" uses a canine image and Darius's trickster potential to lampoon Earn's relation to tricksterism to pronounce a broader social critique and to suggest Darius's environmental knowledge, the gun-range subplot in "Nobody Beats the Biebs" builds on the presence of such knowledge as it employs the urban African American trope to attack environmentalist double standards and critique the effects of racialized environmental stereotypes and affects. The power of *Atlanta*'s dog-themed satirical elements lies both in the elaborate ways in which it embeds its (environmental) critiques within the plots of individual episodes as well as in the unobtrusiveness and ambivalence of the canine images of dogs as weapons, pets, shooting targets, or cartoon characters that convey these underlying satirical messages. The series' aesthetic redirection of canine iconography coupled with its concrete representations of socioeconomic and affective realities creates a space for addressing some of environmentalism's racialized legacies.

NOTES

1. This focus is not to suggest that *Atlanta*'s representations of nonhuman animals involve only dogs, whether generally or specifically in relation to Darius. In regard to the implication of the show's use of animals other than canines, see O'Brien's essay herein.

2. See K. Smith 3–4; Hicks 206. For a recent overview of environmentally oriented work on African American literature and culture, see the introduction in Claborn. On the relationship between ecocriticism on African American perspectives and animal studies, see L. Johnson's introduction and Boisseron's first chapter.

3. Besides playing into the character's evocation of an African American–trickster tradition, this subtle association with nonhuman animals is one of the central environmentally relevant differences among *Atlanta*'s male leads. Darius's representation in this regard contrasts significantly with what O'Brien identifies in her essay herein as a tendency in Earn and Alfred to distance themselves from animals to assert their belonging in domestic space.

4. See Boisseron xxv–xxvii, 6–11.

5. See Giltner; L. Johnson.

6. For further discussion of the complex racial and ethnic implications of this episode, see Lee's essay herein.

7. The specter of dogfighting likewise implicitly recurs in Michael Vick's brief—and surreal—appearance at the end of "Money Bag Shawty" (s2e3), but there does not seem to be any overt connection with such activity on Darius's part here.

8. For further discussion of this episode and the gun-range scene in particular, see Brooks's essay herein.

9. See Mohai.

10. See L. Johnson 1–7; Boisseron x–xi.

"THAT'S YOU"

Reflections on Human-Animal Doublings in *Atlanta*'s Televisual Satire

SARAH O'BRIEN

Atlanta is structured by traffic and is about traffic.[1] Through carefully framed title sequences, establishing shots, and other interstitial images that visualize mobility and stasis, the series considers how bodies, goods, and services move—or don't move—through the city, the music industry, and especially through domestic spaces. The slow-moving story stages the characters' spiritual and economic strivings in the streets, sites of commerce, institutional spaces, and residential interiors of Atlanta, the capital of the New South and a city that rarely receives its due in television or film. Much of the first season follows Earn, backpack on, traveling between his dead-end job (he's initially stuck selling credit cards at Hartsfield-Jackson, one of the world's busiest airports), local fast-food chains and nightclubs, and the houses and apartments of his family and friends. *Atlanta*'s narrative web is spun from his and the other characters' halting movements through the city: premonitory encounters on MARTA (the city's public transportation system), Uber rides that lead to police shootings, and friendly carjackings. Faltering shots of thresholds punctuate these mobile sequences, and their recurrence underscores the guarded precarity of the home as a space built on inclusion and exclusion.

An array of nonhuman animals—purebred and stray dogs, exotic pets, vermin, hunted wildlife, birds via omnipresent birdsong—circulate in the series and introduce many of its most memorable, enigmatic moments. These animals confound the roles typically afforded animals on television: the only pet to appear in the first two seasons is a caiman named Coach, and he is set loose by his human companion-captor, Uncle Willy (Katt Williams), the episode's titular "Alligator Man" (s2e1); the plot frequently involves dogs, but they take the decidedly uncompanionable forms of apparitions, icons, and commodities—almost all of them[2] associated with the character Darius (LaKeith Stanfield).[3] The only animals "Old McAlfred" has on his "safe farm" in "Andrew Wyeth: Alfred's World" (s4e9) are a dead rat and a murderous, cannabis-devouring feral hog. Wildlife comes into view outdoors, in the green spaces enfolding the city, yet it is likewise at odds with conventional TV images of vast vistas of untouched nature: birdsong accompanies ubiquitous police sirens, an eviscerated deer turns up in some suburban woods behind a gas station, an imaginary slithery "snipe" proves all too real, and a lethal (and embodied) undertow tugs at recurring scenes of male bonding through fishing. Often fleeting and always cryptic, these animal incursions comment on the (im)possibilities of mobility for the African American characters, particularly the male leads, Earnest "Earn" Marks (Donald Glover) and Alfred "Paper Boi" Miles (Brian Tyree Henry).

I locate *Atlanta*'s traffic in human and nonhuman animals at the intersection of the mode of satire, the televisual genre of the sitcom, and the geographic setting of the city of Atlanta.[4] Placed at this juncture, the series can be understood as a narrative that is distinctively serialized across a varied field of intertextual references such that it becomes hospitable to subversive human-animal pairings. Scholars have recently traced, across divergent threads of African American literary history, instances in which Blacks and animals join, in Lindgren Johnson's analysis, in "mutually supporting resistances to both white *and* human exceptionalism" (25), forging what Bénédicte Boisseron calls "interspecies alliances" that allow them to "assert their dignity" (xx). When recognition of one's humanness/humanity is never assured, such moves carry enormous risks. It is remarkable, Joshua Bennett observes specifically of Black male writers, that "even from within the midst of their own, systematic dehumanization—the hypersexualization of their bodies from childhood onward, lowered academic expectations, as well as the constant imposition of mortal fear from the outside world— . . . they are nonetheless willing to turn toward the nonhuman world and read fugitive possibility where others might only see confinement or despair" (32). *Atlanta*, a series featuring an exclusively Black (though, importantly, not exclusively male) writing room, demonstrates the potential of this affiliative turn to animals to germinate in the audiovisual, serial form of television.

The aforementioned "alligator man," the various canines connected with Darius, the "owl's casket" ostrich egg and intimations of human breeding and training in "Teddy Perkins" (s2e6), the beastly Schnappviecher of "Helen" (s2e4), the mockumentary excavation of the underappreciated cartoon animal and its underacknowledged authors at the center of the Disney universe in "The Goof Who Sat by the Door" (s4e8), and other moments orient *Atlanta* as a series that is guardedly interested in nonhuman collaborations. Attentive to these gestures, this essay builds to a reading of the interspecies affiliation that emerges between Al and a dead deer in "Woods" (s2e8), a coupling that is born of and turns back on the longstanding racist trope of the "black buck." Reading this pairing at the crossroads of African American satire, the historical conventions of primetime American television, and the cultural geography of the titular city allows us to understand it as a more complex and specifically televisual commentary on southern Black masculinity in a series held together in large measure by its critique of the invisibility-hypervisibility dialectic that governs Black cultural production. And while it would be a stretch to suggest that *Atlanta* likewise condemns the violent regimes of (in)visibility that structure animal life, its idiosyncratic serialization of human-animal metaphors goes beyond the traditional use of animal ciphers in satire, a mode whose long history Tom Tyler sums up as invariably treating animals as "empty, transposable placeholders who fulfil a vital function but have no significance in their own right."

What makes *Atlanta* stick as satire is the duality of its registers and the persistence with which it positions doubleness as an experience of identity and place systemically conditioned by racial and economic inequality. It captures what W. E. B. Du Bois describes as "double consciousness": "this sense of always looking at one's self through the eyes of others, of measuring one's soul by the tape of a world that looks on in amused contempt and pity. One ever feels his twoness,—an American, a Negro; two souls, two thoughts, two unreconciled strivings; two warring ideals in one dark body, whose dogged strength alone keeps it from being torn asunder" (*The Souls* 8). Characters in *Atlanta* see themselves being seen as Black and specifically seen as Black stereotypes. "I scare people at ATMs, boy, I *have* to rap," Alfred sighs to Zan (Freddie Kuguru) in "The Streisand Effect" (s1e4). As it expresses the characters' constant weighing of their sense of self against how they are seen, the series elaborates a double consciousness that also juxtaposes the shimmering images that the city offers up of itself with less idyllic views of its sprawling and variegated environs. Remarking on the continued relevance of double consciousness to *Atlanta* and to "black Atlanta's development in proximity to white America," Maurice Hobson highlights how the series brings into focus the dualities of a city that is simultaneously imaged in popular culture as the Black Mecca and home to some of "the most discontented and deprived circumstances for black people in the South and nation." The specificity of *Atlanta*'s satire lies in the doubleness of its reflections on Du Boisian doubleness—making clear that Black Americans' burden of split vision is embedded in place.

Yet *Atlanta*'s satire expands even further if we linger on Du Bois's description of the special kind of strength required to endure double consciousness: "dogged" (from the transitive verb "dog") indeed means "to follow like a dog on the heels of."[5] Du Bois's choice of adjective to express the persistence with which African Americans must shoulder split vision insinuates an animal association, as if to underscore Boisseron's observation that "there exists another form of double-consciousness for the universal black folk, which is the feeling of being both human and animal in the eyes of others" (84). *Atlanta* satirizes this double consciousness in the shooting-range scene[6] in "Nobody Beats the Biebs" (s1e5) when a white man in a camo baseball hat repeatedly informs Darius, who has just riddled his dog-shaped shooting target with bullets, "you . . . you can't shoot a dog." As Matthias Klestil observes in his essay in this volume, the ambivalence of this second-person address is significant, yet a blunter double meaning circulates alongside the nuanced interpretation he unfolds: "you" (indefinite) refers to people (it is inappropriate or immoral for us humans to pretend to kill dogs), while "*you*" (definite) hails Darius as a Black man, for whom it is doubly wrong to kill an animal insofar as, in this man's eyes, Darius is not definitively *not* an animal. Being seen in this way is degrading and dangerous, but Darius is dogged in more ways than one: while survival dictates suppressing his affective response here, as Klestil points out, he navigates other moments by ensnaring his interlocutors (and viewers) in confounding commentary that leads them astray, down dead ends, and sometimes into new spaces of thought.

As satire, *Atlanta* holds together these multiple and frequently overlapping dualities through its use of genre. As Jonathan Greenberg explains, "satire combines, inhabits, or transforms other genres" (10). *Atlanta* takes up and satirizes multiple genres but inhabits the sitcom and, in doing so, satirizes that genre's abiding investment in idealized forms of white middle-class domesticity. When viewed as a sitcom, *Atlanta* emerges as a post-postracial sendup of the classic "mirror sitcoms" of the 1980s and 1990s, like *The Cosby Show* (1984–1992) / *Family Ties* (1984–1989) and *Living Single* (1993–1998) / *Friends* (1994–2004) that Bambi Haggins identifies as racially inverted "[American] dream mythology morality plays" (31). *Atlanta* resides in the subgenre of sitcoms about twentysomething creatives making it in the city, specifically the *Living Single* / *Friends* dyad, telling the story of an alternative family anchored around two biological cousins whose members periodically retire to a couch to reflect on their existence. Mirror sitcoms extend a decidedly uncritical split vision: they acquiesce to the "separate-but-equal-discourses" that Herman Gray ascribes to series like *Family Matters* (1989–1997) and *The Fresh Prince of Bel Air* (1990–1996), with the reflecting series "situat[ing] black characters in domestically centered black worlds and circumstances that essentially parallel those of whites" and thereby "maintain[ing] a commitment to the universal acceptance into the transparent 'normative' middle class" (87).

These racially homogenous sitcoms gave way, in the early postnetwork era of the 2000s and early 2010s, to series with comparatively diverse ensemble casts—*Scrubs* (2001–2011), *Community* (2009–2015),[7] *Parks and Recreation* (2009–2015)—that arguably court an even more naïve belief that universal access to the American dream has finally been unlocked (Beltran). As any lingering fantasy of a postracial society was extinguished in the waning days of the Obama presidency, a new era of Black-produced television emerged, led by series like *Black-ish* (2014–), *Empire* (2015–2020), *Queen Sugar* (2016–2022), and *Insecure* (2016–2021). *Atlanta* stands out among this second golden age of Black-produced television, largely because, as Sierriana Terry points out, it "shifts the perspective to the black poor and working classes" (31) and, in its rejection of middle-class drama, insists on the realities of separate but decidedly not equal Black worlds. Simultaneously, and more distinctively than these other series, it inhabits the familiar televisual space of the sitcom.

Atlanta's satire subverts the sitcom's domesticity through its focus on a character who is unhoused and its settings in unhomely interiors and quietly menacing exteriors. The first season casts Earn as a Goldilocks figure who doesn't quite fit in the homes of his friends and family members, finding refuge in that quintessential space of suburban transition turned stasis, the storage locker. Yet this fable remains rooted in realism. Satire "makes reference to the real world," after all, and "its disruptive force depends upon this referentiality" (Greenberg 21). *Atlanta*'s intro and transitional sequences insistently locate these homes in the "real world" of Atlanta. Specifically, the opening sequences of the season openers (except for the third season, which splits its time between Europe and an assortment of standalone episodes seemingly separate from the main cast) splice together aerial shots of McMansions and urban blight, creating a juxtaposition that points at "real-world" circumstances, such as the disproportionate effects of and uneven recovery from the Great Recession on housing in Black neighborhoods, a disparity that is particularly acute in metro Atlanta (Markley et al. 316). Whereas other episodes use situational type to inscribe the title *Atlanta* into the space of the city, these opening sequences conclude by positioning stylized flyover credits over long shots that offer up the city's skyline as a vista of opportunity: a fortress of skyscrapers encircled by verdant foliage and bisected by Interstate 285 punctuates "The Big Bang" (s1e1); "Alligator Man" (s2e1) culminates in the iconic view of the skyline from the Jackson Street Bridge, which overlooks the forking paths of Interstate 75 and Freedom Parkway, a stretch of inner-city highway that hugs the Martin Luther King Jr. National Historic Park; and "The Most Atlanta" (s4e1) frames the city's skyline at a greater distance, suggesting the characters' potential turn away from the city in the final season. A lit-up, fast-motion version of the view from the Jackson Street Bridge recurs in the promotional images for the mock talk show *Montague* in "B.A.N." (s1e7). Through this mise en abyme of postcard images of the city refracted by glimpses of the divisions embedded in its built environment, *Atlanta* asserts the inextricability of the city's televisual representation and its material reality.

Situating *Atlanta* as a satirical take on the sitcom—a genre set and destined for consumption in domestic space—underscores the significance of these transitory views of city spaces and, in doing so, offers a way to understand the many material and metaphorical animals that move through *Atlanta*'s (un)homely spaces. Its (self-)referential edges recall Charles Rutheiser's use of "imagineering"—the Walt Disney Company's term for its approach to engineering picture-perfect theatrical and theme-park spaces, which it often cast as "nature" and "wilderness"—to describe Atlanta's self-image making in preparation for hosting the 1996 Olympics. Greater Atlanta is, in his view, "a polynucleated sprawl of sylvan suburbs, slums, and shopping malls surrounding a central archipelago of fortified fantasy islands rising out of a sea of parking lots—the whole tenuously linked by expressways, television, and a fragile sense of imagined *communitas*" (Rutheiser 4). Produced over twenty years later, *Atlanta* centers its critique of this imagineered geography on the appropriation and commodification of Black popular culture, an ever-intensifying strain of the city's "intense form of boosterism" (4). By situating this critique within a constructed geography that is shot through with decidedly un-Disneyfied views of the nonhuman world and citations of Disney's less celebrated animal icons—for example, the desultory and seemingly inescapable Goofy hats in "New Jazz" (s3e8), Loquareeous's return home to *The Tortoise and the Hare* after surviving his foster-parents' murderous intentions in "Three Slaps" (s3e1), and every moment of "The Goof Who Sat by the Door"—*Atlanta* asks viewers to consider how the commercialization of Black culture, and specifically Black music, is shaped by familiar binaries separating inside from outside, city from nature, and human from animal. As Boisseron observes, "the human-animal divide is put into question when the unfamiliar intrudes upon the familiar in a sort of *unheimlich* (uncanny) effect" (82–83).

Atlanta's uncanny effects accumulate and amplify in its second season, the title of which, "Robbin' Season," plays on dual human and animal meanings: winter in the city sees an uptick in robberies to keep up with holiday spending ("Everybody gotta eat. . . . Or be eaten," Darius and Earn explain in the season premiere), as well as the arrival of American robins that come to Georgia to breed (T. Johnson). In its coupling of violent symbiosis and pastoral passage, this pun inheres in the season's ten-episode arc. The significance of this diffused wordplay comes into focus if we consider *Atlanta*'s content and form as traffic. Traffic circulates in *Atlanta* in all senses of the word: in the audiovisual backdrop of vehicles moving through a city that is synonymous with sprawl and deadlock; in plotlines that foreground the frequently illicit and always complicated transmission of commodities (CDs, drugs, guns, phones, purebred dogs, pianos); in narrative detours into surrealist or magical realist modes sneaking in metaphorical meanings; and in *Atlanta*'s structure as serial television. With this last meaning of traffic, I am thinking of Raymond Williams's identification of "flow" as the defining condition of television: we experience TV not as a discrete text but rather as an assemblage of "increasing variability and miscellaneity" that, by dint of the medium's fundamentally sequential structure, generates meaning intra- and intertextually (88). *Atlanta*'s enigmatic animals play outsized roles in connecting the pieces of its serialized narrative—they conduct its flow. Take, for example, the business of dogs: in "The Streisand Effect," Darius helps Earn trade his phone for an ancient-seeming sword and then a cane corso, yet Earn doesn't "come up off" the trade—the sale of the puppies bred by the dog—until "Sportin' Waves" (s2e2), by which time he's all but forgotten that he's in line for $4,000. Or consider Yvonne, the human who Uncle Willy holds captive alongside Coach in "Alligator Man": she is played by Monique Grant, who appears (as Yvonne or some other character—it's unclear) in Ahmad White's commercial for his psychic services in "B.A.N." The Nutella-sandwich-eating White (Emmett Hunter), of course, also appears on the bus in "The Big Bang," only to disappear into the woods after the dog that will witness the parking-lot shooting that nominally sets off the series. These serial iterations introduce narrative connections that alternately appear to be utterly inconsequential and massively important—and, occasionally, both poignant and patently absurd, as with the cutaway to forensic photos of a bloated Goofy glove floating in the scum of the lake where Thomas Washington presumably drowns in "The Goof Who Sat by the Door." As such, they introduce and sustain the possibility of meaningful meetings between humans and animals.

As if to introduce them as an unknown quantity, animals first appear in *Atlanta* as palpably absent signifiers: one of the show's promotional images presents the three male leads with peaches plugging their mouths, as if the city's commercial imaginary is gagging them, readying these hip, young Black men for the proverbial spit.[8] Earn and Alfred both invoke animals in early episodes to assert what they are not. Earn makes his first and only explicit reference to his housing status in "The Big Bang," when he, Darius, and Alfred leave the latter's apartment to smoke weed on a couch that's been tossed outside: "I'm not *real* homeless," Earn assures them, "I'm not using a rat as a phone or something." In "Streets on Lock" (s1e2), Alfred explains to Darius his preference for getting takeout while they wait for their wings at J. R. Crickets: "I don't like people watching me eat; make me feel like I'm in a zoo." In these jokes, Earn and Alfred distance themselves from animals in ways that at once resist visual objectification and assert their belonging in domestic space. Yet as *Atlanta* develops its unhomely spaces, this realm emerges as at odds with the homogenous, hermetically sealed homes of sitcoms past, and its assortment of animals in fact becomes essential to establishing these spaces as permeable and hospitable to difference. Indeed, Alfred gamely eats a "zoo pie" in "The Most Atlanta" on the first stop of the scavenger hunt that the idiosyncratic rapper Blueblood has concocted to lead mourning fans to his funeral. Doing so seems to signal Alfred's acceptance of Blueblood's invitation to surrender to chance encounters. The animals of *Atlanta* are "commensal," Boisseron's term for animals that do "not abide by a dichotomy of private-public space" (xxiii). Boisseron has in mind species such as urban deer and rats, both of which circulate in *Atlanta*, along with other, more dangerous animals moving outside their conventional categories (undomesticated dogs, feral hogs, the house-pet caiman). Through their marked presence in, outside, and at the threshold of the characters' homes, these animals establish Atlanta as a city that, built on sharp divisions of racial and economic inequality, nevertheless holds within it unlikely possibilities of encounter and exchange.

"Alligator Man," "Woods," and "Andrew Wyeth: Alfred's World" stake out complementary realms of commensality. These episodes, particularly the first two, hinge on "condensed" human-animal doublings, to use Glenda R. Carpio's term for the various temporal moves that the series makes to refurbish figures that might otherwise appear hackneyed ("B.O.S."). With reference to Coach and Uncle Willy, she writes: "*Atlanta* invokes the spirit of the much-sentimentalized trickster, a figure so over-determined it signifies saccharine banality at worst, romance at best, [and] it does so strategically. The show uses longstanding tropes in the Black tradition in condensed fashion—compressed to better re-gather their potency and reclaim them from overuse." Carpio understands these compressions as balanced against moments of "dilation"—here, the succinct use of slow motion paired with the Delfonics's "Hey Love" to express Coach's "swag"—that enable moments of visual yet not uncritical pleasure. I further locate these thickenings in *Atlanta*'s layered traffic, which stitches together frayed planes of reality to meld a televisual space-time in which it becomes possible to imagine the bright lines between nature and city, home and not-home, and external performance and interior thought coming undone.

When situated in this traffic, the condensation of "Woods" can be understood as satirizing an animal metaphor with deep historical connections to southern Black masculinity and a particularly enduring presence in American media. If Willy embodies the trickster, deploying Coach as "his avatar but also his decoy" (Carpio, "B.O.S."), then Wally (Reggie Alvin Green) serves as one of several incarnations of the "magical Negro," a stereotypical Black character who, having no narrative arc of his own, offers kindly assistance, often of the spiritual sort, to a leading white character who has been set adrift. *Atlanta* satirizes this Hollywood trope through its serial insertion of characters like Wally and Ahmad White, who appear out of nowhere to minister to the main characters, only the magic they traffic in is likely derived not from "folk wisdom" but from hallucinogens and psychic quackery—and the men they pretend to help are Black (Glenn and Cunningham 138). With its parallel pairing of a magical Negro alongside the flash of an animal, "Woods" offers a callback to "The Big Bang," with the dustup that sends Alfred into the woods—quick cuts of four bodies in motion, shouting; a MARTA train hurtling past; shots fired—recalling the pilot's parking-lot shooting. In light of this visual rhyme, the dead deer acts as a return of the repressed or at least a reminder that the narrative's nominal motive remains, eighteen episodes in, not just unresolved but also largely unmentioned. In summoning this earlier violence, the eviscerated deer remind viewers that it is Alfred, not Earn, who remains most susceptible to its consequences.

The first season's tracing of Earn's search for a leg up and a place to stay gives way, in the second season, to Alfred's pursuit of frustratingly unattainable basics like a haircut and a hold on "realness." Alfred's journey comes into full view in "Woods," which opens with a stock sitcom moment: a mother chiding her son for not doing his chores. Alfred's mother, Lorraine (Diane Sellers), appears in the background of his dining area, scolding him as he sleeps on the couch in the foreground. Yet as the pilot's exposition of Alfred's residual anger at Earn established, his mother has been dead for a year. Her presence, then, is of a piece with *Atlanta*'s intermittent slippage into different metaphysical spaces, here stylistically signaled only by the slow dimming of the kitchen light as she recedes. Reality resumes with the buzzing of Alfred's phone, and a text from an unnamed number and a call from Earn indirectly reference the anniversary of Lorraine's death by asking if Alfred is okay. Alfred rouses himself and enters the kitchen to find Darius making pasta from scratch, and this largely unmarked transition back to mundane reality turns the ongoing joke of Darius's unlikely domesticity (he is introduced in the series wielding a knife and plate of freshly baked cookies) into a sharper suggestion that he fulfills a substitutive maternal role as Alfred's housemate.

Alfred then goes on a perambulatory date with Ciara (Angela Wildflower), a woman embracing her influencer status who scorns Alfred's discomfort with it; when this tension boils over while the two are getting pedicures, Alfred angrily decides to walk home. En route, three younger Black men posing as admiring fans rob him at gunpoint. Alfred manages to fend them all off and takes refuge in some woods, where he crosses paths with Wally. They stumble on and then circle back by a deer carcass, causing the following exchange:

> WALLY: That's you. Deer guts. That's what I'll call you. Big ol' Black-boy deer guts. [Laughs.] You're stubborn. You're stubborn, and you're Black. [Laughs.]

ALFRED: I'm serious man. Leave me the fuck alone.
WALLY: Boy, you is just like your mama.
ALFRED: What?
WALLY: [Laughs.] What's the matter? You lookin' all crazy.

Time passes and Wally continues to trail Alfred until he eventually takes a boxcutter to Alfred's throat, confirming that the most dangerous thing in the woods is human. Alfred escapes and tumbles out of the woods into a brightly lit gas station, where he gets a cold drink and invites a selfie with a white kid.

Wally's exclamation that Alfred is "deer guts," made the instant the two encounter the animal remains, equates Alfred and the deer, summoning the racial slur and trope of the "black buck." This stereotypical image of a hypersexualized Black man defiant of white authority has deep roots in American culture and literature, gaining a particularly strong currency in film, where, as Donald Bogle explains, it plays a defining role in two moments pivotal to the representation of Black men: D. W. Griffith's *Birth of a Nation* (1915) and the Blaxploitation era of the 1970s (10, 210). Whereas Griffith's film is blatantly racist in its portrayal of Gus and Lynch as "brutal black bucks," films made in what Bogle dubs "the age of the buck" are more insidious in their use of "tenacious buck protagonists" styled to appeal to Black audiences and affirm Black identity, as they were made mostly by whites in pursuit of commercial profit (10, 219). In pairing a deer carcass and a can't-win (at least until later seasons, though even then his "victory" may be somewhat pyrrhic) rapper, *Atlanta* satirizes the figure of the black buck, expressing a specifically televisual form of the "buck theory" that Joshua Bennett traces in recent work by and about Black men. Observing that "the buck—in all of its power, grace, and vulnerability to unexpected, untimely death at the hands of another—has appeared in the work of Black men from the nineteenth century up until the present day" (28), Bennett proposes, from his vantage point as a Black male writer, that poets such as Tommye Blount and Terrance Hayes, along with the filmmaker Jordan Peele in *Get Out* (2017), approach "the buck not only as figure or animal familiar, but as pharmakon. The poison and the cure. The enfleshment of what we, necessarily, refuse and what has been refused us" (31). Alfred is all too aware that, in the eyes of many, he embodies the stereotype of the black buck. Through Al's self-aware performance of this role and the particularly gory enfleshment of deer guts, "Woods" stakes out a satirical cure for this poisonous view of Black masculinity.

Recalling buck figures from in and outside the series, the dead deer in "Woods" collects several satirical challenges to the buck stereotype. The secondary meaning of "a buck" as a dollar is also always there given that Alfred needs to make money. The episode picks up on a scene in "The Club" (s1e8) when the DJ plays Crime Mob's "Knuck If You Buck," and no one dances, a reaction to the hometown hit that, Terry notes, Black Twitter found perplexing and which she explains as "possibly a subtle challenge to the expectations of blackness by black people" (67). This quiet refusal to comply with expectations to exuberantly perform an aggressive sociality—expressed in the lyrics' literal meaning, "knuckle up if you're buck wild"—finds an echo in Paper Boi's "Mucking" (though that song title is, Alfred explains, a comically absurd portmanteau of other words[9]), which so laughably fails at the sexual bravado expected of Black rappers. Along with these aural echoes, the deer carcass recalls an obscure animal remainder from TV history: an upended buck trophy that appears, inexplicably, in an investigation room in the pilot of *Twin Peaks* (1990–1991). If David Lynch's prestige drama seems far afield from the sitcom lineage this essay has thus far staked out, it's worth recalling *Twin Peaks*'s driving fascination with exploring horror in the everyday domestic—as well as Glover's remark that making "*Twin Peaks* with rappers" was the impetus for *Atlanta* (Cwik).

The dead guts of *Atlanta* and the trophy of *Twin Peaks* appear in medium shots that are markedly similar in their composition, with the torso and head splayed horizontally and the antlers tipping into the screen's righthand third of visual interest. In all other ways, they differ. Indeed, *Atlanta*'s shot of deer guts flashes a mirror image to the stately trophy of *Twin Peaks*, much as *Atlanta*'s Atlanta presents the inverse of the fabricated, almost exclusively white town of Twin Peaks. Special Agent Dale Cooper (Kyle MacLachlan) and Sheriff Harry S. Truman (Michael Ontkean) momentarily acknowledge the upturned trophy, and it remains in the scene as a surreal invocation of the association between hunting and detective mastery, their job being to find the murderer of Laura Palmer, the beauty queen whose status as "trophy" is established in the intro sequence's framing of her photograph in the high-school trophy case ("Pilot"). The revelatory shot of the deer guts in *Atlanta* is handheld, from Alfred's perspective, which, coupled with Wally's assertion—"That's you"—identifies Alfred with it. *Twin Peaks*'s trophy is a classically naturalist mount, fastidiously crafted to recreate the animal in the throes of "liveness" (it's also a large deer or, more properly, a stag). The deer guts of *Atlanta* are just that: guts, aswarm with flies. The limbs have been removed, leaving only the eviscerated torso and head. This isn't roadkill (cars don't do this) but, more likely, a hunting spoil—the meat taken and the rack, small and unimpressive, abandoned.

If we understand *Atlanta* as an African American satire woven from conversation with television and place, then the deer guts emerge as a subversive incarnation of the buck, one that Alfred tentatively takes on when he coaches the wan teen to "give, like, a mob face, man" in the convenience store. Alfred grimacingly smiles here, showing his teeth, still bloodied from the attack hours earlier. The pose makes him look tough yet, in recalling the deer guts, also declares that he won't be dressed up (contrary to Ciara's insistence that he trade in his "sweaty hoodie") and made to represent something he is not. The scene cuts to black, and a credit reads "In Loving Memory of Willow Dean Kearse." As many recaps and tweets have noted, Kearse is the mother of actor Brian Tyree Henry; she died suddenly in 2016, just as the crew was wrapping the show's first season. This dedication thus forms a bookend with the opening scene's reverie of Lorraine such that "Woods" unfolds as a story about Alfred's/Henry's disorientation not just with self and celebrity but also with grieving and vulnerability. The existential struggles of Alfred and the other principal characters take on increasing importance in the series' later seasons: a worldly trans woman named Lorraine[10] (Ava Grey) takes an especially stoned Alfred under her wing for a strange night in Amsterdam; significant portions of the last two seasons are devoted to Vanessa (Zazie Beetz) figuring out where she belongs, particularly as a mother; and the series finale unfolds a string of on-brand dreamlike vignettes that broach the previously unmentioned death of Darius's brother and conclude with Darius contemplating his chosen family—and possibly the ontological status of the entire series—from his perch atop Alfred's burnt-orange velvet couch (a far more luxurious version of the ratty furniture both inside and outside his apartment in the show's early seasons).

J. Bennett understands Black male writers' turn to the figure of the buck as "a unique form, we might say, of Du Boisian second sight" (31). In the poems he reads and in *Get Out*, this split vision acknowledges the spectacular connections between the most hunted humans and animals in the United States, yet it also demands that we "think instead about the interior worlds of Black men as they live and breathe, their childhood dreams and critical optimism, their lifelong fears and unimpeachable joy" (30). Black mothers, he points out, are central to those childhood dreams and the lives they inspire (33). In gesturing to the ongoing presence of Lorraine and Kearse in Alfred's and Henry's lives, the framing of "Woods" invites attention to these men's interiority, underscoring that they are not just homebodies, but having recently lost their mothers, they are profoundly homesick. This detour in "Woods" is just one route through which *Atlanta*, in moving through spaces that are satirical, televisual, and Atlantan, invites viewers to think deeply about its characters, their dreams, and their grasp on home.

NOTES

1. This essay is indebted to the thought-provoking conversations about *Atlanta* that I had with students in my Writing about Television and Writing Home courses at the University

of Virginia and in the "Serial Formations: Species, Race, Structure, Screens" panel convened by Ted Geier at the 2019 meeting of the Society for Cinema and Media Studies. A version of this essay appears in my book *Bits and Pieces: Screening Animal Life and Death* (2023).

2. Among the few exceptions are a pair of dogs—Cornpop and Gizmo—both of whom are pets of problematic white women in "Three Slaps" (s3e1) and "The Homeliest Little Horse" (s4e2), respectively. Disney's cartoon dog Goofy features prominently in the form of a hat sold to tourists (including Alfred) in Amsterdam in "New Jazz" (s3e8) and as the star of the "Blackest movie of all time" in "The Goof Who Sat by the Door" (s4e8).

3. For further discussion of canine-human relationships, see Klestil's essay herein.

4. For further discussion of this conjunction, see this volume's introduction.

5. See "Dog," as in definition 1a.

6. For further discussion of this episode and this scene, see the essays by Brooks and Klestil herein.

7. Donald Glover played the character of Troy for the first five seasons of this show.

8. For further discussion of this image, see Parks's essay herein.

9. For further discussion of this song's larger significance, see Boorman's essay herein.

10. Her first name is surely not a coincidence, especially considering *this* Lorraine offers Alfred existential career and life advice while he is wearing his Goofy (and goofy) hat. In very different ways, both of these metaphysically ambiguous Lorraines are manifestations of Alfred's conscience at fraught moments in his life and artistic career.

DeKalb County

"YOU CHOSE BLACK"

Atlanta's Gendered Politics of Black Respectability and Representation

KEYANA PARKS

"You chose Earn ... I chose Dave ... I chose white ... you chose black." These words, delivered in "The Streisand Effect," the fourth episode of *Atlanta*'s initial season, prompt the question of what it means for a Black woman to "choose Black." In the context of this declaration, it means sacrifice and subordination. However, the process by which the show's Black female lead fashions her own self-worth across the show's four seasons punctuates *Atlanta*'s exploration and indictment of Black gender politics informed by the contradictions of stereotype, respectability, and masculinity. The show itself presents as hypermasculine, with the first season's promotional material depicting the three Black male main characters in a receding line with Georgia peaches in their mouths.[1] Accordingly, most discussion of *Atlanta* thus far has been focused on Earnest "Earn" Marks (Donald Glover), his cousin Alfred "Paper Boi" Miles (Brian Tyree Henry), and their friend Darius (LaKeith Stanfield). The show's one prominently featured woman character is Vanessa "Van" Keefer, played by German-born actor Zazie Beetz. Van only features in ten of the first two seasons' twenty-one episodes, and although Beetz is credited on every episode of the final two seasons, Van is on camera in less than half of them.

Van nevertheless plays a central role in conveying the show's satirical critique of Black gender politics and its investment in portraying a twenty-first-century "progressive Black gender ideology" beyond hegemonic norms of respectability.[2] *Atlanta*'s pointed attention to constructions of Black masculinities is heavily informed by stereotype.[3] Less so is the show's interrogation of how misogynoir[4] contributes to a Black gender politics in which Black women remain undervalued and misunderstood, particularly regarding the presumption that they make choices contrary to their best interests.

Through a close reading of Van's presence, I investigate how *Atlanta* employs a kind of satiric surrealism that imaginatively engages with Patricia Hill Collins's assertion that "to confront social inequality, African Americans need an analysis of Black masculinity and Black femininity that questions the links between prevailing Black sexual politics, their connection to Black gender ideology, and struggles for African American empowerment in response to the new racism" (7). I argue that the show achieves this through a convergence of the satiric, the surreal, and the hyperreal that makes intelligible the absurd ways respectability limits a progressive Black gender politics of choice, particularly when coupled with stereotypes that reflect both white gender norms and Black pathologies.

In *Hokum: An Anthology of African-American Humor*, Paul Beatty describes the complementary utility between the absurd and surreal: "The funniest, and oftentimes the saddest, folks realize that if it weren't for absurdity, life wouldn't make any sense" (299). He goes on to describe the surreal as the space Americans inhabit to escape confronting the absurd: "All contradictions must be rectified. All wrongs must be righted. The problem with making things rational is that it's a lot of work. It's much easier to ignore absurdity than to deal with it. So when someone is confronted with irrationality, they'll say, 'Wow, man, that's so surreal.' If something happening is surreal, you're absolved. Can't make the surreal real, dude" (300). *Atlanta*'s blend of the satiric absurd and the surreal confronts audiences with "irrationality" while also withholding absolution. Even as viewers encounter critiques of oppressive gender ideologies that pigeonhole Black men, they are also forced to recognize how intraracial constructions of Black masculinity reinforce oppressive ideologies. In the context of the show's surrealism, what becomes satirized is not so much Van's stereotypical characterization as an "angry Black baby mama" as the occlusion of her right to possess *any* of those stereotypical characteristics or her existence being predicated on choosing Earn, choosing Black.[5] *Atlanta* engages with Wahneema Lubiano's assertion that "the problem of addressing the construction of reality can[not] be answered by more claims to realism without considering how and why both hegemonic realism and resistance to or subversion of the realism are constructed" (264). Van's character does little to "resist" stereotype; *Atlanta* instead subversively represents the angry-Black-baby-mama stereotype and the conditions of its existence as simultaneously real, absurd, and—with the encroachment of the surreal—irrational.

Notions of "prevailing Black sexual politics" often manifest in popular culture through stereotypes dialectically depicting "broken" familial homes, lazy baby daddies, lecherous baby mamas, and/or wholesome nuclear, working- or upper-middle-class Black families. Historically, Black women's sexual stereotypes have been viewed as particularly pernicious. When hypersexual, they are jezebels, gold diggers, or welfare queens; when asexual, they become mammies or strong Black women; when emasculating, they are angry Black women or overbearing baby mamas and so on.[6] Van's character follows in the footsteps of Sapphire from *The Amos 'n' Andy Show* as an angry Black woman, with much of her ire directed toward her baby's father, Earn. As such, she reads as the angry Black baby mama. I contend that *Atlanta* deliberately employs such stereotypes to interrogate a "problematic Black gender ideology coupled with an unattainable hegemonic (White) gender ideology [that] leaves heterosexual Black men and women struggling to develop honest, affirming love relationships" (Collins 258). Stereotype thus employed unravels the hegemonic representation of Black gender norms that elide the complex political, economic, racial, and sexual realities of Black cishet relationships.[7]

Terri S. Francis's definition of the surreal also proves instructive for such a process of unraveling:

> Surrealism here, the *Afro*-surreal . . . is actually a realism so real, so contrary to the norms of publicized blackness, that it represents a rupture, a radical break from ordinary understanding such that the old feels new—because it was never known. When what seemed real is revealed to be a farce—that disjuncture, this sudden crash with reality realer than accepted truth forces a total reorientation to self and society. (101)

Atlanta's satiric surreal embraces stereotype not only as real but also as fresh and acceptable. It subverts the audience's expected recognition of and resistance to stereotype and compels viewers to contend with the absurd ways Black representation assumes the burden of realism.

Although stereotype has perpetually been a central apparatus on the satirical playground, in such a male-dominated genre, Black-women stereotypes rarely appear as subversive. Bell hooks notes that in establishing an "oppositional gaze . . . black looks were mainly concerned with issues of race and racism, the way racial domination of blacks by whites overdetermined representation. They were rarely concerned with gender" (*Black Looks* 117–18). Ishmael Reed's *Flight to Canada* (1976), for example, excoriates the white-dominated publishing industry and capitalist markets. However, while the incorporation of Mammy Barracuda's character upends the asexual attribute of the stereotype, his representation of Barracuda's "choice" to serve Master Swille uncritically reifies stereotypes of Black women as hypersexual, angry, and complicit with white masculine power.[8] Reed's Black-woman stereotype in a neo-slave narrative intent on demonstrating the "past as contemporary"[9] undermines what Darryl Dickson-Carr describes as the degenerative mode of critique operating within African American satire (*African American*).[10] On screen, Spike Lee's

Bamboozled (2000) offers a complex approach to representing Black women and Black gender politics. His film demonstrates how racist corporate structures and sexist assumptions surrounding Black women's success and choice impact Sloan's (Jada Pinkett Smith) psyche. Yet even as Sloan acts as the voice of Black reason in the film, she never causes the audience to question her resistance to stereotyping or her belief that Blackness is only comprehensible through respectability.

Some contemporary male satirists appear more willing to fulfill Dickson-Carr's degenerative mission, turning their satiric barbs toward Black masculinity. Marpessa, the main Black woman character in Beatty's *The Sellout* (2015), certainly adopts aspects of popular stereotypes about Black women. Still, her voice and critique of oppressive systems are not only present but also meditated on and valued by the text's main character. Unlike Barracuda, Beatty portrays Marpessa's choices within the context of her individual desire for freedom—sexual and otherwise—and the constraints informing them. Like the satires of Reed and Beatty, *Atlanta* intentionally subverts representations of Black masculinity through critiques of racist and capitalist white hegemonies. When contemplating gender norms, respectability, and stereotypes, *Atlanta* follows the degenerative spirit of Black women writers such as Fran Ross, Carlene Polite Hatcher, Issa Rae, and Kaitlyn Greenidge in subversively critiquing how such hegemonies shape Black gender politics.[11]

It is important to note that *Atlanta*'s very construction presents contradictions that refuse to be neatly solved. For example, the majority of episodes heavily featuring Van are written and/or directed by "black female cultural producers whose practices," Nicole Fleetwood argues, "highlight the troubling presence of the black female body both to dominant public culture and to black masculinist debates about race, subjectivity, and visuality" (9).[12] One can read Van's centrality to the show's critique of gender politics as simultaneously commenting upon the irony of her absence. By no means should the representation of Van in *Atlanta* or recognition of Black women's roles in writing and shaping Beetz's character foreclose engagement with critiques of Glover's misogyny.[13] Instead, it metanarratively reflects the fraught nature of contemporary progressive Black gender politics and the persistently "troubling presence of the black female body."

Over the course of the first two seasons, Van navigates establishing her value separate from being Earn's baby mama.[14] I primarily focus here on three episodes centering Beetz's character: "Value" (s1e6), "Juneteenth" (s1e9), and "Helen" (s2e4). In each of these episodes, Van's private conversations with other Black women strike upon the gender norms and stereotypes informing their choices. The relative absence of the surreal in these scenes confers a sense of hyperrealism compared to other pivotal moments in the show.

Atlanta's first season develops the satiric irony of the angry-Black-baby-mama stereotype and its historical ties to the patriarchal norms that disadvantage Black men and women. As an unemployed Black man who sometimes lives with his baby mama, Earn's name immediately signals the irony undergirding prevailing Black gender norms mandating a male head of household. In both "Value" and "Juneteenth," Van expresses a need for financial stability because, despite her baby father's nickname, she is ironically the only one *earning* money. As the primary source of income, Van fits stereotypes perpetuated after the 1965 release of Daniel Patrick Moynihan's *The Negro Family: The Case for National Action* (commonly known as the "Moynihan Report"), which was used to cast Back families with a Black woman head of household as abnormal, dysfunctional, and the source of ruin for Black familial life. However, the very fact that Earn can variously be described as Van's baby daddy, occasional boyfriend, friend with benefits, and co-parent speaks to the show's investment in reworking the terms of respectability that maintain norms of Black gender politics and representation. Van and Earn tellingly struggle to adhere to norms of masculinity and femininity that reject Black women as providers.[15] Indeed, understanding Earn as itinerant and jobless yet also an occasional lover and an engaged, loving father requires an examination of the stereotypes that fundamentally devalue alternative familial structures.

While the second scene of the pilot introduces the dynamics of Van and Earn's relationship, it is not until "Value" that Van develops into one of the show's main characters.[16] As the title indicates, the episode explores various formations of value and the ways Black women can transcend them in order to recognize their own worth. As Van reconnects with her friend Jayde (Aubin Wise), the two women greet each other with superficial warmth, though the tension between them is palpable. Their dinner conversation casts them respectively as the baby mama and the gold-digging jezebel, two options through which they can exercise an autonomy always already circumscribed by, but never wholly subsumed within, patriarchal valuation. Wearing an all-white tailored suit with a slicked-down middle-part ponytail, Jayde physically appears to epitomize norms of respectable and classy Black womanhood. Jayde initially compliments Van on her natural hair, but comments such as "looks better than last time," "you should have went to Fernando's," and "he will fix those roots" expose her passive-aggressive undertones. Van retorts, "How much does Fernando charge?" and follows up with "Well, who's paying for yours . . . because I actually have to pay for mine," thereby implying recognition of Jayde's ability to perform respectability precisely because of how she sits outside of it as a de facto courtesan. Irony reigns as both women espouse fundamentally differing views about what it means to be valuable, and yet neither fit within traditional boundaries of "valuable" womanhood.

Their mutual disapproval takes on a hyperrealism as they both discuss value on their own terms while occupying recognizably stereotypical positions. The episode's nuanced juxtaposition of stereotypes avoids entering what Terrion L. Williamson describes as "stereotype discourse . . . the preoccupation with locating pathology or righteousness in certain cultural actors or texts that . . . often function to position black female iconography along a continuum of 'positive' or 'negative' representations" (17). While it might be laughable and ironic to some that an "Instagram escort" is lecturing Van about her "value" as a woman, Jayde's serious, emphatic statement that "Women need to be valuable. Black women need to be valuable" betrays her vulnerability. It not only indicates an understanding of her vulnerable, devalued position but also how, as an escort, she refuses to be governed by its attachment to respectability as she lives out her own criteria for value.[17] Although Jayde sees Van's relationship with Earn as devaluating, Van counters the idea of her passively accepting male valuation by claiming her own agency and desire. Similar to the first episode, in which Van and Earn lie intimately in bed together before Van matter-of-factly reveals that she has a date with another man, Van refuses to allow her choice to be with Earn in any context to be viewed as her only option. Neither woman's position appears fundamentally right, wrong, positive, or negative, and though they both disagree with each other's life choices, their disagreement neither reifies nor upholds Black women's choices as valuable only in the context of respectability.

While the conversation between Van and Jayde appears to revolve around the valuation of Black women's sexual freedom, the rest of the episode chronicles Van's subsequent dismissal from her teaching job and emphasizes the absurd ways Black women are punished both for adhering to and transgressing respectability. Against her better judgement, Van agrees to smoke weed with Jayde; the next morning, she receives a notification that random drug tests are being administered at her job. The first person she calls is none other than Earn's cousin Alfred, the up-and-coming rapper Paper Boi, drug dealer, and alleged murderer.[18] Alfred's brief inclusion in the episode, particularly his supine, relaxed figure rolling a blunt, brings into focus the differing hegemonic norms informing gender relations. His voice mocks her for needing him, for stepping outside of the bounds of respectability, but her response—"I am all we have" (even if she is not valued as such)—emphasizes her impetus to maintain respectability because of its impact on her family's economic stability. Her ensuing actions—pressing out pee from Lottie's diapers, filling an empty condom with it, and taping it to the inside of her thigh—verge on the absurd as she is ironically compelled to move further outside of respectability to keep her job.

The surreal forces its way onto the screen when the job in question comes into full view as a coworker abruptly interrupts Van's resolute walk toward the testing room to inquire if she is responsible for supervising in-school suspension (ISS). In a flashback, this same colleague calls attendance in a droning, unengaged way. She is forced to look up after receiving no reply for "Tobias Walner" and finds him sitting silently at his desk in whiteface. The whiteface instantiates a disruption to the norm of whiteness that would render Tobias invisible if he adhered to the expectations of Black respectability and normalcy. Echoing Faedra Chatard Carpenter's reading of a young boy photographed in whiteface at a 1965 Selma civil rights march, Tobias's "insistent black presence [breaks] through a whiteness that previously obscured black political visibility" (2). Black respectability's collusion with normative values would mark Tobias as disobedient, sentence him to invisibility, and deem him a criminal for deviating from those expectations. Without the introduction of the surreal, Tobias goes unnoticed by not only his teacher but also the system that reduces both him and Van to invisibility if they respond and act appropriately.[19]

The surreal flashback to Tobias's whiteface interrupts a fast-paced dolly shot of Van's progression from her house and through the school's halls toward her drug test. The intrusion returns the episode to its normal pace and provides the audience with time to question Van's absurd plan of action, even if she does not. She resumes her path toward the testing room, and after unsuccessfully attempting to untie the knot in the baby-pee-filled condom—it pops between her teeth and splashes down the front of her dress—Van dejectedly walks into her principal's office and confesses, "I smoked." Her principal's response marks a return to hyperrealism. She calmly and matter-of-factly relays: "Urine samples aren't sent off. The county can't afford quarterly drug tests for its employees, so after the first one, they're really just to keep people on their toes. Listen, everybody smokes weed. The system isn't made for these kids to succeed, and you gotta shake it off somehow—I get it." She then summarily fires Van for admitting to her drug use; the inevitability of this termination conjoined with the surrealism of Tobias's whiteface exposes the real absurdity of "the system" designed to oppress and penalize.

Van must comply with an absurd ethics of respectability that not only condemns her as an unwed mother but also disciplines any attempt to "shake it off." The puzzled look on Van's face registers the absurdity of the idea that she still needs to be fired even though the tests are not analyzed. In the context of her principal's words, Van is indeed wrong but not for smoking weed. Instead, Van is punished for telling the truth, for openly stepping outside the bounds of respectability that delimit her ability to earn money. Van is forced to walk the gendered lines of respectability that refuse to value her as her family's sole provider.

The surreal returns to conclude the episode and further solidify the parallel devaluation of Van and Tobias. The camera pans to Van sitting at a teacher's desk and then cuts to a close shot of Tobias in whiteface. His mischievous smirk and quick, upward eyebrow flick comprise the final shot. The satiric surreal endows the show with what Danielle Fuentes Morgan describes as a core tenet of twenty-first-century African American satire, the refutation of "traditional respectability politics [that] shifts the concept of ethics away from vague notions of right and wrong and opens up what ethical behavior might really look like in practice—the ethics involved in creating space for authentic ways of being without assigning value to portrayals" (*Laughing* 6). Van and Tobias's shared space in ISS registers the absurdity of the actions Van undertakes to keep from being fired as well as the fact that she is still terminated. The inevitability of her firing satirizes the idea that respectable "choices" result in being recognized as valuable. The satiric surreal posits strict dichotomies between right and wrong as concomitant with values that carry retributive consequences for Black women.

"Juneteenth" is the next episode that centers Van, and its opening scene continues to underscore the differing gendered relations to power that Van and Earn experience even though both of them are impacted by stereotypes and respectability. The scene depicts Earn "waking and baking" beside a sleeping, naked, brown-skinned woman. His relaxed, unbothered repose is interrupted by the soft vibrating sound of a phone call from Van, who is waiting outside for him and visually agitated. Unlike when Van wakes up in imminent danger of losing her job on the morning after smoking with Jayde, Earn faces no such distress. This scene rehearses a stereotypical trope wherein the angry baby mama is waiting for or has business with her baby daddy who is in the arms a "floozy."[20] However, the show makes plain that Van's ire is unrelated to Earn's sexual life, thereby simultaneously challenging the overbearing-Black-matriarch type, the deadbeat-Black-father type, and the desirability of a traditional nuclear-family structure.

The episode more explicitly satirizes and contextualizes a system of value predicated on respectable Black gender politics that merely reproduces current power structures. As they begin driving to a Juneteenth celebration hosted by Monique Allen (Cassandra Freeman), a wealthy and well-connected Black woman, their conversation explicitly reveals what is at stake and for whom. For Van, the potential opportunities awaiting her at the party could open doors of future employment. It could be "really good" for her, but it is only when she follows up with "It's also good for Lottie" does Earn respond "Why else do you think I'd be here?" Earn's words communicate his detachment from this event, and his actions in the early stages of this episode corroborate this sentiment. Viewing Van as valuable only insofar as it relates to her being the mother of their child is indicative of the ways Black masculinity can work in concert with white patriarchal power to elide Black women's individuality and stifle independence. Monique's warm greeting when they arrive—"Oh you must be Mr. Hubby!"—unmistakably defines the requirements of respectability that must be met in order to access the domain of the upper-crust elite Black society and further values Van only in presumed matrimonial connection to Earn. While all that is required of Earn is to "be here," Van is transparently only eligible to enter because she is "married" to a "respectable" Black man who attended (but did not graduate from) Princeton.

This bourgeois domain, however, is one into which neither Van nor Earn truly desire entrance; the contradictions between displays of Black pride and freedom amid opulence and wealth take on bizarre features of the satiric surreal, rendering it ridiculous to both viewers and the protagonists. Earn describes the party as a Spike Lee–directed version of Stanley Kubrick's *Eyes Wide Shut* (1999). Unseen baritone voices harmonize a spiritual; liveried bartenders craft cocktails with names like "Emancipation Eggnog," "Plantation Master Poison," and "Forty Acres and a Moscow Mule"; and hors d'oeuvres served from slave ships contribute to a bewildering pastiche that comments on the holiday's recent cultural renaissance and ahistorical appropriation. The episode satirizes the ways in which upper-class Black respectability contributes to the capitalist consumption of Black history and works against a progressive Black gender politics. It appears they have entered not the home of a Black woman, but the home of a southern planter.

What solidifies this peculiar satiric shift into surrealism is the introduction of Monique's white husband, Craig (Rick Holmes). He enters the scene by way of a grand staircase and greets Earn with a hearty exclamation of "Happy freedom day!" while clasping him on the shoulder in a gesture that presumes a brotherly familiarity, which Earn clearly does not share. Craig continues by asking Earn, "You're familiar. Cherokee?" Although Craig later explains he was referencing a country club, the interaction and Earn's response—"Uh, no. Just Black"—touches on several different historical and contemporary racist stereotypes, appropriations, and erasures. More importantly, the scene establishes a dynamic in which Craig is somehow an expert on Black masculinity, while Earn is expected to authenticate Craig's authority even as his own is undermined. Earn wanders into Craig's private study, which is awash with Black cultural artifacts, like Thomas Dunwitty's corporate office in *Bamboozled*. Adding to the scene's surrealism is the placement of Childish Gambino's *Redbone* album. It at once alludes to Glover's own contentious relationship with masculinity, Blackness, and its consumption. The record's placement substantiates the scene's surreal comment on Craig's appropriation of Black masculinity, one that occurs in both the real and the absurd. Unlike Tobias Walner, who can only visually take on whiteness but not disrupt or assume its privileges, Craig's cultural appropriations lead to no such reprimand.

This scene's focus on the challenges to Earn's Blackness and masculinity highlights both his gendered privilege in relation to Van and his oppression as a Black man. While wandering around Craig's office, Earn's eyes alight upon an outlandish painting of what appears to be a muscled Black man with a sword battling the mythical gryphon. Craig's voice breaks into the scene, claiming the painting was inspired by Malcolm X's words: "Nobody can give you freedom. Nobody can give you equality, or justice, or anything. If you're a man you take it." Earn, however, recognizes Craig's misappropriation of this exhortation; Craig's emphasis on "man" elides the context of Malcolm X's speech and speaks to the construction and vision of freedom within Black communities and movements along lines of phallic power. Craig, a twenty-first-century liberal version of "the man," is juxtaposed against Earn, whose Blackness continues to mark him as not man enough while his distance from Craig's stereotype of Black masculinity marks him as not Black enough. Craig's patronizing comment about Earn's need to visit Africa and quip that "it's nice to see a Black man on the management side" of music, draws attention to Earn's compounding inter- and intraracial status as an outsider. Interestingly, what is never challenged is his respectability.

Even as the episode criticizes stereotypes of Black masculinity and appropriations of Black cultural knowledge and production, it also communicates how respectability manifests differently in Van's and Earn's gendered relationship to the Black elites surrounding them. Earn's masculinity and perceived educational pedigree provide a privileged space in which he can complain, while Van must exasperatedly ask, "Do you think I'm happy here, having to prostitute myself for an opportunity? . . . Do you think that I'm happy that I need you here in order to do that?" Greeted with Earn's nonchalant shrugs and "maybe," Van charges Earn to "for once just pretend that we aren't who we are? I mean because we both know that you're good at pretending." She receives more than anticipated when Earn finally leans into his expected role as "Mr. Hubby" from Princeton and further exposes the party's surreal absurdities through his performance. Although neither wants to remain at the celebration, Van's use of "prostitute" not only recalls her interaction with Jayde but again foregrounds gender within an intersectional relationship to power Earn does not experience. She communicates her vulnerability as a Black woman in a way Earn does not or refuses to comprehend, acknowledge, or value.

The satiric surreal and the real collide when a group of older women, wearing similar floral dresses and spread out in a somewhat menacing rank, ask Earn what he does for a living. He responds by launching into a brief encomium about Van:

> Nothing. I mean that. Van does everything. She works, she raises our child, she's smarter than me, better than me. I mean that's why I married her. She honestly doesn't get the credit she deserves. I mean, ever.

But that doesn't deter her from being what she is, which is a mother, a provider, and a partner. Gun to my head, I don't think I could even look at another woman.

The painful irony, of course, is that the underlying veracity of Earn's words does not characterize her reality and value inside or outside the surreal. She is baby mama, not wife; she "does everything," but her sacrifice remains undervalued and often unacknowledged. Van is "a mother, a provider, and a partner" but is not, as the opening scene makes explicitly clear, the only woman for whom Earn has eyes. The reality of their relationship conflicts with what the people at the party expect; therefore, it must be told within the confines of the surreal. Again, it becomes clear that Van does not need Earn, but according to respectable Black gender politics, she *should* need him. Earn's surreal act of "pretending" at Van's request exposes the gendered structures of power that oblige Van's dependency on him when, in fact, both he and Lottie depend on her. Ironically, Earn seems unbothered by the ways his masculine presence is required to make Van legible. Yet, he remains disturbed by Craig's appropriation of Black masculinity and alternately Monique's deprecation of it.

Van's recognition of Earn's performance must be contextualized within the private exchange she shares with Monique. Unlike Earn, Monique is fully embedded in the surreal and speaks the truth without pretense:

> MONIQUE: Craig, Craig, Craig, Craig. You don't think I know how crazy my husband is? This whole "Black people as a hobby" shit? Slam poetry? *Martin* reruns? That nigga told my ninety-five-year-old grandmother that she was cooking her collard greens wrong.
> VAN: Well, girl, you married him.
> MONIQUE: Yeah, I did. Can't eat if you don't open your mouth. I get this big-ass house, and he gets the Black wife he always wanted. That's marriage. I like Craig, but I love my money.

Without excusing or endorsing Monique's choice to inhabit the role of gold digger, the exchange highlights her decision to obtain what she desires in a system that would continue functioning with or without her. When Van queries if Monique is sorry she cannot have both "understanding and security," Monique's response that "it's redundant to be both Black and sorry in the world" more or less accurately recalls the lady in orange's monologue in "no more love poems #1" from *for colored girls who have considered suicide when the rainbow is enuf*.[21] Unlike Craig's misappropriation of the Malcolm X quote, Monique's paraphrase captures the lady in orange's realization that her attempts to defy the world's definitions of her do not matter as much as finding value and love in herself. Monique is hyperaware of the same Black gender politics of choice informing her, Jayde's, and Van's subjugation. Like Jayde, Monique embraces stereotype as a space of hyperrealism that acknowledges the conditions informing her value and choices.

To close this article, I examine "Helen"—the episode from which I drew inspiration for my essay's title—alongside two episodes from the final season, "Work Ethic!" (s4e5) and "Snipe Hunt" (s4e7). All three episodes remain eminently preoccupied with representing a progressive Black gender politics, but what does it mean that "Snipe Hunt," in which Earn not only chooses Van but acknowledges that he desires her as a woman outside of her role as Lottie's mom, is one of the least surreal episodes?

Before analyzing the juxtaposition of "Helen" and "Snipe Hunt," it is necessary to briefly discuss how "Work Ethic!" degeneratively critiques the Black entertainment industry's contradictory gender politics of representation, including *Atlanta*'s own participation therein. Written by Janine Nabers, the episode offers a surreal parody of Tyler Perry and his studios through the character of Kirkwood Chocolate, who is played by Donald Glover in heavy makeup. When Van visits his Chocolate Land studio for a bit part in which she stereotypically presents as a "ratchet" friend,[22] Lottie's unscripted interruption of a scene draws Mr. Chocolate's attention, and she is whisked away from her mother and moved from set to set to appear in several of the seemingly endless concurrent productions underway on the lot. Searching desperately for Lottie, Van forces her way in to see Mr. Chocolate, who for the majority of the episode is only seen as an omnipresent disembodied voice issuing commands over an old-fashioned loudspeaker. When Chocolate remains unfazed by Van throwing hot grits on him in an allusion to *What's Love Got to Do with It?* (1993),[23] she proceeds to tell him: "You're a con man. You just make unrelatable shit that takes advantage of the people you say you're trying to help." Mr. Chocolate scoffs at her characterization of his work and narrates a litany of ways Van's life both on and off his sets mirrors the characters he creates: "You're a single mother who can't afford to feed your daughter. Phaedra [a hairdresser at the studio] is your hip girlfriend. You have a formerly incarcerated, light-skinned love interest, a Christian, gun-toting grandmother, and let me guess, you have a dark-skinned baby daddy? . . . And you threw grits at me, unprovoked. Face it, Vanessa, you're a Kirkwood Chocolate woman." Although this speech clearly parodies Perry's characters (particularly his women characters), Chocolate's character reflects *Atlanta*'s commitment to portraying Black realities whether they are ultimately "good" or "bad."

Similar to Van's hyperreal conversations with Jayde and Monique, Van's ensuing conversation with a disappointed Lottie accentuates the complicated negotiations Black women must undertake when approaching Black gender politics of representation. Van tells Lottie that, although it is unfair, she carries a burden of representation and that Van "just really want[s] Lottie to be old enough to decide what [she] want[s] to represent" instead of having it dictated to her, least of all by someone like Chocolate. In some ways, *Atlanta*'s surrealism insists that, although it may be unfair that Black cultural producers bear a responsibility to represent a progressive Black gender politics, the reality is that they do.

Reading "Helen" and "Snipe Hunt" together helps illuminate the ways *Atlanta* wrestles with the burden of representation while also trying to imagine progressive Black gender politics. In "Helen," Van and Earn leave Atlanta to attend Fastnacht, a German carnival celebration held in Helen, Georgia. The entire episode addresses multiple aspects of Black gender politics through Van's and Earn's interactions with each other as well with the predominately white festival attendees; however, the juxtaposition of two ping-pong matches Van and Earn play against each other best exemplifies the show's use of the satiric surreal and hyperreal to reveal the masculine-centered Black gender politics of choice that leaves Black women feeling like they "chose Black" over "being valued as a human being." "Helen" is one of the few episodes in which Van appears genuinely happy and feels recognized as valuable outside of Earn. Her happiness dissolves when her girlfriend introduces her as "Lottie's mom" and Earn refuses to participate fully in festival activities because, he says, "it isn't me." His statement says more about his inability to articulate his discomfort in a predominately white space and Van's independence within it. Jayde and Monique may be objects of satiric critique, but their choices in partners reinforce the way they value themselves within a patriarchal system that otherwise subordinates them.

In the first game of ping-pong, Van lightheartedly and easily wins. The surreal again abruptly intrudes onto the screen in a manner similar to Tobias's unsettling interruption in whiteface. As Earn asks Van why she publicly upbraided him for his surliness, the camera cuts to a solitary figure in a slasher mask who seems to materialize out of thin air. The reality is that with or without a spectator, Earn does not want to confront the idea that Van does indeed have a choice other than him. The second time they play, the game takes on an air of seriousness and, like the conversations Van has with other Black women throughout the series, hyperreality. Van's decision to choose herself leaves Earn with the choice to value her on her own terms or not. Although Van and Earn may no longer be a couple at the close of "Helen," they are moving toward being honest about their desires and needs, as well as coming to terms with the fact that their choices may not align. Van chooses herself over a relationship with Earn that no longer meets her needs nor offers her value as a person; that she does so while continuing to co-parent with Earn expresses a progressive Black gender politics that respectability disavows. It is important to note that Earn is not castigated for wanting to keep the status quo of his relationship with Van, but he must accept that he can no longer expect Van to meet his needs while refusing to meet hers.

In "Snipe Hunt," one of the least surreal episodes in the entire series, Earn finally lives up to his nickname. It is not, however, his ability to provide financial security for Lottie and Van that illustrates the show's progressive gender politics. Instead, it is Earn's exploration of Black masculinity and his insecurities as a Black man excluded from white male privilege that creates room for their relationship's growth. Despite being ribbed by Alfred in "The Homeliest Little Horse" (s4e2) for foolishly "giving [his] money away," Earn has been attending therapy during the early episodes of season 4, partly because of his internal struggle with the possibility of moving to LA for work without Van and Lottie. In "Snipe Hunt," Earn makes several attempts to convince Van to join him. Van, however, is skeptical of his grand gestures of love and states: "I can't just pack up my whole life because you love me as Lottie's mom. It's not enough for me." Her response illuminates how the issue is not choosing Black in and of itself, but rather the fact that choosing "Black" often problematically means choosing a gender politics that fundamentally denies your own value. It takes Earn's vulnerable acknowledgement of his desire for and need of Van beyond being Lottie's mother for Van to agree to the move. Through the maintenance of her right to choose or not choose Earn, *Atlanta* shifts the burden of respectability onto systems of oppression, whether intra- or interracially imposed, instead of on people forced to exist within them. Van's choice to be with Earn may be a happy ending, but it is neither a predetermined or compelled one. *Atlanta*'s characterization of Vanessa recognizes that a twenty-first-century examination of Black gender politics, masculinity, and stereotypes necessarily requires an intersectional analysis of Black gender politics and Black women's place within them.

NOTES

1. The peach is an homage to the city and state of the show's namesake, Atlanta, Georgia, but also a popular moniker for women and a metaphor for their buttocks.

2. For a discussion of respectability politics, see Higginbotham. Credited with the term's coinage, Evelyn B. Higginbotham describes respectability politics as a set of standards adopted by Black women in the early twentieth century to "combat racist images and structures" (187). Also see White.

3. For further discussion of this, see Murray's essay herein.

4. In her *Misogynoir Transformed: Black Women's Digital Resistance*, Moya Bailey writes, "Misogynoir describes the uniquely co-constitutive racialized and sexist violence that befalls

Black women as a result of their simultaneous and interlocking oppression at the intersection of racial and gender marginalization" (1).

5. Claudia Rankine explores this denial of the right to choose anger through her examination of tennis legend Serena Williams in *Citizen: An American Lyric* (2014).

6. For further analysis of these stereotypes, see Harris-Perry; Jewell.

7. I focus on the cishet relationship between Van and Earn, but the show also contemplates progressive Black gender ideologies through queerness. See Avilez's essay herein for more on this subject.

8. Another Black woman character in the novel, Aunt Judy, has a relationship to freedom that is, at best, indifferent (Reed 170–71).

9. Reed describes the use of anachronism in his work as his manifestation of a vodun theory of time in which the past is the contemporary. See Domini.

10. Dickson-Carr's analysis draws from Steven Weisenburger's description of degenerative satire as a "radically subversive mode of satire" (2) that "delegitimize[s] . . . [and] functions to subvert hierarchies of value and to reflect suspiciously on all the ways of making meaning, including its own" (3).

11. For further discussion of women and Black satire, see the essays by Morgan, Boorman, and Horhn and Maus herein.

12. See the episode listing in this volume's composite bibliography.

13. Glover has been called out for the ways he speaks about Black women. In a recent interview with himself, he asks, "Are you afraid of Black women?" and responds, "Why are you asking me that?" (Glover, "Donald").

14. Darius even reinforces this specific stereotype somewhat later in "Sinterklaas Is Coming to Town" (s3e2) when he responds to news of Van's unexpected arrival in Amsterdam as a sign of "baby-mama drama."

15. For example, in "Go for Broke" (s1e3), Van and Earn attempt to have a date night. Earn does not have enough money for the bill and tip but still refuses to let Van pay.

16. For further discussion of this episode, see Cortes's essay herein.

17. This theme recurs in "Tarrare" (s3e10), which contains a subplot in which a friend of Van's from Atlanta finances a trip to Paris by agreeing to urinate on a willingly submissive and wealthy client.

18. All these roles garner him respect—"street cred"—if not respectability.

19. This connection between the absurd, the surreal, Black masculinity, and the visualization of whiteness is further explored in "B.A.N." (s1e7). The entire episode plays with the surreal through a fake talk show called *Montague*, complete with commercials, special guests (Paper Boi and fictional transgender activist Dr. Deborah Holt), and interviews. During the show, Montague introduces Antoine Smalls, who identifies as white, although he is clearly a dark-skinned Black man. The episode intersectionally critiques the homophobia and transphobia of both Black masculinity and whiteness while also drawing attention to the racism Black men experience; as Antoine explains in his interview, they "don't get the respect [they] deserve." That Antoine identifies as transracial but is visually Black and transphobic signifies on the ties between whiteness and Black masculinity, highlighting the absurd alliances between the two even as Black masculinity can never benefit from that alliance.

20. The chapter "Baby Mama (Drama) and Baby Daddy (Trauma)" in Mark Anthony Neal's *Soul Babies* provides a comprehensive overview of popular cultural refences to these

tropes, particularly in relation to the music industry. It should be noted that the very fact of Earn's presence in his daughter's life deviates from the negative stereotypical confines of the absent Black baby daddy. See Neal 57–98.

21. "i cdnt stand bein sorry & colored at the same time / it's so redundant in the modern world" (Shange 57).

22. For more on "ratchet" as a contemporary stereotype, see Warner; Pickens.

23. It is important to note this allusion not only because of the ways it references violence against Tina Turner but also because of the popular cultural dissemination of the scene as a joke or funny despite Turner's recent revelation about the difficulty grappling with the representation of violence against her.

ATLANTA AND THE INSTABILITY OF RACIAL PERFORMANCE

TIKENYA FOSTER-SINGLETARY

Just over half a decade since its first episode aired, *Atlanta* is being examined by scholars and television critics, particularly regarding its use of magical realism, surrealism, and satire. Such readings invite viewers to consider *Atlanta*'s complex representations of Blackness that transcend the familiar realms of straightforward comedy and "gritty" realism. The show's creative choices deliberately push viewers to consider discomforting issues surrounding Blackness and its expression, specifically ones that involve the hidden costs accompanying the social expectations of performing racialized identity in circumscribed ways.

Two episodes from season 2 highlight how *Atlanta* attempts to destabilize race by inviting the audience to examine "incorrect" presentations of Blackness and, ultimately, to recognize both the capriciousness of racialized identity and the corresponding fragility of Black life. "Teddy Perkins" (s2e6) hyperbolizes a performance of Blackness to depict and to complicate Black pain, revisiting implied questions about the fullness of Black humanity. "FUBU" (s2e10) contrasts the absurdism of "Teddy Perkins" with a deceptively realistic retrospective presentation of Black boyhood. Together, these episodes ask viewers to consider Blackness as spectacle and performance with the always-looming possibility of being misread; the audience sees this misreading as Black fragility laid bare in watching Young Earn,[1] Teddy, and Darius negotiate Black male racial identity in ways that mock not only racial performance but also the stability of race itself. Lisa Guerrero situates such racialized fragility in the context of late capitalism: "African Americans are inherently postmodern subjects whose condition has consistently been one of dislocation . . . [because] in contemporary America, black humanity is a hypothesis" ("Can I Live?" 267). Both episodes invite examination of the postmodern Black condition by engaging a satirical lens that targets and undermines expectations about the concreteness of Blackness by presenting it as something that can always be taken away or shifted.

As is true of many of *Atlanta*'s other episodes,[2] the action in "Teddy Perkins" and "FUBU" takes viewers outside the city proper, a suburban alternative to the gritty and desperate urban space. The disruptions to place highlight the characters' struggles to project Blackness in recognizable ways. These episodes perform "comic critique" through "black satire [that] serves to both critique society *and* legitimate black rage" (Guerrero, "Can I Live?" 268, emphasis original). The result of this satirical lens is what Danielle Fuentes Morgan calls "kaleidoscopic Blackness," "those multifaceted, private recesses of Black identity and selfhood that are often unknown to or overlooked by those who would simplify Blackness to render it consumable and commodifiable" (*Laughing* 2). Thus, the series expands and complicates an understanding of Black people and Black bodies as subjects. In *Crazy Funny: Popular Black Satire and the Method of Madness*, Guerrero further argues that the body of the Black subject "signals a panoply of trauma whose meaning shifts depending on who it is that is reading his body" (7); so, the shifting meaning of Black bodies points to instability in expressing and understanding presentations of Blackness to interrogate it as spectacle. Lastly, Mark C. Jerng's *Racial Worldmaking* argues that "race works with genre in building, anticipating, and organizing the world" for establishing what is plausible (18). Even without an overtly racialized social structure, race is reified and reflected by the worlds we experience and imagine here through a satirical lens that is (especially in "Teddy Perkins") at risk of being misrecognized. Taking Morgan, Guerrero, and Jerng together, the Black subject is acted upon—interpreted—in the context of narrative worlds that both create meaning and invite critique by questioning whether and how we can "know" Blackness. These episodes use satire to illustrate that viewers "*participate in genres*" in order to form and organize our sense of the world" (Jerng 9, emphasis original). These ideological moves thoughtfully negotiate Black humanity and its presentation on screen.

It is also useful to consider Melissa V. Harris-Perry's concept of a "crooked room" in examining these episodes. In *Sister Citizen*, Harris-Perry recounts a psychological study focused on how individuals navigate space. The study finds that some participants who "were placed in a crooked room and then asked to align themselves vertically . . . perceived themselves as straight only in relation to their surroundings," while others "managed to get themselves more or less upright regardless of how crooked the surrounding images were" (29). She posits that the crooked room represents race and gender stereotypes that pose "warped images of [Black women's] humanity" (29). *Atlanta* confronts viewers with "crooked rooms"; it contorts characters into curious, hyperreal, or uncomfortable ideological (and physical) spaces, and the protagonists struggle to situate themselves beyond/outside the relationship to external definitions. This confrontation exposes the illogical nature of America's racial hierarchy, using satire to turn the Black subject into the creator instead of the created. Guerrero proposes a Black satiric epistemology that is rooted in "the construction of black subject formation through a lens of exaggeration that specifically highlights how the absurdity of the racial logic of white supremacy determines the very (im)possibilities of an actualized black subjectivity" (*Crazy* 12). Harris-Perry's crooked room together with Guerrero's Black satiric epistemology explains why the protagonists of these episodes have difficulty both in projecting themselves and in being recognized. They are forced to negotiate subject formation that cannot escape the interpolation of capitalist white supremacy. Viewers watch as the characters attempt to maintain their individual racialized identities when faced with destabilizing racial landscapes. Those same viewers, however, may struggle to properly interpret what they see—which parts are meant as literal representations of reality and which as satiric commentary?

Challenging the show's title, both "Teddy Perkins" and "FUBU" invite viewers to move outside the city of Atlanta itself.[3] At the beginning of "Teddy Perkins," Darius (LaKeith Stanfield) is in a moving truck, presumably driving along one of the many tree-filled, pastoral roads that extend beyond Interstate 285, the so-called "Perimeter" encircling the city. Correspondingly, an early scene in "FUBU" shows a teenaged version of Earn (Alkoya Brunson) boarding a school bus that takes him to a high school in a suburb, albeit a mostly Black one,[4] outside the Perimeter. Both characters' movement indicates the physical mobility that often marks freedom for African Americans. However, it also gestures less encouragingly toward structural boundaries related to Atlanta's history of white flight, as well as both its de facto and legal forms of segregation.[5] Much as the use of Stevie Wonder's "Sweet Little Girl" in the opening scenes of "Teddy Perkins" provides a sonic cue, shifting the action out of the city's core signals to viewers that they are not in the Atlanta of southern hip hop. Neither, though, are they looking at the direct legacy of Scarlett O'Hara's Atlanta. In doing so, the series obscures and complicates the boundaries of race and place that might otherwise be assumed. The series itself resists linear structure, and examining these episodes out of the order in which they aired highlights contrasts intrinsic to their commentary on Black humanity and identity. This reordering reconstructs a passage from adolescence into adulthood, which also emphasizes how and why cloudy expectations about racial performance can instigate an internal and external chaos that ultimately leads toward madness.

The opening of "FUBU" finds Earn reluctantly accompanying his mother (Myra Lucretia Taylor) during a shopping trip to Marshall's. Having wandered away from her into racks of clothing, he is awestruck upon finding a bright-yellow FUBU shirt. His body language shifts instantly from boredom to excitement when he asks her to buy it. Without looking at it, she mutters, "It better not have no craziness on it," before putting it in her cart. Although her remark is clearly not meant in these terms, it nevertheless foreshadows how the expectations about performing Blackness can instill a "craziness" whose consequences are later (within the chronology of Earn's life) reflected in the person of Teddy Perkins. His unmistakable delight at wearing the shirt to school suggests his certainty that it will provide him with the street-smart ease that his cousin Alfred (Abraham Clinkscales) seems to have learned by the time they are in high school. Both the disheveled Reserve Officers' Training Corps uniform that we see him wearing in the school's hallways and his skillful verbal manipulation of an administrator unsuccessfully attempting to discipline him signal Alfred's ability to move confidently between disparate spaces and still own each of them.

Earn is obviously proficient in his schoolwork; his lab partner, Racheal (A'Nya Schofield), confirms as much by telling him, "You're pretty smart, Earn." However, he is far less comfortable in his social interactions. The FUBU shirt marks a clear—if also superficial—Black identity and provides Earn with an instant poise that he previously lacks. Almost immediately after boarding the bus to school, a classmate named Mike (Anthony Jaylon Mayfield) notes his "cool shirt," and Earn quietly revels in this observation until a violent interaction between two other students on the bus reminds the viewer of the adolescent hierarchies of power that Earn must navigate daily. The FUBU shirt's potential talismanic qualities are unmistakable less than four minutes into the episode.

Earn strides into his classroom with the same smile he has been wearing since spotting the shirt at Marshall's. His classmate Chris (Austin Lowe), who towers over the shorter and portly Earn, immediately identifies him as "the n***a with the FUBU shirt," thereby affirming the shirt's ability to confer in-group authenticity. Chris's approval is echoed by another male classmate, Mark (Treylan Newton), who remarks that "Earn out here tryna jump fresh! I see you!" And a young woman named Erica (Brianna Adamson) amiably says, "Hey Earn . . . I like your shirt" as she sits down at her desk near him. All these interactions combine to form a near-complete validation of Earn's intentions in wearing it. The shirt both reflects and creates the confidence Earn needs to protect himself from ridicule and to perform masculine social prowess. He is literally clothed in the structure of burgeoning Black masculinity, as expressed by a commodity perceived to be monetarily and socially valuable.

Everything shifts, though, as the camera shows another classmate, Devin (Myles Truitt), taking his seat in the background. As Devin unzips his jacket, he is shown wearing what at first glance looks like the exact same shirt as

Earn's. The same classmates who moments before had been offering Earn their endorsement suddenly shift to questioning the authenticity of both his and Devin's shirts:

> CHRIS: One of y'all got a fake shirt. Look, this one has more stripes than that one, and that one got a patch.
> MARK: Oh, no, y'all wearing fake FUBU now? [Class erupts in laughter.]

Devin, who has barely had time to sit down, matter-of-factly replies that "My shirt ain't fake. Talk to Earn," who naturally also denies that his shirt is not the genuine article it claims to be (and which he clearly needs it to be). Reveling in his role, Chris performs a showy comparative examination of the two shirts but ultimately declares without further explanation that another student named Johnny Lee is "definitely gonna know which one fake."

As Earn walks in the hallway with a white classmate named Alex (Grady Port), their conversation demonstrates the stakes of the racialized semantics of authenticity:

> ALEX: Your shirt looks fine to me.
> EARN: But if it's fake, everybody's gonna roast me. Forever. Remember how Thomas got his nickname?
> ALEX: Who?
> EARN: Thomas Jones. Doo-doo Jones.
> ALEX: Oh. Yeah. Well, is your shirt fake?
> EARN: I don't know.
> ALEX: Doesn't seem like a big deal to me. I've worn this shirt twice this week.

Although Alex's T-shirt—a souvenir from the Salty Dog Cafe in Hilton Head, South Carolina—might itself convey particular class or racial implications in a different context, Alex is not among those to whom Earn's shirt signifies anything beyond an individual sartorial expression; as FUBU's acronym suggests, it is neither *for* him, nor *by* him.

When Earn's lab partner points out a thread hanging from his shirt, the implication is that Earn's racial self is similarly becoming "loose." He pulls at the thread, and it creates a larger hole. As the camera pans right to a subtly grinning Devin, Earn's anxiety about failing to authentically mark his body grows. The looming suggestion is that *he* will be read as fake, that his very racial identity is in jeopardy. He can easily use a microscope to distinguish a plant cell from an animal cell, but he genuinely cannot tell the difference between the authentic shirt and the knockoff. The large sign hanging in the back of the classroom that reads "Under the Microscope" takes on a much darker double entendre as it frames Earn's predicament; the loose thread on his shirt signals the unraveling of his racial authenticity and the corresponding destabilization of his social identity. He is at physical and psychological risk, as is made clear in the subsequent scene in which two older and larger students aggressively ridicule his "fake-ass FUBU" that they presume came from a "thrift store." They explicitly link the authenticity of his clothes to the authenticity of his Blackness by labeling him as the "type of n***a to wear four-line Adidas and shit." Furthermore, the precarity of Earn's Blackness extends beyond his peers, as shown by the silent, disdaining looks he gets from two older Black cafeteria workers while wearing his shirt in the lunch line.

Earn enlists Alfred's help in extricating himself from the situation. As Alfred nonchalantly rifles through other students' lockers, Earn confesses that he is "freaking out" because he is "not cool like [Alfred]" and is concerned that "if the older kids find me, they're gonna beat me up." In response, Alfred asks about Devin's comparative status:

ALFRED: How cool is the other kid?
EARN: He's pretty cool. He always has dope clothes. His dad is like thirty.

As David E. Kirkland and Austin Jackson observe, "cool" posturing is often used to traverse the social landscape of Black manhood with resilience and power (281). Moreover, "young men [use] their clothing as a subversive tool . . . [to] communicate their ideas on their terms despite being entrenched in a contested educational domain that is commonly hostile to black males" (291). Such subversion of institutional authority does not, however, exempt such young Black men from the judgment of their peers. To wit, Devin's "cool[ness]" in this context is clearly synonymous with his acceptance among the other Black students and correlates with the "dope[ness]" of his outward appearance. The influence of this logic is apparent when the same two students who previously harassed Earn turn their attention to Devin. He defends himself using the circular logic that links clothing and authentic Black selfhood: "I don't wear bootleg clothes. I got all the [Air] Jordans, everyone knows that. And Earn come in here every day looking like a bum, so y'all know his shirt is fake."

After Earn admits that his shirt came from the sale rack at Marshall's, Alfred exasperatedly replies, "Bro, you got to get some money," but also reassures Earn by suggesting a trick that demonstrably worked for him earlier in the episode: "Man, don't be actin' nervous. I mean, people try to come at you, just deny it. Confidence is the key." In Alfred's view, communicating the self-assurance that Earn exuded at the episode's outset is far more important than the actual authenticity of his shirt.

Despite being visibly Asian American—and thus seemingly not being "us" like Alex—Johnny Lee becomes the unquestioned judge of which shirt is authentic upon his arrival in the episode at the end of the school day. Over the course of the day, Earn has increasingly covered up his shirt with a grey hoodie and is attempting to slip out of school unnoticed when Mark pulls him into a side hallway to undergo Johnny's examination. Johnny quickly looks at the tag of Earn's shirt and grinningly declares: "This one's fake! It says 'Made in Bangladesh.' It should be China." Chris's immediate reaction emphasizes that Johnny's judgment invalidates Earn substantively; *he*, not just his shirt, is "wrong as hell" in Chris's view. Earn's dead-eyed stare acknowledges his imminent social exile, but Alfred steps in and employs his previously articulated tactic to rescue Earn from certain humiliation. Like Johnny, he looks at the tag on Earn's shirt, but he reframes precisely the same piece of evidence found there to work in Earn's favor by linking it to Johnny's ethnic identity instead: "Man, this one the real shirt. It's supposed to say 'Made in Bangladesh' on this one. Of course this fool gonna say 'Made in China.' He is Chinese." Alfred gestures toward Devin's shirt and states bluntly: "That one the fake one. Trust me, I know." Nothing that Devin says or does thereafter can rescue him from the instantaneous shift of the boys' ridicule ("Yo, this n***a homeless!"). Alfred's assessments of both the shirt and Johnny's ethnicity—he weakly shouts, "I'm not Chinese, I'm Filipino" down the hall as Chris and Mike pursue Devin—are questionable at best, but the conviction with which he expresses them seems to be all that is needed to decide the matter in Earn's favor.

Although Alfred's supplanting of Johnny *could* be read as a preference for ingroup determinations of racial authenticity, such a reading ignores the undisputed trust that such Black characters as Chris and Mark previously placed in Johnny's abilities to spot the fake shirt. A more compelling interpretation involves the manner in which Alfred's intervention speaks to the unsteady—and thus perilous—grounds on which these performances of Blackness take place. While Earn has largely been concerned with his fragile social status, Devin's fate illustrates that the concrete nature of the danger facing these Black boys. After Earn's renewed social standing is confirmed by Erica giving him her phone number, Mike tells him that the "twelfth graders just found out [about Devin's shirt]. They're going in on this man." As Earn watches from the back of his bus, the same older boys who tormented him earlier ruthlessly torment Devin verbally and physically as he boards his own bus for home. The next day, a somber school administrator informs the class that Devin took his life overnight. Throughout the episode, the shirts consistently raise the question of who gets included in FUBU's "us." The incidents of intraracial challenges to racial classification in the episode make it clear that belonging is an issue that is always in flux.

Earn's is a quintessential coming-of-age dilemma, but it has rarely been presented on screen in the context of Black boys' lives.[6] Still less frequently has it affirmed the interiority that "opens up a place for kaleidoscopic Blackness to emerge despite its seeming denial" by satirically "acknowledging and subverting expectations of racial performance" (Morgan, *Laughing* 59, 3). The episode's final scene begins with Earn returning home after learning about Devin's suicide. Along with the opening scene in Marshall's, it forms an exterior frame for all the other scenes depicting Earn's direct interactions with his peer group. After he walks in the door, Earn's mother and his aunt Lorraine (Diane Sellers) question him about Devin, after which they give him well-intentioned directives about how to handle himself in similar circumstances:

> EARN'S MOTHER: You better say something if somebody tries harassing you. People will bully you your whole life if you let 'em. You got to stand up for yourself.
> LORRAINE: Mm-hmm, and you and your cousin got to look out for each other.

Of course, Earn *has* already been harassed, and Alfred *did* look out for Earn but not as much by helping him "stand up for [him]self" as by setting Devin up as a sacrifice in trade. As the women's instruction shifts to why Earn should wear a suit to his upcoming piano lesson, their words continue to contrast jarringly with the lived reality depicted in the previous scenes:

> EARN'S MOTHER: You want to make a good impression. Our mother always said, "You got one chance to make a first impression."
> LORRAINE: Mm-hmm. True indeed.
> EARN: But it's gonna be all hot . . .
> EARN'S MOTHER: I don't care. You are a Black man in America, and when you meet people, you need to look good. Your clothes are important.
> LORRAINE: That's true, Earn. You need to wear the suit.

Their advice presents a different perspective on how clothes can serve to communicate and confirm social acceptability. The episode's wider context, though, recalls Guerrero's epistemology of Blackness in the context of racialized capitalism, in which neither a tie nor a designer shirt will ever offer adequate security. As Leigh-Ann Jackson notices, "Between school and home, [Earn is] getting two different takes on respectability politics." At school, being respectable is about correctly navigating a naïve-yet-powerful capitalistic expression of Black masculinity; in the view of his older relatives, the message is about performing Blackness in ways acceptable to white America.

Either a genuine FUBU shirt or a suit will, at best, satisfy only one of these performances of acceptable Blackness, never both. No article of clothing can make a "good [enough] impression" because Blackness is constantly at risk of being misread and having its authenticity invalidated. Theri Pickens notes: "To be respectable is to be policed by oneself and a larger black community so that one is deemed worthy of equal treatment. Implicit in the ideology of respectability lingers the idea that it is not possible to remain individualized as a black person: one's individual will and desires must be subordinated to the political and social uplift of the collective" (42). Earn's efforts to navigate these competing expectations are a manifestation of his own struggle to stand upright in a crooked room. He is trying to create himself as best he can while other forces are simultaneously trying to construct, reconstruct, and/or deconstruct him. The final bit of dialogue satirically drives home the absurdity of his situation. As he walks to his room, Earn's mother states: "I got you another one of those FUBU shirts. It was on sale. Don't say I never did anything for you." Although she clearly means this as a loving accommodation of Earn's stated desires, her comprehension of the volatile dynamics of his life at school is inadequate for interpreting the undertones beneath his halfhearted reply of "thanks" upon seeing this new shirt laid out on his dresser.

The fragility illustrated by the younger characters in "FUBU" is also apparent in the adults of "Teddy Perkins." The line between reality and illusion is deliberately blurred in a confusing, plot-twisting narrative focused on the secondary character of Darius. The episode teasingly plays with light and dark imagery, probing Blackness as an unstable spectacle and performance. Ultimately, the characters in "Teddy Perkins" are constantly adjusting to the crooked room of racial expectations and are only able to "right" themselves if they resist the kinds of simple definitions of Blackness found in "FUBU" that are grounded in capitalism and defined by trauma.

Darius's brief stop at a convenience store in the beginning of the episode foreshadows an overarching theme: seeing what may or may not be readily visible. Noticing a cap that reads "SOUTHERN MADE," Darius purchases it and darkens several letters until it reads "U MAD," with an implied interrogative that foreshadows Teddy Perkins's madness.[7] The startled reaction of the store clerk and several white patrons cements the perhaps obvious point that the hat was not intended to be worn by a Black person. However, Darius's creative revision disrupts its message to convey an alternate idea. Originally intended as a declaration of culturally conservative whiteness (if not outright white supremacy), Darius's revision interrogates that same audience. Moreover, because he extracts this idea from the very letters already on the hat, he implies that southern identity does not belong solely to the white descendants of the Confederacy.

This scene echoes "North of the Border" (s2e9), in which Earn and Alfred find themselves in a white college fraternity house. They are seated beneath an enormous Confederate flag and surrounded by naked pledges whose heads are covered in white hoods. The pledges are compelled to dance around to "Laffy Taffy" by Atlanta hip-hop group D4L. The racialized violence suggested by the gigantic flag is somewhat neutralized both by the submissive posture of the pledges and by the strangely hospitable treatment that the Black men receive in this presumably hostile environment. Both scenes suggest the "postmodern racial trauma" that animates much of contemporary Black satire. Using Guerrero's Black satiric epistemology, Darius makes "new meaning through dissonance as a central mechanism in forging radically different ways of knowing" (*Crazy* 12). Darius's use of African American Vernacular English in modifying the hat serves to center Black rhetoric as a mode of resistance, a double meaning that ridicules white supremacy (Tucker 10). He puts the hat, with its new message, on his own head and, in doing so, claims a new South whose presumed racial equality would make defenders of the old one "mad" (in both senses of the word). The hat now speaks with Darius's voice, but neither the previous iteration nor its traumatic effects are erased. As a commodity, it visually represents a response to the "social anxiety of madness and the racial anxiety of blackness [that] have become interlinked through modes of commodification and consumption" (Guerrero, *Crazy* 17). It collapses multiple versions of the South—the antebellum "Dixieland," the Confederate States of America, the New South, the Dirty South, etc.—that may be in conflict but which also coexist, however unsteadily.

As Darius walks up to a mansion to pick up a free piano he found through an online message board, he is framed by a large wrought-iron door. The daylight is behind him, casting him in shadow. Entering the house, he is enveloped by still more darkness, both literal and figurative. The curious figure of Teddy Perkins verbally slices through the darkness before he emerges bodily from his position against a wall. The only light comes from a nearby window, but the skin on Teddy's unnaturally lightened face is also visually jarring. This interplay between light and dark both destabilizes racial boundaries and establishes the episode's critical commentary on race as a performed spectacle. Darius has already set the episode's visual leitmotif in motion by darkening the letters on the hat to illuminate his message, thereby reversing the usual association of dark and light. This reversal is underscored again inside Teddy's mansion when Darius is blinded by a camera's flash. Instead of casting a light that illuminates, the light of the flash is blinding and "darkens" Darius's sight. The episode's play with light and dark speaks to the larger concerns of Black racial fragility that emerge throughout *Atlanta* and particularly in the two episodes highlighted here. Audience expectations are manipulated and ridiculed to force a reconsideration of how Blackness is performed, created, and surveilled. Both episodes feature darkly satirical narratives that unmask the unevenly defined ideas about Blackness and expose the ways they create both external and internal anxiety (Guerrero, *Crazy* 17).

"FUBU" is grounded, at times agonizingly so, in the reality of Black adolescence in ways that are reminiscent of the middle section of Barry Jenkins's film *Moonlight* (2016). "Teddy Perkins" serves as a comparably abstracted and absurd companion piece. Both episodes center Blackness as spectacle with which Black people themselves must grapple. In "Teddy Perkins," this is made clear by the cameras Teddy has placed throughout the house. Blackness is both highly observable and unstable in its visibility. When Darius stumbles onto the massive bank of video screens on which Teddy can watch nearly every area of the house, it reminds viewers that Black bodies are surveilled in formal and informal ways; they are always "under the microscope," as Earn finds out in "FUBU." This surveillance exemplifies the ways in which "madness projected onto white bodies has the power to redeem or recuperate the white subject [but] madness projected onto black bodies only has the power to accuse and indict the black subject" (Guerrero, *Crazy* 4). Black characters, then, are meant to absorb the madness and trauma of society, not to reflect or to transform it. Teddy's unmistakable display of trauma inverts that formula; he is watching rather than being watched.

However, the artifice of his physical presentation (e.g., his dark wig and blanched skin) makes him a spectacle as well. His exaggerated appearance inverts the blackface tradition that puts artificial Blackness on display for audiences to ridicule. Instead, Teddy's performance of whiteness is meant as the target of the audience's scorn (as well as perhaps some of its empathy). Seeing Teddy slice open a comically large ostrich egg, erupt into unwarranted anger, and display his "museum" dedicated to "great fathers" (all of whom, like Teddy's own, are examples of abusive parenting of children who grew up to be celebrities), the audience is meant to see him as odd, but perhaps they might also identify with his pain. What viewers see is not recognizable Blackness (or whiteness, for that matter) but a clumsy caricature that tries to navigate around expectations of racial stability.[8]

Teddy's ghost-like appearance forces a contrast between whiteness and Blackness; and he is clearly not white. Teddy does not represent "an instance of *passing*, because this person is not ultimately *misread* or *accepted* by anyone as white, but instead a related performance of racial essentialism without the racial ambiguity or phenotypic sameness that passing in all its forms necessitates" (Morgan, *Laughing* 68, emphasis original). Teddy destabilizes the spectacle of race by embodying a Black self that is both "hidden" and seen beneath a thin veil of what appears to be whiteness. Because the audience knows that almost nothing they see is authentic, the idea of race itself is revealed to be unsteady. The complicated presentation of Donald Glover in prosthetics and whiteface as a parody of Michael Jackson (and his deflection of credit for this virtuosic performance[9]) echoes Guerrero's claim that the "black experience in the twenty-first century exists in the interstitial space between the real and the hyperreal: the postmodern version of double consciousness" ("Can I Live?" 277). Teddy represents a kind of extreme double consciousness that ridicules assumptions about Blackness and its performance, even in private spaces, like his mansion. The result is a dissociative experience that much contemporary Black satire illustrates (Guerrero, *Crazy* 17). However, because Blackness is assumed to be suspiciously unstable—mad even—Black subjects may be rendered incapable of forming fully integrated selves; disintegration becomes unavoidable (Guerrero, *Crazy* 3, 16). Teddy is a visual manifestation of that disintegration, a confrontation with the struggle to be seen accurately that may externally be perceived as insanity. His body is difficult to read, perhaps even to himself, and it critiques the assumed stability of race making. What seems like madness, then, is a tension around how "race composes expectations for what the world might look like and activates rules for knowing the world" (Jerng 16). Teddy exists inside Harris-Perry's crooked room, where he struggles to adapt to the expectations of the world around him; his failure has seemingly driven him insane.

A question in the second half of the episode is whether Benny, ostensibly Teddy's brother, is real. In another play with light and dark (as well as another nod to Michael Jackson), a supposed medical condition prevents Benny from being in the sun. He is literally hidden from light, both by head-to-toe bandages and by confinement inside the house. Much as Black bodies have been physically contained resulting from housing segregation and mass incarceration, Benny is confined to the basement. Just as Black people in America have had their overall mobility obstructed by laws and lack of access to transportation and economic means, Benny's mobility is symbolically challenged by his wheelchair and body-encasing bandages. In some ways, he—like Teddy—satirizes the view of Blackness as a concrete, fixed idea attached to people. It's difficult to pin down exactly who or what Benny is. Is he an imaginary manifestation of Teddy's fractured self? Is he a real, separate person? Or is he the fragile, sick version of Michael Jackson for whom audiences can muster empathy? Teddy concedes to Darius that Benny does not actually exist, immediately after which Benny emerges from his lair to kill both Teddy and himself. All this obscurity and internal contradiction creates even more volatility surrounding race, and the episode leans into this nebulous space without providing a definitive answer to the questions it raises.

Teddy tells Darius late in the episode that Benny "plays pain" but also that "he just played what he knew." He furthermore suggests that their father imparted to them a sense that pain is the definitive signifier, asserting that "great things come from great pain." Darius rejects this formulation, though, responding: "Not all great things come from great pain. Sometimes it's love." His emphasis reframes the images and ideas presented in both this episode and in "FUBU" concerning the performance of racial identity and its consequences. Darius attempts to see upright in a crooked room, and viewers are invited to look at the world through his more nuanced lens. His rejoinder to Teddy bridges the episode's satirical overtones with the generative promise of what Tucker calls "comic rage"—humor combined with anger that indicates the potential for healing (23). The violent ending of "Teddy Perkins" is certainly not wholly optimistic, but while Teddy and Benny are both consumed by unsuppressed rage, Darius emerges from the episode to point toward the healing that Tucker suggests is possible though not guaranteed.

Whereas "FUBU" suggests the threat of destabilized racial identity is largely within a microcosm—school—"Teddy Perkins" confirms that when American racial dynamics become unmoored, race is rendered illegible, unreadable, absurd (Guerrero, "Can I Live?" 276). The audience is left to wonder whether Teddy's body should be understood as a performance of whiteness, a performance of Blackness, Blackness transparently masquerading as whiteness, or something indiscernible. These two episodes allow room for both realistic and absurdist examinations of Black humanity and vulnerability. Questions emerge about how and if Blackness can be a knowable reality, but reading these episodes satirically also reminds the viewer that Black humanity cannot be presumed and must be asserted in the way that Darius does in "Teddy Perkins." Although both episodes depict madness and death, there is also a hopeful strain in *Atlanta*'s contemporary setting that points toward the potential to thrive amidst racial instability.

NOTES

1. The capitalization and usage here correspond to the character's identification in the credits. He will simply be called Earn hereafter for the sake of brevity.

2. Seasons 3 and 4 extend the show's depiction of racial performance into new contexts. In particular, "Crank Dat Killer" (s4e6) returns to the notion of a commodified, wearable performance of Blackness in the form of designer sneakers. Similarly, in "Rich Wigga, Poor Wigga" (s3e9), white students don the "accoutrements" of contemporary Blackness—do-rags, hip-hop dance, etc.—to access scholarship money meant only for Black students. Finally, in "White Fashion" (s3e6), Blackness is also a consumable artifact that can be purchased and utilized for any purpose, including legitimizing whiteness and forgiving its transgressions.

3. Other episodes in the second season do likewise. For example, "North of the Border" (s2e9) inverts geographic orientation to travel south from Atlanta to Statesboro, Georgia,

while "Helen" (s2e4) moves outside the city to a quasi-German space that is radically unlike most of the southern United States. The third season, in turn, moves the entire principal cast to several different cities in Europe.

4. Miller Grove High School (located in Dekalb County, Georgia) gets a shout-out in the episode's description on hulu.com.

5. See McGehee.

6. "Rich Wigga, Poor Wigga" likewise examines somewhat older adolescent boys; commodities are used to mark a façade of racial identity, but the people who attempt to pass as Black are quickly sorted out. At the episode's end, though, the main character, Aaron, manages to slide into a veneer of Blackness through sartorial and grooming clichés (as well as the preference for white girls he expresses in the episode's final line). His ease—devoid of either adolescent angst or the burdens and fears of Blackness—betrays his imposture to the audience.

7. For further discussion of this scene and the episode in general, see the essays by Brooks and Nishikawa herein.

8. In "The Goof Who Sat by the Door" (s4e8), a Black Disney employee who is inadvertently promoted to CEO also attempts to create an "authentic" depiction of Blackness through *A Goofy Movie* (1995). It likewise fails, having been bowdlerized by the studio, and the executive disappears.

9. The episode's credits indicate that Teddy Perkins starred "as himself."

"WHAT THE HELL IS MUCKIN'?"

Mistranslation and Linguistic Pessimism in *Atlanta*

LOLA BOORMAN

The first season of *Atlanta* opens with an incident of linguistic misunderstanding. Idling in their car while they negotiate their newly minted manager-client relationship, Earnest "Earn" Marks (Donald Glover) and his cousin Alfred "Paper Boi" Miles (Brian Tyree Henry) are interrupted when a passerby (Renell Gibbs) knocks off their driver's-side mirror. Alfred jumps out of his car to confront the offender, who ignores him and continues to walk away. Finally, Alfred blocks his path, asking: "Don't you hear me talking to you? I'm speakin' English." The conflict continues along linguistic lines when the man—identified in the episode's credits only as "Dude"—recognizes Alfred as Paper Boi and begins to question the meaning of his song's lyrics:

> DUDE: What the hell is muckin', Paper Boi?
> ALFRED: Man, you know what it is, I explain in the hook, n***a. Man, why we even talkin'?

The linguistic breakdown caused by the Dude's rejection of Paper Boi's definition and Alfred's subsequent refusal to translate "muckin'" (a clumsy portmanteau for "massage" and "fucking") is a precursor to more immediate, life-threatening violence as Alfred draws his gun on the mouthy Dude. This opening scene establishes the interlocking relationship between humor and violence that defines *Atlanta*'s aesthetic mode, where distinction between comedy and horror often hangs in an uncomfortable and arbitrary balance. It also establishes a pattern of linguistic untranslatability governing the logic of *Atlanta*'s satire.

This spat between Alfred and the Dude interrupts the negotiation between Earn and Alfred that launches the characters on their very weird, series-spanning ride together toward rap stardom. The linguistic disintegration within this conflict becomes the point of origin—and the site of perpetual malfunction—for *Atlanta*'s various racial, social, political, and economic critiques. But as this scene demonstrates, *Atlanta* refuses to orient its linguistic worldview around a process of code-switching between Black and white vernaculars, between "non-standard" and "standard" forms of English; such strategic fluctuation has been a prominent feature of contemporary Black satirical works. Resisting this familiar opposition, *Atlanta*'s satire emerges instead from repeated instances of linguistic misunderstanding and mistranslation from *within* its enclosed "community."

As Angelica Jade Bastién notes, the show does not "unpack blackness for an audience, white or otherwise, that's unfamiliar with its vernacular" ("In Its Second Season"). Pushing this observation further, I explore how *Atlanta*'s formal rendering of code-switching, competing linguistic systems, and untranslatability ultimately resists the notion of a unified and knowable "vernacular" entirely. Throughout *Atlanta*'s four seasons, we see characters repeatedly collapse into miscommunication as they try to translate their experiences and desires into various socially legible discourses. If traditional satire seeks to provide a corrective to societal ills by asserting, as Maynard Mack suggests, "the validity and necessity of norms, systematic values and meanings that are contained by recognizable codes" (58), then *Atlanta*'s critique of linguistic stability and common meaning exposes those codes as contentious, manipulable, and, often painfully, *un*recognizable. Indeed, *Atlanta* appears to demonstrate the impossibility of generating normative values around a shared language, choosing instead to present what Howard D. Weinbrot identifies as characteristic of the Menippean mode: "a precarious universe of broken or fragile national, cultural, religious, political, or generally intellectual values" (7).

Lisa Guerrero identifies this degenerative function as a defining characteristic of Black satire that "create[s] social narratives about race that expose the fact that there is no shared language or understanding about race in US society. When black subjects attempt to engage these polyglot racial narratives, the result is a state of dissociation" (*Crazy* 17). Guerrero's linguistic metaphor for Black satire's political and affective targets takes on new resonances in light of *Atlanta*'s specific attention to language, grammar, and translation; the incompatibility of various forms of linguistic communication becomes the basis of *Atlanta*'s comedy, but it is also at the root of its pessimistic tenor.

This essay closely examines moments of linguistic exchange and (mis)translation in order to position *Atlanta*'s satire in between competing narratives of optimism and pessimism within the African American literary canon. Does *Atlanta* offer a disconnected grammar of "psychic surrender" (Guerrero, *Crazy* 8) or a new satirical language for registering social and political fragility? I explore how a dynamic of linguistic inclusion and exclusion plays out, interrogating how moments of disagreement on language use and translation form the basis of the show's critiques of the commodification of Black art, social mobility, and gender politics. Incidences of linguistic misunderstanding in *Atlanta* manifest predominantly as various forms of dispossession, which I read in keeping with contemporary scholarship that interprets Black satire as a mode that expresses collective and individual mourning. However, I also look to models of Black multilingual satire, namely Fran Ross's *Oreo* (1974), to consider how such characters as Vanessa "Van" Keefer (Zazie Beetz) use linguistic instability and untranslatability as productive openings for self-expression beyond mourning and as a means of interrogating the show's representations of masculinity.

I take as my starting point Dustin Griffin's claim that Menippean satire adopts dialogue as its principal form (40). This is relevant for *Atlanta* not only because of its sketch-like, character-based structure but also because of how the show foregrounds its interrogation of shared meaning through the breakdown of linguistic norms. Disjuncture and dissonance constitute the affective and intellectual foundations of the Menippean mode, whether it be what Northrop Frye calls its "violent dislocations" or what Mikhail Bakhtin identifies as its "joyful relativity" (qtd. in Weinbrot 11). According to Frye, the Menippean satirist targets the "diseases of the intellect, as a kind of maddened pedantry" (*The Anatomy* 309). As Derek C. Maus suggests in his analysis of Percival Everett's Menippean aesthetics, such satire offers "neither prescription nor solution for the ills it depicts," and in Everett's particular case, these kinds of intellectual deficiencies are "cured by new and more productive uses of one's intellect, rather than simply by following a different set of imposed rules" (*Jesting* 60). The inability to locate meaning in shared moral codes or normative values is significant for theorizing *Atlanta*'s distinct interest in language and miscommunication. The show frequently features moments of linguistic discord in which two competing meanings, discourses, or language systems are placed in tension. Such moments are rarely resolved through an effective or smooth translation from one language (or vernacular) to another or by one definition winning out. Instead, like many Menippean satires, this dialogic mode always ends up in a "stalemate" (Griffin 40).

As my reading of the opening scene suggests, this kind of linguistic "stalemate" structures the relationships among individual characters, institutions, social classes, and racial groups. This pattern also constitutes the show's central relationship between Earn and Alfred. Before Alfred's confrontation with the Dude (which both opens the episode and recurs as its chronological end point), Alfred dismisses Earn's request to manage Paper Boi. Their disagreement arises out of their contrasting etymologies for the word "manage":

ALFRED: Manage. You know where the word "manage" come from?
EARN: *Manus*, Latin for "hand."
ALFRED: Probably, but I'm gonna say no for the purpose of my argument: "manage" come from the word "man," and that ain't really your lane.

What initially appears to be a simple and predictable "dis" also hints at a more complex linguistic confrontation that reveals how *Atlanta*'s satire is derived from a breakdown of consensus. Alfred doesn't deny that Earn's definition is correct, but he instead asserts that correctness is beside the point; what matters is the manipulation of language for "the purpose of [the] argument." When he breaks "manage" down to what he considers its root ("man"), Alfred mirrors Earn's etymological logic yet refuses to translate the word through Latin to access its underlying, historical meaning. Confining Alfred's definition to "man" is not just a way of setting up the characters' misguided conceptions of masculinity but also signals that resistance to translation and interpretation will be a motif in *Atlanta*'s satirical technique. Although Alfred's armchair etymology descends into a punchline, the linguistic affinities between the two definitions and their aural resonances again present the problem of linguistic consensus and ultimately label Earn as hopelessly unmanagerial, regardless of his reply. What Alfred needs, he says, is "a Malcolm," whereas Earn is just "too Martin." This analogy places Alfred and Earn's disagreement about language within the context of a broader search for consensus that defined much of twentieth-century African American political struggle. More pointedly, however, it evokes a Black rhetorical tradition against which these problems of definition play out. Rejecting both Malcolm X and Martin Luther King Jr. as linguistic, political, or masculine touchstones, Earn instead offers to be a "silent wildcard." Earn's refusal of (or perhaps indifference toward) the dichotomous presentation of Black masculinity and political agency conveyed through the opposition of these two historical figures manifests in the realm of language; Earn's silence stands in stark contrast to the oratorical traditions evoked by the references to both "Martin" and "Malcolm." The Black rhetorical tradition is first called upon and then usurped, albeit with nothing except silence to take its place.

This interaction among linguistic stalemate, mistranslation, and silence becomes a defining feature in *Atlanta*'s style and articulates both its allegiances to and its divergences from other Black satirical works. Alfred's and Earn's degenerative evocation of the Black political and rhetorical tradition in this scene suggests a logic of "signifyin(g)" as Henry Louis Gates Jr. theorized it in *The Signifying Monkey* (1989). For Gates, African American literary works are always already ironic and "double voiced" (*The Signifying Monkey* 19); they are textual "mulattoes" (17) that speak simultaneously—if also differently—to

Black and white readers. Black texts "revise" both the African American literary tradition and the Western canon, repeating recognizable tropes "with a black difference" (17). Although Gates's analysis focuses on the intertextual relationships of revision and repetition *within* the Black tradition, his presentation of Black writing *as difference* mapped out a fundamental dissonance between Black and white linguistic and literary modes. For Gates and for the Black writers he explores, Blackness is "not an absolute or metaphysical condition . . . nor it is some transcending essence that exists outside of its manifestations in texts. Rather, the 'blackness' of black American literature can be discerned only through close readings. By 'blackness' here I mean specific uses of literary language that are shared, repeated, critiqued, and revised" (139).

Atlanta troubles such identification of the Black text as inherently "double voiced," instead resisting a straightforward opposition between Blackness and whiteness and becoming deliberately unwieldy in its polyvocality. Unlike immediate contemporaries playing on the intersections between linguistic and racial doubleness, *Atlanta*'s satire does not emerge from the tension between Black articulation and white understanding as it does in *Key & Peele*'s recurrent "Obama's Anger Translator" sketches, Spike Lee's *BlacKkKlansman* (2018), and Boots Riley's *Sorry to Bother You* (2018), in the latter of which the protagonist's (played by LaKeith Stanfield) ability to "use [his] white voice" transforms him from a lowly telemarketer into an elite "power caller."[1] Characters in *Atlanta* do not "translate" for a white audience; in fact, they frequently ensure that the racialized presumptions underlying white speech acts are made unnervingly legible (for example, Dave's overly relaxed use of the *n*-word with Earn in "The Big Bang"). *Atlanta*'s episodes are instead "born translated," to use Rebecca Walkowitz's terminology (*Born Translated* passim). Born-translated texts move beyond Bakhtinian heteroglossia, encompassing a multiplicity of "multiregional, continental, and planetary" languages at "even greater scale[s]" (24). Such texts do not seek to "expand belonging" but "striv[e] to keep belonging in play" (25). By adopting a sense of "internal multilingualism" (42), born-translated works make English perpetually foreign. This state of being always already translated helps to navigate *Atlanta*'s tonal strangeness (season 3, the bulk of which takes place in a variety of European cities, is a particularly good example of this), but it also offers a way to theorize the show's structure of dialogic stalemate as a form of mistranslation or untranslatability, in which the untranslated represents "what one keeps on (not) translating" (Cassin xvii). The show features numerous moments of loaded silence—e.g., the strange interaction with a student in whiteface after Van is fired from her job in the wake of owning up to smoking weed in "Value" (s1e6); as Darius's drives away at the end of "Teddy Perkins" (s2e6); as Alfred realizes that the kids he thought were fans are about to mug him in "Woods" (s2e8); as Alfred refuses to talk to Earn about the violent encounter with the feral hog in "Andrew Wyeth: Alfred's World" (s4e9)—that represent a refusal to translate, to live in partial knowing and perpetual alienation. Such scenes echo Gates's contention that "if to communicate is an essential and social function of all language, so is to conceal, to leave unspoken, to mask" (*Figures* 171).

This constant state of translatability—and the social and political slippages that it causes—correlates with what Walkowitz calls a "postlingual" condition:

> Migrant writers no longer agree that possessing a dominant language is the best way of contesting the multilingualism and racism of national literatures. . . . They are unpossessing languages; repudiating the goals of fluency and comprehension, including their own. . . . Unpossessing involves veering away from the rhetoric of permission and obligation: who can use a language, who has to use a language, how many languages one may use, and what competent or proper use looks like. It also involves shifting from monolingual expertise to gradations of fluency across and within several languages. ("On Not Knowing" 323–24)

A similar kind of "unpossession" takes place in *Atlanta*, but it does not result in what Walkowitz describes as an experience of "linguistic hospitality" (234). Unpossession complicates the politics of linguistic mastery at play in African American cultural traditions, which privileges, on the one hand, code-switching, linguistic trickery or mimicry, verbal sparring, rhetorical misdirection, and, on the other, the notion of linguistic authenticity associated with Black vernacular English. Unpossession rejects the logic that the speaker can and should master as many codes as possible. But in *Atlanta*, rather than leading to an openness of linguistic registers, unpossession takes on a distinctly pessimistic tone as our characters find themselves in a world where mastery over various codes and discourses no longer matters and where any attempt to use language results only in widespread *dis*possession. This pattern of linguistic unmooring structures what Sheri Harrison compellingly describes as the aesthetics of "the new black Gothic" in which texts interweave horror with comedy in rendering the "inescapability and the eschewal of hope for the future" and the "near-constant vulnerability of black life."

Atlanta uses the stylistic trappings of translation—for example, the subtitles in "The Club" (s1e8)—to advance a foreignizing and defamiliarizing vibe that leaves both the characters and viewers in a consistent state of partial incomprehension. In *Atlanta*'s world, whiteness is perpetually trying to translate itself into Blackness, cannibalizing and commodifying it. We witness white characters either trying to assimilate themselves into and/or appropriate Black discourse—e.g., Dave, the aforementioned radio DJ (Griffin Freeman); Craig

Allen (Rick Holmes) via his spoken-word performance in "Juneteenth" (s1e9); the parasitic "Socks," who insinuates himself into Paper Boi's crew in "The Old Man and the Tree" (s3e3) and incomprehensibly reps himself as "the white Liam Neeson" in "Cancer Attack" (s3e5); the various YWAs (young white avatars) that Paper Boi and his Black rapper colleagues cultivate in "Born 2 Die" (s4e3)[2]—or remaining largely silent, like Clark County's white manager, Lucas (Matthew Barnes), who functions as a mute symbol for white mobility, power, and influence. Non-English languages present themselves on the periphery, as in the cases, for example, of Drake's absurdly fictional Mexican *abuelo* (Carlos Guerrero), who resides in the basement of his Atlanta mansion in "Champagne Papi" (s2e7), or the man identified in the credits only as "Crying Chinese Bro" (Talbott Lin), who is briefly shown sobbing and shouting hysterically into his cell phone in Mandarin midway through "The Streisand Effect" (s1e4). Although these languages occur at the show's spatial and narrative margins, their nature confounds interpretation, which helps scuttle the interrelated possibilities of conventionally coherent storytelling and mutual understanding. These untranslated foreign languages also gesture toward the invisible dynamics of untranslatability and dispossession at play both within English and within the supposed linguistic "community," which presents itself as persistently foreign both to the viewer and to the show's central characters who help construct it.

Therefore, while *Atlanta* is a "born-translated" text, it uses the techniques and effects of (mis)translation to help generate its darkly comic tone. The connection (or, more accurately, the disconnection) between language and various forms of racial, political, and economic dispossession is thrown into stark relief at various points across the first two seasons: from the indecipherable glossolalia of a detention center's processing area in "Streets on Lock" (s1e2) to the malfunctioning wireless sound system at a streaming service's corporate office that is incompatible with Earn's phone in "Sportin' Waves" (s2e2) to almost all of the utterances by the delightfully unfiltered and untranslatable Darius, such as this one from "The Big Bang":

> DARIUS: Hey, look, I know you don't know me . . . My name's Darius. Um, I was just wondering, could I measure your tree?
> EARN'S FATHER [Isiah Whitlock Jr.]: No, not right now.
> DARIUS: Not right now? That basically means no, man.

Atlanta parallels *Sorry to Bother You* in relying on a tragicomic formula of translation between Black and white discourses, particularly in circumstances in which white dialects are closely tied to narratives of social or economic mobility.

Already in "The Big Bang," language is closely aligned with financial gain. When we first meet Earn, he is working on commission, signing people up for credit cards at the Atlanta airport. In fact, though, Earn is *not* working in this scene because his work depends on his ability to engage a customer in conversation, in generating dialogue. Earn's labor and his value is, therefore, constituted by and contingent on his ability to communicate effectively. Earn's attempts to engage passersby result in violent verbal rejection. One man even tells Earn to "fuck off," to which Earn responds, "I know, right?" Earn paradoxically negates his own original speech act through his overly animated affirmation of the man's hostility. The extended silence that follows renders a profound and abject humiliation that is untranslatable, at once deeply private and crushingly public, schadenfreude mixed with shame, disgust, and exhaustion. This abortive dialogue has a knock-on effect in Earn's conversation with his coworker, Swiff (Harold House Moore), whose almost incomprehensible monologue about his night at the club hums in the background of Earn's tortured silence: "That was just rude man. Hey yo . . . Compound was lit last night. Man, my cousin had, like eight bottles up in that bitch. They found with, like, three ho's a piece, my n**. Shit was crazy. . . . Earn? Earn?" Earn's inability to "possess" language here leads directly to his economic dispossession, which is itself (re)framed by Swiff's narrative of excess and consumption.

The relationship between language and money plays out most legibly in the characters' relationship to rap, here viewed not as a form of artistic expression or as a political statement but merely as a way to "get paid." In its representations of Alfred's career, and the music industry more generally, *Atlanta* strips rap of its power and significance as a linguistically dexterous and subversive social form. Rap has long been considered a politically and linguistically subversive art form in its ability to use "signifyin(g)" and coded languages to "tur[n] the stereotypes of black and white American culture on their heads" (Gates, "2 Live Crew," A23). More recently, critics have suggested that rap has played into the same market forces it once sought to parody, presenting a version of authenticity that conforms to the commercialization of Blackness in the mainstream (Nishikawa 38). Kinohi Nishikawa identifies a group of contemporary "hip hop satirists" (including Glover's own exemplary alter ego, Childish Gambino) "who lampoon, ironize, and otherwise point up the folly of society's hegemonic understanding of rap" and "advanc[e] the funniest, and often most profound, critique of rap's investment in 'keeping it real'" (39).

Atlanta works in a similar mode, but the show accomplishes its censure by evacuating rap of its creative, linguistic potential and thereby exposing it as nothing more than a commodified and commercialized discourse. The finer points of Alfred's musical artistry often remain in the background with the exception of the opening confrontation with the Dude, in which the clumsy and ineffectual nature of Paper Boi's wordplay is painfully evident. The Dude's close reading of Paper Boi's rap exposes its lack of invention and the one-dimensionality of its sexual innuendo. Wordplay and literariness become objects of suspicion, particularly when they serve an obvious commercial purpose. Suspicion of commodified Blackness takes place in a radically different context in "Juneteenth" as Earn surveys the bizarre range of cocktails on offer at a ritzy party hosted by a mixed-race couple: "Emancipation Eggnog... it's June." His mutterings are interrupted by a Black bartender, who has, until now, maintained a professional, if also detached, attitude: "N***a, do I got to explain alliteration? Hmm?" As with Alfred's lyrics, a facile attempt at linguistic creativity is here implicated in systems of commodification, threatening to permanently blur the boundary between art and kitsch.

The linguistic flatness of Alfred's rap is intensified by one of the show's most recognizable hooks, the catchy refrain from Paper Boi's mixtape which recurs and repeats throughout seasons 1 and 2: "Paper Boi, Paper Boi, all about that Paper Boi." This refrain is repetitive and empty in both its initial suggestion of success and its later signification of fame's meaninglessness. Moreover, the linguistic conventionality and inelegance of the chorus, in which "paper" signifies a deadening confluence of money and textuality, exposes Alfred's persona as a rapper to be paper-thin.

The literary and philosophical hollowness of Alfred's rap—at one point in "B.A.N." (s1e7) he confesses, "I don't think about what I'm rapping half the time. Look, I'm just tryna get paid"—reaches its logical conclusion in Paper Boi's rival, Clark County, whose vapid hit single, "YooHoo," retreats even further away from linguistic complexity into a form of hip hop that is always already commodified. As suggested in "Sportin' Waves" (s2e2), the song seemingly originates as an advertisement for a chocolate-flavored drink that exemplifies what Bastién calls Clark County's "brand of unthreatening black cool" ("*Atlanta*'s Silly Yoo-hoo") and the implications of that brand in a white financial and creative system. It seems almost irrelevant that the song denigrates the very beverage it is intended to be marketing as "dirty Sprite" and is replete with corny insinuations (for example, "Saw your baby mama like... Yoo-hoo... and then I sent her home with a good night") that fit awkwardly, at best, into a soft-drink advertisement; ultimately, the words don't sell Yoo-hoo, but Clark County's curated image does. Alfred's somewhat lesser (at this point in the series) degree of fame is likewise sparked not by the quality of his music but by his "hard" persona, which marks him as one of the "last real rappers," according to a waiter who uncomfortably praises him thusly after he is arrested in connection with the shooting ambiguously depicted in "The Big Bang." Throughout the series, the linguistic content of rap is completely submerged by its social and commercial effect, which demands—as a reporter makes clear to him in "Nobody Beats the Biebs" (s1e5)—that Alfred "play [his] part" as the "asshole" rapper if he hopes to make any "paper" within the commodified hierarchies of the music business.[3]

Atlanta's preoccupation with (mis)translation and linguistic dispossession are most palpable and revealing in "Helen" (s2e4), which focuses on the unravelling relationship between Van and Earn against the uncanny backdrop of a carnivalesque German Fastnacht celebration. "Helen" places issues of language front and center both as a means of generating the show's characteristic tonal blend between comedy and horror and, more crucially, as way of exploring Van's linguistic *repossession* of her various, often-conflicting identities. In "Helen," Van assumes control, if not mastery, over various language games in ways that destabilize the prevailing pessimism of *Atlanta*'s worldview. Van's ability to move between languages—as well as between gendered and racialized roles and identities—not only unsettles representations of Blackness and whiteness but also offers a corrective to *Atlanta*'s predominantly masculine logic, complicating and mediating the show's linguistic cynicism.[4]

The episode's emphasis on Van's linguistic and racial hybridity resonates with another great work of bilingual satire, Fran Ross's novel *Oreo* (1974). A postmodern retelling of the myth of Theseus, the novel follows its mixed-race protagonist, Christine (a.k.a. "Oreo"), as she engages in a series of absurd, erudite, and utterly confounding language games in order to reveal the "secret of her birth" to a Black mother and an estranged Jewish father (Ross 8). As Marlon James—himself a producer of linguistically fecund fiction—notes in the preface to the novel's 2018 reissue edition, *Oreo* often reads "as the smartest and wildest conversation you've ever had" (x). Told through a heady mix of "Yidlish," Black dialect, Wittgensteinian proverbs, etymological jokes, mathematical formulas, and advertising jargon, the novel transforms various cultural lingua francas into "unrepresentable . . . heteroglossia[s]" (Mullen 113). Christine/Oreo becomes, as Tru Leverette argues, a "traveler, translator, and mediator," who is not interested in translating for her audience but, instead, in weaving together a constantly shifting language that expresses "the various possibilities of being two together" ("Traveling Identities" 80).

While elsewhere in *Atlanta* the kind of linguistic experimentation that occurs in *Oreo* only furthers an overall degeneration of social consensus, "Helen" walks the line between linguistic empowerment and dispossession, a process that manifests in Van's role as a reluctant and selective translator. "Helen" offers a rare view of Earn and Van's relationship in isolation from the show's usual cast of characters and outside of the geographical boundaries of urban Atlanta.[5] The couple travels to the actual northeastern Georgia town of Helen, where, for reasons that remain unexplained, Van has been attending a German-language Fastnacht since she was a child. A few hours into the evening, Van reflects on her racial identity in a conversation with her mixed-race childhood friend Christina (who is in a relationship with a white man):

> VAN: I don't know why you have to introduce me as Lottie's mom. You know my first name. . . .
> CHRISTINA: But you make that shit look good. Like, it's different for you.
> VAN: What do you . . . what do you mean?
> CHRISTINA: You know, it just seems like something that you're more ready for.
> VAN: What do you mean?
> CHRISTINA: Because . . . you know, like, you chose Earn. I chose Dave.
> VAN: Mm-hmm.
> CHRISTINA: Yeah, like, since we were kids. Like, I chose white. You chose black.

Van's linguistic oscillation between English and German in the episode also positions her between Black and white cultural spaces and delineates the stark gender expectations that both cultural positions entail. Christina's wider implication is that Van "chose" to become a young mother, something she associates clearly with her relationship with Earn and her "Blackness." Throughout the episode, however, Van resists these attempts to fix her within a specific racial and cultural identity, using her linguistic in-betweenness as a means of being "two together," like Christine/Oreo.

From Earn's perspective, the episode makes the show's logic of linguistic dispossession painfully literal. Earn spends the episode in a cycle of perpetual incomprehension, fully dependent on Van to translate not only the German that is spoken among the festivalgoers but also the bizarre customs and traditions of the celebration—and the surreal events that haunt its margins. Earn's linguistic insecurity is tightly linked to the racial discomfort that Earn feels as one of only three Black people in the room[6]; one tipsy attendee even briefly assumes he is in blackface because, as Van has warned him in advance, the festival traditionally features a "Moor."

Another dimension of his verbal anxiety, though, involves the sexual dynamics of his and Van's relationship. The episode begins with Earn performing oral sex on Van in her apartment in Atlanta. In the car on their way to Fastnacht, Van suggests Earn smoke weed next time because it may give him more "tongue confidence." Although this comment works simultaneously to assert Van's sexual agency and to destabilize Earn's,[7] it also prefigures Earn's more direct and explicit linguistic marginalization later in the episode. Whenever Earn attempts to reassert control of his surroundings at the Fastnacht festival, his contributions invariably lead to uncomfortable stalemates. For example, a long and clearly flirtatious conversation in German between Van and a handsome bartender is not subtitled, leaving both Earn and the presumably sizable non-German-speaking portion of the audience suspended in unknowing. As occurs elsewhere in *Atlanta*, Earn's attempt to reclaim social and linguistic mastery manifests as an act of economic repossession; he interjects abruptly: "Ding, ding. How about some service?" In keeping with his experience throughout the show, his failed assertion of economic and social dominance serves only to solidify his alienation from both the festival crowd and Van, a point she drives home by telling him "you really should learn German."

Against the eerie carnivalesque quality of Fastnacht, Earn struggles in "Helen" to master the rules of various literal and figurative games as his immediate linguistic incomprehension becomes a stand in for his gross misunderstanding of his relationship with Van. The episode degenerates into a series of competing and obscure rituals, from the incomprehensible parlor game that involves bouncing a ball around a plastic cup and which Earn unexpectedly wins when he ignores Van's advice to "follow her lead" to the more sinister *Schnappviecher* (an anonymous and silent figure dressed in a wolf suit) who steals from one unlucky festivalgoer each year (this year Van is his victim).[8] The episode is punctuated by two climactic moments in Van and Earn's unravelling relationship, both of which play out over competitive games of ping-pong. While the first game represents Earn's attempt to regain control over his surroundings and of Van, given he believes he'll have the upper hand, it quickly becomes a proxy for Van's autonomous expression. The second game takes place after a conversation between Van and the German bartender (subtitled this time) and after Van reclaims her phone from the *Schnappviecher*. Before they play, Van asks Earn what he wants from their relationship; when he doesn't give a direct answer, she both states what she wants and makes the termination of their relationship contingent on her winning the game.

Van's growing sense of "tongue confidence" derives from her role as translator, from her ability to adapt to and assimilate various codes, linguistic or otherwise. Unlike Earn and Alfred—each of whom is repeatedly displaced and silenced by language—Van's linguistic fluidity in "Helen" affords her ownership over her racial identity and her sexual agency. The episode, in many ways, intentionally mirrors "Juneteenth," which also centers on the dynamics of Van and Earn's relationship during an awkward outing. In an inversion of the opening of "Helen," the episode begins with Earn waking up beside an unknown naked woman just before he gets picked up by Van to go to an elaborate Juneteenth celebration at the home of a wealthy interracial couple. Van and Earn, who plays up his as-yet-incomplete time at Princeton, pretend to be married in order to project an air of middle-class respectability that Van thinks will gain her greater opportunities in this influential social circle.

In this episode, however, it is Earn (ironically rebranded as "Earnest") who wields the linguistic currency, slipping into a mimicry of bougie qualities and its attendant social capital.

Like "Helen," this episode offers an uncomfortable confrontation with class and whiteness, but Van is far less in control of her language and identity in "Juneteenth." In their conversations with various party guests, Van generally follows Earn's verbal cues. In one particular scene, she directly repeats his sentences in a vain attempt to convince their interlocutor, a quintessential bougie matriarch, that they are not only highly cultured but also a cohesive couple:

EARN: We were just saying this the other day . . .
EARN AND VAN: [Stammering] The quality of theatre . . .
EARN: . . . is just gone
VAN: . . . is just not there . . .
EARN: . . . it's just not there . . .
VAN: . . . anymore.
EARN: It's just not there.

Here, Earn initiates and originates the couple's joint response only to appropriate Van's words as his own. In "Juneteenth," Earn functions not only as an interpreter of middle-class cultural capital but also subsumes Van's speech into his performance. Although attending the party does not achieve Van's desired result, it does end with the couple finding common ground in mocking the party's many pretensions and having sex in her car on the way home. This is a marked contrast to "Helen," which started with Earn performing oral sex on Van but which ended with Van foreclosing any further possibility of intimacy with Earn; their relationship moving forward will seemingly be defined by the comparatively mundane details of transporting their daughter to and from school (a dynamic that only changes after significant upheaval for both of them in seasons 3 and 4).

Van's ability to move between languages in "Helen" offers a fleeting and unsatisfactory return to older, more optimistic accounts of code-switching and linguistic invention as a form of power and self-expression. But, like other moments of self-affirmation in *Atlanta*, it remains marred by cynicism and sadness.[9] Van's act of claiming her independence from Earn results in what Joseph Winters might call a form of "melancholic hope" (17), in which the discourses of optimism and pessimism, progress and mourning are irrevocably intertwined. Although Van and Earn reach a kind of consensus at the end of "Helen," it is born out of a fundamental, irreparable misunderstanding. *Atlanta*'s linguistic pessimism emerges from this complex double bind, in which the true cost of repairing and transcending such misunderstandings, of being heard, of translating oneself from one language into another is profoundly and painfully felt by the show's central characters.

NOTES

1. Recent Black-authored literary works that tread similar ground satirically include such works as Colson Whitehead's *Apex Hides the Hurt* (2006) and *Sag Harbor* (2009), Danzy Senna's *New People* (2017), and Mateo Askaripour's *Black Buck* (2021).

2. In "White Fashion" (s3e6) this impulse is taken to its logical conclusion when Alfred is asked to join a "diversity advisory committee" for a popular streetwear brand embroiled in self-inflicted racial controversy, having produced an item of clothing that seems to reference the "Central Park Five" without any understanding of that term's historical significance. For the board, comprised of Black influencers and artists (and some white imposters) this is not an opportunity to make change in the fashion industry but a meal ticket for extending their own fame and capitalizing on free samples. Alfred's idea for a "Re-Invest in Your Hood" campaign, for which he records as a video pitch, is quickly co-opted and becomes the soundtrack to a "colorblind" advertisement featuring a compendium of stylized minorities.

3. For further discussion of this episode and this theme, see the essays by Britt and Cortes herein.

4. Beetz's biography amplifies this episode's interrogation of essentialist notions of whiteness and Blackness. The uncanny whiteness of the somewhat German town of Helen, Georgia, is focalized largely through Earn's paranoid perspective, but both the town and Earn's view of it are destabilized by Van's ability to occupy both cultural positions (and Beetz's ability to portray this flexibility credibly). Born in Berlin to a German father and an African American mother, Beetz effectively reflects Van's idiosyncratic ties to Fastnacht, which, in the episode itself, are a source of its surreal and "untranslatable" tone.

5. For further discussion of this episode and Van in general, see the essays by Parks, Morgan, and Cortes herein.

6. This anxiety is revisited by Earn's disclosure to his therapist in "The Homeliest Little Horse" (s4e2) that he felt isolated and out of place at Princeton because of being "one of twelve Black kids" there.

7. One is reminded of Alfred's comment from the pilot episode about Earn's relationship to being a "man."

8. It also transpires that Fastnacht is largely a game to be won, seemingly through a traditional German dance competition. This is the first year that Van, the self-proclaimed "Serena Williams" of the festival ("they hate, but they can't deny the stats"), has not won the trophy, her loss of which occurred because of her fight with Earn. Instead, the trophy is won by Christina's white boyfriend, Dave, who, according to Van, "can't dance for shit."

9. In "Tarrare" (s3e10), Van's linguistic competence—she can also speak French—facilitates her attempted erasure of self as she seeks to leave her old life in Atlanta behind. Her desire to be "like Amelie" leads her astray as she becomes a chef for a strange cult of hand eaters (another reference to *manus*, perhaps?) in Paris, which includes Alexander Skarsgård among its members.

IRONIC MINSTRELSIES OF AFFECT IN *ATLANTA*

PHILLIP JAMES MARTINEZ CORTES

In *Atlanta*, the figure of the minority ironically embodies the figure of the minstrel. Donald Glover's series features minority characters, such as the rising rapper Alfred "Paper Boi" Miles (Brian Tyree Henry) and the single mother and middle-school teacher Vanessa "Van" Keefer (Zazie Beetz), who are pursuing meaningful lives by subversively imitating the racist minstrelsy roles that pervade public and private discourse. *Atlanta* reveals that the nineteenth- and early twentieth-century tradition of minstrelsy governs the social codes and expectations of diverse contemporary contexts, such as the music industry and educational institutions in which Alfred and Vanessa, respectively, work. As a result, minstrelsy promulgates a sacrificial discourse that exchanges empathetic sensitivity for minorities' lived emotional experiences in favor of unempathetically coercing them into acting as passionately unhinged objects. *Atlanta* imagines the inclusive possibilities of irony wherein minority characters embody minstrelsy's emotional minimalism as well as its stereotyped emotional excess to build affectively recuperative and resistant moments, which are otherwise excluded by contemporary minstrelsy.

Traditional minstrelsy enforces this regime of affective sacrifice through pictorial representations or actors in blackface makeup exaggerating African Americans' physical features into stereotyped, negative behaviors of excess.[1] Luvena Kopp argues, "Black stereotypes function as symbolic forms that configure a white supremacist national mythology" (215). Scholars such as Kopp, Derek Conrad Murray, and Danielle Fuentes Morgan (among others) show how African American artists unsettle this racist mythology. Kopp analyzes the ways that Spike Lee's *Bamboozled* (2000) "spotlights the interchangeability of racial [and minstrel show] categories by having his main black character, Delacroix, act stereotypically white and his main white character, Dunwitty, act stereotypically black," achieving, in turn, "a denaturalization of the racial concept and its hierarchical order" (221–20). Similar to Kopp's conclusion regarding the "interchangeability of racial categories," Murray demonstrates that the visual art of Glenn Ligon envisions a "post-Black" aesthetic whose "malleability" reveals the "inability [to] fully encapsulate the complexity of the African-American experience" (*Queering* 30). These scholars' claims of "racial interchangeability" and "post-Black malleability" anticipate Morgan's contention that African American minstrel actors of the nineteenth and early twentieth centuries implemented an "ironic emancipatory performance" of adopting "negative stereotypes of Blackness . . . while negotiating a sophisticated critique of the oppressor" (*Laughing* 15).[2] The ironic minstrels of *Atlanta* may amuse the gatekeepers of national affect and may cause them to justify their own need to police the affective comportment of minorities, but at an ironic level, their performances fortify, rather than sacrifice, their emotional worlds.

Extending these scholars' accounts, I approach *Atlanta*'s ironic minstrelsies through affect theory. I argue that *Atlanta* contends with the white "national affect" of minimal empathy associated with traditional and contemporary minstrelsy. In making this claim, I adapt José Esteban Muñoz's analysis of the affective performances in Latino/a drama. Muñoz identifies majoritarian affects as the " 'official' national affect, a mode of being in the world primarily associated with white middle-class subjectivity" that "reads most ethnic affect as inappropriate" (69). Muñoz explains that "the affective performance of normative whiteness is minimalist to the point of emotional impoverishment" and that the "affective code" of whiteness reads ethnic others as bound to express "affective excess" (69, 70). Even though this "affective code" judges Latino/a dramatic performances as excessive, Muñoz contends that minoritarian perspectives envision them as "decidedly dissident in relation to structuring codes of US national affect" (78). The "US national affect" relevantly describes minstrelsy's affective investment in preserving what Brian Roberts calls the racial hierarchy that elevates "whiteness and moral respectability" (20). Muñoz's framework has applications for interrogating the relationship between the sacrificial discourse of modern minstrelsy and the performative actions of Black and minority persons in *Atlanta*. The series portrays characters challenging minstrelsy's exclusive national affect because these characters inclusively embody both minstrelsy's white minimalism and its stereotyped Black affective excess to forge tentative yet recuperative relationships with their inner selves.

I treat irony as inviting both exclusive and inclusive modes of interpretation. Irony is generally defined as a rhetorical figure of speech wherein "the intended meaning is the antithesis of the literal meaning of the words used" (Macey 206) such that this antithesis creates, as Ross C. Murfin and Supryia M. Ray put it, "a contradiction or incongruity between appearance or expectation and reality"

(251). Such approaches result in unequal binaries wherein an interpreter understands irony through an exclusive method that privileges what is perceived as the intended reality over the surface meaning. In certain respects, minstrelsy's national affect evokes such an exclusivist reading of irony; it innately rejects the empathetic understanding of minorities as affectively complex beings in favor of a forced nonempathetic interpretation of them as affectively excessive caricatures. Racist hierarchies impose regimes of such exclusive ironies, wherein the national affect's desire for minstrel tropes is a conditional affect rooted in coercion. In *Atlanta*, there are indeed characters who primarily embody minstrelsy's exclusive brand of irony, and my analysis of the show's depiction of an African American version of Justin Bieber (Austin Crute) in "Nobody Beats the Biebs" (s1e5) exemplifies the extent and purpose of its role within *Atlanta*'s broader discourse on race.³

In contrast to the impoverishing irony of conventional minstrelsy, though, a relationally inclusive version of irony can richly incorporate oppositions. Linda Hutcheon introduces this latter form of irony by stating that "ironic meaning comes into being as the consequence of a relationship, a dynamic, performative bringing together of different meaning-makers, but also of different meanings, first, in order to create something new and . . . to endow it with the critical edge of judgment" (58). Hutcheon formulates irony as an "inclusive (both/and)" technique wherein the superficial and intended meanings are not antithetical but rather work together to create an ironic meaning that is "*simultaneously* double (or multiple)" (58, 60, emphasis original).⁴ The power of inclusive irony, therefore, rests in how its gesturing toward multiplicity affords the ironist opportunities to transform the incorporated meanings into new meanings. In theory, inclusive irony can be endlessly generative and semantically fluid.

In the following analysis, I examine the exclusively affective ironies of Black Bieber and the inclusively affective ironies performed by Alfred and Van. Despite making this distinction, I acknowledge that the two kinds of irony can and do overlap with each other since both Alfred's and Van's appropriations of tropes related to minstrelsy inevitably import and signify upon these tropes' exclusivist origins. Nevertheless, my distinction serves as a heuristic by which my discussion can juxtapose these two characters' respective subversions of minstrelsy. Whereas Alfred's ironic minstrelsy responds to the minstrel types of the "c**n" and the "brute," Van's ironic minstrelsy addresses the patriarchal expectations implicit in the "m*mmy" character and the ideal of the "strong Black woman." Their distinctive performances collectively estrange contemporary minstrelsy's sacrificial logic, exposing in turn the fictiveness and tenuousness of racial stereotypes.

Among the stock characters from minstrelsy that Black Bieber emulates is the docile c**n. Ronald Jackson II informs us that this character type includes the "youthful and unaware pickan***y" and the "complacent storytelling Uncle

Remus" and that all representatives of this category "embodied the most overtly hurtful stereotypes of Blacks as innately inferior, lazy, shiftless, illiterate fools" (31). In "Nobody Beats the Biebs," Black Bieber's exclusivity is evident in how he performs the happy-go-lucky, youthful, and obedient pickan***y version of the c**n.[5]

While playing in a charity basketball game, Alfred and Bieber have an on-court altercation, which is at least partly related to Alfred's (mis)perception that he has been invited to play because of his self-identification as "a legend at two games" (rapping and basketball). Upon entering the venue where the game is to be played, Alfred even approaches a television journalist named Valencia Joyner (Paloma Guzmán) with a flirtatious and presumptuous suggestion: "You should go ahead and interview me now 'cause I'ma be MVP of this thing." Her nonplussed reaction does little to dampen his ardor, even when she refers back to an incident from the show's pilot:

> VALENCIA JOYNER: Oh, I know who you are. You're the guy who shot someone.
> ALFRED: See what . . . see, well, it ain't really happen like that. You know what I'm saying? The internet, it just run with stories, so. So, you need to get to know the real me.
> VALENCIA JOYNER: Oh, yeah?
> ALFRED: Oh, yeah, yeah. Look, I'll even let you interview me somewhere fly like Benihanas.

Needless to say, she does not accept his invitation and Alfred fails to recognize that neither she nor her television audience nor the crowd at the game has any interest in knowing "the real [him]." The eventual on-court confrontation between Alfred and Bieber arises both from Alfred's frustration at what he sees as Bieber's unjustified monopolizing of both the ball and the crowd's esteem during the game and from Bieber's self-absorbed mugging for the cameras at Alfred's expense beforehand:

> REPORTER: You look like you're ready for the game.
> [Bieber puts his hand in the Reporter's face]
> JUSTIN BIEBER: [Turning toward the assembled crowd] I'm gonna dunk on a bitch!
> ALFRED: I don't like this n***a.

After the two trash-talk and show each other up repeatedly on the court, Bieber finally metaphorically hits Alfred below the belt by calling him "broke in real life and basketball." Alfred responds by fouling Bieber brutally as the latter drives to the basket—potentially to dunk, and thereby transitively suggesting that Alfred is a "bitch"—and the two begin pushing, screaming, and wrestling as their teammates and a shocked crowd look on.

At a press conference after the game, Bieber demonstrates the conciliatory aspects of his pickan***ny façade when he declares before the press: "I just want to say, um, sorry about what happened today. It's not who I am. I guess I been trying to be so cool. . . . This is the real Justin. I'm not a bad guy. I actually love Christ. I guess I've just been hanging out with the wrong people." As soon as his speech ends, he transitions to singing from his forthcoming album "Justice,"[6] the soundtrack of which plays in the background. His audience of reporters and members of the press are enchanted by his apologetic speech and upbeat song. The exclusive minstrelsy of Bieber emerges in the ways that his claims to revealing "the real Justin" and loving Christ as well as his c**n-like subservience to the press become absorbed into his promotion of both his commercial album and his personal brand.

His exclusively ironic usage of "real" and "actually" reveals otherwise that his affective "love" is artificial and ultimately transactional. And as part of this performative exchange, he separates himself from "cool" and "wrong people," code words that within the context of the episode refer to the excessively physical "asshole" or "thug" minstrel types that rappers like Alfred are made out to be. The episode's title takes on another meaning in this light, given its play on the title of rapper Biz Markie's 1988 single "Nobody Beats the Biz," which itself puns on a well-known advertisement for a New York electronics store. *Atlanta*'s revision of Biz Markie's title suggests that Bieber's ascendancy is attributable largely to having commodified himself as a caricature from minstrelsy.

The media's role in reifying this distinction is made explicit as Alfred again tries to proposition Valencia Joyner for some reparative publicity:

> ALFRED: Hey, look, I just want to apologize to people, you know, for how I was acting. Think they got the wrong idea of me. Maybe . . . you can interview me sometime? Get to know the real me.
>
> VALENCIA JOYNER: Listen, I want to give you some advice. Play your part. People don't want Justin to be the asshole. They want you to be the asshole. You're a rapper. That's your job.

Bieber's performance thus echoes, albeit in euphemistic terms, the national affect's prejudice against the aberrantly "cool" affects of certain minorities, even as *Atlanta*'s Black version of him both literally and performatively embodies them at times. In these respects, Black Bieber performs ironically but in a way that *exclusively* sacrifices communal "love" for minoritarian "wrong people" and betrays instead a submissive "love" for the national affect's majoritarian biases as well as its monetary benefits.

We can further unpack Black Bieber's "love" by examining the lyrics from the album that he promotes. He sings: "Girl, / whatever I did / doesn't matter. / You know that I'll always be better. / Sometimes I'm crazy and I know it. / That's how I show you that I care." The ironic dissonance is striking; the lyrics "whatever I did / doesn't matter" abdicate responsibility for his "crazy" actions, yet these words ironically occur in an album whose title, "Justice," connotes the sense that individuals or institutions *should* face the consequences for any "crazy" injustice they commit. Bieber alliteratively equates unjustly acting "crazy" with showing the supposed justice of his own "care." Although he inclusively pairs two opposing ideas, Bieber's statement exclusively renounces a just "care" for any damage that his "crazy" mistreatment has done to his female partner. His love and care betray an exclusivity in which these affects forsake one kind of meaning (empathy for women) to revel instead in the unequal meaning of the irresponsible c**n figure.[7] Black Bieber acts as a beloved darling of the national affect, through which the exclusively ironic regime of contemporary minstrelsy resonates. The feelings communicated by his closing performance ultimately intend the domination of marginalized groups while negating the possibility of unconditional love and care.

In contrast to Bieber, Alfred strives to resist tropes of minstrelsy, displaying a particularly fraught relationship to the figures of the c**n and the brute. R. Jackson explains that the brute is "scripted to be nothing less than an indiscreet, devious, irresponsible, and sexually pernicious beast" and embodies racist and patriarchal fears about the rape of white women (41); this figure has evolved, in contemporary media, into rap music's "thug" persona, characterized by lewdness, violence, and territorial protectiveness. Whereas the c**n emotes excess idleness and obedience, the brute or thug expresses overflowing sexuality and physicality, presumably with the intent to titillate and also threaten, according to the majoritarian perspective.

Alfred's ironic inclusivity decenters Black Bieber's exclusivity. *Atlanta* demonstrates this contrast through the brawl that instigates Bieber's performative mea culpa. As Alfred and Bieber are grappling together on the court, Bieber yells, "I'm MVP [most valuable player]! I'm MVP!" while Alfred exclaims, "I hate you! I hate you!" Although Alfred plays into the media's minstrelized expectations of him as the violent thug, he expresses contempt toward Bieber's commitment to the manner in which the music industry and the media perceive and value him as the "MVP." Alfred's aggression becomes inclusively ironic inasmuch as his wrestling embrace with Bieber potentially resonates visually as a gesture of affectionate intimacy (though the audio that accompanies this visual obviously counteracts such an interpretation). Hutcheon claims that irony forges an "inclusionary" connection between ironist and interpreters. To elaborate, she cites Kenneth Burke's statement that "dialectic irony" depends "upon a sense of fundamental kinship with the enemy, as one *needs* him, is *indebted* to him" (Hutcheon 514, emphasis original). Alfred's aggression signals an "indebtedness" to the trope of the brute; however, instead of sacrificially paying this debt with submissive love, he derides Bieber's MVP status, even if few in the audience share his perspective. Perversely echoing the laziness of the c**n type, Alfred shirks his expected labor of emoting counterfeit care for his minstrel bedfellow and, consequently, interrupts minstrelsy's sacrificial process.

Alfred's hatred crystallizes his c**n-like resistance to the demands of minstrelsy. The following lyrics from his song "Paper Boi" elaborate what this hate might mean: "Paper Boi, Paper Boi, always 'bout that paper, boy. / If you ain't on your grind and you flexin', you's a hater, boy. / Paper Boi, Paper Boi, always gettin' paper, boy. / If you ain't makin' money, then you ain't a moneymaker, boy." Here, a "hater" signifies someone who opposes pursuing profit (i.e., "paper") and "flexin' " their materialistic gains, yet the rhymed pairings of "hater" with "paper" and "moneymaker" ironically suggests that any hate can transform into a dependence on or love for these capitalist interests. When Alfred wrestles with Black Bieber, he does not announce his love for capitalism or minstrelsy; instead, his hate represents a c**n-like distaste for such indebtedness to Bieber's "flexin' " as the ostensible MVP. Alfred's attempts at taking him down—literally and figuratively—illustrate that the violence of the brute and the laziness of the c**n can be inclusively repurposed into affects of dissident contempt. Indeed, the supplementary sense of "flexin' " as "acting flexibly" resonates in the ways that Alfred frees his minstrelsy to allow divergent affective expressions of hatred.

Alfred also evidences his inclusive flexibility through his imitation of the affectively unempathetic minimalism that characterizes the national affect, often putting on an eye-rolling deadpan glare that both opposes and mimes the empathetic minimalism of the music industry. His blank gaze expresses a dearth of such conventional affects as happy submission or enraged violent intent. This minimalism contrasts sharply with his explosive response to Bieber's minstrelsy, yet because Alfred emotes both maximally and minimally, he proves his affective fluidity in unsettling the majoritarian affect of white minimalism. In particular, Alfred ruptures the national affect by repeatedly conveying an intentionally weak imitation of it.

Alfred's minimalism becomes a subtle performance of ironic mediocrity. Evoking the indolence of the c**n, he undersells expectations as part of his parodic mimicry of the national affect. Alfred's mediocrity is especially resonant when he visits the offices of an online streaming service in "Sportin' Waves" (s2e2). While there, Alfred records a radio announcement, reciting his corny scripted lines—"This is Paper Boi, and you're tuned into the Fresh Rap Mix Playlist. Long live fresh"—in a subdued affect that is wholly unsuitable for the service's marketing purposes. After the white recording engineer suggests that he deliver another line reading in a "cool" way, Alfred repeats it in the same tone but adds a slight, yet significant, vernacular modification: "This is Paper Boi, and you're tuned into the Fresh Rap Mix Playlist. Long live fresh ... n***a." For his third take, the engineer encourages him to sound as though he's at a "crazy" party, and Alfred's body language suggests that he can no longer tolerate this assignment.

What do we make of Alfred's appending "n***a" to signify coolness? The original slur of "n****r" unmistakably degrades Black people, but because Alfred uses the African American vernacular of "n***a," he satisfies the white engineer's racialized expectations of what is "cool" at a superficial level. Also, the engineer's use of "crazy" can connote similar racist undertones. Through his deliberate mediocrity, he mimes the minimalism of whiteness and, at the same time, suggests that the euphemistic sense of "coolness" the engineer invokes repressively conceals the historically loaded heat and racist offensiveness of "n****r." On the whole, Alfred's response to these euphemisms echoes his earlier encounter with the Black Bieber's euphemistic use of "cool," "wrong," and "crazy" in his performed apology. Bieber's euphemisms can function as code words for minstrelized behaviors of stereotyped excess. These words reveal that white minimalism thrives by refashioning explicit racism into the benign veneer of civil discourse.

Because Alfred affects the bare minimum while at the streaming service's offices, he resists playing it too "cool" and too much like the crazy-brute or shirking-c**n stereotypes of minstrelsy; however, his affective minimalism still somewhat recalls the c**n just as his affective maximalism in his fight with Bieber echoes the brute. Overall, he emulates brutish violence and c**n-like laziness to decenter his ironic indebtedness to minstrelsy's exclusive love and counterfeit care. His subsequent performance on a tiny stage for the streaming service's office staff is one more example in which we can delineate the nature of this decentering. As he begins his song "Paper Boi," he dispassionately mutters, "Yo ... Hey ... Paper ... ," before abruptly walking off the stage and dropping the microphone in a white staffer's hand. In a different context, this final act would be a "mic drop," which typically serves to boast about the wit and quality of one's performance. However, Alfred's "mic drop" here signifies that he sacrifices not only the "paper" (i.e., money and publicity) he can earn from the streaming service but also any sense of emotional investment in his performative labor. Moreover, handing off the microphone may signify him mockingly passing the labor of singing onto the white staffer. Reversing the roles, Alfred subtly assigns the white man a performative role, in this case, one that is deeply associated with a particular type of Blackness the man is seemingly in no way prepared to adopt (unlike, say, the real-life Justin Bieber).

The threefold nature of Alfred's ending flourish demonstrates that inclusive minstrelsy multiplies beyond exclusive minstrelsy's imposition of affective minimalism. Alfred's ironies enable him to achieve the integrity of emotional self-fortification while decentralizing, even if only for a fleeting moment, the pervasive supremacy of the national affect. If there is a labor that Alfred performs in imitating the c**n, it is his constant "flexin'" of affect whereby his aggressive hate and mediocre cool precariously balance yet also unbalance the unrelenting demands of whiteness with the fundamental right to dignity.

Much as Alfred performs this delicate labor, Van—Earn's intermittent girlfriend and sexual partner, a middle-school teacher, and a (mostly) single mother—pursues a related yet different labor of inclusive irony. Van's ironies respond to the ways that minstrelsy seeks to limit the freedom of Black women, and her inclusive irony therefore exposes how race and gender intersect in traditional minstrelsy. Through Van's actions, *Atlanta* again demonstrates that irony precariously supports the emotional intimacies of marginalized people, regardless of what aspects of their identity have led to their marginalization.[8]

Two stereotypes from minstrelsy that Van struggles against are the "baby mama" and the "strong Black woman." The former evokes the stock character of the m*mmy, who is represented typically as an overweight single mother devoted to fulfilling domestic responsibilities. Although not exactly a figure of traditional minstrelsy, the strong Black woman is another figure echoing minstrelsy's demand for feminine sacrifice. Melissa V. Harris-Perry argues that the "particular histories of slavery, Jim Crow, urban segregation, racism, and patriarchy . . . have created a specific citizen imperative for African American women" to be the self-reliant "strong black woman," who is "a motivated and hard-working breadwinner," "sacrificial and smart," and "suppresses her emotional needs while anticipating those of others" (22). However, this ideal's emphasis on autonomous strength and emotional altruism creates the damaging consequences of making "routine human weakness and fragility" into "sources of potential shame" and discouraging "attention to the structural sources of inequality" (Harris-Perry 186, 190). Van's inclusive minstrelsy affords us the opportunity to examine how she resists both the baby-mama and the strong-Black-woman stereotypes and rejects minstrelsy's national affect of sacrificing empathy for the emotional suffering and structural inequities that beset Black women.

We can observe Van's dissident attempts in "Value" (s1e6), in which Van dines with her friend Jayde (Aubin Wise). Although her actual profession is never specified, the women's dialogue over drinks and dinner implies that Jayde provides some form of companionship service to wealthy patrons, such as professional athletes. Throughout their meeting, Van rebuffs Jayde's invitations to accompany her on one of her luxurious overseas trips or even just to come with her to an elite patron's listening party by invoking her family: "I have a daughter. I can't leave. . . . I have Lottie [her daughter]. . . . We [Van and Earn] have a daughter." Jayde sneers that Van is like a "grandma" before admonishing her to become more concerned about her value: "I mean, you used to make fun of girls like you. . . . You know, you really need to think about your value. . . . Black women need to be valuable . . . the NBA players that I fuck with, they fuck with me because I provide a service, and I am worth it. I am cultured, intelligent, and beautiful." For Jayde, being "valuable" means pursuing the strong-Black-woman ideal because, as Harris-Perry puts it, she "suppresses her emotional needs while anticipating the needs" of her NBA players, and she treats her culture, intelligence, and beauty as signs of her independent strength. At the same time, Jayde's use of "fuck with" in relation to the NBA players suggests that her pursuit of this ideal bears inclusively subversive elements. "Fuck" at once insinuates that her affluent patrons must sexualize her body in order for her to actualize her value, yet "fuck with" implies that Jayde in turn exploits this sexualization to reap financial benefits. The paired construction of her verbal "I fuck with, they fuck with" stresses that the materialistic and sexual exploitation goes both ways and that Jayde, in a somewhat inclusively ironic way, appropriates patriarchal sexualization for her personal gain.

However, Jayde's manipulations inevitably rest on the sacrifice of her emotional needs; Van responds, "That kind of black-and-white mentality might work for you, but for those of us who don't live on whether a linebacker swipes left or right . . . there's a gray area." Van counters that Jayde can only achieve her value through a sacrificial "black-and-white mentality" that demands adherence to the strong-Black-woman ideal or consignment to the dependent role of the "m*mmy." What's more, Van highlights that Jayde's strong-Black-woman persona inevitably thrives on the objectifying gaze or "swiping" (as in the affirmative gesture on a dating app) of men. Alternatively, Van insists upon an inclusive value, a "gray area" that exceeds minstrelsy's patriarchal attitude toward Black women's value and affirms a both-and ethos of incorporating yet still subverting minstrel stereotypes.

Van later shows what such alternative value might look like when, after having smoked marijuana the night prior with Jayde, she attempts to pass a drug test that her middle-school teaching job requires. Van first solicits Jayde's help and then Alfred's, but neither of them proves a reliable source of assistance. Van takes the initiative and improvises by filtering her infant daughter's urine into a condom that she tapes to the inside of her leg, intending to pour it into the specimen cup as a substitute. Ultimately, this ploy fails: the condom she uses to contain her daughter's urine ends up tearing apart when she tries to transfer the contents into the specimen cup and the urine spatters onto her face. With no other options available to her, she admits her weed smoking to her supervisor, who promptly fires her. Despite her failure, Van asserts an inclusive value that simultaneously expresses *both* her self-reliant independence from Alfred, Jayde, and presumably her casual partner Earn (whose help she does not seek at all) *and also* her domestic reliance on her daughter in the somewhat unusual form of Lottie's urine. Further significant, the messiness of being sprayed with urine especially perverts the stereotypes of both the m*mmy devoted to (and preternaturally proficient at) household duties like cleaning, and the strong Black woman obsessed—like the mother, Lena, in Lorraine Hansberry's *A Raisin in the Sun* (1959)—with the supposed purity of self-sufficiency. Van's tactics reveal that pursuing these ideals involves a grotesque messiness that women like Jayde may repress or prefer to excrete. Van's splattering by Lottie's urine, then, represents the impossibility of sacrifice as affective traces of other people's bodies inevitably find their way back. While the national affect fundamentally excludes affective excess, Van's inadvertent failure demonstrates otherwise.

Her urinary baptism, if you will, awakens Van from the false consciousness of blindly pursuing a sacrificial model, and as a result, she confesses her transgression to her supervisor and exposes her vulnerability, a quality excluded from both the strong-Black-woman ideal and the national affect. Her confession is especially significant because her supervisor—who is Black—subsequently informs her, in a different kind of confession, that the county government cannot afford drug tests for their employees and only administers them "to keep people on their toes." The supervisor is momentarily understanding, believing that Van smoked weed "to shake . . . off" the fact the "system isn't made for . . . kids [from minority backgrounds] to succeed," but she nevertheless fires her on the basis that she needs "to cover . . . [her] own ass, as well as the school's." The supervisor's confession underscores the educational system's exclusive irony; because this official wants to "cover" the school's "ass" (yet another indirect reference to excretion), she signals that the educational institution functions to erase or "cover" the affectively excessive "shit" of smoking and in-school disobedience that employees and students, respectively, commit in response to the school's constipated assemblage of bureaucratic rules and systemic biases. From the school's perspective, a strong Black woman must be affectively pure, but Van cannot "shake off" her vulnerability. Instead, Van's urine-tainted body impurifies her into excreta of sacrifice. Willing to confess her transgressions, Van wears such perceived weakness as marks of her value.

In "Helen" (s2e4), we can witness in finer detail the limits of Van's inventively inclusive minstrelsy. Van and Earn travel together to a small (and real) town named Helen in rural Georgia to attend a Fastnacht festival celebrating the hitherto-unmentioned German part of her heritage. Van gradually becomes exhausted with Earn's noncommittal attitude both to the festivities and to her emotional needs overall and ultimately ends her sexual relationship with him by the end of the episode. The broader context for her decision is her growing frustration at being tied to the baby-mama role imposed on her by her friend Christina (Jessica Tillman) in this episode and previously by Jayde in "Value." The initiation of Van's breakup with both Earn and the dependent-baby-mama role is ironic and creative. She announces her desire to separate by proposing a ping-pong match to Earn; if she wins (and it immediately becomes very clear that she will), she will stop having sex with Earn. In response to Earn's skepticism about what winning the match will prove, Van states bluntly, "It's gonna prove that I'm tired." Her expression of emotional exhaustion is also another expression of vulnerability, so the game and her victory at it again perverts the idea that a strong Black woman must repress weakness.[9]

The ironies of Van's enterprise are manifold. First, the game becomes a kind of trial by which she uses victory at ping-pong to gauge her victory over the minstrelized baby-mama and strong-Black-woman stereotypes and her victory over Earn's patriarchal notions about his sexual license over her body. Second, she uses the positive outcome of her victory, which typically connotes strength, to emphasize the negative affect that she is "tired" of the emotional labor of appeasing Earn's desires. Third, instead of effusively emoting her fatigue through expressive gesticulations, she does it through a deadpan glare, mirroring both the national affect's minimalism and Alfred's signature response. Fourth, the coordinated maneuvers of hitting a ping-pong ball—the style and form of a sport—serve as another medium through which she conveys her feelings or explicit lack thereof; the resounding manner in which she strikes the ball in winning the game's final point underscores the ironic combination of vigor and fatigue that she feels at this moment. Although not as grotesque as her urinary ingenuity, the ironies of her game are an entangled mess of conflicting senses: minstrelsy and antiminstrelsy, patriarchy and antipatriarchy, victorious strength and exhaustion, excess tiredness and deadpan minimalism, and affective expression and the predetermined rules of the game. Van's minstrelsy signifies her refusal to accept how minstrelsy and patriarchy seek to read Black women as domestically dependent or purely self-reliant entities. Instead, she strives beyond exclusivist readings and toward an irreconcilably complex identity. Managing the morass of race, gender, and minstrelsy discourse becomes Van's labor of achieving and emoting her freedom.

Atlanta imagines alternative modes of dissidence that invite the audience's empathetic interpretation. Acting wildly emotive would render these ironists readable according to oppressive minstrelsy tropes of minority excess. However, *Atlanta* urges its audience into closely acknowledging the subtle affective registers of irony and feeling the unconditional compassion that the national affect denies. Inclusive irony may fail in the eyes of persons like Jayde or the

Black Bieber, but its failure reveals the further failure of minstrelsy to master the uncontainable passions of minority individuals.

NOTES

1. For a discussion of minstrelsy's past and present stereotypical characters, especially the brute, c**n, and m*mmy types that this essay discusses, see R. Jackson 23–47. Because of my discomfort, I've censored parts of racial slurs with asterisks.

2. For additional discussion on the liberating possibilities of African American minstrelsy, see Taylor and Austen.

3. Although my analysis focuses primarily on episodes from the show's first two seasons, its fourth and final season is replete with direct and indirect references to minstrelsy as well. Kirkwood Chocolate in "Work Ethic!" (s4e5) is at least partly a parody of Tyler Perry, whose work has been characterized by Spike Lee and others as modern-day minstrelsy. "The Goof Who Sat by the Door" (s4e8) is a brilliantly nuanced mockumentary that reimagines Disney's *A Goofy Movie* (1995) as "the blackest movie ever made" instead of as a vehicle for a character often interpreted as a racist caricature, particularly in his earliest incarnations. Finally, the series finale features a Black sushi chef who is livid that African Americans seem to prefer Popeye's fried chicken—which he characterizes as "c**n chicken" in a lengthy diatribe—over his culinary experiments.

4. For her full discussion of inclusive irony, see Hutcheon 57–88.

5. For further on this episode, see Brooks's essay herein.

6. The real-life Bieber actually did issue an album with this title in 2021, though neither he nor Donald Glover have suggested publicly that there is any direct connection—ironic or sincere—between it and the fictional one from *Atlanta*.

7. It's worth noting that Black Bieber's promotional actions are comparable to those of the real-life Justin Bieber. The episode seemingly presumes the audience's awareness of his frequent participation in such games, including a 2011 game that was billed as a showdown between Bieber and famed Atlanta rapper Ludacris. Despite the admirable intention of raising money for worthy causes, it is hard not to impute a secondary, more personal motive considering the frequent charges of appropriating Blackness that have been leveled against Bieber for such public behaviors as using the *n*-word (which Black Bieber also does during the game) and sporting Black-associated hairstyles, such as dreadlocks and cornrows. That Black Bieber wears a jersey with the number twenty-three seems to further suggest such a satirical reading given that number's associations with both Michael Jordan and LeBron James. *Atlanta* implicates Black Bieber as a minstrel submitting to majoritarian interests while, at the same, indirectly satirizing the white Bieber as a minstrel profiting from Black imagery. For a summary of the latter's offenses from 2014 to 2021, see Karimi.

8. For more on Van's characterization, see the essays by Parks and Morgan herein.

9. For further discussion of both "Value" and "Helen," see Parks's essay herein.

"IT'S A SIMULATION, VAN"

Atlanta, *The Twilight Zone*, and the Uncanniness of Black Womanhood

DANIELLE FUENTES MORGAN

Atlanta has rightly been praised for its inventiveness and investment in the interior life of elder Black millennials as the characters navigate young—but not so young anymore—adulthood. The satirical impulse of the series reveals the inherent absurdity and surreality of Black millennial life, in which self-actualization is still elusive despite seemingly greater access to social mobility. I focus here especially on "Champagne Papi" (s2e7), which is concerned with a satirical interrogation of the millennial "pics-or-it-didn't-happen" ideology as a way to engage questions about "the real" and to reveal the confines of seeing and believing in the twenty-first century, particularly for Black women. Reimagining precursors like *The Twilight Zone* (1959–1964) and its interest in the uncanniness of American life in general, *Atlanta*'s surreality opens up into the specific uncanniness of young Black American life, in which the real and the imagined form a symbiotic satirical relationship that reveals limited options for self-actualization for Black millennials.

Within African American satire, *Atlanta* is a particularly apt example of the permeability of the line between comedy and horror given that both comedy and horror are founded on the unexpected, the absurd, or the surreal, as well as the reframing of that which is already—or *seems* already—familiar. The series leans into existing anxieties around race, gender, and class to heighten a sense of uneasiness by negotiating the line between what could be and what is. This disquiet is why the series makes us both shudder and laugh out loud—we never know, from moment to moment, what response the show might elicit. "Champagne Papi" is broadly engaged with the (im)possibility of real experiences within the hyperchronicling of the twenty-first century, while also offering a satirical critique of these stakes in practice for Black women in the context of an unsatisfying girls' night out at a New Year's Eve party at Drake's mansion. The episode reveals the surreality of millennial life and, specifically, the uncanniness of Black women's existence. Just in the episode's opening minutes, the uncanny encounters include the following: an unsettling driver who tells a shuttle bus full of young women, "Y'all pretty. I'ma take y'all home with me. Just kidding"; a male security guard requiring the women to put on disposable booties in order to enter the mansion; and a charming guy who initially seems to be an "insider" as he flirts with the episode's protagonist, Vanessa "Van" Keefer (Zazie Beetz[1]), but might just be a creep. Nothing has quite the glitz and glamour the women expect from the night, and they find themselves objectified in ways that suggest both imminent danger and mundane materiality. By the end of the episode, wishes are unfulfilled: one friend has a bad reaction to a gummy cannabis edible, another finds her Black male celebrity crush cozied up with his white girlfriend, another disappears for the evening, and the men at the party are almost uniformly sketchy. And in the ultimate disappointment, we discover along with Van that Drake isn't actually there—in fact, he's not even on the same continent.

In this episode, the absurdity of Black life—of Black selfhood as always already unattainable—brings reality into stark satirical relief. If the uncanny is that which is strangely familiar or unsettles us as a result of its recognizability, *Atlanta*'s satirical surreality unsettles because it lays bare the uncanniness of contemporary racialization, the inability of elder Black millennials to self-actualize despite supposedly equitable access to the means of doing so in both the surreal world of fiction and in real-life experiences. Unlike similar comedy-dramas focused on elder white millennials, such as *Girls* (2012–2017), *Love* (2016–2018), or even *Fleabag* (2016–2019), there is an implication, in "Champagne Papi," that self-actualization is foreclosed for our Black protagonists; honesty is punished, and aspirations lead to violence.[2] This episode instead is more directly connected to Issa Rae's *Insecure* (2016–2021), which also offers a satirical reading of the Black female millennial struggle for self-actualization. While the characters in *Insecure* are often stymied in their efforts at finding romance and financial success, each of its episodes and each of its seasons' arcs demonstrate the continued necessity of Black female friendships for self-hood and survival.[3] What *Insecure* suggests about the necessity of Black female friendships via comedy-drama *Atlanta* imagines through the uncanniness of episodes involving Black women.

The avenues that are supposed to provide a way out are a dead end for young Black adults. For this reason, consideration of uncanniness in contemporary African American satire provides a way to think about the series not only in view of the recent explosion of Black speculative fiction[4] but as a continuing examination of the line between comedy and horror in the twenty-first century. These satires reject preeminent ideologies of the postracial as a safe space and refuse to imagine a move past categorization as necessary or even desirable. In the context of *Atlanta*, race matters, gender matters, and class matters, even if these demarcations are unclear and can be transgressed. Ultimately, the series engages the satiric mode to demonstrate the insufficiency of the postracial, the postgender, or even class skepticism in the actual lived experiences of Black millennials. It is the *post*-postracial, *post*-postgender, class-asserting impulse of this African American satire that opens into Black uncanniness and brings Black womanhood into stark relief.

Recontextualizing Van—a somewhat ancillary figure among *Atlanta*'s four main characters—as a potential, albeit only temporary, protagonist makes clear that her established lack of centrality can be read as a satirical statement on the subordinate treatment of Black women more broadly. "Champagne Papi" opens with Van and her girlfriends preparing to go to a party hosted by superstar, recording artist Drake. Although each woman has her reasons for going, Van's focus is singular: to take a picture with Drake to boost her Instagram clout in large part to make Earn (Donald Glover)—the show's primary protagonist, her on-again, off-again partner, and father of her daughter—jealous after he posted a video with another woman on his own Instagram.[5] I read this episode as a twenty-first-century Black reimagining of messaging typified by that exemplar of televisual satire, *The Twilight Zone*, which similarly plays upon recognizable tropes to critique the contemporary realm. In this sense, rather than treating *The Twilight Zone* as a comparative lens, I examine tropes from that series as a theoretical framework through which we can better understand *Atlanta*.

Although *The Twilight Zone* might seem an unlikely precursor for *Atlanta*, I want to remind audiences of *Atlanta*'s potential reading as speculative fiction not only because much speculative fiction invites satirical interpretation but also because of the overwhelming absurdity and surreality of the second season of *Atlanta*, particularly the three-episode arc at its core—"Teddy Perkins" (s2e6), "Champagne Papi," and "Woods" (s2e8). "Teddy Perkins" is perhaps the show's most famous and unsettling episode; in it, Darius (LaKeith Stanfield) goes to pick up a multicolored piano from a reclusive performer, a sort of surrogate Michael Jackson figure, disturbing in both appearance and interaction. The plot of "Champagne Papi" has already been summarized above, leaving only "Woods," which follows Alfred/Paper Boi (Brian Tyree Henry) on a nightmarish journey through a suburban forest, during which he meets both potential caretakers and executioners as he tries to make his way back home. Each episode focuses on a different character who significantly is *not* the protagonist of the series as a whole, adding a sense of surreality in these episodes in which Earn may not even fundamentally appear. The stand-in protagonist of each of these episodes survives their own uncanny existence as distilled into a single day. Like *The Twilight Zone*, *Atlanta* can be read as nihilistic but certainly not *only* nihilistic. It is true that we may not expect the characters to get a traditional happy ending or achieve self-actualization, but this is not because the world lacks meaning. Instead, we imagine a scenario where the characters might attain Abraham Maslow's basic needs of physiology and safety *if only* they were able to assert themselves fully, even as the series suggests that such an assertion is impossible. In this way, *The Twilight Zone* offers a way to decode *Atlanta*'s more surreal moments, which might otherwise be dismissed as nonsensical or weird for the sake of being weird. It provides a blueprint for understanding the significance of these uncanny moments in a series that is otherwise grounded in recognizable reality.

While *Atlanta* largely focuses on questions of Black masculinity, episodes focusing on Van[6] demonstrate the particular concerns of Black women within the satirically rendered context of Black uncanniness. In *The Unconcept: The Freudian Uncanny in Late-Twentieth-Century Theory*, Anneleen Masschelein writes of the inherent difficulty in defining the "uncanny": "This entails that the uncanny is marked by the unconscious that does not know negation or contradiction; even when something is negated, it still remains present in the unconscious. According to this reasoning, the contradiction resulting from negation is not exclusive or binary: denying something at the same time conjures it up. Hence, it is perfectly possible that something can be familiar and unfamiliar at the same time" (8). Perhaps this is why the series opens in "The Big Bang" (s1e1) with Darius immediately noting his sense of "getting some crazy déjà vu right now" not only as an uncanny feeling but also in terms of the literalness of what he's actually already seen. That déjà vu may allude to the violence that occurs here and recurs throughout the series in both real and surreal iterations. In this way, Darius's articulation likely matches that of viewers who are conditioned to assume this sort of violence to be quotidian between Black men while also, by calling it déjà vu, calling out and resisting the pathologization of Black men as naturally savage. For audience members, the ingenuity of *Atlanta* might be found in the fact that it reveals without pretense what we might instinctively already know to be true—racism is real, sexism exists, and people are generally disappointing. While the events of each episode may be shocking, this takeaway is not. The framing is important when we consider "Champagne Papi" as a continuation of this interrogation: How do you satirize real-life experiences when real life is already absurd enough to seem self-satirizing?

Responding to this question, "Champagne Papi" takes cues from *The Twilight Zone* through two critical misdirections: the overt turn in which audiences become aware that the Drake that Van saw in Instagram photos from the party is, in fact, a cardboard cutout and the series' more subtle ironic tendency to reveal the most about Van when it decenters her within its storytelling. While the satirical impulse of *The Twilight Zone* reminds us that the horrors depicted on the show are real, the satirical impulse of *Atlanta* shows us that, within the context of Black millennial life, reality is *horrible*. Whereas *The Twilight Zone*'s characters shout that "this is a gag!" to signal their distressed desire to return to reality, "Champagne Papi" offers Van's resignation that perhaps there is no reality at all or at least that seeing isn't necessarily believing.

"Champagne Papi" parallels *The Twilight Zone*'s similarly slow-building revelations that put reality under erasure. For instance, in "Stopover in a Quiet Town" (s5e30), a married couple wake up in a strange house after a night of drinking; the evening is blurry, and although they knew better, the husband attempted to drive home. As they struggle to make sense of their whereabouts, they discover the entire town is filled with real-looking but fake items—a stuffed squirrel, a prop telephone, and, most damningly, a train that only goes in a loop around the small town itself. Finally, a looming shadow appears, and a giant hand picks them up. A woman's voice says: "Be careful with your pets, dear. Your father brought them all the way from Earth." The protagonists are captive in a giant child's terrarium on another planet. The moral, as Rod Serling elucidates in his closing monologue, is not to drink and drive, but the larger fearsome revelation is that reality could break way into a nightmarish surreality in which things look comfortably familiar but are horrifically uncanny.

Using the satirical instability of the real-surreal boundary in *The Twilight Zone*[7] as an entry point for thinking of *Atlanta*'s own satirical impulse, we recognize that "Champagne Papi" demonstrates the particular challenges faced by Black women through the uncanniness of Van's disappointingly mundane experiences with men—both the hard-to-shake stranger who knows the layout of Drake's house a bit too well and the absent Drake himself—over the course of one girls' night out. Kathleen Rowe in *The Unruly Woman* writes, "More often, the conventions of both popular culture and high art represent women as objects rather than subjects of laughter" (3). Here, the women have subjectivity, and men are rendered as objects through their various absences; whereas we have consistently seen the men of *Atlanta* disappointed and disillusioned, we now witness the ways men themselves can be disappointing and disillusioning in situations where they maintain (limited) power.

We see a similar letdown resulting in the midst of would-be glamour in "Value" (s1e6). Van impulsively smokes weed with her friend Jayde after a tense, fancy dinner together, and what initially seems to be a girls' night out devolves into a comedy of errors in the morning when Van belatedly recalls that she will be drug tested at her job. After some valiant efforts to pass her test, she confesses to her boss, who is sympathetic but nevertheless fires her straightaway. The episode initially seems to be a quotidian commentary on Black women's existence—damned if you do, damned if you don't—with Van serving as a proxy for Black women in general. However, a twist worthy of *The*

Twilight Zone occurs in one of the most iconic images of the series to date: a Black boy sits in Van's classroom in crisp whiteface, a sly smile on his face as he looks at Van and awaits her returned gaze. The camera closes in on his steady face, and when she finally looks at him, he subtly raises an eyebrow before the cut to the credits. Rather than ending the episode on the downturn toward dystopia, another way to read this peculiar and seemingly unrelated scene is as a brief crystallization of that *Twilight Zone* impulse in which the reality of fakeness and the fakeness of reality fused together reveal a surreal affective terrain of new possibilities.[8] For Van, this Black student in whiteface might briefly signal that there are other ways to self-actualize and exert your limited power whether others accept it or not, an idea she returns to a season later in "Champagne Papi."[9]

In her own words, Van hopes to "replace Earn" by getting a photo with Drake; this language of replacement is critical here not only because it suggests a commodification of reality but also because it reveals her belief in a sort of synonymity between visuality and virtuality. Seeing is believing, but in both *The Twilight Zone* and *Atlanta*, the truth lies in a deeper, more critical analysis of that cliché. Seeing is never simply about cataloguing the facts of what is presented before us; we see what we need to see, and then our beliefs follow accordingly. The real question is, Can these beliefs hold? This episode asks us what Drake represents for Van in the context of Instagram and its curated version of personhood. Near the end of the episode, Van comes across a long line of women waiting to enter a room with cardboard cutouts of Drake and is herself presented with an offer to take a photo with one of them for twenty dollars. All the Instagram photos she has scrolled through during the course of the evening are revealed as nothing more than women posing with cheap, two-dimensional simulacra of Drake. It is all uncanny on multiple compounding levels. Drake's house is superficially beautiful, and the women all look like models, but the women ride in a nondescript rented van to get to an undisclosed location, put booties over their designer shoes, and spend most of the night avoiding sketchy men. In the end, none of this is particularly significant since Drake himself is not even there, except of course in the form of the cutouts that could just as well be part of a marketing display in a record shop. In *Twilight Zone* episodes like "Stopover in a Quiet Town," such revelations of hollowness provoke unexpected terror. For Van, this revelation is met with forbearance rather than panic. Drake was going to be used as a prop one way or the other at this party; as a cutout, he is simply literalized in that role.

Van's new understanding of the illusory nature of the fake-real boundary is an epiphany. She is unceremoniously informed by the two women taking money at the door that the fake is as good as it gets: "Look, they're real to everyone else. I mean, this your best option, anyway. You thought you was gonna have a meaningful convo with Drake or some shit? . . . You was gonna come to the party, ask for a pic and post it on the Gram, so here you go." Initially skeptical, Van walks away, prompting one of the women running the photo shoot to dismiss her by saying to her coworker, "Girl, she ain't *real*." This is a moment of surprising witness, an articulation that what is now fake to Van is real to everyone else. This sort of revelation may be familiar to fans of *The Twilight Zone*, but rather than falling into despair, Van is steadied by the recognition that the boundary between what is and what might be is permeable (not coincidentally, a major premise of much speculative fiction). What's the difference between meeting someone famous and pretending to meet them if you're just "doing it for the Gram" anyway? Ashleigh Wade argues that "Black girls form complex digital kinship structures that reveal how digitality enters into discourses on Black relationship formation and communication practices" (81). Such digitality provides a space for self-articulation and power that may be otherwise unavailable to young Black women. Thus, although doing it for the Gram might serve as the proxy for the surreality of life in the twenty-first century, it might also surprisingly create the most *real* way to gain some autonomy over life as well.

An interaction at the party between Darius and Van's friend Nadine (Gail Bean) is particularly instructive as Darius articulates a theory that life is a simulation.[10] Nadine and Darius first meet while she is having a paranoid response to a cannabis edible. In a seemingly incongruous—and possibly imprudent—attempt to calm and reassure her, Darius begins to explain Nick Bostrom's simulation argument, the idea that all existence may be a computer simulation. Darius's engagement with and concise description of Bostrom in the context of his appearance at Drake's party and a conversation with a person he's just met (notably while she is high) is, on its face, comedic until it isn't. The revelation that nothing is real, that "[she] is nothing" as she later reiterates to Van, alleviates the paranoia she was otherwise experiencing: if you're scared, learning that what you're afraid of is not only out of your control but also fundamentally not real offers a revelatory relief in the moment itself, regardless of whether or not you believe it in the morning. A theory that might depress a sober or more self-assured person and make them question their successes and the meaning of life almost ironically gives Nadine a way to steady herself. For Nadine, being "nothing" might be more desirable than being afraid. More broadly, the recognition that none of it is real potentially offers Black millennials, especially Black women, an escape from being constantly denied subjectivity, a way to remind them that the odds are stacked against them and it's not their fault.

Darius is arguably the most intuitive and introspective of all the characters in the series and, for this reason, perhaps simultaneously the most and the least likely to be seen at Drake's party. Donald Glover says of the episode: "That moment [of Darius's explication of Bostrom's argument] is like the hook in music. It's what tells you why you're there" (Friend). Such significance belies Darius's stated reason for attending the party—"I know Drake's chef, Guillermo, from the glorious days of pick-up soccer"—which is a perfectly guileless explanation compared to the status-motivated rationales voiced by Van and her friends in the episode's opening scenes; Darius is there for Guillermo, so whether this is Drake's party or not is inconsequential to him. When Nadine tells Van that the world isn't real—"it's a simulation, Van"—the latter's response is ultimately resigned: "It's all fake. There is no Drake. So don't ruin your high, and just enjoy yourself."[11] It is what it is and also what it isn't. One scene removed from paying to take a picture with a carboard cutout,[12] it is indubitably through acknowledging the surreality of the surrounding world that Van and her friends find subjectivity. After all, isn't Instagram itself just a simulation anyway? So, if you're being like the calculating online influencer Zan (Freddie Kuguru) in "The Streisand Effect" (s1e4) or like Van in "Champagne Papi" and "doing it for the Gram" because social media offers you your best possibility for self-actualizing, aren't you living in the simulation in a near-literal sense? This explanation is particularly compelling in light of the episode's title; not only is Drake himself not actually there, but "Champagne Papi" is a nickname taken from Drake's own Instagram handle and thus a reference to his flashy and curated online alter ego.

The episode revels in depicting a collective Black womanhood that belies the lack of options actually afforded to Black women. Even as we see that these friends don't quite get the celebrity experience they are seeking, there is a clear sense of support for and valuation of camaraderie among *most* of the women involved.[13] Things fall apart when they are separated, and they are saved only after finding each other again.[14] Imperfect as its expression might be in "Champagne Papi," sisterhood is perhaps *the real*, the thing to hold on to despite the instability and/or artificiality of the surrounding world. This scene between Van and Nadine may remind viewers of *The Twilight Zone*'s "The Midnight Sun" (s3e10), which likewise posits the necessity of friendships with other women as a mechanism for survival in both reality and surreality. Two women, Norma and Mrs. Bronson, decide to stay in an apartment alone together as the Earth spins closer to the sun, their death from the intense heat imminent. The women share their limited resources and operate as a protective dyad against would-be male intruders in the midst of climate crisis. However, we learn that Norma was in a fever dream; the Earth is not moving closer to the sun but away from it, and she and Mrs. Bronson will soon freeze, alone together. Norma remarks in a haze, "Isn't it wonderful to have darkness and coolness?" Mrs. Bronson replies with sadness in her eyes that somewhat contradicts her emotionless voice: "Yes, my dear. It's wonderful." Mrs. Bronson allows Norma the momentary comfort of believing that a cold world offers sanctuary that the nightmarish heat cannot, particularly in the midst of the personal heatwave of Norma's fever. It is an act of kindness to give her friend relief from an oppressive reality, even if the fantasy is transitory.

We see this same sort of female allegiance in *Atlanta*. What is perhaps most striking in "Champagne Papi" is the subjectivity with which these women are endowed and the ways that subjectivity is still shown to be powerful in some contexts and insufficient in others. Here, their subjectivity and even status as a protagonist still only opens up into a reactive and highly gendered frame—within the trope of the night out; the "girls-only" articulation belies an almost perfunctory interest in men.[15] "Champagne Papi" satirically uncovers women's imperfect options for self-actualization in a world where posing with a cardboard cutout of a famous man for an Instagram photo might be the *most real* way to actualize rather than being a sign of *fakeness*. Shardé M. Davis argues that because Black American women "have shared experiences in—and possibly shared perceptions of—the social world, they might also devise similar strategies to fight back. While it is inconceivable to resist institutionalized oppression at the structural level, Black women can resist manifestations of power and dominance as they occur day to day" (303). There's a parallel here with the end of "The Midnight Sun" in which female friends gently allow each other the peace of their fantasies,[16] even if the frame cannot hold.

Compare this with "The Club" (s1e8) and its hypermasculine concern with reality, with performatively "keeping it real." Van is noticeably absent from this episode in which Earn has secured a club appearance for Paper Boi, which goes awry when the club manager first tries to evade paying them altogether and then refuses to pay in full until Paper Boi himself storms into the manager's office and violently demands his money. Throughout the episode, Paper Boi and Earn both meet women who expose, in different ways, these men's inability to get what they want, be it money, sex, or respect. After Paper Boi gets paid and the men celebrate at an early morning diner, they see on the news that Paper Boi is wanted for questioning in a shooting in which he was not a participant (presumably *not* the one indirectly depicted in "The Big Bang"). Even when they win, they can't help losing, and this is no real surprise. If anything, this episode is an inversion of *The Twilight Zone*'s sensibility in its devotion to realism at the end. Here, while in the surreal fantasy of would-be ballers, the mundanity of reality comes crashing back down upon them.

Season 2, particularly in the episode "Champagne Papi" (along with "Teddy Perkins" and "The Woods"), closely follows the narrative arc set up by classic episodes of *The Twilight Zone* in making legible the line that demarcates what utopia may or may not be, who is empowered within it, and what reality is—to address the conundrum raised in the song "Compared to What" by the singer Roberta Flack: "Tryin' to make it real, compared to what?" For these women, it is this indecipherability between the real and the imagined, between horrifying absurdity and the comedic absurd, indeed, even between survival and death that requires a nuanced and carefully articulated satire, which inspires both laughter and discomfort in its depiction. What is reality, and does it matter? In *The Twilight Zone*, recognition of such inscrutability is often followed by the protagonist's life-or-death choice: Will they accept their new understanding or opt out through disorientation or death? For Van, surreality is less a condemnation and instead a confirmation that the world is, in fact, absurd. Ultimately, Drake's absence from what purports to be his own party is no more nonsensical than having to take a shuttle bus from an empty parking lot to a mansion that lacks outlets at which Van can charge her phone.

Van and her friends, now accompanied by Darius, close out the episode still dressed in their party clothes and holding their shoes as they stumble home at sunrise. Even here, it is uncanny; the scene holds all the visual trappings of a "walk of shame" the morning after a sexual encounter, but nothing of the sort occurs. Yet Van somehow finds one more moment of defiance in matter-of-factly stating that "Drake's Mexican."[17] She infers this knowledge from having met an older, Spanish-speaking man in the basement of the mansion. From contextual clues during their encounter, she comes to presume that the man is Drake's "*abuelo*," thereby contradicting the "reality" of Drake's well-publicized Canadian, Jewish, and Black-and-white biracial self-identification. Echoing the sudden appearance of the whiteface student in "Value," Van asserts her own way of understanding the world. While this moment ends the episode on the upswing of laughter, it also opens into new futures[18] where, like in "The Midnight Sun," embracing the fantasy of control might be a way to assert your own power. In "Champagne Papi," this girls' night out is mundane compared to the rest of the series and certainly the Grand Guignol of "Teddy Perkins" and "Woods" that it is bracketed by in season 2. However, the episode demonstrates that there is no real need for science-fiction horrors; the absurdity of reality is enough to unsettle. In this way, *Atlanta* examines what Rod Serling describes, in his opening narration of *The Twilight Zone*, as "the pit of man's fears and the summit of his knowledge." In *Atlanta*, that space between fear and knowledge is productive for Van, opening into an affective terrain that resists what would otherwise perhaps result in dispossession.

NOTES

1. Beetz also stars in an episode of the most recent iteration of *The Twilight Zone*.
2. We see a similar impulse in Michaela Coel's brilliant *I May Destroy You* (2020), which follows a group of elder Black millennial Londoners as they attempt self-actualization. As

in *Atlanta*, the primary figures face the realization—and the frequently grim physical and psychological consequences thereof—that the best of all worlds may not align with their expectations.

3. Although romantic desires play a large part in the series, *Insecure* is ultimately much more interested in the homosocial, companionate love between protagonist Issa and her best friend, Molly, as the relationship endgame. For further discussion of *Insecure*, see Horhn and Maus's essay herein.

4. While definitions of speculative fiction vary, these texts are perhaps best described as narratives containing magical or supernatural elements not found in real life or realistic fiction. I'm thinking here certainly of the twenty-first-century resurgence of Octavia Butler's novels but also N. K. Jemisin's *Broken Earth* series (2015–2017) and Colson Whitehead's *The Intuitionist* (1999) and *Zone One* (2011) in literature as well as Jordan Peele's films *Get Out* (2017), *Us* (2019), and *Nope* (2022) and Misha Green's televisual adaptation (2020) of Matt Ruff's novel *Lovecraft Country* (2016).

5. The exploitative and/or manipulative nature of social media—especially Instagram—is a recurrent theme in *Atlanta*. For further discussion of this topic, see Lee's essay herein.

6. "Value" (s1e6), "Helen" (s2e4), and "Tarrare" (s3e10) all feature scenes with Van in conversation with another Black woman over questions of self-identity and self-preservation and with conflicts occurring in the context of chosen romantic relationships with men. Van also plays a major role in "The Most Atlanta" (s4e1), "Work Ethic!" (s4e5), and "Snipe Hunt" (s4e7), the last of which seems to resolve the series-spanning tension about the prospects for her relationship with Earn.

7. For instance, consider "The Lonely" (s1e7), in which a wrongly convicted man in solitary confinement on a lone planet is given, as his only company, a robot, who becomes *real* to him but to no one else; consider also "Shadow Play" (s2e26), in which a man who is sentenced to death argues that he is dreaming, and when executed, all those with whom he's come in contact will no longer exist.

8. This is similar to "A World of Difference" (s1e23) in which an actor, unhappy with his real life, seems to opt into assuming the life (and the imaginary world) of the character he is playing, even though his decision to opt in cannot be accepted by others in the context of the world in which he exists.

9. For further discussion of this episode, see the essays by Rutter and Parks herein.

10. The series finale—"It Was All a Dream (s4e10)—ambiguously implies that Darius, a frequent visitor to a sensory-deprivation tank, could be having difficulty distinguishing between reality and fiction and may have dreamed the events of the entire series. If so, this framing offers an explanation for why the interior life of Van, the character Darius primarily knows only as "Earn's girl" and "Lottie's mother," is less frequently examined than that of the other male characters.

11. Van's statement that there "is no Drake" perhaps foreshadows Earn's strange meeting with someone who may or may not be D'Angelo (Enoch King) inside a surreal Rally's franchise in "Born 2 Die" (s4e3). This experience culminates in Earn being told that D'Angelo is a kind of cosmic, gestalt personality: "A D'Angelo is a complex network of men, women, and D'Angelos spread across countries, earth, and light. You have proven yourself worthy of our visage."

12. Although we don't see it happen, viewers may note that Van *does* end up taking the photo because she leaves the party wearing the Puma slides that come with the thirty-dollar photo package.

13. The two brief moments where we don't see this real camaraderie is in the quiet schadenfreude we read on the women's expressions when one woman is denied entrance into Drake's mansion and in the profit-driven women who offer photos with Drake's cutout.

14. We see this again in the bizarre Van-centered episode "Tarrare" (s3e10), in which Van has been apparently living as a French model and sous chef, acquiring and preparing severed human hands for elite diners. It is not until a chance encounter with and emotional prodding by Candice, one of the friends from "Champagne Papi," that Van breaks down and begins to reevaluate her life and direction; Candice offers support as Van decides it is time to return to her real life, whatever that may be.

15. Ironically, Nadine is the only one who doesn't enter the party seeking out a man and ends up having the most meaningful—although not sexual or romantic—connection with a man via her conversation with Darius.

16. Contrast this with *The Twilight Zone*'s "Mirror Image" (s1e21), an episode that served as inspiration for Jordan Peele's film *Us*. A woman continues to see her own doppelganger at a bus station. When she seeks the camaraderie and protection of a man at the station, he feigns understanding before betraying her and clandestinely calling the police to escort her away. It isn't until he sees his *own* doppelganger that he realizes too late that she was telling the truth.

17. This also suggests a surreal explanation for the presence of "Papi" in Drake's Instagram moniker.

18. This moment occurs significantly as the sun rises on January 1, the start of the new year.

East Point/College Park

BECOMING INHUMAN

Donald Glover, Hiro Murai, and the Self-Alienation of Celebrity

KINOHI NISHIKAWA

On December 6, 2013, the first music video for Childish Gambino's second studio album, *Because the Internet*, was released online. The video's single, "3005," had come out in October, and its lovelorn lyrics situated the rapper in R&B territory: "No matter what you say or what you do / when I'm alone, I'd rather be with you. / Fuck these other n****s. / I'll be right by your side 'til 3005, hold up" (Glover, "Childish Gambino—3005"). Yet unlike most R&B music videos, where the beloved addressee often has a starring role, "3005" shows Childish Gambino riding a carnival Ferris wheel with only a giant stuffed teddy bear sitting next to him. As the wheel goes around, Childish Gambino raps with an expressionless face, his mouth spitting lyrics as if on autopilot. He is going through the motions. The bear, meanwhile, moves and blinks in a way that suggests it is alive. But this potential vehicle for cuteness is offset by the fact that the bear becomes visibly worn—soiled, tattered, even beat up—with each revolution. Absent the beloved, it bears the emotional wounds of the relationship. Visually, the video transfers feelings typically reserved for a person to an object. As that object shows signs of wear, we come to feel its pain, all the while wondering how a toy came to feel in the first place.

The object's ability to generate pathos underscores Childish Gambino's seeming lack thereof. Compared to the teddy bear, his character looks disinterested, withdrawn. What does it mean, then, that the object displays more "human" traits than the rapper? Perhaps we are looking at not two separable figures here but one—a single character marked by an internal conflict or cleavage. This reading is lent support by the fact that the lyrics are only partly about standing by a girl through thick and thin.[1] They also bespeak Childish Gambino's insecurities about fame, career, family, and friendship: "Got a house full of homies, why I feel so the opposite? / Incompetent ain't the half of it. / Saturdays we're Young Lavish-ing. / Saddest shit is I'm bad at it." Though having achieved the outward trappings of success, Childish Gambino attests to feeling like he is an imposter: a rapper without a block to call home, someone who performs the part of "living large" poorly. The bear may represent this deep ambivalence within himself, where the pressures attendant to success have displaced the wide-eyed naïveté with which he began his career.

The split subjectivity of "3005" culminates in the video's conclusion. As the chorus cycles on repeat, we see from the wheel's perch that an area just beyond the carnival is on fire. We only get snatches of the view, so it's unclear what is transpiring. When the camera returns to the passenger car's seat and the soundtrack switches to baby-voiced singing, we see that Childish Gambino's character has disappeared, leaving the bear alone in its most ruined state, its stuffing falling out and its fluff looking singed by flame. After a beat, the camera rotates outward again, and the soundtrack turns to a robotic voice freestyling a strange incantation. From the bear's perspective, we get a better view of the fair and fire. Alone in the fairway is a single figure—a shadow—who may well be the person we just saw in the Ferris wheel. But if his voice is being thrown onto the scene, then the video leaves us with the unsettling proposition that Childish Gambino is no longer himself. Man and bear now appear alien to each other. What we are witnessing, then, is the process of the rapper *becoming inhuman*.

I first wrote about Childish Gambino, Donald Glover's musical stage name, in an essay that appeared in *Post-Soul Satire: Black Identity after Civil Rights* (2014). There, I consider how the rapper's early indie releases were committed to satirizing what was then a dominant trend in hip hop: mass commercialization around a narrow set of images of Black masculinity. By the early 2010s, mainstream hip hop had been caricatured by the media as being obsessed with "babes, bullets, and bling" (C. Lee). Childish Gambino's career took off from a position of rejecting what hip hop had become. In his early albums, he weds an underground artistic sensibility with emergent online distribution to sidestep corporate record labels and fashion a new kind of Black male rapper, one who is hyperaware of the way media shape his persona. I argue that Childish Gambino "alternates between performing the object of critique," as in parodying hip-hop stereotypes, and "deploy[s] the autobiographical self to contest the regime of commodified stereotypes," as in drawing on his own feelings and experiences (and here the slippage between Glover and his persona is intentional) to cut through the manufactured image of hip-hop "reality" (Nishikawa 47). In both cases, the rapper's "real" self is never coincident with the persona he performs. That may have been why Glover came up with his moniker not from "the street" or from a childhood nickname but from the online Wu-Tang Clan name generator. The idea is that there is *nothing* behind Childish Gambino; all we have to go by is how we encounter him in performance.

This chapter extends the argument of that earlier essay by showing how Donald Glover has transformed his critique of hip-hop mimesis into an overarching aesthetic that characterizes not only his mid-career music but also his work writing, producing, and acting in *Atlanta*, particularly the show's two prepandemic seasons.[2] What began as an outside-looking-in satire of hip-hop conglomeration at the height of its global reach has had to adapt to Glover's becoming a major cultural figure in his own right. As "3005" demonstrates, and as even cursory knowledge of *Atlanta* can confirm, Glover has retained his irreverent perspective on the music industry. The difference is that the nature and object of his satire have changed to match his position as an artist. I argue here that his recent work moves beyond the autobiographical to explore the conceptual and aesthetic affordances of becoming inhuman. Rather than pointing out the contradiction between stereotype and speaking subject, the "insider" Glover radically alienates the speaking subject from himself. At stake in this performance of self-division is not simply the fabrication of hip-hop gender codes but, more fundamentally, the fantasy structure that conducts how Black male celebrities are consumed.

Glover often advances this self-division as an actual feature of his music. Recall the switch to a squeaky, babyish voice at the end of "3005," which is then replaced by a deep, monotone voice whose rap sounds as though it is issued by a walkie-talkie.[3] With no other vocals credited in the song, these shifts reflect Childish Gambino's multiply remixed voice, a sonic layering that confounds any clear identification of the speaking subject. But beginning with *Because the Internet*, we see Glover rely more pointedly on visual forms to convey alienation from his own celebrity. Consider the cover art for the album, a self-dissolving portrait of the artist. Glover originally released the cover image online as a GIF, thus making the dissolve a function of digital manipulation. To replicate that effect for the CD, his label Glassnote used lenticular printing technology, which creates an illusion of a changing image as you move it around. As these promotional materials suggest, the all-consuming visuality of internet culture is both a major source of Glover's fame and a significant driver of his obsolescence. The image literalizes the project of becoming inhuman, which has been a hallmark of Glover's aesthetic since.

Glover's key collaborator in developing this aesthetic is the Japan-born filmmaker Hiro Murai. Known for combining elements of horror with flourishes of noir, Murai has cultivated a visual style that dovetails with Glover's self-reflexive critique of twenty-first-century race relations. The son of a famous Japanese popular-music composer, Murai moved to Los Angeles as a boy and eventually earned his degree from the famed University of Southern California

School of Cinematic Arts. After directing his first music video in 2005, Murai gained experience as a director of photography on several more videos, all in the indie-rock and pop genres. In 2009, Murai began directing videos for R&B and hip-hop artists, including Raphael Saadiq, Usher, Lupe Fiasco, and Earl Sweatshirt. This expansion of his portfolio coincided with hip hop's turn away from the "thug" style that had dominated the 2000s. Indeed, the Black male rappers whose videos he directed were misfits, nerds, and weirdos in their public personas—a far cry from the hardened dealers and hustlers portrayed by 50 Cent and Jay-Z. No wonder, then, that, in 2013, Murai directed Childish Gambino's "3005" as well as the short film *Clapping for the Wrong Reasons* that accompanied the release of *Because the Internet* (Hamada; Ettenhofer). This was just the beginning of a fruitful and ongoing collaboration between two artists who, though ensconced in Hollywood's celebrity culture, refuse the terms of Black male idolization.

Consider the music video for "Telegraph Ave.," another single from the album, released online on October 10, 2014. Like "3005," "Telegraph Ave." is riddled with self-doubt. The issue here concerns Childish Gambino's ability to commit to a girl and settle down with her: "And I'm nervous truth be told. / I never saw me growing old / in Oakland, in Oakland" (Glover, "Childish Gambino—Telegraph Ave"). People who know her are leery—"All the girlfriends saying, 'Here we go again'"—so the track record for both may not augur good things. Unlike "3005," however, which contrasts professions of love with a scene absent the beloved, "Telegraph Ave." expresses romantic wariness while the beloved is featured prominently in a tropical paradise. Childish Gambino and the girl (Jhené Aiko) are not in Oakland but on an island, enjoying a vacation in a lush rainforest and on the beach. The bright greens of grass and trees stand out sharply from cloudy skies and red earth, creating a visual landscape far removed from the Oakland of which the song speaks. In this way, Murai creates a disjuncture between the song's lyrics and their visual representation, turning Black cultural associations with urban space (such as concrete references to Telegraph Avenue in historically Black Oakland) into a self-questioning mindset. Everything seems to be going well for the couple—except that this disjuncture suggests that things are not what they seem.

First, there is the fact that the video begins in a Jeep with Childish Gambino getting behind the wheel and driving off. In the side-view mirror and from behind his seat, we only get to see his face from just below the eyes down. It's not until a full minute into the video that we realize the girl is in the passenger seat. Murai shows her eyes glancing at Childish Gambino from the perspective of the rearview mirror. Although their surroundings may suggest relaxation and comfort, this is a couple that clearly doesn't see eye to eye. Their estrangement is lent further support during an interlude in which the girl watches her lover swim in the ocean from the shore. Murai takes us underwater and shows Childish Gambino encountering a monk seal. Strange, muffled sounds travel through the water until he comes back up for air. This is shortly followed by an instrumental section in which electronic beats mark Childish Gambino's dancing alone in a seeming trance. The incantation of "3005" that signals a process of becoming inhuman returns here to notable effect.

These oddities culminate in the video's final sequence. In the dead of night, a pair of headlights takes the couple by surprise as they walk through the woods. The vehicle accelerates and smashes into Childish Gambino's character. Two men whom the couple encountered earlier get out of the car, but one of them seems concerned for the girl's safety. We see why: when the Black man stands up, the torn left side of his body reveals a tentacled monster lurking beneath his skin. With slimy appendages shooting out from his body, Childish Gambino dispatches the two hunters with ease, but instead of running away screaming, the girl takes in the chaos, holds the gaze of the lover she thought was human, and steps toward him. It is as though she finally recognizes Childish Gambino for who—or what—he is.

The lyrics and visuals make sense together as a comment on the figurative monster that lurks within a man who cannot get over his doubts about a romantic relationship. But in 2014, they also served an extratextual purpose: to rebuff gossip that Glover and Aiko—collaborators on each other's musical projects at that time—were dating. The social-media-fueled speculation constrained what both felt like they could express as artists. The importance of resisting such gossip for Glover can be insinuated from the fact that the phrase that forms the album's title appears in the lyrics of "Telegraph Ave.": "And they're saying it's because of the internet. / Try her once, and it's on to the next chick. / X-O the O faces on your exes, right? / And we can do the same thing if you wanna have at it." The strain under which Glover raps, even partly obscured by a stage name, reflects the fact that any relationship he has is bound to come under online scrutiny. While the reference to "O faces" isn't definitive—they could express orgasm or surprise—the fact is that fame keeps "exes" in the picture. Such unwanted attention is the price of celebrity; its inevitability comes across with a resigned shrug.

As a media format that relies on collapsing any border between artistic performance and commercial promotion, the online music video courts gossip by casting Glover and Aiko in the main roles only to subvert the fantasy that it would confirm or deny those rumors.[4] Murai's use of classic horror tropes, like the "body snatcher" and the "last girl standing," turns the imagined attachment into the stuff of a midnight movie. In some ways, these familiar yet pleasurable cinematic moves ensure that any subtext about Glover and Aiko is exposed as generic wish fulfillment. At the same time, Murai's direction introduces a fresh perspective to the horror genre itself. In particular, the long opening sequence in which Childish Gambino's eyes are concealed takes on new meaning in light of his becoming inhuman. The seeds of his monstrous turn are already there, which is why the two locals look askance at him before he steps into the water. Thus, as with "3005," the male character in "Telegraph Ave." is self-alienated—not one with himself or with his body—from the beginning. On this frequency, the lyrics and visuals work together to show how the couple's love is thwarted by events set in motion long before their arrival in paradise.

In visual style, lyrical substance, and metadiscursive commentary, the collaboration between Glover and Murai on "Telegraph Ave." is reminiscent of one of the most famous music videos of all time: *Michael Jackson's Thriller*. The video is in fact a nearly fourteen-minute short film directed by filmmaker John Landis and cowritten by Landis and Jackson. The film was conceived by Jackson as a way to jump-start sales for his album *Thriller* (1982), with the hope of returning it to the top of the charts after it had spent most of the previous year there. He picked Landis to direct after seeing his mixed-genre horror-comedy movie *An American Werewolf in London* (1981). After its release on December 2, 1983, *Michael Jackson's Thriller* played on constant rotation on MTV and did indeed revive the album's sales. The album's success and that of the film were mutually reinforcing. *Thriller* became the bestselling album of all time, while the film, distributed for retail on VHS, became the bestselling videotape of all time. In many respects, the Michael Jackson whose fame we now take for granted was born out of the wager that his persona was the perfect vehicle for a groundbreaking fusion of commercial, musical, and visual cultures.

At its core is a storyline that playfully subverts audience expectations for Jackson's performance of Black masculinity. The film opens with a shot of Jackson and "Michael's Girl" (Ola Ray) driving through the secluded woods in a Cadillac convertible. The car runs out of gas, he says, so they start walking. He is wearing a varsity jacket and jeans, she a long skirt and bobby socks. On their walk, Jackson formally asks the girl out and gives her a ring. But he utters this warning: "I'm not like other guys." She professes her love, thinking he only wants to emphasize his superiority over her other choices. He corrects her: "No, I mean I'm different." At that point, the full moon peeks out from behind the clouds, and Jackson lets out a shriek as he keels over. In conjunction with Rick Baker's astonishing special makeup effects, Landis then shows Jackson morphing into a werewolf, each part of his face becoming disfigured by animal features. Once the transformation is complete, Jackson chases the girl around and eventually pins her to the ground. Just as his clawed hands are about to assault her, Landis cuts to a movie theater where an audience, which includes Jackson and the girl, is terrified by what they see on the screen.

Kobena Mercer's early analysis of the film remains the most attuned to its contemporary critique of Jackson's idolization.[5] The mass publicity of his slippery racial, gender, and sexual identification is, for Mercer, both the pretext and the subtext of the film. Once we see Jackson and the girl in modern clothing, seated in and then leaving the movie theater, we come to understand the opening as a parody, a film within a film (one that the marquee outside calls "Thriller," fittingly enough) and thus "a simulacrum of a story in its stylistic send-up of [horror] genre conventions." The parody becomes a way for Jackson, the artist, to deflect rumors about his identity. For Mercer, the film "presupposes a degree of self-consciousness on the part of the spectator, giving rise to a supplementary commentary on the sexuality and sexual identity of its star" (44). The line "I'm not like other guys" cuts multiple ways, acknowledging "the gossip which circulates around his star image" while teasing the idea that his "difference" could mean that he is "homosexual, transsexual or somehow *a*sexual" (46, emphasis original). In other words, the film uses the horror genre's investment in the norms of 1950s youth culture (the projected innocence to which terror is contrasted) to stage the ambiguity of Jackson's sexual persona. No wonder Jackson tapped Landis, whose *American Werewolf* likewise relied on audiences' recognition of its parodies of horror conventions, to direct his video.

But what to make of the fact that, after this crucial turn, the film goes on to show Jackson and the girl confronted by another terror—a phalanx of zombies? During the couple's walk home from the theater, Jackson begins to sing the lyrics to *his* "Thriller," which compares the "thrills" of watching a horror movie to those that the boy promises to show the girl. After Vincent Price recites a campy rhyme, the undead rise from a cemetery and surround the couple. To the girl's horror, Jackson—now a zombie himself, with bulging eyes and sallow cheeks—joins them as their front man and performs an incredibly choreographed dance to the song's infectious beat. The girl runs from the scene and escapes to her house. However, the undead follow her and break in. Just as Jackson and the other zombies close in on her, the film cuts once again to show the girl in the confines of an unmolested home, her boyfriend reaching his hand out to comfort her. Except just as Jackson leads her away, he turns back to the camera and flashes a smile that is topped by menacing yellow eyes—the same ones that appeared when he turned into a werewolf earlier. Here, Landis's frame narrative is confounded as a trait from the fictional film finds itself expressed in the actual boyfriend. So, the zombie infestation cannot be passed off as a nightmare, and the B movie "Thriller" seems to have crossed over into real life. Meanwhile, any conception of finding the "real" Jackson is deferred in a play of generic recombination.

Far from stifling interest in Jackson, Landis's film built up his mythos. Jackson's star power afforded him the opportunity to hold a mirror up to the mass media's obsession with that very same trait. Audiences were mesmerized by the hall of mirrors into which *Michael Jackson's Thriller* delivered them. Landis's reliance on prosthetics and special-effects makeup was perfectly suited for a celebrity whose physiognomy had already become a topic for sensationalized coverage. "As the monstrous mask is, literally, a construction made out of makeup and cosmetic 'work,'" writes Mercer, "the fictional world of the horror film merely appropriates what is already an artifice" (49). The slippages between 1950s Michael, werewolf Michael, 1980s Michael, and zombie Michael dramatize the fact that there is, finally, no "real person or private self" behind the persona but only Michael Jackson as an image. By reveling in its use of special effects, thematizing what is usually left implicit, the film serves as "an allegory for the fascination with which the world beholds his reconstructed star image" (49). Getting lost in the artifice and being able to enjoy the camp are part and parcel to securing Jackson's success.

While Mercer's reading of *Michael Jackson's Thriller* remains trenchant, it does not account for what might be called the film's satirical edge: its delight in seeing us—recall those final yellow eyes—try to find the real Jackson only to end up in a hall of mirrors.[6] This strain in Landis and Jackson's collaboration is picked up by Glover and Murai in the work they have done for *Atlanta*. Of the forty-one episodes, Murai has directed twenty-six of them, suggesting how important his vision is to the realization of the series. To be sure, the entire show could be said to explore the alienation at the heart of social media, celebrity culture, and the contemporary music industry. In a canny act of displacement, Glover plays Earnest "Earn" Marks, the learn-as-you-go music manager of rapper Alfred "Paper Boi" Miles (Brian Tyree Henry). Whatever associations we bring to the series through Childish Gambino—on whom Michael Jackson's music and choreography have had a profound influence—are suspended as Alfred navigates a music scene that consumes Black male talent with jaded familiarity. Alfred is on the cusp of making it, but from what he is able to see on the other side, celebrity exacts an awful toll on those fortunate enough to achieve it. This is where Murai's vision comes in: his episodes are notable for framing the theme of self-alienation with a peculiar blend of satire and horror. And like *Michael Jackson's Thriller*, Murai aims not to expose the "real" Glover or Henry to audiences but to scramble our coordinates of what even counts as reality for Earn and Alfred.

Consider the episode "Nobody Beats the Biebs" (s1e5). Earn and Alfred attend a charity basketball event, where the headlining celebrity is Justin Bieber. The Canadian pop star and former teenage heartthrob constitutes a touchstone of overhyped, social-media-driven fame in the music industry today. But rather than give viewers a straightforward comparison between Paper Boi and Bieber—one trying to break in and get a taste of what the other has—Murai, Glover, and writer Stephen Glover (Donald's brother) create a scenario where the sheer unreality of celebrity is thematized. In this episode, Bieber is portrayed as a cocky young Black man (Austin Crute) who uses his charm to get away with uttering silly inanities and behaving obnoxiously toward others. For his part, Alfred cannot understand the appeal: in shots from his point of view, we see Bieber urinate in front of adoring fans and push his hand in the face of entertainment reporter Valencia Joyner (Paloma Guzmán). Murai's framing allows us to recognize the irony in the fact that Bieber acts with impunity while Alfred cannot shake off his "criminal" reputation—his bad rap, so to speak—no matter how well he comports himself. The hopelessness of his situation manifests when Alfred provokes an on-court fight with Bieber. Though the fight leaves both men looking bad, it is Bieber who takes the occasion to announce his regret, offer himself up for redemption, and promise that his "real" self has emerged out of the scandal. While Bieber revels in his impromptu press conference (where he also performs a single from his new album *Justice*), Alfred is scorned by Valencia who notes, cynically: "Play your part. People don't want Justin to be the asshole. They want you to be the asshole. You're a rapper. That's your job."

Black Bieber is made possible by Murai's body-snatcher aesthetic and the Glovers' choice to have the character played as an inhuman version of the "real" Justin Bieber. Murai's shots from Alfred's point of view create a sense of unease, as if he is the only one able to see Bieber's fraudulence while everyone laps up his abuse. Though the episode retains a lighthearted tone, it generates thriller-style suspense in Alfred's increasing isolation from what the world considers to be true and authentic. That Bieber is played as a young Black man transmits that feeling of isolation—Am I really seeing this? Am I the only one not in on the joke?—to viewers themselves. By the end, the Glovers leave us wondering whether Bieber had calculated the fracas all along for it ended up being a boon to his celebrity. In this way, Black Bieber calls up the metadiscursive ironies of white pop stars' appropriation of Black musical and choreographic talent and of the same group's ability to have their bad behavior escape racial judgment. Thus, though Valencia's final words are harsh, they are the one moment in the episode where Alfred's suspicions are confirmed—and where the reputational price of Paper Boi's success is clarified in no uncertain terms.[7]

The satirical edge of "Nobody Beats the Biebs" may sound like it contrasts an authentic Black self to the whitewashed fantasies of a corporate media machine. But Murai and Glover resist essentializing Alfred's position in the series, as if he embodies the "real real" over and against the manufactured reality of the music industry. Not coincidentally, their most inventive deconstruction of this presumption makes use of horror tropes. "Woods" (s2e8) begins with Alfred on a date with a companion named Ciara (Angela Wildflower). On a drive around town that ends at a nail salon, Ciara shows herself to be an expert "influencer," constantly generating content and narrating her activities as if watched by another. Alfred remains aloof from her brash, market-attuned advice; he would rather not have to deal with these aspects of modern life. His fidelity to a notion of authenticity expresses itself most forcefully when, after Ciara takes a photo of him in the salon chair without his permission to share on social media, he walks out on the date and vows to walk home. For Glover and writer Stefani Robinson, this is Alfred's stand for "keeping it real," remaining true to himself in an age where self-exposure is often misconstrued as the truth.

Alfred would seem to be vindicated when he meets a group of three Paper Boi fans near a wooded area. Though he is flattered by their recognition, he soon realizes that they intend to mug him. The young men beat Alfred, who fights back and manages to avoid being shot. An assailant chases him into the woods, where, in a trope taken from countless horror and thriller movies, the victim is forced to run for his life. Murai stays tightly focused on Alfred's face as the terror of being caught plays across it. Darkness falls; fear intensifies. He wanders aimlessly and runs into an older Black man in tattered clothes. The man, who gives his name as Wally (Reggie Alvin Green), is a nuisance Alfred wants to avoid. After losing him, the camera zooms out over the scene to show a surprisingly deep forest, which makes it seem as though Alfred were not in the city at all. He encounters Wally again when it becomes clear he has been walking in circles. This time, in the face of Alfred's disrespect, Wally draws a knife to his throat, saying: "Keep standin' still. You're gone, boy. You're wastin' time. And the only people who got time are dead." The fear instilled by the threat serves as renewed impetus to get out of the woods, which Glover and Robinson mean for us to take both literally and figuratively, as Alfred needs to stop making excuses and jump-start his career as Paper Boi.[8] He manages to scramble out of the trees and ends up at a gas station, where he takes refuge in its store. While Alfred searches for something cold to hold to his face, a white fan recognizes him and asks for a selfie. This time—worn, exhausted, and bloodied—Alfred grins for the camera phone in a version of keeping it real that traverses the fantasy of authenticity not outside of fandom but through the way it operates today. Actively negotiating the compromises one has to make in a cutthroat industry is, for Alfred, a way of moving forward without losing himself. Notably, this realization is afforded by Wally, whose presence proves to be not an explicit threat but a spectral haunting.[9]

Though the travails of Alfred as Paper Boi are the most sustained way Glover meditates on his own stardom through the series, his art of becoming inhuman is epitomized in a single episode that has little to do with the rapper. Instead, "Teddy Perkins" (s2e6), which helps set up the storyline of "Woods," offers metadiscursive commentary on the psychic perils of Black male idolization through a thinly veiled representation of Michael Jackson himself. The episode follows Darius (Lakeith Stanfield) as he answers an online offer for a free vintage piano, free so long as it can be moved off the property. He discovers that the instrument is housed in a looming, dimly lit mansion inhabited by Theodore "Teddy" Perkins, an unsettling figure who possesses a pale, mask-like face and who speaks in a lilting, high-pitched tone. Teddy claims to be the brother of the piano's owner, the once-famous musician Benny Hope. He explains that Benny abandoned his career after coming down with a rare skin condition. When Teddy steps away, Darius sees Benny's career trajectory in a series of photographs in the hallway: from young Black soul singer with dark skin and an afro to pop icon with lightened skin and straightened hair to a wheelchair-ridden man whose face is completely obscured by bandages. Hearing the piano playing from a room only Teddy seems to occupy, Darius suspects that Teddy is in fact Benny, the former an alter ego he has created to deal with his lost celebrity. He tells his friends Alfred and Earn as much when he calls them, comparing Teddy to the former baseball player Sammy Sosa, whose skin has been noticeably lightened from his use of bleaching cream.

But this suspicion is challenged when Darius tries to move the piano out by way of the elevator only to end up in the basement. There, he encounters Benny (Derrick Haywood), who writes on a chalkboard "teddy kill us both" and asks him to retrieve a gun from the attic. Darius tries to ignore this family trouble only to find Teddy's car blocking his moving truck. When he goes to ask Teddy to move his car, Darius finds him watching an old film reel of his father reprimanding Benny while playing the piano. The scene echoes an earlier one in which Teddy approvingly cites their father's belief that "great things come from great pain," likening Benny's experience to that of other Black celebrities—Michael Jackson, Marvin Gaye, Serena Williams—who had notoriously exacting fathers. It then takes a harrowing turn when Teddy swings the gun toward Darius, saying that he has chosen him as the "sacrifice" his father long said was required to be a Black artist. Teddy has Darius handcuff himself to a chair in the main foyer. Darius tries to save his life by sympathizing with Teddy, insisting that "not all great things come from pain," that beauty can also come from love, and that "your dad should've said sorry." Teddy coldly rejects this appeal, but right when Darius seems doomed, Benny wheels himself out of the elevator, picks up the gun, and shoots Teddy dead. He then turns the gun on himself and blows his brains out. The episode ends with coroners taking the bodies away and Darius leaving the mansion without his piano.

This extended synopsis allows us to understand how Glover and Murai encode figural monstrosity in the very process of young Black men *becoming famous*. Whereas their video collaborations tend to deploy what Mercer would call "metaphorical monsters" to reflect self-alienation, "Teddy Perkins," like

"Nobody Beats the Biebs" and "Woods," draws on horror and thriller genres' formal properties to cultivate a sense of dread around the characters. A strictly metaphorical reading might hone in on the fact that Benny as Teddy embodies many things we associate with Jackson: the soft, affected voice, the musical career marked in equal measure by trauma and success, the excruciating loneliness of his (faded) stardom, and, not least, the face that has turned into a smooth white surface. As the episode itself thematizes, this reading would follow a correspondence between the pain inflicted on Black boys by their fathers and the art that propels them to international fame. Yet the way Murai frames Teddy creates uncertainty about such a reading. Early on, in the parlor of the mansion, Teddy invites Darius to share a giant soft-boiled ostrich egg with him. Murai lingers on the orb and shows Teddy thumping it with a small hammer. Upon peeling it open, thick embryonic goo oozes out, causing Darius to gag. The viscous liquid provokes disgust in the viewer, too, yet it doesn't faze Teddy, who seems to relish tasting it in front of his guest. The stillness of his face, which Murai frames through wide-angle shots, only adds to the disorientation as it betrays no affect, no motive, nothing except its sheen. Throughout the episode, these shots make the face appear like a floating mask. In observance of Benny's photosensitivity, Teddy keeps the mansion in a state of near darkness. By framing Teddy as an ethereal presence in this gloom, Murai disturbs viewers' ability to read him at all. He seems less a cover for Benny's pain than an uncanny figure in his own right, not a monster so much as a character who provokes estrangement whenever we think we know who he is.

The noncorrespondence between Teddy and Benny is hinted at well before Darius heads to the basement (a depth metaphor if there ever was one). In the second hallway photograph, Benny is shown standing next to then president Bill Clinton in the foreground. Although their faces are slightly blurred, viewers can clearly see a figure between them in the background: a faint silhouette of a Black man in a suit. The man's bright yellow eyes reference the ending of *Michael Jackson's Thriller*, where the "real" Jackson shows himself to be the monster, his alter ego, all along. Yet just as that meaning requires us to traverse different narrative frames in Landis's film, so do the glowing eyes here multiply the personae in question. For one, if that eerie figure isn't Benny, who is he? If he's Teddy, then that means they are indeed two distinct characters, not one, as Darius has come to presume. But if this malevolent force is somehow external to Benny, then what can account for his supposed self-hatred? How does he end up, in the next photograph, disabled and wrapped up, looking like the iconic invisible man of horror movies (most notably, James Whale's 1933 production of *The Invisible Man*)? Benny appears to be haunted by an actual evil, not simply one internal to his psyche. The detail recalls the shadow we see for a split second at the end of the video for "3005." But it also raises the questions of imposture and body snatching that are at the heart of "Nobody Beats the Biebs." In *Atlanta*, figural monstrosity leaves metaphoricity (of the teddy bear, for example) behind for the thing itself: irresolution over who is human and who is the shadow.

Whether Benny as Teddy or Teddy as uncanny double of Benny, Glover and Murai tease viewers' sense that Teddy essentially represents Benny's divided self. But that impression is itself called into question when Darius happens upon Teddy in the screening room. In the old footage of his father berating Benny, there is a constant audio refrain: a hand pounding the top of the piano. The father expresses his frustration with his son by slamming the very instrument of Benny's artistic talent (and the object of Darius's quest). The detail echoes an earlier moment when Darius, convinced that Teddy is Benny, tries to finalize paperwork for the transfer of the piano. After loudly objecting to Darius's effort to sympathize with Benny's plight, Teddy slams the pen on the top of the piano. The fact that this act is repeated with force in the film reel— and *after* the discovery of the man in the basement—suggests that Darius is on the wrong track and that there is a malevolent force emanating from this family's traumas. It also leaves open the possibility that Teddy is not Benny but his father, which, given their fraught and codependent relationship, could be another way of imagining the father as always already the son. This reading foreshadows the scene in "Woods" when Wally, in his first rambling dialogue and apropos of nothing, admits, "I lost my baby." Alfred doesn't think anything of the statement—at this juncture he thinks the old man is crazy—but the confession may indicate a paternal haunting (rather than an uncanny doubling) that rhymes with the refrain of the slamming of the piano.

In the end, though, it remains ambiguous whether Teddy is really Benny, his brother, or his father. There are two corpses, as suggested by the coroner's body bags, but the statement that lingers after the murder-suicide is Teddy's succinct response of "exactly" to Darius's claim to knowing that "there is no fucking Benny." Darius thinks he's got Teddy's number, but the rejoinder only serves to provoke questions rather than provide answers. Is there no Benny because Teddy is Benny? Or is there no Benny because Benny was always already a construct, a stage name, a figure other to himself? Or is there no Benny because Benny is dead to Teddy, whether as his brother or his father? The ambiguity at the heart of Teddy's affirmation calls into question the episode's entire symbolic order. As such, it leaves us with the option of understanding Teddy not as one person or another but as the inhuman "Real" that haunts the Benny Hope legacy. Teddy is the traumatic core out of which the motto "great things come from great pain" springs.[10]

What makes this figuration of becoming inhuman a capstone achievement in Glover and Murai's art is the way it obliquely redounds on Glover's own celebrity. I did not previously specify the actor portraying Teddy because the episode's closing credits say that Teddy Perkins appears "as himself." Although media coverage of *Atlanta* is content to point out that Glover did, in fact, play Teddy, it also notes that Glover stayed in character for the entire shoot and that the prosthetics that went into his makeup rendered him unrecognizable to many of the cast and crew. In other words, Glover embodied Teddy's uncanniness as part of the production process. This literalization of the inhuman—where Glover does not just represent monstrosity but embodies it—is further registered in the fact that the episode contains Glover's usual character, Earn, in the backseat of Alfred's car. Thus, the illusion that Teddy plays "himself" is supported by viewers who expect to recognize Glover as Earn. The desire to read the celebrity into the character—something that accounts for the mise en abyme effect of *Michael Jackson's Thriller*—is, in "Teddy Perkins," confounded by a meta-metareflexivity. Teddy doesn't just challenge who we think Glover is (as the monsters in *Thriller* do for Jackson). Teddy instead turns Glover inside out, exposing in viscous (real) and prosthetic (artificial) forms the divided subject himself. The episode traverses Glover's star image to dwell in the "Real" of his own image making, which has been both a creative and a coercive process.

Teddy Perkins is neither a metaphor nor an allegory. Rather, he is both the performance and the embodiment of the contradictions of Black male celebrity. This literalization of becoming inhuman sharpened its satirical edge at the seventieth Primetime Emmy Awards ceremony held on September 17, 2018. Glover was nominated for Outstanding Lead Actor in a Comedy Series for playing Earn and Teddy in that episode. However, Teddy showed up to the ceremony, as did Glover (Desta). The dual appearance surprised everyone and left observers flummoxed as to who was really behind the mask. To this day, no one has been able to figure it out. Indeed, the fact that Glover and Perkins could be seen in the audience at the same time reframed media coverage away from the televised episode and toward the live broadcast. Suddenly the question became, Who was this person *separate* and *apart* from Glover? The nomination may have been for a dual performance, but the dual appearance staged its own logic, one that denied there had ever been one actor playing two roles to begin with. Two bodies, rather than two roles, became the talking point of the evening.

To the extent that Glover and Murai continue to collaborate on their artistic endeavors, the latter will help visualize an outside to the celebrity culture that envelops the former. From Childish Gambino's early music videos to television episodes that achieve something like the status of performance art, Glover and Murai have experimented with visualizing the traumatic "Real," the living monstrosity, of manufactured star images. Now an A-list celebrity whose 2021 deal with Amazon Studios promises more creative control and larger audiences

(Goldberg), Glover no longer can rely solely on lyrical invention and comic wordplay to articulate his difference from the mainstream. Contending with our image-saturated celebrity culture requires someone like Murai to execute his satirical intent. We can expect their combined work to further rebuff audiences' wish to know Glover, to consume Glover, to make him theirs.

NOTES

1. In an interview with Fuse TV, Childish Gambino reveals that he wrote "3005" not (just) as a love song but as a reflection on existential loneliness. He ties his feeling "scared of being alone" to the memory of a big dog on the street where he grew up. He overcame his fear of the dog only when he had someone next to him—namely, his sister, whom he "knew [he] had to protect" (Fuse).

2. In my view, the song and video "This Is America" (2018) and the latter two seasons of *Atlanta* mark a third stage of development in Glover's career. As such, I leave it to others to focus on that as my interest here is on his development into the second stage.

3. Behind this second voice is yet another, one that belts out what sounds like a dirge.

4. Online music videos perfect a promotional dynamic pioneered by cable music videos in the 1980s and 1990s. While the genre as a whole depends on consumers' awareness of (and participation in) celebrity culture, online music videos are guided by even greater degrees of consumer targeting and personalized consumption (Edmond).

5. Mercer's essay was first published in *Screen* in 1986.

6. The kind of playful self-awareness we see in this video is not sustained for the rest of Jackson's career. Indeed, as his own celebrity grew to enormous proportions, Jackson took on a persona of dour self-seriousness and isolated eccentricity. The turn in his public presentation may have sought to mask what is now recognized as a pattern of preying on vulnerable children. When Jackson returned to the horror genre for the Stephen King–scripted, forty-minute video *Michael Jackson's Ghosts* in 1996, the tone he struck was self-righteous and indignant. The video, as Robin R. Means Coleman explains, "focuses on the odd 'Maestro' who is liked by children, but is misunderstood by adults who want to see him ejected from their community. . . . In a seemingly semi-autobiographical tale, Maestro proceeds to transform himself into various demon figures in an effort to scare the adults away, leaving him alone with the children to play in his home" (160). This essay distinguishes the satirical intent of the earlier film from the aesthetics of Jackson's later works, which are marked by the use of power and influence to conceal serial abuse.

7. All these readings come out of an imposter scenario that does not reveal itself as such. But the episode does announce imposture as a controlling theme when Earn plays along with a white female agent's mistaking him for another agent named Alonzo. Here the woman's favors and flattery gain Earn a foothold in the world of high-powered celebrity management. After some half-hearted resistance to her mistake, he is content to go along with the impersonation. The ruse turns sour, however, when the woman finally turns on him (as Alonzo), calling him out for undercutting her business and stealing her clients. She promises to ruin him, using venomous, homophobic language. The sudden reversal

frightens Earn, who, along with Alfred, cannot wait to leave the charity event. For further discussion of this episode, see the essays by Rutter and Parks herein.

8. In this, Wally's counsel is reminiscent of the riddle-like advice given to the narrator by his grandfather in Ralph Ellison's *Invisible Man* (1952).

9. For further discussion of this episode, see O'Brien's essay herein.

10. For further discussion of this episode, see the essays by Glavanakova, Foster-Singletary, and Lee herein.

STREETS ON LOCKE

The Volition of *Atlanta*

THOMAS BRITT

Hip hop and rap, among the most significant cultural influences on *Atlanta*, have historically been concerned with turning dreams into reality, most obviously in the lyrics and lyricism that are central features of such musical expression. For example, "Juicy," the lead single of the Notorious B.I.G.'s debut album *Ready to Die* (1994), begins with a spoken introduction—directed at detractors who threatened to impede Christopher Wallace's ambitions—that segues into the first half of the first bar: "It was all a dream." In the chorus, Total reiterates the theme, singing "reach for the stars . . . you had a goal." A decade later, Atlanta rapper (Young) Jeezy emerged with *Let's Get It: Thug Motivation 101* (2005), his major-label debut featuring a trap-star mantra to stir the ambitious listener in the song "Thug Motivation 101": "You gotta believe, you gotta believe. Let's get it!" Fellow Atlanta rapper Future couched his ambitions in a pointedly cinematic form, titling his label's first compilation mixtape *F.B.G.: The Movie*. On the track "See It to Believe It," Future alternates verses with another rapper named Test, who proclaims, "I'm setting goals, I'm reaching achievements," while Future affirms having "Left the trap in a Phantom. / And I ain't coming back."

To varying degrees, each of these rappers exist at the nexus of drug dealing and rapping, a situation featured in several films preceding *Atlanta*. Craig Brewer's *Hustle & Flow* (2005) and Damon Russell's *Snow on tha Bluff* (2011) use such characterizations to establish a relevant polarity for *Atlanta*'s satirical viewpoint. Both films feature individual antiheroes whose personal drives propel the single-minded narratives; they lionize their respective main characters to such an extent that there is no inherent critique or disapprobation of their vice, folly, and violent behavior. The films differ from one another tonally, as *Hustle & Flow* plays out as a fantasy and *Snow on tha Bluff* as a tragedy.

The intersecting activities of dealing and rapping are both tentpoles and satirical targets for *Atlanta*'s depiction of broke, Princeton dropout Earn Marks (Donald Glover) and his attempts to manage the ascendant rap career of his weed-dealing cousin Alfred "Paper Boi" Miles (Brian Tyree Henry). *Atlanta* departs significantly from the chimerical *Hustle & Flow* and the nihilistic *Snow on tha Bluff* in part because its dual-protagonist narrative approach provides an opposition of drives, which leads to complications and consistently grounds the characters in the frustrating realities of the economy and social mobility. The parallel—though not always integrated—paths trod by Earn and Alfred are ripe for satirical critique and commentary as each man's arc serves as a check on the other. Both are trying to "level up" in life. Within the context of *Atlanta*'s first two seasons, neither Earn nor Alfred experiences a rags-to-riches narrative.[1] Earn has no permanent residence and is co-parenting a daughter with a partner who, like Earn, is seeing other people. Alfred is only materially comfortable when his marijuana supply chain remains unbroken, and he learns repeatedly that his growing fame does not make him impervious to being robbed or threatened.[2] Neither sees a satisfying return on their investment in Paper Boi's career during the show's first two seasons, which are my exclusive focus in this essay (partly because the show intentionally elides the middle—and perhaps most important—section of Paper Boi's ascendancy to stardom).

Although unlikely to have directly influenced *Atlanta*, John Locke's *An Essay Concerning Human Understanding* (1689) includes a specific philosophical context for this breakdown of action in meaningful service of an ambition. Locke distinguishes notions of the mind and body from the active exercise of power:

> This power which the mind has thus to order the consideration of any idea, or the forbearing to consider it; or to prefer the motion of any part of the body to its rest, and vice versa, in any particular instance, is that which we call the Will. The actual exercise of that power, by directing any particular action, or its forbearance, is that which we call volition or willing. (Locke 186)

In an extensive interview and profile of his career, Glover offers an insight into his profession as an entertainer, parsing the concept of will in a Lockean fashion: "'Before my first album [as Childish Gambino] came out, I wanted people to like me, and to realize that I had good intentions. . . . Then I realized that no one has good intentions—we all just have incentives'" (Friend). Furthermore, Locke's evocative focus on rest and motion provides a framework for characters' choices in *Atlanta* as well as in the films considered here given that the parlances of the drug and rap games respectively emphasize *moving* product and making *moves*. In both contexts, those who do not move do not thrive.

Earn and Alfred perceive themselves as strivers putting forth great effort to succeed, but their movements often reveal them instead to be slackers failing to take advantage of opportunities that would more likely lead to success (or at least forestall failure). Moreover, they face numerous obstacles outside themselves that further constrain their options and agency. Many of the show's most absurdist moments involve the fallout from miscalculations by Earn and Alfred as they attempt to negotiate both internal and external stumbling blocks. For example, a major setback in Earn's life arises from what initially seems like a success after he books a university gig for Alfred in "North of the Border" (s2e9). Earn's choice to forgo hotel rooms and instead to crash at the apartment of a young woman he barely knows ultimately results in the destruction of his and Alfred's possessions, setting their entire enterprise back, both in terms of material assets and reputation. Likewise, although Alfred is hungry for financial success as a rapper, he routinely fails to take advantage of such lucrative opportunities as social-media partnerships or media events that could significantly boost his profile and therefore his income. Through both actions and inactions, Earn and Alfred tend to sabotage their individual and collective success throughout seasons 1 and 2.

There are several classical sources that, like Locke, may not be direct influences on *Atlanta* but are nevertheless useful in analyzing the theme of ambition in the show's character-driven satire. One is the writing of satirist and moralist Jean de la Bruyère, whose *The Characters, or the Manners of the Age, with "The Characters of Theophrastus"* (1688) builds on the moral typology found in the influential *The Characters of Theophrastus*. John T. Gilmore highlights two opposing strands in de la Bruyère's satire, one that implies "human nature was essentially unchanging" and another with a more edifying "moral purpose" (117). Gilmore finds this combination irreconcilable: "La Bruyère's work seems to suggest that these two elements are mutually contradictory. The satirist claims that his purpose is to bring about the improvement of society by making people aware of their failings, but if it is claimed at the same time that human nature is unchanging, this could be read as suggesting that all such efforts will be in vain" (Gilmore 117–18). De la Bruyère's observations on "Mankind" in *The Characters* are an especially fitting intertext for considering *Atlanta* expressly because they illuminate the corrupted/corruptible nature of people that causes a person's actions to deviate from those notions and aims that would otherwise take them toward the achievement of their goals. For instance, in his second characterization on humankind, de la Bruyère concludes that, despite some changes that individuals make to "their habits, language, outward appearance, their rules of propriety, and sometimes their taste[,] . . . they always preserve their bad morals, and adhere tenaciously to what is ill and to their indifference for virtue" (154).

As previously stated, the ambitions that Earn and Alfred have within the music industry are constantly filtered through and affected by their vacillation between striving and slacking and/or the perceptions thereof. Another relevant classical source is Aristotle's *Ethics*, in which the philosopher writes about the double-edged sword of ambition, commenting: "In the desire for honor there are degrees of too much and too little, and a right source and a right manner. We blame the man who loves honor for seeking it too much or from the wrong source; and the man who is indifferent to it for not choosing to be honored even for fine actions" (Aristotle 159). There is a through line linking Aristotle to Theophrastus and de la Bruyère insofar as "the character sketches of Aristotle and Theophrastus . . . were clearly intended to be morally instructive" (Kemp 62) and Theophrastus "situate[d]" characters "in the context of an Aristotelian golden-mean morality" (Knutson 55). *Atlanta* perhaps inadvertently continues this thread by revealing a significant interest in moral examination, if not instruction, and by treating striving and slacking as two extremes that frame characters' potential actions. Critical commentary on Aristotle's writing about ambition observes that even he struggled with locating vice and virtue relative to ambition, which is evident in his nuanced descriptions in the passage above. It is therefore unsurprising that Earn and Alfred struggle to properly embody ambition in a contemporary setting.

Classical antecedents are not, however, the only intertexts that help explicate the ways *Atlanta* satirically treats its protagonists' "moves." The two aforementioned twenty-first-century films also present character, setting, and plot details that offer comparative insight into *Atlanta*'s depiction of Earn and Alfred. *Hustle & Flow* romanticizes the dreams of its protagonist at the expense of vulnerable characters within the narrative. Specifically, a Memphis drug dealer and pimp named DJay (Terrence Howard) enjoys a character arc that brings him to the cusp of rap stardom, a realization of dreams that minimizes the harm he has caused to at least three women in his life, as well as to their babies. In the opening scene of the film, DJay explains to Nola (Taryn Manning), a young woman working for him as a prostitute, that the only way they will get a "move on" in the world is if he sells her body to strangers. This rationalization of his own failure to provide for them contradicts his stated philosophy, which insists that although individual men like him operate on instinct, like dogs, humanity is also capable of a higher existence that asks the question, "What if?" and presumably answers it idealistically rather than cynically. DJay's goal of becoming a successful rapper is a form of socially higher existence that depends on the exploitation of those around him. However, if his actions were consistent with his own philosophy that humankind can elevate to an ethically or even existentially higher plane of speculation and accompanying action, he would be able to achieve his goals without doing so much obvious harm to those around him. His response to "What if?" is a projection that serves only his individual wants, resembling pure animal instinct more than collective uplift.

Furthermore, many of the most significant opportunities that buoy DJay's quest to become known as a rapper occur serendipitously, with minimal intent or exertion on his part. For example, in the midst of a comically frustrating drug deal, he acquires a musical keyboard that almost magically aids his own composition process. Likewise, an old friend who now works as a recording engineer approaches him at a convenience store, initiating a musical partnership that turns DJay's house into a recording studio. In another instance, DJay's most favored associate, a pregnant prostitute named Shug (Taraji P. Henson), sings the hook that provides his track with the missing element it needs to garner radio play. Despite all this, the film uncritically focalizes the narrative on DJay's perception of his own struggles and outsized sense of his own effort. For example, he prioritizes his "mode" above all else, insisting that everything in life is secondary to the inner drive (which he likens to a drumbeat) that keeps him focused on his dreams. In truth, DJay's striving is consistently fueled by others' unappreciated or outright unacknowledged labor. DJay's selfishness and unrepentant vice seemingly invite a satirical reading of his character (and thus the film as a whole), but Brewer entirely avoids targeting his behavior for overt mockery, exposure, or disapproval.

Compared to *Hustle & Flow*, *Snow on tha Bluff* is even more closely identified with (and therefore likely to be seen as sympathetic toward) the perspective and bad behavior of its drug-dealing protagonist, Curtis Snow, who appears simultaneously as himself and as a fictionalized version of himself. The film is an unusual sort of pseudodocumentary[3] set in the Bluff district on the west side of Atlanta. In an early scene, a group of shockingly naïve college students are using a camera to film their trip into the Bluff to buy drugs. They meet Curtis, who gets in their car to conduct such a transaction, but he pulls out a gun and robs them of their money and their camera, which he subsequently orders one of his associates to use to document everything Curtis does. The streets of the Bluff are not unlike the limited pathways of a video game, with Curtis encountering the same places and characters but modifying his strategies to earn rewards and defeat his enemies. The quasi-documentary visualization results in several action sequences that resemble first-person-shooter games, further contributing to this analogy. The fictionalized internal explanation for how the film came to be recorded in the first place as well as a final scene that suggests how the film was edited and made available cannily solve David Bordwell's contention that "the problem of the pseudo-documentary is to motivate the fact that someone is filming these dramas" alongside a secondary issue of "motivating how the film has been made public."

Snow on tha Bluff's fidelity to the documentary format helps reveal the nihilistic reality of life in this particularly rough section of Atlanta. From the opening scene onwards, Curtis is constantly searching for the next "move" he will make, resulting in a series of robberies, assaults, and shootings that are as troubling as they are visually chaotic. Like DJay, Curtis explicitly states his philosophy of life, but Curtis eschews instinct or aspiration in favor of survival: "In the street, either you gonna be the one that doin' it, or it gonna get done to [you]." In *Snow on tha Bluff*, destructive patterns of the past haunt the present. Even the deaths of loved ones do not deter Curtis from his ceaseless criminal movement. As with *Hustle & Flow*, this scenario is ripe for satirical treatment, but in production, marketing, and reception, the primary emphasis of the film is to seem real, to seem raw,[4] and not to remark on or repair the brokenness on display.

One of the defining characteristics of *Atlanta*'s satirical mode involves the recurring situation of Earn and Alfred being stopped or stilled and thereby being forced to consider the causes and effects of their actions. This contrasts with *Hustle & Flow* and *Snow on tha Bluff*, whose narrative designs are mostly to maintain, and then to accelerate, the moves of their ambitious characters toward material rewards. In those films, even being locked up—ostensibly a near-complete stasis—is presented either as a way to burnish DJay's street cred or as an elliptical setup for Curtis's triumphant homecoming. *Atlanta*, however, exposes the vagaries of experiencing success in the intertwined rap and drug games, realities in which forward progress is constantly impeded by outside forces, underscoring the precarity and capriciousness of lifestyles that too often look like certain avenues to wealth in popular culture. The series also satirically alludes to several current events in the rap industry, a sphere of entertainment that Glover knows well thanks to his parallel career as Childish Gambino. These allusions offer alternate personas[5] or origin stories and thereby both criticize the commercial and critical power structures within which rap exists and mock some of rap's least self-aware consumers; however, they *never* delegitimize rap as an art form.

Atlanta's first two episodes offer variations on hindering forces. The structure of "The Big Bang" (s1e1) is circular, the plot beginning and ending with Earn, Alfred, and their friend Darius (LaKeith Stanfield) enjoying a celebratory moment in a vehicle. The occasion for celebration is that Alfred's persona-defining song "Paper Boi" is being played on the radio for the first time, partly thanks to Earn's unusual doggedness. But a verbal dispute with a passerby quickly turns physical, followed by a shooting depicted in a deliberately vague manner. This framing primes the viewer for subsequent interruptions to the protagonists' trajectories. The satirical technique here reverses expectations for celebratory scenes that appear in more straightforward narratives about aspiring musicians. For example, the happy ending of *Hustle & Flow* is a montage of DJay's long-suffering colleagues overjoyed at hearing his song's radio premiere. The irony of such a scene in "The Big Bang" arises from the structure and visual execution of the shooting incident, leading the audience to believe that Earn and/or Alfred has been shot. Hence, this moment denotes not the beginning of a successful professional partnership but the potential ending of the cousins' lives.

The title of "Streets on Lock" (s1e2), which alludes to a 2006 (Young) Jeezy Atlanta trap song of the same name, has a dual meaning. In one sense, through his alter ego of Paper Boi, Alfred has "locked down" the attention and respect of the streets, not only with a song that has blown up but also with a well-publicized shooting (the one depicted in the previous episode) that augments his perceived "realness" in ways that echo Jon Pareles's 1994 comments about Tupac Shakur: "Hip-hop has always prided itself on its street-level authenticity, and putative gangster rappers . . . may feel compelled to act like roughnecks even when the microphone is off" (34). In another sense, though, a consequence of their activity is to be locked up, at least temporarily, at the Atlanta Detention Center. Although Alfred is released almost immediately, Earn spends several awkward hours in processing, stuck in a situation mirroring the holding pattern of his personal life.[6] He is neither free to go, like Alfred, nor is he, as a clerk gruffly points out, "in the [legal] system yet." The language here parallels how Earn also consistently fails to register as legitimate or authentic within the "system" of rap music; his role as management is treated with contempt (or, at best, as a necessary evil) by street-level players, like Alfred.

The episode thoroughly satirizes the nonsensicality of the two men's experiences in jail. The episode's opening dialogue suggests that the police officers who arrested Earn and Alfred do not have sufficient evidence to charge them for the shooting indirectly depicted in "The Big Bang" and, moreover, that they unsuccessfully attempted to coerce confessions/denunciations before arresting them on possession charges:

EARN: Never been arrested before, man.
ALFRED: Yeah. Should've ditched that weed, though.
EARN: Yeah, there was a lot going on, so I kind of forgot to do that. It was just, like, half a blunt. Like, you've been arrested for weed. It's not that bad, right?
ALFRED: Well, it's not as good as not getting arrested for weed.

Unlike Alfred, Earn has no criminal record, yet he lacks both the finances and knowledge of the system in which he finds himself to be freed from detention as quickly as Alfred. As he sits awaiting processing, the cinematography and production design reduce Earn to a small figure, dwarfed by bureaucracy and physically and verbally stuck between other detainees. Earn is eventually released after several hours, but his thorough lack of agency while detained alludes to the realities of incarceration: "Black men are . . . disproportionately held pretrial as a result of an inability to post monetary bail[,] . . . [and though] their bail amounts are similar to bail amounts set for whites, black men appear to be caught in a cycle of disadvantage" (Subramanian et al. 15).

By satirically exposing the absurdities, inequalities, and contradictions of this aspect of the legal system, "Streets on Lock" predicts (and possibly influences) both the actions and art of Atlanta rapper Young Thug, whose 2021 single and music video (with Gunna and YTB Trench) "Paid the Fine" chronicles his posting bond for thirty inmates at Atlanta's Fulton County Jail. Gunna specifies that this philanthropic gesture arises from both him and Young Thug "tryna put my people on," thereby echoing another interruption in Alfred's life.[7] As Paper Boi's reputation ascends, Alfred is repeatedly stopped in public by strangers who dream of doing what they perceive him to have accomplished. In "Streets on Lock" alone, Alfred is imposed upon because of his fame by both the corrections officer who escorts him from the detention center and a restaurant server, whose ardent reverence strikes Alfred as insane. The former demands a selfie with Paper Boi seemingly to add to his collection of photos of famous Atlanta rappers given that he gleefully announces that he previously locked up Gucci Mane. While delivering an order of hot wings to Alfred's table, the latter praises Paper Boi for being "a rapper that would just blow a n***a's brains out on the street" and ominously exhorts Alfred not to "let me down" because "I don't know what I'd do." Although both of these figures are themselves satirized for their parasitic fandom, another significant irony arises from the fact that Alfred knows that their projections of his status are illusory. Each encounter of this sort not only interrupts his life but also reminds him of his lack of actual success, which he increasingly attributes to Earn's mismanagement. This irony is heightened in season 2 by giving Paper Boi a foil, a hard-charging young rapper named Clark County (R. J. Walker), whose duplicity was inspired by a real-life rapper Glover once observed in the studio.[8]

"Money Bag Shawty" (s2e3) finds Alfred in the recording studio with Clark County. Alfred declines the opportunity to get in the booth and perform a verse. He instead smokes and drinks with Darius on the couch while Clark County not only berates and physically threatens his recording engineer but also disingenuously appropriates Alfred's lifestyle by referencing "Hennessy plus the herb" in his lyrics after professing neither to drink nor smoke. Subsequently, he breezily discusses the extraordinary endorsement offers he has received, which he attributes to the efforts of his white manager, Lucas (Matthew Barnes). Lucas's race illustrates Atlanta's ongoing commentary on racial advantage and points out the pressures Black entertainers face regarding racialized associations of commercial and cultural acceptability. This encounter with Clark County ultimately does nothing for Alfred except to rouse his sense of Earn's shortcomings, a resentment that intensifies even as Alfred himself continually underwhelms in his efforts to build his brand and showcase his music at industry events for which Earn arranges his attendance.

Properly examining Earn and Alfred within the slacker/striver paradigm requires acknowledging that they often lack the agency to turn their ambitions into actions. Although the underlying racial inequities that disenfranchise Earn and Alfred in various ways are the target of many of *Atlanta*'s most barbed satirical moments—e.g., the aforementioned "Streets on Lock" as well as "B.A.N." (s1e7) and "Juneteenth" (s1e9)—the psychological toll of the decisions they feel forced into is also frequently addressed. Earn has departed Princeton for reasons that remain unknown until the final season, but his unwillingness to discuss the specifics of this break in his higher education highlights how much it weighs on him (as does the fact that he eventually reveals it during a session with a young Black therapist in "The Homeliest Little Horse" [s4e2]). He and his partner Vanessa (Zazie Beetz) exist in tenuous personal and professional circumstances as they attempt to raise a gifted child, whose best prospects involve a private education they cannot yet afford.

Alfred's somewhat introverted nature conflicts with the public persona demanded by what feels like his only path to success not predicated on dealing drugs. In "The Streisand Effect" (s1e4), he explains his perceived constraints to Zan (Freddie Kuguru), an eccentric social-media influencer, entrepreneur, and pizza-delivery driver: "I scare people at ATMs. I have to rap." In contrast, Zan shamelessly hustles his way across various gigs and regularly breaches boundaries, justifying his exploitation as an activity he believes everyone—including Alfred—to engage in. Alfred sees the threatening cultural associations of Black masculinity as something he embodies without wanting to, prompting his movement into the rap industry in which he could exploit, rather than be punished for, those associations. Zan seems to revel in (and trade on) the instability of his own visual racialization and the flexibility it affords.[9]

Earn's striving is evident in his reconnection with Alfred at the start of the series, a move Alfred immediately recognizes as opportunistic: "You want in on Paper Boi." Much like DJay in *Hustle & Flow*, who sees accomplished rapper Skinny Black (Ludacris) as his vehicle toward stardom, Earn latches onto Paper Boi to avoid pursuing other more mundane—and also more stably remunerative—kinds of employment. The difference is that Earn's success depends on a sustained mutual journey with Alfred, whereas DJay encounters Skinny Black in a kind of competition that only one of them can win. In "The Big Bang," Earn is initially shown unenthusiastically performing his menial job pitching credit cards to passengers at Hartsfield-Jackson International Airport. He stands next to a placard touting the credit card's incentive to "Earn Miles." This becomes both a pun and a cue as Earn goes to work for [Alfred] Miles. As Alfred and Earn walk through the same airport on their way to Europe in "Crabs in a Barrel" (s2e11), the same placard is altered to read "Earn Miles Forever," suggesting both the correctness and durability of their collaboration, as well as their ensuing joined fates. Earn insists on being Alfred's manager as if he has a natural right to that position, a familial obligation that Alfred explicitly validates. Earn's simultaneous striving and slacking bring to mind Aristotle's observation about "the man who loves honor . . . seeking it too much or from the wrong source" and foregrounds *Atlanta*'s satirical juxtaposition of intentions and incentives. As Alfred's manager, Earn succeeds in arranging publicity appearances for Paper Boi at a nightclub, in a celebrity basketball game, at the offices of a Spotify-like streaming service, and at a college social event. Yet the return on their investments of time, energy, and money proves insufficient, nonexistent, or even counterproductive on each of these occasions. The resultant impression is that such venues are venal and/or corrupt, reinforcing *Atlanta*'s general skepticism toward the way the entertainment industry favors those (like Clark County) who play by the corrupt game's rules.

Earn's difficulties at coping are exacerbated by and to some extent explained by the personal hang-ups he carries with him wherever he goes. In "The Big Bang," Earn unloads in a question-filled soliloquy: "I just keep losing. I mean, are some people just supposed to lose for balance in the universe? I mean . . . like, are there just some people on Earth who are supposed to be here just to make it easier for the winners?" Subsequent episodes confirm his defeatist suspicions. For example, in "Go for Broke" (s1e3), Earn is mortified by not being able to purchase a kid's meal for himself as well as being "broke on payday" thanks to his ninety-six-dollar paycheck. His relationship to Vanessa involves similar setbacks. Both his material contributions to and his presence (physical and emotional) in their life together are inconsistent.

In "The Jacket" (s1e10), rather than acknowledging how his present (relative) steadiness with Vanessa and his daughter provides an opportunity to pivot toward a more stable career, he maintains a distance that fuels the dream of music-industry success. Earn typifies the twenty-ninth figure in the "Of Mankind" section in de la Bruyère's *The Characters*: "There are certain things which we most passionately desire, and of which the mere thought carries us away. . . . [I]f we happen to obtain them, we are less sensible of them than we thought we should be, and we enjoy them the less because we aspire to get some of greater importance" (163). Earn walks out of Van's apartment wearing a designer sweatshirt, whose imprinted legend—"Strivers Row and Co."— invokes an iconic site of Black achievement and "respectability." Outkast's song "Elevators (Me & You)" (1996) plays over the scene, emphasizing Earn's precarious situation. André 3000's statement that he "live[s] by the beat like you live check to check. / If it don't move your feet, then, I don't eat, so we like neck to neck" testifies to his dependence on listeners' response to his music, a situation that Earn likewise faces since the start of his collaboration with Paper Boi. His destination is ultimately revealed not to be a majestic brownstone on Harlem's Strivers Row but rather a storage unit in which he is both storing his possessions and sleeping. His inability to reify his lofty ambitions has reduced him to an object on standby.

Alfred's status as a striver/slacker is considerably more tilted toward slacking, though when pressed, he is also able to make moves with more vigor than Earn. This is evident in "The Club" (s1e8) when he forcefully retrieves money owed to him by an unscrupulous promoter and in "Nobody Beats the Biebs" (s1e5) as he manhandles a fictionalized (and Black) version of pop singer Justin Bieber. Alfred is arguably limited in the moves he makes, but he frequently embodies the very stereotype of violent Black masculinity that unsettles him when the waiter praises him for it in "Streets on Lock." The key problem with his use of physical force is that it supports the characterization he is ostensibly trying to escape, that of the "gangster" scaring people at ATMs. As an attractive reporter with whom Alfred is unsuccessfully flirting in "Nobody Beats the Biebs" bluntly tells him: "Play your part. People don't want Justin to be the asshole. They want you to be the asshole. You're a rapper. That's your job." Alfred's apophatic preoccupation with stating what he does not want to be or do results in an insecure, noncommittal, and ultimately ineffectual approach to becoming a public figure.[10]

Alfred can be understood through de la Bruyère's observation: "Idleness is the mother of listlessness, and chiefly induces men to hunt after diversions, gambling, and company. He who loves work requires nothing else" (174). Alfred does not particularly enjoy working, causing him to fill his time with unproductive pursuits. That he is nevertheless able to make enough money to live comfortably contrasts with *Snow on tha Bluff*'s evocation of stagnancy.[11] An especially memorable sequence of that film finds Curtis's wise grandmother encouraging him to change his ways while he can. Her exhortation is followed by a monologue in which Curtis says: "It's a still life. Still smoking, still drinking, still standing in lines. Still taking care of children. . . . Still strapped. We just still. We just still." Curtis is not going to change his life because the grim stillness (not to be confused with "stillness," its opposite) that grips his particular district of Atlanta is an episodic, hopeless routine of violence that never ends.

Such violent cyclicality is emphasized by the title of *Atlanta*'s second season, which Darius defines, in "Alligator Man," as follows: "Robbin' season. Christmas approaches, and everybody got to eat. Or be eaten." The season's opening adapts certain elements of a real-life armed robbery and shooting at a fast-food restaurant by a teenaged Texas rapper named Tay-K in 2017. However, by restricting such (self-)destructive activity to minor characters in a parallel story, *Atlanta* situates Alfred and Earn at enough of a distance from the city's harshest realities to give them a deceptive quasi comfort in which dreams of stardom and riches seem attainable. Such dreams are routinely exposed throughout the season as illusory, as in "Champagne Papi" (s2e7), or toxic, as in "Teddy Perkins" (s2e6) and "Woods" (s2e8).[12]

Alfred wants the rewards of public recognition without putting in the necessary work or making the necessary sacrifices. Two conspicuous strands of *Atlanta*'s satirical view of this condition are Alfred's physical comportment and his relationship to music. Alfred sitting on a couch is among *Atlanta*'s most recurrent images. Sometimes he sits on the couch in his apartment and eats, plays video games, and sends texts. Other times, he occupies a couch outside like a throne, usually flanked by Earn and Darius. In "Money Bag Shawty," he stays on the couch throughout Clark County's recording session, never moving into the booth to show his skills. His general lassitude directly relates to his somewhat curious depiction in the show's first two seasons. Despite the centrality of his profession to his character and to the plot of most episodes, Alfred is actually only seen performing in short installments, mostly in the low-budget music video for "Paper Boi" and during his half-hearted (and ultimately aborted) effort to entertain the mostly white employees of a music-streaming service in "Sportin' Waves" (s2e2), whereas Clark County is perfectly willing to perform for the same audience, incentivized by the material and practical rewards they offer him. By contrast, the most remarkable scenes in *Hustle & Flow* are those that chronicle, in loving detail, the process of composition and recording of DJay's raps. *Hustle & Flow* is a movie in which constructing songs is depicted as both hard work and its own reward, as befits the plot's optimism. In *Atlanta*, Paper Boi's songs simply exist, alienated from both his labor and his emotion. His reaction to his single's first play on the radio in "The Big Bang"—saying "[I] kind of hate this song" and turning the radio off—further attests to this distancing.

A mystical experience reminiscent of a horror film in "Woods" finally provokes Alfred to stop sitting around and to move forward. The arrival of this tipping point also intensifies his dissatisfaction with Earn's performance as his manager to the point that Earn's firing seems imminent. The episode's resolution, though, suggests that his existential crisis in a dark urban forest may have only provoked Alfred's instinct for physical survival rather than any commitment to taking control of his musical career. A concluding scene in a convenience store reveals the dirty, bloodied Alfred as grateful to be alive. He agrees to take a selfie with an earnest young fan, recalling the scene with the officer in "Streets on Lock." His smile in the selfie brings to mind the revealing third-act Polaroid image of a momentarily contented Leonard Shelby (Guy Pearce) in *Memento* (2000), an image that is evidence that he has temporarily overcome his demons yet is damned to confront them all over again. Given his track record of returning to bad habits, the same might be true of Alfred. Indeed, "New Jazz" (s3e8) plays like an urban European retelling of "Woods," putting Alfred through a similarly distressing, drug-induced wringer in Amsterdam, which exposes the cyclicality of his condition.

Alfred and Earn have what seems to be an epiphany near the end of "North of the Border." The unpaid gig at the university that Earn booked for Paper Boi is a disaster, though in keeping with his invisibility as a performer, the reasons have nothing to do with Alfred or his music. Forced to flee the site of the concert after an incident instigated by their friend—and Paper Boi's nominal bodyguard—Tracy (Khris Davis), Alfred and Earn sit on a couch in a white fraternity house with a giant Confederate flag hanging on the wall behind them. The scene is loaded with symbol and ritual, inviting readings of the protagonists' situation in relation to slavery, their lack of agency, and the choice to humiliate themselves in exchange for acceptance.[13] Those symbols and rituals are themselves unstable given that the fraternity brothers are aficionados of southern rap and, thus, completely in awe of Paper Boi. They are far more threatening toward the naked and hooded pledges that kneel on the floor before Alfred and Earn than toward the Black guests, who they ply with weed and praise in their house. Within this bewildering setting, Alfred tells Earn that "I gotta make my next moves my best moves" before expressing his belief that Earn is not "cut out for" managing his career. Both men's insecurities have been building for two seasons, and this scene lays bare the distinction between the will to achieve and actuating volition. As much as Earn *wants* to succeed as Alfred's manager, he has not demonstrated the ability to make it happen. As much as Alfred *wants* commercial and cultural success as a rapper, he trails his competition, Clark County, in both aspects, even if the artistic quality and relative inauthenticity of Clark County's particular brand of success—exemplified by a cheesy commercial for Yoo-hoo—is not likely to be a path that would satisfy him.[14]

Similar to being still versus moving and slacking versus striving, another dichotomy informing *Atlanta*'s satire is being "stunted" on versus "stunting" on others. Earn and Alfred are so preoccupied with considering the vagaries and mechanisms of stunting that it distracts them from more productive work. To understand stunting and its place within the show's satirical orientation, it is necessary to briefly review the urtext of stunting, the song "#1 Stunna" (2000) by southern hip-hop duo Big Tymers (consisting of Birdman/Baby and Mannie Fresh). The lyrics to "#1 Stunna" envision a successful rapper's lifestyle so grand that his body and those of his female companions are encrusted with diamonds and everything he touches turns to platinum. In the introduction to the song, Baby asserts that a rival "can't out-stunt" him in showing off cars; other signifiers of wealth and success accrue across the remaining verses. The chorus playfully links this type of showing off to famous stuntmen, including Evel Knievel, Jackie Chan, and others. Big Tymers not only provided the language and template for stunting but also later illustrated, in "Still Fly" (2002), how rappers could still stunt even when they were broke. The entirety of "Still Fly" is a statement about faking a wealthy lifestyle to keep one's personal brand (and hip-hop career) moving forward despite setbacks. *Atlanta*'s conception of stunting is consistent with Big Tymers' ostentatious display of real or feigned riches, and the show extends those modes to include various attempts to advance one's position.

Much could be said of the various plot reversals that revolve around stunting, especially in "Money Bag Shawty," but the most consequential example takes place in "Crabs in a Barrel," in which both Earn and Alfred seem to get another chance to correct their respective courses. At the beginning of the season, in "Alligator Man," Earn is passed a mysterious golden gun by his Uncle Willy (Katt Williams), himself a cautionary figure suggesting Earn's future if he fails to find a better path.[15] Having largely vanished from the plot in the intervening episodes, the gun returns in "Crabs in a Barrel" to threaten Earn's most significant move yet. Despite his seeming desire to cut Earn loose at the end of "North of the Border," Alfred agrees to let Earn accompany him for his stint as the opening act on Clark County's European tour. Realizing far too late that he left the gun in the bag that he hurriedly packed for the trip, Earn improvises an act of stunting that ultimately bests Clark County's manager, Lucas—Earn's rival, as Clark County is Alfred's. Earn shrewdly transfers the gun out of his bag at the airport security check, planting it on Clark County, who, in turn, pins it on Lucas.

Earn's move gains Alfred's approval to a greater degree than anything he has previously done in his role as his cousin's manager. As Alfred explains in a quiet, certain manner on the plane, Earn had no other choice but to pass the gun. By doing whatever it takes to survive—and especially by hanging his rival out to dry in the process—Earn has finally acted in a way that validates the potential of his ambitions, a development that lays the groundwork for Paper Boi's rise to the stardom that they experience in the show's latter two seasons. In the end, *Atlanta*'s dual protagonists, Alfred and Earn, are playing a zero-sum game in which their mutual wins necessarily occur alongside others' losses, a point that is dramatically foreshadowed in a flashback to their adolescence in "FUBU" (s2e10). This episode features a dispute over the authenticity of a shirt by the popular clothing brand FUBU, which significantly factors into a schoolmates' suicide.[16] Young Alfred uses his guile to help extricate young Earn from a situation in which the possible revelation of his shirt's inauthenticity will open him up to mockery and possibly physical abuse, but in doing so, another boy named Devin with a similar (and possibly authentic) shirt becomes the scapegoat. Earn survives another day in the harsh school environment but must live with the understanding that his victory has cost another young boy his life. One episode—and more than a decade in Earn's life—later, the visual metaphor of the plane's incipient takeoff suggests that the leveling up that Earn and Alfred have sought might also be about to happen. But the memory of "FUBU" and its resolution inherently reminds the viewer of potential ancillary consequences; gaining the world involves losing some souls.

Repeatedly, *Atlanta* signals its satirical exposure of the rap game's precarity, frequently (and somewhat ironically) infusing prominent voices of hip hop and rap into its soundscape as it does so. For example, as Earn is settling in for the night in his storage unit at the end of "The Jacket," the camera starts pulling back just as a significant line from "Elevators (You & Me)" plays over the soundtrack and presumably also through the headphones that Earn is wearing. André 3000's words—"this ain't gon' stop, so we just gon' continue"—express an attitude that reflects the "Keep On Keepin' On" motto that appears on a T-shirt that Earn wears in multiple episodes. The themes of ambition and achievement present in hip-hop and rap lyrics are part of a tradition that goes back a century to Langston Hughes's "Mother to Son" (1922). In that poem, a mother charts her life's hard journey along a staircase marred by tacks, splinters, torn-up boards, and bare places where carpet should be. Despite these conditions, she has continued to climb and encourages her son not to sit down and drop out of the ascent. *Atlanta* seemingly suggests that this staircase and even the elevators alluded to in the title of Outkast's song have been replaced by a kind of tightrope across which only the "stunter" can pass; success is not guaranteed, and there is no safety net, particularly for those like Earn and Alfred, who struggle to align their ambition and volition.

NOTES

1. Although this essay is exclusively focused on the first two seasons, it should be noted that this changes radically in the latter two seasons once Paper Boi has become an international superstar, who is on at least his second tour of Europe at the start of season 3. Not only has he become rich enough to fling 20,000 Euros casually at hordes of adoring fans upon being released from an Amsterdam jail in "Sinterklaas Is Coming to Town" (s3e2), but he is also so financially secure that he worries, in "New Jazz" (s3e8), about owning the masters of his recordings, suggesting that they are an investment and not just evidence of his artistry.

2. His brush with death in "Crank Dat Killer" (s4e6) even leads him to take Soulja Boy's advice and get himself a rural "safe farm" to which he can escape in "Andrew Wyeth: Alfred's World" (s4e9), though even that bucolic space ends up being invaded by feral pigs and recalcitrant farm implements.

3. One of the film's producers notes that the "film follows real-life criminal Curtis Snow as he robs drug dealers and attempts to provide for his child. The most controversial element of our film is that some of the footage is real while other scenes are staged." He also insists that it "is not a celebration of hood life, but rather an expose on the current condition. Our goal was to illuminate a forgotten neighborhood, an underworld that lives next door" (Knittel).

4. "Keeping our message authentic, I felt that it was important to project from the perspective of those entrenched in this neglected community. This is their story and *we must keep it hood at all costs*" (Knittel, emphasis added).

5. See, e.g., the storylines involving the rap group Migos in "Go for Broke" (s1e3) or Drake in "Champagne Papi" (s2e7).

6. For further discussion of this episode, see Avilez's essay herein.

7. That both Young Thug and Gunna were subsequently arrested and charged in a Racketeer Influenced and Corrupt Organizations Act–related case and denied bond multiple times—the evidence against them including the lyrics of their songs—is an irony stranger than fiction.

8. See Tharpe.

9. For further discussion of this episode and Zan's characterization, see the essays by Glavanakova and Lee in this collection.

10. For further discussion of both this episode and this scene, see Cortes's essay herein.

11. Alfred's stagnation seems to arise much more prominently once he has reached stratospheric heights of success and fame in the latter two seasons. "Born 2 Die" (s4e3) even suggests that he—like all the rappers who came before him—will soon be supplanted and that he should cash in on his fame while he can by mentoring a YWA (young white avatar).

12. For further discussion of these episodes, see the essays by Morgan, Nishikawa, O'Brien, and Rutter herein.

13. For further discussion of this episode and this scene in particular, see the essays by Brooks and Rutter herein.

14. Multiple episodes in season 3—e.g., "Cancer Attack" (s3e5), "White Fashion" (s3e6), and "New Jazz"—reinforce this supposition.

15. Williams's casting in this role satirizes the persistent real-life legal troubles of the comedian and actor, who won a Primetime Emmy Award for his performance in the namesake role as Uncle Willy.

16. For further discussion of this episode, see Foster-Singletary's essay herein.

Hartsfield-Jackson International Airport

PLAYING ON THE BORDER

Racial Ambiguity, Passing, and Possibility in *Atlanta* and Charles Yu's *Interior Chinatown*

ABIGAIL JINJU LEE

Race, like satire, is relational. Racialization unfolds through complex, multidimensional relationships encompassing our social and political contexts, the histories between porous racialized groups, and hierarchies of power and violence. Satire is an effective tool for a relational analysis of racial hierarchies as so much of satire's critical edge depends on a complex network of absurdities and ironies that function primarily in relationship to one another and to a given work's cultural context(s). Taking up this relational approach to racialization—rather than, for example, a comparative approach that assumes discrete racial groups that can be weighed and measured against one another—invites us to understand Asianness and Blackness formed in association not only with white supremacy but with each other, reclaiming a history of relationality between these groups. Examining the relationships among Asianness, Blackness, and whiteness in American culture, this chapter takes up satire along ostensible racial borders in *Atlanta* and Charles Yu's novel *Interior Chinatown* (2020). The unsettled and paradoxically edgeless dimensions of Blackness emerge as sites of experimentation and biting satire in *Atlanta*'s four seasons. Analyzing *Atlanta*'s satirical strategies—especially in regard to racial ambiguity and racial passing—alongside those of *Interior Chinatown* underlines the contrast between the desire to *become normative* and the assertion of *being otherwise*. The former involves either trying to assimilate into normative whiteness and achieve a supposed universality or superficially (and exploitatively) performing selected aspects of racially marked identities that are acceptable to dominant white society. The latter, a radical state of racialized life, involves experimentally transcending the bounds of the normative altogether.

Interior Chinatown is a novel in the form of a metafictional screenplay featuring Asian Americans playing different stock characters and attempting to land breakout roles on a police procedural called *Black and White* filmed in a generic, unplaced Chinatown. Yu's novel teeters between sympathy with and satire of its subjects. It employs a layered tone in depicting the protagonist's professional goal to become "Kung Fu Guy" on the TV show that films in his Chinatown, inviting the reader to sympathize and to identify with his inner conflict—including his desire to become a normative "American"—while also satirizing the absurdity of the system in which he is trapped. *Interior Chinatown*'s commentary on American culture and its media landscape is mirrored by the protagonist's inner conflict between envying the benefits of his wife's racial ambiguity and desperately wanting to pass into a racially unmarked normative. This ambivalence contrasts with the strategies used in *Atlanta*, a series which aims its satirical arrows directly at the desire to become normative, satirizing it without any corresponding sympathy. Through the "transracial" character Harrison Booth/Antoine Smalls (Niles Stewart), the spectral and damaged musician Teddy Perkins (Donald Glover), and the racially ambiguous social-media influencer Zan (Freddie Kuguru), *Atlanta* sharply rejects becoming normative as a viable strategy for liberation. However, *Atlanta* also offers glimpses of being otherwise through the improvisational means of existence and self-expression, which reaffirms Fred Moten's assertion that "the history of blackness is testament to the fact that objects can and do resist" (*In the Break* 1).

I examine representations of racial ambiguity and racial passing in two texts using satire to expose the messy, impossible edges of supposedly unequivocal racial categorizations. Before doing so, I briefly trace a lineage of satire concerned with challenging racial borders in both African American and Asian American literature and performance. Thereafter, I take up *Atlanta*, arguing that, through its satire of racial boundaries, the series articulates Blackness as a radical break from normative, unmarked whiteness—a way of being otherwise. Finally, I unravel the borders of Asianness, Blackness, and the racially ambiguous in *Interior Chinatown*, exploring the ambivalent ways in which the novel constructs Asianness, sympathetically upholding a dream that Asian Americanness could become normatized while also still satirizing the stereotypes into which Asianness is constrained. By looking along these multiple vectors that associate Blackness, Asianness, and whiteness, racialization appears not as a reflection of distinct, bounded, and immutable identities but rather as a dynamic, multivalent process of exerting power and violence that necessarily conceptualizes racialized groups in relationship to each other.

Transgressing arbitrary racial boundaries and exploring racial ambiguity through humor has always been an integral element of African American satire. From Bob Cole's "Willie Wayside" performances in the 1890s through Melvin

Van Peebles's *Watermelon Man* (1970) to Keenen Ivory Wayans's *White Chicks* (2004) and beyond, whiteface has been employed to highlight the absurdity of racial boundaries while also affirming the belonging of the Black "in-group" that understands the humor inherent in imitating and satirizing whiteness (McAllister 16). However, another distinct thread within African American literature involves satire occasioned and/or enabled by the relationship between Blackness and Asianness. For example, Ishmael Reed's *Japanese by Spring* (1993) uses a Japanese takeover of an American university as the background for the protagonist's quest to ascend within corporatized higher education while satirically exposing hollow multiculturalist academic discourses. Paul Beatty's work has also often played with Afro-Asian connections. His novel *Tuff* (2000) embodies disidentification and strategically alters racist tropes of Black masculinity through the relationship between a stereotypically tough, drug-dealing African American youth named Winston and Inez Nomura.[1] Not only is Inez modeled on the radical Asian American activist Yuri Kochiyama, but also Winston's "thug" persona is unsettled in no small measure by his affinity for neorealist Japanese film (Schalk 56). On television, the "Racial Draft" (s2e1) sketch on *Chappelle's Show* (2003–2006) depicts delegations representing various identity groups laying claim to celebrities in order to "determine their racial standing . . . once and for all" ("Samuel Jackson Beer"). The ostensible ambiguity of the various draftees originates from a variety of circumstances, including phenotypic characteristics, cultural and parental heritage, and artistic appropriation. For example, the Black delegation and the Jewish delegation each claim a mixed-race individual as their own by selecting Lenny Kravitz and Tiger Woods, respectively, whereas the Asian delegation chooses the Wu-Tang Clan, whose performed "Asianness" consists entirely of allusions to Chinese pop culture in their music. Further examples of the exploration of Black-Asian relationality and racial representation on TV include *Master of None* (2015–2021), in particular the "Indians on TV" (s1e4) and "Thanksgiving" (s2e8) episodes, and *Insecure*'s (2016–2021) Asian American heartthrob Andrew Tan (Alexander Hodge), who has come to be known as "Asian Bae" by the show's fans.

Although critics have increasingly emphasized the importance of satire in African American literature and art, Asian American satire remains severely undertheorized. Asian American writers such as Frank Chin (*The Chickencoop Chinaman* [1972]), Maxine Hong Kingston (*Tripmaster Monkey* [1989]), Karen Tei Yamashita (*Tropic of Orange* [1997]), David Henry Hwang (*Yellowface* [2008]), and Charles Yu have all approached the relationships among Asianness, Blackness, and whiteness through satire, while performers such as Margaret Cho, Bowen Yang, and Awkwafina have built careers around performances that defamiliarize Asianness and occasionally (especially in Awkwafina's case) appropriate elements of Blackness for comedic effect.[2] Extending these lineages to our contemporary racial landscape, we see, emerging in the satires examined here, a set of questions concerning racial ambiguity, the incommensurability of Blackness, and the ambivalent place of Asianness in a society shaped both by the unmarked, supposedly universal (paradigmatically white) American ideal and the forces of anti-Blackness.

Performing along and across the putative Black-white color line has been a prominent source of humor and satirical commentary on the instability and absurdity of such a line while also asserting Blackness as a break from Western humanist modernity. *Atlanta* picks up this tradition in the spoof episode "B.A.N." (s1e7), in which Alfred "Paper Boi" Miles (Brian Tyree Henry) reluctantly appears as a guest on an episode of *Montague*, a fictional talk show on a network clearly modeled after Black Entertainment Television (BET). Alfred has been invited to discuss comments he made on Twitter about Caitlyn Jenner's transition and as something of a scapegoat for transphobia within the rap community generally. His appearance is prefaced by a segment about Antoine Smalls, a "transracial" Black teenager who identifies as a thirty-year-old white man named Harrison Smalls and dresses the part in ill-fitting khakis and New Balance sneakers. Harrison/Antoine says that "race is just a made-up thing," bemoans the fact his peers do not accept his white identity as he engages in such typical-white-guy behavior as going to the farmer's market, and encourages the police to harass Black men. He also reveals he is planning to surgically change his physical appearance and complete his transracial transition.

Harrison/Antoine's transracialism is ultimately ridiculed because it bespeaks an understanding of race as a sort of property that can be traded, exchanged, and acquired. His transracialism is a parodic reversal of the fungibility of Blackness as Harrison attempts to exchange his racialization for the dominant one simply by claiming and performing what he understands whiteness to be. In so doing, Harrison/Antoine attempts to assert his ownership of whiteness. As Cheryl I. Harris argues, whiteness has been constructed not solely as a shade, a race, or an identity but as *property*, arguing that "whiteness and property share a common premise—a conceptual nucleus—of a right to exclude," the origins of which lie in "the parallel systems of domination over Black and native American peoples" (1714). *Atlanta*'s satire of Harrison/Antoine's attempt at passing points to the inevitable failure of simply claiming whiteness as a normative path to liberation—a strategy that Yu's protagonist adopts in a somewhat different manner (see below)—when one is structurally excluded from such a position of ostensible universality or whiteness. Instead, his transracialism is used to mockingly challenge the idea that racial identity can be possessed or exchanged like property.

Throughout the episode, Alfred asserts that he isn't transphobic but also that he doesn't like Caitlyn Jenner. He wholly rejects the parallels between the Black struggle and the difficulties confronting Jenner, a rich and famous white trans woman. When Dr. Deborah Holt (Mary Kraft), an academic seemingly invited to demonstrate Alfred's intolerance and ignorance, states that he is complaining about chickens coming home to roost, Alfred replies: "No, no, no, no, no. Rap *is* chickens coming home to roost. Look, my life is messed up from [*bleep*] y'all did, okay?" Alfred understands his rap career not as a path to fame or even as a form of artistic expression, but rather primarily as a necessary pushback against the limited possibilities afforded to Black Americans by an anti-Black world. Even as he raps, "It's always 'bout that paper, boi," in his breakthrough single, his tired demeanor and frustration while performing the song again and again belie the lyrics' simple equation of success and satisfaction.

Alfred asserts the necessity of understanding relations of power—not only identity—and the incommensurability of the Black structural (non)position, the absurdity of equating gender and race without attending to their intersections that make Black people of any gender subject to state-sanctioned violence and dispossession. He understands his experience as "phenomenal blackness," a myth of "the black body" that is overlaid onto him, evident in his slouched, reluctant appearance on camera and his disdain for performing the idea of Blackness that is clearly expected of him by the host (Young 12). Black feminist geographer Katherine McKittrick describes the ways in which "the spaces of otherness have hardened through time, often with black, 'wretched' bodies occupying or residing outside the lowest rung of humanness and thus inhabiting what most consider inhuman or uninhabitable geographies" (7). Alfred's discomfort at the expectation that he occupy this "inhuman" space is clear, yet McKittrick offers a redefinition of these "inhuman" spaces centered on Black life and ways of being that reject the given order of things: "This black urban presence—black life—uncovers a mode of being human that ... redefines the terms of who and what we are vis-à-vis a cosmogony that, while painful, does not seek to inhabit a location closer to that of 'the fittest' but instead honors our mutually constitutive and relational versions of humanness" (12). The abjection of Blackness as inhuman makes Alfred vulnerable to violence and death, but he also suggests that he views, in this abjection, the possibility of fugitive world making ("chickens coming home to roost") and alternate ways of being, as well as a break from the logics of property and ownership that inform whiteness. Though anti-Blackness has "messed up" Alfred's life, he has also found a place—albeit perhaps a tenuous and imperfect one—for creative revolt in the exclusion forced upon him; to use Moten's terminology, Alfred embodies being otherwise by improvising "in the break."[3]

"Teddy Perkins" (s2e6) is another instance of playing on the supposed borders between whiteness and Blackness. The episode's opening finds Darius (LaKeith Stanfield) driving outside of Atlanta to pick up a free piano. The ornate home at which he arrives is gently dilapidated, evoking both the idea of whiteness as property and its gradual slippage. Upon entering, Darius meets Teddy Perkins, whose unsettling artificial paleness and strained voice inevitably bring to mind Michael Jackson. Teddy experiences his racial boundary transgressions (evinced by his lightened skin and rococo habits, including eating an almost-raw ostrich egg) through psychic wounds and trauma due to abuse by his father. His piano-playing brother experiences them in a far more physical manner; Benny Hope (Derrick Haywood) is trapped in a wheelchair by a debilitated body and is furthermore vulnerable because of a rare skin condition that leaves him entirely wrapped in fabric. The brothers are pathologized as physically and mentally ill, and their descent into madness alludes to such narratives as Jessie Redmon Fauset's *Plum Bun* (1928) and Nella Larsen's *Passing* (1929) that depict the psychic toll of racial pretense. Teddy and Benny expose the desire to use fame to *become normative* (and thus exit Blackness) through their unsettling exaggeration of various tropes associated with crossing the Black-white color line.

Atlanta offers many satirical commentaries on performing at the intensely policed borders of Blackness. Such performances affirm Moten's contention that "Blackness and black radicalism are not in between but neither one nor the other. New things, new spaces, new times demand lyrical innovation and intervention, formal maneuverings that often serve to bring to the theoretical and practical table whatever meaning can't" (*Black* 10). In *Atlanta*, Blackness is not presented as an "in-between" state or an alternative to the white Western heteronormative. Instead, Blackness is constructed as a break from it, such that Harrison/Antoine's crossing of the supposed border with the white heteronormative is rendered absurd. Displaying the absurdity of attempting such a racial crossing, *Atlanta* satirically criticizes "transracial" figures such as Rachel Dolezal, whose appropriation of Blackness was still very fresh in the public mind when "B.A.N." originally aired in 2016. Teddy, in contrast, doesn't so much perform whiteness as become an eerie, pale, and conflicted echo of a former self, evinced by his violent interactions with his gauze-encased (and, thus, also pathologized in his exterior whiteness) brother. As the audience gradually learns along with Darius, their father irreparably damaged them in trying to harness their musical talents as children; correspondingly, they are now bent on destroying themselves and each other. Teddy's unsettlingly, ambiguous whiteface performance is a satire of the consequences of losing oneself in pursuit of acceptance by the dominant culture.[4]

If *Atlanta* derides the very idea of a simple division between whiteness and Blackness, how does satire addressing the fraught spaces at other racial borders function? As "we know that ideological concepts are defined not by their clear centers but by their ambiguous borders . . . [where] strong declarations about race, racism, and racial belonging can be both broken and made," then looking at the relationships between Asianness and Blackness offers another perspective on the (im)materiality of racial boundaries and possibilities for fugitive world making across such borders (Godfrey and Young 16).

One of the most sustained engagements with Asian-identified characters in *Atlanta* occurs in "The Streisand Effect" (s1e4). The episode's main storyline concerns Alfred's annoyance at harassment by an online influencer and troll named Zan. Zan is ambiguously racialized, and a running joke throughout the episode involves Black characters guessing at his ethnicity, wondering if he is Dominican or Indian or "half-Chinese or something." In the opening scene, Zan inserts himself into a conversation between Alfred and Earn after recognizing Alfred as Paper Boi. While doing so, he explicitly claims racial kinship:

ZAN: Eh, Paper Boi! Good shit, homie! You blowin' up right now, my n***a.
ALFRED: Yeah, I don't know you.
ZAN: But I'm still your n***a, believe me.
ALFRED: Shit, are you even Black?
ZAN: Of course I am!

The cultural stakes of—and doubts about—his perceived racial status are later alluded to by another character: "I don't like Indian dudes who say 'n***a.'" The Black characters' difficulty in placing Zan racially mirrors their struggle to understand his relationship to themselves and to the community; people know *of* him but don't really know who he is or what—if anything—his online schemes amount to.

After being mocked, harassed, and made into a meme by Zan online, Alfred decides to confront him. He spots Zan getting into a car with a young boy—portrayed as indisputably Black—in the back seat and rides along as they deliver a pizza. During the drive, Alfred pointedly contrasts his life with Zan's: "Look man, I don't know if you know what's happening out here, but this ain't no game, a'ight? I'm getting tired of n***as online harassing me.... You messin' with my life, man; this my job." Alfred informs Zan: "There's no money anywhere near rap.... [N]***as die. People are forgotten. Shit is real." Zan predictably asks if he can "use that," and Alfred gets angry at him for being a "salesman." Zan replies that he has to commodify everything and reminds him that Alfred does the same in his rap career: "What's the difference? I mean, it's all in the game. We're all just hustlin'... you too." Alfred's response invokes his large and unmistakably Black embodiment: "'Cause I have to! I scare people at ATMs, boy." Echoing his sentiments in the "B.A.N." episode, Alfred furthermore insists that rap is "making the best out of a bad situation," essentially aligning it with Black improvisation in the break.

When Zan reaffirms his view that their relationship is symbiotic—"You're exploiting your situation to make rap, and I'm exploiting you exploiting that. Money, bro"—Alfred disengages, claiming that he "could say some shit right now" but doesn't want to "go off" on Zan in front of the young boy, who he presumes (in another gesture that tacitly accepts Zan's claim to Blackness) is Zan's son. Throughout the scene, the boy's largely unexplained presence in the car unsettles Alfred, who tells him to wear a seatbelt and looks askance as Zan has the boy repeat comically elaborate obscenities that Zan gleefully claims are "catchphrases" for the online videos they record together as "business partners." Once they arrive to make their delivery, Zan has the boy run out with the pizza. After the boy is robbed by the customer, Zan laughs and continues filming; the fact that he is *already* filming, though, either suggests he knew the robbery would happen or that he is *always* curating his experiences for online consumption. His casual exploitation of this child—especially in light of the boy's Blackness—further casts Zan as an opportunist, and this seems to be the last straw for Alfred, who makes his scorn evident by wordlessly exiting the car—and the scene—while Zan continues filming the boy pounding on the robber's door and shouting obscenities.

Zan's racial ambiguity is used as a fulcrum for humor. The inability to place him firmly in one racial category or another is both humorous and unsettling, pointing to his eschewing clear ties to any community in favor of commodifying everything. Rap, and Blackness in general, is a commodity for Zan, something to performatively attribute to himself when convenient, to trade upon, and to hold as property. Other characters' doubts bespeak their mistrust of his commodity-based approach to Blackness. The fact that Zan seems, at times, to be similarly haunted by Asianness indicates a discomfort with Asian American attempts to appropriate Blackness or understand their racialization by performing Blackness. His racial ambiguity thus becomes a means to explore both the commodification of Blackness and Black culture and the difference between exploitation and fugitive survival, between "selling out" and living as an objectified, commodified body.[5]

Interspersed among Alfred's interactions with Zan in "The Streisand Effect" is a second plotline hinting at a different, less inherently exploitative interaction among Black and Asian characters (and even white ones). Darius drives to a pawn shop where Earn intends to pawn his phone for a small amount of cash that he says he desperately needs. Darius eventually convinces Earn to trade for a samurai sword instead, initiating a labyrinthine scheme that plays out in the remainder of the episode. Throughout these scenes, Darius voices a number of assertions, including "AIDS was invented to keep Wilt Chamberlain from beating Steve McQueen's sex record" and "most Black people don't know who Steve McQueen is." After Earn admits his own ignorance on the latter score,

Darius says that he knows about McQueen but only because he's Nigerian, implying that he is in an oblique relationship with Blackness in the colloquial American use of the term. This points to Darius's eccentricities and his role as a character who pushes back against stereotypes of Black masculinity through his offbeat comments and surreal presence.

While standing beneath a poster for a movie starring Steve McQueen, the African American pawnshop owner (Clark Harris) confirms Darius's assertion:

> EARN: Hey, do you know who Steve McQueen is?
> PAWNSHOP OWNER: Yeah.
> [Earn makes sheepish face at Darius.]
> DARIUS: Would you know who Steve McQueen was if you didn't work here?
> PAWNSHOP OWNER: Black people don't know who Steve McQueen is. I keep that there for protection. If some dude comes in here asking about that poster, I know he's trying to get me to turn around so he can rob me.

This joke sets the tone for the remainder of this plotline, which asserts the arbitrariness (and thus fluidity) of supposedly definitive racial characteristics and establishes a contrast between the ways that characters mobilize such slippages.[6]

Earn and Darius next move to an urban warehouse containing a flourishing Asian underground that verges at times on stereotype but that is also shaped by performances of Blackness. As they walk from their car to the warehouse, Darius and Earn continue conversing about Zan's ethnic identity, with Darius speculating that Zan's shortness marks him as Chinese and citing Genghis Khan's "linchpin" policy of eradicating tall enemies as his evidence. As they walk past a slightly out-of-focus Asian man wearing an Afrocentric T-shirt and sporting cornrows, Darius encourages a disbelieving Earn to "look it up," to which Earn incredulously responds, "In what, *The Racism Book*?" The interior of the warehouse continues this mélange of racialized imagery and sounds: the song "It G Ma" by Keith Ape, a Korean rapper, plays in the background throughout; Darius and Earn walk past stacks of Asian antiques; groups of both Asian and Black people are shown gambling; an older Asian woman with dyed blond hair counts stacks of cash; and an Asian man with a gas mask incongruously perched atop his head walks past as Darius specifies—without further explanation—that the man is "not Chinese." While Darius trades the sword to a Black man (Tyree Edwards) for a large cane corso dog, a figure credited—in unwitting anticipation of *Interior Chinatown*—only as "Crying Chinese Bro" (Talbott Lin) sits awkwardly on a sidewalk in the background while shouting unsubtitled Mandarin into a cell phone. The episode temporarily shifts storylines again but in the episode's construction; immediately after the shot of Alfred leaving Zan's car, the episode cuts to Darius and Earn taking the dog to a rural farm, beautifully filmed in the golden tones of sunset, a distinct departure from the warehouse's (mostly) murky lighting. Darius hands over the dog to a white man (Danny Vinson) who addresses him familiarly as "D." Darius informs Earn that the man plans to breed the dog and give them a substantial cut for each of the puppies in the litter, albeit only "in September."[7]

This elaborate trading up—which increases Earn's payout from $190 to $4000[8]—flows through a series of spaces whose racialized encoding at times superficially suggests strict Black, Asian, or white boundaries but which also subtly reveal themselves to be sites of nuanced and nonexploitative relationships that seemingly provide all participants with an equal share of the benefits. These benefits, though, do not come in time to meet Earn's immediate needs: "See, I'm poor, Darius, and poor people don't have time for investments because poor people are too busy trying not to be poor. I need to eat today, not in September." Darius steps up, though, offering Earn his phone so that Earn can pawn it quickly because, as he succinctly states, "We're friends now." Although the elaborate and underground trades dependent on Darius's relationships are ultimately beneficial, they also do not respond to the urgency of Earn's situation. Darius's gift to Earn reinforces the importance of Black community, operating alongside the relational networks across difference embodied by Darius's unusual transactions.[9] After Darius proclaims them friends, the camera lingers on Earn sitting on the car hood against the sunset with soft lens flare dancing across the image. The song "Home Again" by Michael Kiwanuka begins to play over the shot as Darius and Earn get in the car together, presumably heading home. The combined visual, sonic, and narrative tone here all distinctly contrast with the other unresolved plot line, which ends with Alfred walking away from Zan's car while Zan films the young boy pounding on the door of the man who just robbed him. Although *Atlanta* generally derides the motivations for and/or the means of attempts at racial appropriation, this plotline exemplifies how Darius is frequently the vehicle through which it depicts an unironic—though not always uncomical—form of being otherwise.

Interior Chinatown presents Asianness not so much as a break from Western humanism but rather as a sort of vestibule connected to but not fully a part of it. Yu's genre-bending novel is written in the form of a screenplay—including being printed in Courier font—that is set in the Golden Palace Restaurant in "int. Chinatown." This somewhat generic space is itself also a set for *Black and White*, a buddy-cop show starring Miles Turner, a hypermasculine Black detective,[10] and Sarah Green, a white female detective. The novel's protagonist,

Willis Wu, is addressed throughout the book in second-person narration as he moves through various roles on *Black and White*, from such minor parts as "Background Oriental Male" and "Guy Who Runs in and Gets Kicked in the Face" all the way to his dream role as "Kung Fu Guy" (Yu 7).

The physical setting of the novel is an ambiguous, liminal space between a stock set and an actual locale. For example, Golden Palace is both the set for *Black and White* and a functioning restaurant. The single-room-occupancy (SRO) housing tower above the restaurant is likewise both a set on which inhabitants perform such stock roles as "Young Dragon Lady" and "Inscrutable Grocery Owner (in a Soiled T-Shirt)" and a domicile for people hailing from numerous Asian countries and cultures who have discrete names, relationships, and desires. *Black and White* so fully conditions the Asian characters' existence, though, that everyone is fixated on landing a bit part on the show. Dashing his father's hopes of breaking this cycle, Willis has embraced a flattening, stereotyped persona, including a fake accent "so he [can] be part of this, part of the American show, black and white, no part for yellow" (Yu 91). Willis either ignores or misses the inherent paradox of this phrasing and suppresses all traces of the belonging that he believes should accrue to him for being "born here, raised here . . . [and getting] As in every subject, including English" in order to "mak[e] a living as Generic Asian Man" (91).

Interior Chinatown is deeply invested in the politics of representation and the possibilities—or lack thereof—for Asian American men. Though Asian American women are at times addressed, the central theme of the novel is the limited representational possibilities for Asian American masculinity in not just Hollywood but the broader context of American culture, in which "everyone starts out as Generic Asian Man. Everyone who looks like you, anyway. Unless you're a woman, in which case you start out as Pretty Asian Woman" (Yu 10). In the world of the novel, Black masculinity (as embodied by Miles Turner) is cast in a distinct and leading role alongside the whiteness instantiated in the costar Sarah Green. For much of the novel, Willis sees the forces of Black masculine hypervisibility and white supremacy collaboratively squeezing out Asian Americans except as limited, marginal, and stereotypical characters. Green largely takes Willis's side when he and Turner argue, leading Turner to comment wryly, "It feels good to have White on your side, doesn't it?" (97). Although Blackness is also somewhat constrained on *Black and White*, it is nevertheless figured as occupying a starring—if also exoticized—role. *Interior Chinatown* suggests that the hypervisibility of Blackness reduces the possibilities for Asian representation in a kind of zero-sum game that largely does not address white supremacy's specific forms of violence. As Willis is working his way up into becoming a more significant character on the show, Turner tells Willis: "You're going along with it. Look where we are. Look what you made yourself into. Working your way up the system doesn't mean you beat the system. It strengthens it. It's what the system depends on" (95). *Interior Chinatown*'s literalization of the limited social roles available to racialized people satirizes Willis's initial unquestioning acceptance of the narrow options available to him, laying bare the absurdity of pursuing liberation by becoming a normative "model minority" in roles prescribed by white supremacy.

At the novel's climax, though, Willis realizes that "Kung Fu Guy is just another form of Generic Asian Man" and articulates a desire to trade his invisibility for the universality of simply being "Generic Man" (Yu 245). This latter category is coded as white "with an unthreatening amount of color sprinkled in" (210). "Unthreatening" here implies the exclusion of Blackness and its historically intertwined resonances of allure and menace for white audiences. In fact, *Interior Chinatown* suggests that Asian American politics is *overly* focused on anti-Blackness, that Asian Americans like Willis feel "somehow ... [t]hat the wrongs committed against your [i.e., Asians'] ancestors are incommensurate in magnitude with those committed against Black people in America.... Your oppression is second class" (233). This is articulated by "Older Brother" after he has finally broken out of his stock role and become a lawyer; this statement argues that Asian Americans are limiting themselves by believing that anti-Blackness is distinct from and incommensurate with anti-Asian racism and that this belief somehow means minimizing one's own suffering as an Asian in America. Older Brother goes on to argue: "Using the Black experience as the model for the Asian immigrant is necessarily going to lead to this. It's based on an analogy, on a comparison, on something quantitative. But the experiences of Asians in America isn't just a scaled-back or dialed down version of the Black experience. Instead of co-opting someone else's experience or consciousness, he must define his own" (234–35). Older Brother points out an irony in the way that Asian Americans have defined themselves in relationship to Blackness and anti-Blackness but does so by disavowing the material ways that Blackness, anti-Blackness, and white supremacy have each conditioned the racialization of Asianness, mocking this "derivative" understanding of Asianness without addressing the foundational role of anti-Blackness in shaping US society.

Yet understanding anti-Blackness as both relational to Asianness and as a foundational element of both the actual institutions of the nation and of "Americanness" writ large would bankrupt the unmarked American identity for which Willis longs. He wants "to be treated like an American ... [a] real American," and his aspiration calls to mind another of Donald Glover's satirical projects, the Childish Gambino song "This Is America" (2018) and its powerful music video directed by Hiro Murai,[11] in which "Americanness" is performed as a chaotic, violent farce, a stark contrast to Willis's unironic romanticization of a normative sense of American identity (Yu 228). Willis never seeks liberation from oppressively narrow identities by redefining the roles that are possible and breaking down the systems that create them in the first place.[12] His struggle to climb the ladder up to "Kung Fu Guy" is presented as satirical, mocking those limited roles.

After Willis shifts his sights from attaining the peak of "ethnic-character" roles to assimilation as an American everyman, though, the novel earnestly couches this desire in sympathy and pathos, connecting it to his complicated relationship to his racially ambiguous nuclear family. Willis's "White-ish" (Yu 164) wife, Karen Lee, and his daughter, Phoebe, can each exist beyond stereotypes of Asianness partly because of their mixed heritage. Karen is both racially mixed—she plays "Ethnically Ambiguous Woman Number One" (164)—and is also presented in some ways as more Taiwanese than Willis because she speaks Taiwanese more fluently than he does (a lack he earlier identifies as "the great shame of his life" [90]). He calls her a "magical creature" and envies her ability to "pass for anything," believing that she fuses "the consciousness of a contemporary American . . . [and] the face of a Chinese farmer of five thousand years ago" (166). His daughter Phoebe's ability to "move freely between worlds" is similarly a source of hopeful possibility for Willis; the novel ends with him wondering if she can assimilate: "Why can't you?" (266). The "worlds" that Phoebe passes among, though, are those of Chinatown and the paradigmatically white suburbs of children's television. Willis briefly improvises a role of "Kung Fu Dad" that might portend a form of being otherwise, but he ultimately abandons it: "That was just another role. A better role than I've ever had, but still a role. I can't keep doing the same thing over and over again" (251). Although Willis's desires in relationship to racialization and ambiguity are firmly oriented toward a liberal humanist Americanness that values his light-skinned, white-proximal female relatives, his desire to assimilate is ultimately presented as a genuine effort to get an answer to the question of why "we're trapped as guest stars in a small ghetto on a very special episode. . . . After two centuries here, why are we still not Americans? Why do we keep falling out of the story?" (251).

Willis's desire to assimilate through his family, though, also causes the police—including Turner and Green—to arrive at his door to arrest him for trying to escape from *Black and White* (and the limitations it represents) in a stolen car. The novel questions whether such a transformation—that is, leaving one's personal interior Chinatown—is possible but does not satirize or undercut the desire. Instead, it suggests that the path to breaking out of stereotypical roles may run toward assimilation. It also presents assimilation as a potentially legitimate path to liberation for Asian American masculinity that nevertheless remains barred by racist structures, such as the police and justice system that the novel narrates as functioning to keep Asian Americans "in their place," physically and culturally, and thereby preventing them from becoming what Willis desires: equals in America, without questioning the acceptance of white supremacy that such a vision of equality necessitates.

Although racial ambiguity is often celebrated in critical texts as "a potential antidote to racism . . . [that] destabilizes race" (Ho 21) and popular narratives construct multiracialism as "at the cutting edge of social and demographic change in the U.S.—young, proud, tolerant," *Interior Chinatown* questions the intended telos of such change (Parker et al. 5). Is racial ambiguity being operationalized to destabilize race or to affirm the supremacy of the normative? The novel oscillates between these two paradigms but never engages fully with the possibility of racialized life as being otherwise in the ways that *Atlanta* occasionally does. While *Atlanta* satirizes the mixed-race character of Zan as a grifter exploitatively trading on his ambiguity, *Interior Chinatown* extols racial ambiguity as a means of assimilation into a vaunted Americanness. Yu uses satire to illuminate how racial roles are stifling, limiting, and suffocating, and the possibility of slipping beyond one's prescribed roles into the universal is desired as liberation from such limitations—but that vision of liberation is only the relative, compromised relief of becoming normative. This contrasts with *Atlanta*, which satirizes various strategies for becoming normative in ways that expose the inherent violence of anti-Blackness and assuming liberal Western humanism as universal. The series constructs both the desire to pass into the supposedly unmarked (paradigmatically white) universal and the desire to manipulate ambiguity cynically as pathological and, in turn, explores radical possibilities in being outside the normative, in the spaces deemed by white supremacy as inhuman.

Examining satire playing along the Black-white color line reveals how *Atlanta* asserts Blackness as not a shade away from whiteness and its fictive, unmarked universalism, but rather as a break from it, a potential way of being otherwise. Satirical interrelations of Asianness and Blackness in both *Atlanta* and *Interior Chinatown* are somewhat less clear about how being otherwise as Asian Americans might function. As Willis holds on to the dream of becoming normative, he finds his own Chinatown to be a "holding cell, purgatory, a vestibule, the anteroom, the waiting room. It's the United States, but not quite America" (Yu 265). He cannot make the jump to considering that *not* being "in America" is potentially a site of possibility and not just a liminal "purgatory." Following Moten's lead, this positioning of Asianness as barred from the normative and stuck in the vestibule can be embraced as a space in the break from which to reject normativity. In understanding Asianness as relational (not competing or in comparison) with Blackness, the political project of Asian America can transform Willis's "vestibule" into an experimental realm for ways of being together conditioned by the infinite and edgeless possibilities among us.

NOTES

1. Another example of Beatty's use of Afro-Asian connections is *White Boy Shuffle*'s (1996) protagonist Gunnar Kaufman's frequent allusions to Japanese literature and relationship with his Japanese mail-order bride, Yoshiko.

2. Although there is plentiful discourse on social media and popular social-commentary websites concerning Awkwafina's performance of a Queens "blaccent," it—and the issue of Asian American appropriation of Black culture more broadly—has, thus far, rarely been addressed by scholars.

3. For further discussion of this episode, see the essays by Glavanakova and Parks herein.

4. For further discussion of this episode, see the essays by Brooks, Foster-Singletary, and Nishikawa herein.

5. For further discussion of Zan's characterization, see the essays by Glavanakova and Morgan herein.

6. There is, of course, embedded here another joke about the Black British director Steve McQueen as he does not come up at all in these conversations. His absence, perhaps, indicates a joke about his earlier films such as *Shame* (2011) and *Hunger* (2008), which centered white protagonists, and his film *Twelve Years a Slave* (2013), which has been criticized for catering to the white gaze and for perpetuating white-savior narratives.

7. For more on this subplot, see Klestil's essay herein.

8. Earn receives—and almost immediately squanders—the money from this deal in "Sportin' Waves" (s2e2).

9. The series' finale "It Was All a Dream," which also features plots following Darius on a layered journey and Asian-Black relationships, this time through a visit to the "first Black-owned sushi restaurant in Atlanta," also ends with shots reflecting Darius's perspective on the community and friendship that Van, Earn, Alfred, and Darius have formed.

10. Given his temperament, it is perhaps significant that his name is an amalgamation of two celebrated Black musicians who were also notorious for their mistreatment of the women in their lives: Ike Turner and Miles Davis.

11. For more discussion of Glover's collaboration with Murai, see Nishikawa's essay herein.

12. Directors, the larger capitalist enterprise of Hollywood, and viewing audiences are all mostly absent from this novel, which primarily focuses on the actors.

COMPOSITE WORKS CITED

EPISODES OF *ATLANTA* (ALL ORIGINALLY AIRED ON FX TELEVISION NETWORK)

Season 1

"B.A.N." Written by Donald Glover, directed by Donald Glover, 11 Oct. 2016.
"The Big Bang." Written by Donald Glover, directed by Hiro Murai, 6 Sept. 2016.
"The Club." Written by Jamal Olori, directed by Hiro Murai, 18 Oct. 2016.
"Go for Broke." Written by Stephen Glover, directed by Hiro Murai, 13 Sept. 2016.
"The Jacket." Written by Stephen Glover, directed by Hiro Murai, 1 Nov. 2016.
"Juneteenth." Written by Stefani Robinson, directed by Janicza Bravo, 25 Oct. 2016.
"Nobody Beats the Biebs." Written by Stephen Glover, directed by Hiro Murai, 27 Sept. 2016.
"Streets on Lock." Written by Stephen Glover, directed by Hiro Murai, 6 Sept. 2016.
"The Streisand Effect." Written by Donald Glover, directed by Hiro Murai, 20 Sept. 2016.
"Value." Written by Donald Glover and Stefani Robinson, directed by Donald Glover, 4 Oct. 2016.

Season 2: Robbin' Season

"Alligator Man." Written by Donald Glover, directed by Hiro Murai, 1 Mar. 2018.
"Champagne Papi." Written by Ibra Ake, directed by Amy Seimetz, 12 Apr. 2018.
"Crabs in a Barrel." Written by Stephen Glover, directed by Hiro Murai, 10 May 2018.
"FUBU." Written by Stephen Glover, directed by Donald Glover, 3 May 2018.
"Helen." Written by Taofik Kolade, directed by Amy Seimetz, 22 Mar. 2018.
"Money Bag Shawty." Written by Stephen Glover, directed by Hiro Murai, 15 Mar. 2018.
"North of the Border." Written by Jamal Olori, directed by Hiro Murai, 26 Apr. 2018.
"Sportin' Waves." Written by Stephen Glover, directed by Hiro Murai, 8 Mar. 2018.
"Teddy Perkins." Written by Donald Glover, directed by Hiro Murai, 5 Apr. 2018.
"Woods." Written by Stefani Robinson, directed by Hiro Murai, 19 Apr. 2018.

Season 3

"The Big Payback." Written by Francesca Sloane, directed by Hiro Murai, 7 Apr. 2022.
"Cancer Attack." Written by Jamal Olori, directed by Hiro Murai, 14 Apr. 2022.
"New Jazz." Written by Donald Glover, directed by Hiro Murai, 5 May 2022.
"The Old Man and the Tree." Written by Taofik Kolade, directed by Hiro Murai, 31 Mar. 2022.
"Rich Wigga, Poor Wigga." Written by Donald Glover, directed by Donald Glover, 12 May 2022.
"Sinterklaas Is Coming to Town." Written by Janine Nabers, directed by Hiro Murai, 24 Mar. 2022.
"Tarrare." Written by Stefani Robinson, directed by Donald Glover, 19 May 2022.
"Three Slaps." Written by Stephen Glover, directed by Hiro Murai, 24 Mar. 2022.
"Trini 2 De Bone." Written by Jordan Temple, directed by Donald Glover, 28 Apr. 2022.
"White Fashion." Written by Ibra Ake, directed by Ibra Ake, 21 Apr. 2022.

Season 4

"Andrew Wyeth: Alfred's World." Written by Taofik Kolade, directed by Hiro Murai, 3 Nov. 2022.
"Born 2 Die." Written by Jamal Olori, directed by Adamma Ebo, 22 Sept. 2022.
"Crank Dat Killer." Written by Stephen Glover, directed by Hiro Murai, 13 Oct. 2022.
"The Goof Who Sat by the Door." Written by Francesca Sloane and Karen Joseph Adcock, directed by Donald Glover, 27 Oct. 2022.
"The Homeliest Little Horse." Written by Ibra Ake, directed by Angela Barnes, 15 Sept. 2022.
"It Was All a Dream." Written by Donald Glover, directed by Hiro Murai, 10 Nov. 2022.
"Light Skinned-ed." Written by Stefani Robinson, directed by Hiro Murai, 29 Sept. 2022.
"The Most Atlanta." Written by Stephen Glover, directed by Hiro Murai, 15 Sept. 2022.
"Snipe Hunt." Written by Francesca Sloane, directed by Hiro Murai, 20 Oct. 2022.
"Work Ethic!" Written by Janine Nabers, directed by Donald Glover, 6 Oct. 2022.

OTHER PRIMARY SOURCES

Beatty, Paul, editor. *Hokum: An Anthology of African-American Humor*. Bloomsbury, 2006.
Beatty, Paul. *The Sellout*. Farrar, Straus and Giroux, 2015.
Big Tymers. "#1 Stunna." *I Got That Work*, Cash Money Records, 2000. CD.
Big Tymers. "Still Fly." *Hood Rich*, Cash Money Records, 2002. CD.
Childish Gambino. "Outside." *Camp*, Glassnote Records, 2011. CD.
Dear White People. Directed by Justin Simien, Lionsgate, 2014.
de la Bruyère, Jean. *The "Characters" of Jean de la Bruyère*. Translated and edited by Henri Van Laun, Lector House, 2019.
Everett, Percival. "The Appropriation of Cultures." *Callaloo*, vol. 19, no. 1, 1996, pp. 24–30.
Flack, Roberta. "Compared to What." *First Take*, Atlantic Studios, 1969. Vinyl.
Future. "See it to Believe It." *F.B.G: The Movie*, Freebandz, 2013. CD.
Get Out. Directed by Jordan Peele, Universal Pictures, 2017.

Glover, Donald. "Childish Gambino—Telegraph Ave ('Oakland' by Lloyd)." *YouTube*, 10 Oct. 2014, https://www.youtube.com/watch?v=p3f-eDzkxcw.

Glover, Donald. "Childish Gambino—3005 (Official Video)." *YouTube*, 6 Dec. 2013, https://www.youtube.com/watch?v=tG35R8F2j8k.

Greenidge, Kaitlyn. *We Love You, Charlie Freeman*. Algonquin, 2016.

"Guilty as Fuck." *Insecure*, written by Amy Aniobi, Issa Rae, and Larry Wilmore, directed by Debbie Allen, HBO, 13 Nov. 2016.

Harris, Jeremy O. *Slave Play*. Theatre Communications Group, 2019.

Hustle & Flow. Directed by Craig Brewer, Paramount Pictures, 2005.

"Insecure as Fuck." *Insecure*, written by Issa Rae and Larry Wilmore, directed by Melina Matsoukas, HBO, 9 Oct. 2016.

Jeezy. "Thug Motivation 101." *Let's Get It: Thug Motivation 101*, Def Jam, 2005. CD.

"The Lonely." *The Twilight Zone*, written by Rod Serling, directed by Jack Smight, CBS, 13 Nov. 1959.

"The Midnight Sun." *The Twilight Zone*, written by Rod Serling, directed by Anton Leader, CBS, 17 Nov. 1961.

"Mirror Image." *The Twilight Zone*, written by Rod Serling, directed by John Brahm, CBS, 26 Feb. 1960.

Notorious B.I.G. "Juicy." *Ready to Die*, Bad Boy, 1994. CD.

OutKast. "Elevators (Me & You)." *ATLiens*, Arista/LaFace, 1996. CD.

"Pilot." *Twin Peaks*, written by David Lynch, directed by David Lynch, ABC, 8 Apr. 1990.

Reed, Ishmael. *Flight to Canada*. Random House, 1976.

Rock, Chris. "A Message for White Voters." *YouTube*, uploaded by Jimmy Kimmel Live, 3 Nov. 2012, https://www.youtube.com/watch?v=EDxOSjgl5Z4.

Ross, Fran. *Oreo*. Introduction by Marlon James, Picador, 2018.

"Samuel Jackson Beer & Racial Draft." *Chappelle's Show*, written by Dave Chappelle and Neal Brennan, directed by Neal Brennan and Rusty Cundieff, Comedy Central, 21 Jan. 2004.

Senna, Danzy. *Caucasia*. Riverhead, 1998.

Senna, Danzy. *New People*. Riverhead, 2017.

"Shadow Play." *The Twilight Zone*, written by Charles Beaumont and Rod Serling, directed by John Brahm, CBS, 5 May 1961.

Shange, Ntozake. *for colored girls who have considered suicide when the rainbow is enuf*. Shameless Hussy Press, 1976.

Snow on tha Bluff. Directed by Damon Russell, Fuzzy Logic Pictures, 2012.

"Stopover in a Quiet Town." *The Twilight Zone*, written by Earl Hamner Jr. and Rod Serling, directed by Ron Winston, CBS, 24 Apr. 1964.

"A World of Difference." *The Twilight Zone*, written by Richard Matheson and Rod Serling, directed by Ted Post, CBS, 11 Mar. 1960.

Yu, Charles. *Interior Chinatown*. Pantheon, 2020.

SECONDARY SOURCES

Allen, Reniqua. "The Missing Black Millennial." *The New Republic*, 20 Feb. 2019, https://newrepublic.com/article/153122/missing-black-millennial.

Appiah, Kwame Anthony. "Racisms." *Anatomy of Racism*, edited by David Theo Goldberg, U of Minnesota P, 1990, pp. 3–17.

Arias, Claudia M. Milian, and Danzy Senna. "An Interview with Danzy Senna." *Callaloo*, vol. 25, no. 2, 2002, pp. 447–52.

Aristotle. *Ethics*. Translated by J. A. K. Thomson, Penguin, 1976.

Avilez, GerShun. *Black Queer Freedom: Spaces of Injury and Paths of Desire*. U of Illinois P, 2020.

Awkward, Michael. *Negotiating Difference: Race, Gender, and the Politics of Positionality*. U of Chicago P, 1995.

Bailey, Moya. *Misogynoir Transformed: Black Women's Digital Resistance*. New York UP, 2021.

Baldwin, James. "The Uses of the Blues." *The Cross of Redemption: Uncollected Writings*, by Baldwin, edited by Randall Kenan, 1964, Vintage International, 2010, pp. 70–81.

Bastién, Angelica Jade. "*Atlanta*'s Silly Yoo-hoo Ad Is a Clever Commentary on Black Art." *Vulture*, 8 Mar. 2018, https://www.vulture.com/2018/03/atlanta-yoohoo-commercial.html.

Bastién, Angelica Jade. "I Am Tired of Films like *Antebellum*." *Vulture*, 22 Oct. 2021, https://www.vulture.com/2020/09/antebellum-movie-review-i-am-tired-of-films-like-this.html.

Bastién, Angelica Jade. "In Its Second Season, *Atlanta* Used Horror to Explore Black Identity." *Vulture*, 18 May 2018, https://www.vulture.com/2018/05/atlanta-horror-second-two-black-identity.html.

Bastién, Angelica Jade. "*Them* Is Pure Degradation Porn." *Vulture*, 14 Apr. 2021, https://www.vulture.com/article/review-them-amazon-series.html.

Bastién, Angelica Jade, et al. "*Atlanta* Season Three Was a Bad Trip." *Vulture*, 27 June 2022, https://www.vulture.com/article/atlanta-season-three-flaws.html.

Beltran, Mary. "Meaningful Diversity: Exploring Questions of Equitable Representation on Diverse Ensemble Cast Shows." *FLOW: A Critical Forum on Media and Culture*, 27 Aug. 2010, https://www.flowjournal.org/2010/08/meaningful-diversity/.

Bennett, Joshua. "Buck Theory." *The Black Scholar: Journal of Black Studies and Research*, vol. 49, no. 2, 2019, pp. 27–37.

Bennett, Michael. "Anti-Pastoralism, Frederick Douglass, and the Nature of Slavery." *Beyond Nature Writing: Expanding the Boundaries of Ecocriticism*, edited by Karla Armbruster, U of Virginia P, 2001, pp. 195–210.

Bergenholtz, Rita A. "Toni Morrison's *Sula*: A Satire on Binary Thinking." *African American Review*, vol. 30, no. 1, 1996, pp. 89–98.

Bhabha, Homi K. *The Location of Culture*. Routledge, 1994.

Bogle, Donald. *Toms, Coons, Mulattoes, Mammies and Bucks: An Interpretive History of Blacks in American Films*. Continuum, 1973.

Boisseron, Bénédicte. *Afro-Dog: Blackness and the Animal Question*. Columbia UP, 2018.

Bordwell, David. "Return to Paranormalcy." *David Bordwell's Website on Cinema*, 13 Nov. 2012, http://www.davidbordwell.net/blog/2012/11/13/return-to-paranormalcy/.

Bradley, Regina M. *Chronicling Stankonia: The Rise of the Hip-Hop South*. U of North Carolina P, 2021.

Bradley, Stefan M. *Upending the Ivory Tower: Civil Rights, Black Power, and the Ivy League*. New York UP, 2020.

Bunche, Ralph. *Ralph J. Bunche: Selected Speeches and Writings*. Edited by Charles P. Henry, U of Michigan P, 1996.

Bunyasi, Tehama Lopez, and Candis Watts Smith. *Stay Woke: A People's Guide to Making All Black Lives Matter*. New York UP, 2019.
Butler, Judith. *Subjects of Desire: Hegelian Reflections in Twentieth-Century France*. Columbia UP, 1987.
Carpenter, Faedra Chatard. *Coloring Whiteness: Acts of Critique in Black Performance*. U of Michigan P, 2014.
Carpio, Glenda R. "B.O.S. 4.1/Alligator Man." *ASAP Journal*, 16 July 2018, https://asapjournal.com/b-o-s-4-1-alligator-man-glenda-r-carpio/.
Carpio, Glenda R. *Laughing Fit to Kill: Black Humor in the Fictions of Slavery*. Oxford UP, 2008.
Cassin, Barbara. Introduction. *Dictionary of Untranslatables: A Philosophical Lexicon*, translated by Michael Wood, edited by Cassin. Princeton UP, 2013, pp. xvii–xx.
Charity, Justin. "'Atlanta' Was Donald Glover's Masterwork." *The Ringer*, 9 Nov. 2022, https://www.theringer.com/tv/2022/11/9/23447133/atlanta-show-finale-legacy-donald-glover-masterwork.
Charity, Justin. "Resist the Impulse to Label 'The Underground Railroad' as Trauma Porn." *The Ringer*, 21 May 2021, https://www.theringer.com/tv/2021/5/21/22447443/underground-railroad-barry-jenkins-black-trauma.
Charles, Julia. *That Middle World: Race, Performance, and the Politics of Passing*. U of North Carolina P, 2020.
Claborn, John. *Civil Rights and the Environment in African-American Literature, 1895–1941*. Bloomsbury, 2017.
Coleman, Robin R. Means. *Horror Noire: Blacks in American Horror Films from the 1890s to Present*. Routledge, 2011.
Collins, Patricia Hill. *Black Sexual Politics: African Americans, Gender, and the New Racism*. Routledge, 2004.
Coscarelli, Joe. "The Cast of 'Atlanta' on Trump, Race and Fame." *New York Times*, 27 Feb. 2018, https://www.nytimes.com/2018/02/27/arts/television/atlanta-fx-season-2.html.
Cousins, Linwood. "Black Higher Learnin': Black Popular Culture and the Politics of Education." *Imagining the Academy: Higher Education and Popular Culture*, edited by Susan Edgerton et al., RoutledgeFalmer, 2005, pp. 247–66.
Crenshaw, Kimberlé Williams. "How Colorblindness Flourished in the Age of Obama." *Seeing Race Again: Countering Colorblindness across the Disciplines*, edited by Crenshaw et al., U of California P, 2019, pp. 128–51.
Crenshaw, Kimberlé Williams. "Race to the Bottom: How the Post-Racial Revolution Became a Whitewash." *The Baffler*, no. 35, June 2017, https://thebaffler.com/salvos/race-to-bottom-crenshaw.
Cwik, Greg. "Donald Glover Wants *Atlanta* to Be '*Twin Peaks* with Rappers.'" *Vulture*, 16 Jan. 2016, https://www.vulture.com/2016/01/donald-glover-on-doing-twin-peaks-with-rappers.html.
Davis, Shardé M. "Taking Back the Power: An Analysis of Black Women's Communicative Resistance." *Review of Communication*, vol. 18, no. 4, 2018, pp. 301–18.
Desta, Yohana. "Emmys 2018: Who Came in Character as Teddy Perkins, *Atlanta*'s Scariest Character?" *Vanity Fair*, 17 Sept. 2018, https://www.vanityfair.com/hollywood/2018/09/teddy-perkins-donald-glover-lakeith-stanfield-atlanta-emmys.

Dickson-Carr, Darryl. *African American Satire: The Sacredly Profane Novel*. U of Missouri P, 2001.

Dickson-Carr, Darryl. "Black Literature Matters; or Making It New." *American Literary History*, vol. 29, no. 4, winter 2017, pp. 790–98.

"Dog." *Oxford English Dictionary*, June 2021, www.oed.com/view/Entry/56407.

Domini, John. "Ishmael Reed: A Conversation with John Domini." *American Poetry Review*, vol. 7, no. 1, Jan./Feb. 1978, pp. 32–36.

Du Bois, W. E. B. *Black Reconstruction in America, 1860–1880*. Athenaeum, 1975.

Du Bois, W. E. B. *The Souls of Black Folk: Essays and Sketches*. Oxford UP, 2007.

Ducotey, Yvelin. "*Atlanta* (FX, Donald Glover, 2016-), vers une transgression générique des frontières géographiques et sociales." *TV/Series*, vol. 18, 2020, pp. 1–21. *Open Edition Journals*, http://journals.openedition.org/tvseries/4571.

Duke, Ellie. "We Need to Talk." *Los Angeles Review of Books*, 8 Mar. 2016, https://lareviewofbooks.org/article/we-need-to-talk/.

Edmond, Maura. "Here We Go Again: Music Videos after YouTube." *Television and New Media*, vol. 15, no. 4, 2014, pp. 305–20.

Edmonds, Brittney M. *Who's Laughing Now? Black Affective Play and Formalist Innovation in Twenty-First Century Black Literary Satire*. 2021. Princeton U, PhD dissertation.

Elam, Michelle. *The Souls of Mixed Folk: Race, Politics, and Aesthetics in the New Millennium*. Stanford UP, 2011.

Ellis, Trey. "The New Black Aesthetic." *Callaloo*, no. 38, winter 1989, pp. 233–43.

Ettenhofer, Valerie. "Hiro Murai Has Mastered the Art of the Gut Punch." *Film School Rejects*, 25 May 2018, https://filmschoolrejects.com/hiro-murai-has-mastered-the-art-of-the-gut-punch/.

Fernandez, Maria Elena. "Why *Atlanta* Season Two Is Called *Robbin' Season*." *Vulture*, 5 Jan. 2018, https://www.vulture.com/2018/01/atlanta-season-two-robbin-season-how-it-got-its-name.html.

Finley, Jessyka. "Black Women's Satire as (Black) Postmodern Performance." *Studies in American Humor*, vol. 2, no. 2, 2016, pp. 236–65.

Fleetwood, Nicole R. *Troubling Vision: Performance, Visuality, and Blackness*. U of Chicago P, 2011.

Francis, Terri S. "Introduction: The No-Theory Chant of Afrosurrealism." *Black Camera: The Newsletter of the Black Film Center/Archives*, vol. 5, no. 1, 2013, pp. 95–111.

Friend, Tad. "Donald Glover Can't Save You." *New Yorker*, 26 Feb. 2018, https://www.newyorker.com/magazine/2018/03/05/donald-glover-cant-save-you.

Frye, Northrop. *The Anatomy of Criticism: Four Essays*. Princeton UP, 1957.

Frye, Northrop. "The Nature of Satire." *University of Toronto Quarterly*, vol. 14, no. 1, 1944, pp. 75–89.

Fuse. "Childish Gambino on Kanye West & Getting Dissed by A$AP Rocky." *YouTube*, 31 Oct. 2013, https://www.youtube.com/watch?v=QVjf9kwMc58.

Gaines, Kevin. *Uplifting the Race: Black Leadership, Politics, and Culture in the Twentieth Century*. U of North Carolina P, 1996.

Gates, Henry Louis, Jr. *Figures in Black: Words, Signs and the "Racial" Self*. Oxford UP, 1987.

Gates, Henry Louis, Jr. *The Signifying Monkey: A Theory of Afro-American Literary Criticism*. Oxford UP, 1988.

Gates, Henry Louis, Jr. *Thirteen Ways of Looking at a Black Man*. Random House, 1997.
Gates, Henry Louis, Jr. "2 Live Crew, Decoded." *New York Times*, 19 June 1990, p. A23.
Gillespie, Carmen. Foreword. *Postracial America? An Interdisciplinary Study*, edited by Vincent L. Stephens and Anthony Stewart, Bucknell UP, 2017, pp. xiii–xv.
Gillota, David. "Black Nerds: New Directions in African American Humor." *Studies in American Humor*, vol. 3, no. 28, 2013, pp. 17–30.
Gilmore, John T. *Satire*. Routledge, 2018.
Giltner, Scott. "Slave Hunting and Fishing in the Antebellum South." *"To Love the Wind and the Rain": African Americans and Environmental History*, edited by Dianne D. Glave and Mark Stoll, U of Pittsburgh P, 2006, pp. 21–36.
Glenn, Cerise L., and Landra J. Cunningham. "The Power of Black Magic: The Magical Negro and White Salvation in Film." *Journal of Black Studies*, vol. 40, no. 2, Nov. 2009, pp. 135–52.
Glover, Donald. "Donald Glover Interviews Donald Glover." *Interview*, 7 Apr. 2022, https://www.interviewmagazine.com/culture/donald-glover-interviews-donald-glover.
Godfrey, Mollie, and Vershawn Ashanti Young. Introduction. *Neo-Passing: Performing Identity after Jim Crow*, edited by Godfrey and Young, U of Illinois P, 2021, pp. 1–28.
Goldberg, Lesley. "Donald Glover Sets Rich Amazon Overall Deal." *Hollywood Reporter*, 17 Feb. 2021, https://www.hollywoodreporter.com/tv/tv-news/onald-glover-sets-rich-amazon-overall-deal-exclusive-4134497/.
Gould, Gaylene. "A Lesson in Awkward." *Sight & Sound*, vol. 27, no. 1, Jan. 2017, pp. 28–30.
Gray, Herman. *Watching Race: Television and the Struggle for "Blackness."* U of Minnesota P, 1995.
Gray, John. *Liberalism*. 2nd ed., U of Minnesota P, 2003.
Greenberg, Jonathan. *The Cambridge Introduction to Satire*. Cambridge UP, 2018.
Griffin, Dustin. *Satire: A Critical Reintroduction*. UP of Kentucky, 1994.
Gross, Terry. "'Awkward' and 'Insecure' Get to the Root of Issa Rae's Humor." *Fresh Air*, National Public Radio, 8 Nov. 2016, https://www.npr.org/2016/11/08/501159971/-awkward-and-insecure-get-to-the-root-of-writer-issa-rae-s-humor.
Guerrero, Lisa. "Can I Live? Contemporary Black Satire and the State of Postmodern Double Consciousness." *Studies in American Humor*, vol. 2, no. 2, 2016, pp. 266–79.
Guerrero, Lisa. *Crazy Funny: Popular Black Satire and the Method of Madness*. Routledge, 2020.
Haggins, Bambi. "There's No Place Like Home: The American Dream, African-American Identity, and the Situation Comedy." *The Velvet Light Trap*, vol. 43, spring 1999, pp. 23–37.
Hall, Stuart. "New Ethnicities." *Stuart Hall: Critical Dialogues in Cultural Studies*, edited by David Morley and Kuan-Hsing Chen, Routledge, 1996, pp. 441–49.
Hamada, Jeff. "An Interview with Director Hiro Murai." *Booooooom*, 19 Nov. 2014, https://www.booooooom.com/2014/11/19/interview-director-hiro-murai/.
Haney-López, Ian F. "Is the Post in Post-Racial the Blind in Colorblind?" *Cardozo Law Review*, vol. 32, no. 3, 2011, pp. 807–31.
Harris, Cheryl I. "Whiteness as Property." *Harvard Law Review*, vol. 106, no. 8, 1993, pp. 1707–91.
Harrison, Sheri. "The New Black Gothic." *Los Angeles Review of Books*, 23 June 2018, https://lareviewofbooks.org/article/new-black-gothic/.
Harrison-Kahan, Lori. "Passing for White, Passing for Jewish: Mixed Race Identity in Danzy Senna and Rebecca Walker." *MELUS*, vol. 30, no. 1, 2005, pp. 19–48.

Harris-Perry, Melissa V. *Sister Citizen: Shame, Stereotypes, and Black Women in America.* Yale UP, 2011.

Hartman, Saidiya. *Lost Your Mother: A Journey along the Atlantic Slave Trade Route.* Farrar, Straus and Giroux, 2008.

Hartman, Saidiya. *Scenes of Subjection: Terror, Slavery, and Self-Making in Nineteenth-Century America.* Oxford UP, 1997.

Hausmann, Leslie R. M., et al. "Sense of Belonging as a Predictor of Intentions to Persist among African American and White First-Year College Students." *Research in Higher Education*, vol. 48, no. 7, Nov. 2007, pp. 803–39.

Hicks, Scott. "W.E.B. Du Bois, Booker T. Washington, and Richard Wright: Toward an Ecocriticism of Color." *Callaloo*, vol. 29, no. 1, 2006, pp. 202–22.

Higginbotham, Evelyn B. *Righteous Discontent: The Women's Movement in the Black Baptist Church, 1880–1920.* Harvard UP, 1993.

Ho, Jennifer Ann. *Racial Ambiguity in Asian American Culture.* Rutgers UP, 2015.

Hobson, Maurice J. "All Black Everythang: Aesthetics, Anecdotes, and FX's *Atlanta*." *Atlanta Studies*, 15 Nov. 2016, https://atlantastudies.org/2016/11/15/all-black-everythang-aesthetics-anecdotes-and-fxs-atlanta/.

Hoggart, Richard. *The Uses of Literacy.* 1957. Transaction Publishers, 1992.

Holland, Sharon Patricia. *The Erotic Life of Racism.* Duke UP, 2021.

hooks, bell. *Black Looks: Race and Representation.* 2nd ed., Routledge, 2015.

hooks, bell. *Killing Rage: Ending Racism.* Henry Holt, 1995.

hooks, bell. *Teaching to Transgress: Education as the Practice of Freedom.* Routledge. 1994.

Hughes, Akilah. "FX's 'Atlanta' Depicts a Truth of Black Experience Unseen on TV." *The Observer*, 9 July 2016, https://observer.com/2016/09/fxs-atlanta-depicts-a-truth-of-black-experience-unseen-on-tv/.

Hutcheon, Linda. *Irony's Edge: The Theory and Politics of Irony.* Routledge, 1994.

Iandoli, Kathy. "Post Malone: Post-Racial or Problematic?" *The Guardian*, 27 Oct. 2017, https://www.theguardian.com/music/2017/oct/20/is-white-rapper-post-malone-post-racial-or-problematic.

"Is Gangsta Rap Hurting America's Children?" *The O'Reilly Factor.* Hosted by Bill O'Reilly, Fox News Channel, New York, 12 Nov. 2003.

Jackson, Leigh-Ann. "'Atlanta' Season 2, Episode 10: 'FUBU.'" *New York Times*, 3 May 2018, https://www.nytimes.com/2018/05/03/arts/television/atlanta-season-2-episode-10-recap.html.

Jackson, Ronald L., II. *Scripting the Black Masculine Body: Identity, Discourse, and Racial Politics in Popular Media.* State U of New York P, 2006.

James, Darius. *That's Blaxploitation! Roots of the Baadasssss 'Tude.* St. Martin's Press, 1995.

James, Marlon. Introduction. *Oreo*, by Fran Ross, Picador, 2018, pp. vii–xii.

Jenkins, DeMarcus A., et al. "The Second ID: Critical Race Counterstories of Campus Police Interactions with Black Men at Historically White Institutions." *Race Ethnicity and Education*, vol. 24, no. 2, 2021, pp. 149–66.

Jennings, Angel. "No Bullets or Body Counts: How 'Insecure' Creator Issa Rae Is Portraying the Sexy Side of South L.A." *Los Angeles Times*, 23 Jan. 2017, https://www.latimes.com/local/california/la-me-southla-perception-20170123-story.html.

Jerng, Mark C. *Racial Worldmaking: The Power of Popular Fiction.* Fordham UP, 2018.

Jewell, K. S. *From Mammy to Miss America and Beyond: Cultural Images and the Shaping of US Social Policy*. Routledge, 1993.

Johnson, E. Patrick. "Black Performance Studies: Genealogies, Politics, Futures." *The SAGE Handbook of Performance Studies*, edited by D. Soyini Madison and Judith A. Hamera, Sage, 2006, pp. 446–62.

Johnson, Lindgren. *Race Matters, Animal Matters: Fugitive Humanism in African America, 1838–1934*. Routledge, 2017.

Karimi, Faith. "Justin Bieber Is Being Accused of Cultural Appropriation over His Hair. Again." *CNN Entertainment*, 29 June 2021, https://www.cnn.com/2021/04/27/entertainment/justin-bieber-dreadlocks-trnd/index.html.

Kaufman, Burton I. *Barack Obama: Conservative, Pragmatist, Progressive*. Cornell UP, 2022.

Kemp, Jerome. "A Moral Purpose, A Literary Game: Horace, 'Satires' 1.4." *Classical World*, vol. 104, no. 1, 2010, pp. 59–76.

Kincaid, Jamaica. *A Small Place*. Farrar, Straus and Giroux, 2000.

Kirkland, David E., and Austin Jackson. "'We Real Cool': Towards a Theory of Black Masculine Literacies." *Reading Research Quarterly*, vol. 44, no. 3, July/August/September 2009, pp. 278–97.

Knight, Charles A. *The Literature of Satire*. Cambridge UP, 2004.

Knittel, Chris. "Irregular Warfare: Marketing *Snow on tha Bluff*." *Filmmaker*, 26 June 2013, https://filmmakermagazine.com/73229-irregular-warfare-marketing-snow-on-tha-bluff.

Knutson, Harold C. "Three Characters in Search of a Vice: The Hypocrite in Theophrastus, Joseph Hall and La Bruyère." *Dalhousie French Studies*, vol. 27, 1994, pp. 51–63.

Kopp, Luvena. "Satirizing Satire: Symbolic Violence and Subversion in Spike Lee's *Bamboozled*." Maus and Donahue, pp. 214–27.

Kunzel, Regina. *Criminal Intimacy: Prison and the Uneven History of Modern Sexuality*. U of Chicago P, 2008.

Lee, Chris. "Donald Glover, Renaissance Man of Comedy and Rap." *Los Angeles Times*, 19 July 2010, https://www.latimes.com/archives/la-xpm-2010-jul-19-la-et-glover-20100719-story.html.

Lee, Julia Sun-Joo. *Our Gang: A Racial History of the Little Rascals*. U of Minnesota P, 2015.

Leverette, Tru. "Re-visions of Difference in Danzy Senna's *Caucasia*." *Obsidian*, vol. 12, no. 1, spring/summer 2011, pp. 110–27.

Leverette, Tru. "Traveling Identities: Mixed Race Quests and Fran Ross's *Oreo*." *African American Review*, vol. 40, no. 1, 2006, pp. 79–91.

Levinas, Emmanuel. "Meaning and Sense." *Collected Philosophical Papers*. Translated by Alphonso Lingis, Duquesne UP, 1998.

Libresco, Leah. "Here Are the Demands from Students Protesting Racism at 51 Colleges." *FiveThirtyEight*, 3 Dec. 2015, https://fivethirtyeight.com/features/here-are-the-demands-from-students-protesting-racism-at-51-colleges/.

Lipsitz, George. *The Possessive Investment in Whiteness: How White People Profit from Identity Politics*. 2006. Temple UP, 2018.

Locke, John. *An Essay Concerning Human Understanding*. Batoche Books, 2000.

Losurdo, Domenico. *Liberalism: A Counter-History*. Verso, 2011.

Lott, Eric. *Love and Theft: Blackface Minstrelsy and the American Working Class*. 2nd ed., Oxford UP, 2013.

Lubiano, Wahneema. "But Compared to What? Reading Realism, Representation, and Essentialism in *School Daze, Do the Right Thing*, and the Spike Lee Discourse." *Black American Literature Forum*, vol. 25, no. 2, 1991, pp. 253–82.

Macey, David. *The Penguin Dictionary of Critical Theory*. Penguin Books, 2000.

Mack, Maynard. *Collected in Himself: Essays Critical, Biographical, and Bibliographical on Pope and Some of His Contemporaries*. U of Delaware P, 1982.

Maltin, Leonard, and Richard Bann. *Our Gang: The Life and Times of the Little Rascals*. Crown Publishing, 1977.

Manning, Brandon J. "Black Millennial Satire." *Post-45*, 22 June 2021, https://post45.org/2021/06/black-millennial-satire/.

Manning, Brandon J. *Played Out: The Race-Man in Twenty-First-Century Satire*. Rutgers UP, 2022.

Markley, Scott N., et al. "The Limits of Home Ownership: Racial Capitalism, Black Wealth, and the Appreciation Gap in Atlanta." *International Journal of Urban and Region Research*, vol. 22, no. 2, 2020, pp. 310–28.

Marriott, David. *On Black Men*. Columbia UP, 2000.

Masschelein, Anneleen. *The Unconcept: The Freudian Uncanny in Late-Twentieth-Century Theory*. State U of New York P, 2011.

Maus, Derek C. *Jesting in Earnest: Percival Everett and Menippean Satire*. U of South Carolina P, 2019.

Maus, Derek C. "'Mommy, What's a Post-Soul Satirist?' An Introduction." Maus and Donahue, pp. xi–xxiii.

Maus, Derek C., and James J. Donahue, editors. *Post-Soul Satire: Black Identity after Civil Rights*. UP of Mississippi, 2014.

McAllister, Marvin. *Whiting Up: Whiteface Minstrels and Stage Europeans in African American Performance*. U of North Carolina P, 2011.

McGehee, Molly. "An Urban Oasis." *Pearl Cleage and Free Womanhood: Essays on Her Prose Works*, edited by Tikenya Foster-Singletary and Aisha Francis, McFarland, 2012, pp. 15–36.

McKittrick, Katherine. "Plantation Futures." *Small Axe*, vol. 17, no. 3, Nov. 2013, pp. 1–15.

Mercer, Kobena. *Welcome to the Jungle: New Positions in Black Cultural Studies*. Routledge, 1994.

Meyer, John C. "Humor as a Double-Edged Sword: Four Functions of Humor in Communication." *Communication Theory*, vol. 10, no. 3, 2000, pp. 310–31.

Miller, Liz. "'Atlanta': Donald Glover Wants You to Feel What It's Like to Be Black." *IndieWire*, 9 Aug. 2016, https://www.indiewire.com/2016/08/donald-glover-atlanta-fx-hiro-murai-trump-1201714877/.

Mills, Charles W. *The Racial Contract*. Cornell UP, 1997.

Mock, Brentin. "Think People of Color Don't Care about the Environment? Think Again." *Grist*, 1 Jan. 2014, http://grist.org/climate-energy/think-people-of-color-don't-care-about-the-environment-think-again/.

Mohai, Paul. "Dispelling Old Myths: African American Concern for the Environment." *Environment: Science and Policy for Sustainable Development*, vol. 45, no. 5, 2003, pp. 11–26.

Montrose, Alex. "Made-Up TV Series on 'Insecure' Is a Commentary on the Lack of Black Sitcom Reboots." *Complex*, 13 Aug. 2018, https://www.complex.com/pop-culture/2018/08/made-up-tv-series-on-insecure-commentary-on-lack-of-black-sitcom-reboots.

Morgan, Danielle Fuentes. *Laughing to Keep from Dying: African American Satire in the Twenty-First Century*. U of Illinois P, 2020.

Morgan, Danielle Fuentes. "Twenty-First-Century African American Satire." *Post-45*, 22 June 2021, https://post45.org/2021/06/introduction-twenty-first-century-african-american-satire/.

Morning, Ann. "Multiracial Classification on the United States Census: Myth, Reality, and Future Impact." *Revue Européenne des Migrations Internationales*, vol. 21, no. 2, 2005, pp. 111–34.

Morris, Wesley. "Why Is Everyone Always Stealing Black Music?" *New York Times*, 18 Aug. 2019, https://www.nytimes.com/interactive/2019/08/14/magazine/music-black-culture-appropriation.html.

Moten, Fred. *Black and Blur*. Duke UP, 2017.

Moten, Fred. *In the Break: The Aesthetics of the Black Radical Tradition*. U of Minnesota P, 2003.

Mullen, Harryette. "'Apple Pie with Oreo Crust': Fran Ross's Recipe for an Idiosyncratic American Novel." *MELUS*, vol. 27, no. 1, 2002, pp. 107–29.

Muñoz, José Esteban. "Feeling Brown: Ethnicity and Affect in Ricardo Bracho's *The Sweetest Hangover (and Other STDs)*." *Theatre Journal*, vol. 52, no. 1, 2000, pp. 67–79.

Murfin, Ross C., and Supryia M. Ray. *The Bedford Glossary of Critical and Literary Terms*. 4th ed., Bedford/St. Martin's, 2018.

Murphy, Chris. "Stephen Glover Thinks Whiteness Is a Curse." *Vanity Fair*, 20 May 2022, https://www.vanityfair.com/hollywood/2022/05/stephen-glover-thinks-whiteness-is-a-curse.

Murray, Derek Conrad. *Mapplethorpe and the Flower: Radical Sexuality and the Limits of Control*. Bloomsbury, 2022.

Murray, Derek Conrad. *Queering Post-Black Art: Artists Transforming African-American Identity after Civil Rights*. I.B. Tauris, 2016.

"NAACP Imposter Sued School over Race Claims: Rachel Dolezal Alleged She Was Discrimination Victim." *The Smoking Gun*, 15 June 2015, https://www.thesmokinggun.com/documents/bizarre/rachel-dolezal-discrimination-lawsuit-786451.

Nakamura, Lisa. "Feeling Good about Feeling Bad: Virtuous Virtual Reality and the Automation of Racial Empathy." *Journal of Visual Culture*, vol. 19, no. 1, April 2020, pp. 47–64.

Nakkula, Michael. "Identity and Possibility: Adolescent Development and the Potential of Schools." *Adolescents at School: Perspectives on Youth, Identity, and Education*, edited by Michael Sadowski, 3rd ed., Harvard Education Press, 2020, pp. 11–22.

Napper, George. *Blacker than Thou: The Struggle for Campus Unity*. Eerdmans, 1973.

Neal, Mark Anthony. *Soul Babies: Black Popular Culture and the Post-Soul Aesthetic*. Routledge, 2002.

Nelson, Victoria. "Addressing Racial Trauma and Hate Crimes on College Campuses." *Center for American Progress*, 9 Aug. 2019, https://www.americanprogress.org/article/addressing-racial-trauma-hate-crimes-college-campuses/.

Nguyen, Hanh. "'Atlanta' Review: 'Teddy Perkins' Is More Nightmarish than 'Get Out,' and We Still Haven't Recovered." *IndieWire*, 6 Apr. 2018, https://www.indiewire.com/features/general/atlanta-teddy-perkins-review-season-2-episode-6-recap-spoilers-theories-1201949701/.

Nigatu, Heben, and Tracy Clayton. "Episode 83: Incognegro (with Jordan Peele)." *Another Round with Heben and Tracy*, WNYC, 1 Mar. 2017, https://www.wnyc.org/story/episode-83-incognegro-with-jordan-peele/.

Nishikawa, Kinohi. "The Lower Frequencies: Hip-Hop Satire in the New Millennium." Maus and Donahue, pp. 38–55.

Painter, Nell Irvin. *The History of White People*. Norton, 2010.

Pareles, Jon. "POP VIEW; How Real Is 'Realness' in Rap?" *New York Times*, 11 Dec. 1994, sec. 2, p. 34.

Parker, Kim, et al. "Multiracial in America: Proud, Diverse and Growing in Numbers." *Pew Research Center*, 11 June 2015, https://www.pewresearch.org/social-trends/2015/06/11/multiracial-in-america/.

Parks, Keyana. "Awkward Prose and Satirical Didacticism." *Post-45*, 22 June 2021. https://post45.org/2021/06/awkward-prose-and-satirical-didacticism/.

Parry, Tyler D., and Charlton W. Yingling. "Slave Hounds and Abolition in the Americas." *Past & Present*, vol. 246, no. 1, 2020, pp. 69–108.

Patterson, Orlando. *Slavery and Social Death: A Comparative Study*. Harvard UP, 1982.

Perry, Imani. *Prophets of the Hood: Politics and Poetics in Hip Hop*. Duke UP, 2004.

Pickens, Theri. "Shoving Aside the Politics of Respectability: Black Women, Reality TV, and the Ratchet Performance." *Women & Performance: A Journal of Feminist Theory*, vol. 25, no. 1, 2015, pp. 41–58.

"Rachel Dolezal Says She Identifies as Trans-Black." *NBC News*, 27 Mar. 2017, https://www.nbcnews.com/video/rachel-dolezal-says-she-identifies-as-trans-black-907981379504.

Raleigh, Elizabeth. "The Color Line Exception: The Transracial Adoption of Foreign-Born and Biracial Black Children." *Women, Gender, and Families of Color*, vol. 4, no. 1, spring 2016, pp. 86–107.

Ray, Sarah Jaquette. *The Ecological Other: Environmental Exclusion in American Culture*. U of Arizona P, 2013.

Roach, Joseph. *Cities of the Dead: Circum-Atlantic Performance*. Columbia UP, 1996.

Roberts, Brian. *Blackface Nation: Race, Reform, and Identity in Popular Music, 1812–1925*. U of Chicago P, 2017.

Robinson, Michelle LaVaughn. *Princeton-Educated Blacks and the Black Community*. 1985. Princeton U, BA thesis. *Politico*, https://www.politico.com/pdf/080222_MOPrincetonThesis_1-251.pdf.

Robinson, Russell. "Masculinity as Prison: Sexual Identity, Race, and Incarceration." *California Law Review*, vol. 99, no. 5, 2011, pp. 1309–1408.

Root, Maria P. P., editor. *The Multiracial Experience: Racial Borders as the New Frontier*. SAGE, 1996.

Ross, Janell. "Larry Wilmore's Take on the 'Unblackening' of the White House." *Washington Post*, 2 Oct. 2015, https://www.washingtonpost.com/news/the-fix/wp/2015/10/02/larry-wilmores-take-on-the-unblackening-of-the-white-house/.

Rowe, Kathleen. *The Unruly Woman: Gender and the Genres of Laughter*. U of Texas P, 1995.

Ruffin, Kimberly N. *Black on Earth: African American Ecoliterary Traditions*. U of Georgia P, 2010.

Russell, Margaret M. "Race and the Dominant Gaze: Narratives of Law and Inequality in Popular Film." *Critical White Studies: Looking Behind the Mirror*, edited by Richard Delgado and Jean Stefancic, Temple UP, 1997, pp. 267–72.
Rutheiser, Charles. *Imagineering Atlanta: The Politics of Place in the City of Dreams*. Verso, 1996.
Ryan, Michael, and Melissa Lenos. *An Introduction to Film Analysis: Technique and Meaning in Narrative Film*. Continuum, 2020.
Schalk, Sami. "Strategic Alterations and Afro-Asian Connections in Paul Beatty's *Tuff*." *Mosaic*, vol. 51, no. 1, 2018, pp. 55–70.
Senna, Danzy. "Mulatto Millennium." *Salon*, 24 July 1998, http://www.salon.com/1998/07/24/24feature_10/.
Senna, Danzy. "To Be Real." *To Be Real: Telling the Truth and Changing the Face of Feminism*, edited by Rebecca Walker, Anchor Books, 1995, pp. 5–20.
Seymour, Nicole. *Bad Environmentalism: Irony and Irreverence in the Ecological Age*. U of Minnesota P, 2018.
Shavers, Rone. "Percival Everett." *Bomb*, vol. 88, summer 2004, pp. 46–51.
Shaw, Todd C., et al. Introduction. *After Obama: African American Politics in a Post-Obama Era*, edited by Shaw et al., New York UP, 2021, pp. 1–42.
Simpson, Tyrone. "The Trope of Awkwardness and Newer Negro Autobiography." *Critical Race Theory in the Academy*, edited by Vernon Lee Farmer and Evelyn Shephard W. Farmer, Information Age, 2020, pp. 227–44.
Smith, Jeanne Rosier. *Writing Tricksters: Mythic Gambols in American Ethnic Literature*. U of California P, 1997.
Smith, Kimberly K. *African American Environmental Thought Foundations*. UP of Kansas, 2007.
Sollors, Werner. *Neither Black nor White, Yet Both: Thematic Explorations of Interracial Literature*. Harvard UP, 1997.
Spike, Carlett. "Major Gift from Mellody Hobson '91 Names New Residential College." *Princeton Alumni Weekly*, 8 Oct. 2020, https://paw.princeton.edu/article/historic-gift-new-residential-college-be-named-mellody-hobson-91.
Stephens, Vincent L., and Anthony Stewart. Introduction. *Postracial America? An Interdisciplinary Study*, edited by Stephens and Stewart, Bucknell UP, 2017, pp. 1–18.
Subramanian, Ram, et al. *Incarceration's Front Door: The Misuse of Jail in America*. Vera Institute of Justice, 2015.
Takei, Carl. "Colleges and Universities Have a Racial Profiling Problem." *ACLU*, 21 Sept. 2018, https://www.aclu.org/blog/racial-justice/race-and-inequality-education/colleges-and-universities-have-racial-profiling.
Tatum, Beverly Daniel. *Why Are All the Black Kids Sitting Together in the Cafeteria? And Other Conversations about Race*. Revised and updated ed., Hachette, 2017.
Taylor, Yuval, and Jake Austen. *Darkest America: Black Minstrelsy from Slavery to Hip-Hop*. Norton, 2012.
Terry, Sierriana. *Black Atlanta: Musical Counternarratives of "Authentic" Blackness in Donald Glover's "Atlanta."* 2018. U of North Carolina at Chapel Hill, MA thesis.
Tharpe, Frazier. "RJ Walker Reveals 'Atlanta' Studio Scene Really Happened to Donald Glover." *Complex*, 1 June 2018, https://www.complex.com/popculture/2018/03/atlanta-robbin-season-yoohoo-rj-walker-interview.

Tillet, Salamishah. "'Insecure' Broke Ground by Embracing Imperfection." *New York Times*, 15 Oct. 2021, https://www.nytimes.com/2021/10/15/arts/television/insecure-final-season-issa-rae.html.

Tillet, Salamishah. *Sites of Slavery: Citizenship and Racial Democracy in the Post-Civil Rights Imagination*. Duke UP, 2012.

Tucker, Terrence T. *Furiously Funny: Comic Rage from Ralph Ellison to Chris Rock*. UP of Florida, 2018.

Tyler, Tom. "Cows, Clicks, Ciphers, and Satire." *NECSUS: European Journal of Media Studies*, vol. 4, no. 1, 2015, https://necsus-ejms.org/cows-clicks-ciphers-and-satire/.

Verhoeven, Monique, et al. "The Role of School in Adolescents' Identity Development: A Literature Review." *Educational Psychology Review*, vol. 31, no. 1, 2019, pp. 35–63.

Verschelden, Cia. *Bandwidth Recovery: Helping Students Reclaim Cognitive Resources Lost to Poverty, Racism, and Social Marginalization*. Stylus Publishing, 2017.

Viruet, Pilot. "'Atlanta' Is Great at Talking about Race without Talking about Race." *Vice*, 28 Sept. 2016, https://www.vice.com/en/article/7bm83a/atlanta-is-great-at-talking-about-race-without-talking-about-race.

Wade, Ashleigh. "Black Girls' Digital Kinship Formations." *Women, Gender, and Families of Color*, vol. 7, no. 1, spring 2019, pp. 80–97.

Waldau, Paul. *Animal Studies: An Introduction*. Oxford UP, 2013.

Walkowitz, Rebecca L. *Born Translated: The Contemporary Novel in an Age of World Literature*. Columbia UP, 2015.

Walkowitz, Rebecca L. "On Not Knowing: Lahiri, Tawada, Ishiguro." *New Literary History*, vol. 51, no. 2, spring 2020, pp. 323–46.

Wanzo, Rebecca. "Precarious-Girl Comedy: Issa Rae, Lena Dunham, and Abjection Aesthetics." *Camera Obscura*, vol. 31, no. 2, 2016, pp. 27–59.

Warner, Kristen J. "They Gon' Think You Loud Regardless: Ratchetness, Reality Television, and Black Womanhood." *Camera Obscura*, vol. 30, no. 1, 2015, pp. 129–53.

We Got Y'all. 2018, https://wegotyall.com.

Weheliye, Alexander. *Habeas Viscus: Racializing Assemblages, Biopolitics, and Black Feminist Theories of the Human*. Duke UP, 2014.

Weinbrot, Howard D. *Menippean Satire Reconsidered: From Antiquity to the Eighteenth Century*. Johns Hopkins UP, 2005.

Weisenburger, Steven. *Fables of Subversion: Satire and the American Novel*. U of Georgia P, 1995.

Wells-Barnett, Ida B. *Southern Horrors: Lynch Law in All Its Phases; On Lynchings*. Arno, 1969.

West, Cornel. *The Cornel West Reader*. Civitas Books, 1999.

White, E. Francis. *Dark Continent of Our Bodies: Black Feminism and the Politics of Respectability*. Temple UP, 2001.

Wilderson, Frank B., III. *Afropessimism*. Liveright, 2020.

Williams, Raymond. *Television: Technology and Cultural Form*. Routledge, 2003.

Williamson, Terrion L. *Scandalize My Name: Black Feminist Practice and the Making of Black Social Life*. Fordham UP, 2016.

Winters, Joseph R. *Hope Draped in Black: Race, Melancholy and the Agony of Progress*. Duke UP, 2016.

Young, Harvey. *Embodying Black Experience: Stillness, Critical Memory, and the Black Body*. U of Michigan P, 2010.

ABOUT THE CONTRIBUTORS

GerShun Avilez is professor of English and associate dean in the College of Arts and Humanities at the University of Maryland, College Park. An award-winning teacher and writer, he specializes in African American and Black diasporic literatures and visual cultures. He is author of two books: *Radical Aesthetics and Modern Black Nationalism* and *Black Queer Freedom: Spaces of Injury and Paths of Desire*. He is the coeditor of *The Norton Anthology of American Literature: 1945–Present*, 10th edition. His work has been published in journals such as *African American Review* and the *Black Scholar* and in edited volumes such as *The Cambridge History of Gay and Lesbian Literature* and *The Psychic Hold of Slavery*.

Lola Boorman is lecturer in American literature and culture at the University of York. Her work focuses on twentieth- and twenty-first-century American literature, intellectual and cultural history, and language politics. Her writing has appeared in *Twentieth-Century Literature*, *The Cambridge Companion to the American Short Story*, *Post45*, and *ASAP/J*.

Thomas Britt is professor and founding member of the Film and Video Studies Department at George Mason University. His film scripts have been awarded or selected by more than one hundred film festivals and screenplay competitions worldwide. Previous publications have appeared in *Savoirs en prisme*, *Refocus: The Films of Albert Brooks*, *New Approaches to Contemporary Adaptation*, *The Routledge History of Death since 1800*, and *Post-Soul Satire: Black Identity after Civil Rights*.

John Brooks is visiting assistant professor in the Department of Comparative Studies and the Department of Theatre, Film, and Media Arts at The Ohio State University. His research and teaching focus on African American literature and Black expressive practices from the nineteenth century to the present, interdisciplinary Africana studies with attention to sound and music, and performance studies. He is the author of *The Racial Unfamiliar: Illegibility in Black Literature and Culture*.

Phillip James Martinez Cortes is an Honors Faculty Fellow at Arizona State University. His research and teaching interests include eighteenth-century satire, moral philosophy, medical literature, literatures of disability and neurodivergence, psychoanalysis, and formalism. He has forthcoming publications on the satires of Tobias Smollett and Jane Collier.

Derek DiMatteo is assistant professor of English at Gannon University. His research focuses on American literary and cultural studies, African American literature, multiethnic literatures of the United States, protest literature, critical university studies, the transnational, English education, critical pedagogy, and first-year writing. His scholarship includes work on Paul Beatty's *Slumberland*, Teju Cole's *Open City*, Mohsin Hamid's *The Reluctant Fundamentalist*, and the film *Higher Learning*.

James J. Donahue is professor and assistant chair of the Department of English & Communication at SUNY Potsdam. He is author of *Contemporary Native Fiction: Toward a Narrative Poetics of Survivance* and *Failed Frontiersmen: White Men and Myth in the Post-Sixties American Historical Romance*. He is also coeditor of *Narrative, Race, and Ethnicity in the United States* and *Post-Soul Satire: Black Identity after Civil Rights*.

Tikenya Foster-Singletary is assistant professor of English at Clark Atlanta University. In addition to teaching literature and writing, she is a frequent presenter at the College Language Association and the Popular Culture Association of the South conferences. Her work has been published in *MAWA Review*, *Obsidian: Literature in the African Diaspora*, and *Southern Quarterly*. Along with Dr. Aisha Francis, she is coeditor of an edited volume focused on the work of playwright and novelist Pearl Cleage entitled *Pearl Cleage and Free Womanhood*.

Alexandra Glavanakova is associate professor in American literature and culture and head of the Department of English and American Studies at St. Kliment Ohridski University of Sofia, Bulgaria. Her teaching, academic research, and publications focus on the culture and literature of the United States, transcultural studies and identity, race, ethnicity, migration, as well as the major cultural shifts in literacy, education, and literary studies under the impact of digital technology. She is the author of two monographs: *Posthuman*

Transformations: Bodies and Texts in Cyberspace and *Transcultural Imaginings: Translating the Other, Translating the Self in Narratives about Migration and Terrorism*. She is also coeditor of *New Paradigms in English Studies: Language, Linguistics, Literature and Culture in Higher Education* and *Swiftian Inspirations: The Legacy of Jonathan Swift from the Enlightenment to the Age of Post-Truth*.

Erica-Brittany Horhn is assistant professor of humanities at North Carolina Central University, where she teaches courses in American humor, African American literature, and English composition. Her primary research centers Black women's lived experiences through humor and communicative patterns, and she has developed a Black women's pedagogy of humor to help Black women make sense of the world.

Matthias Klestil is postdoc assistant in American studies at the University of Klagenfurt, Austria. His research interests include ecocriticism, the Anthropocene, narrative theory, contemporary US fiction and film, and ethnic American literatures. His recent publications include articles on Colson Whitehead's *The Underground Railroad* and Ted Chiang's short fiction, as well as the monograph *Environmental Knowledge, Race, and African American Literature*.

Abigail Jinju Lee is assistant professor in the Indigenous, Race, and Ethnic Studies Department at the University of Oregon. She researches race and Asian American film, TV, and literature, exploring Asian American feminist politics of solidarity.

Derek C. Maus is professor of English at SUNY Potsdam and author of *Unvarnishing Reality: Subversive Russian and American Cold War Satire*. He is editor of *Conversations with Colson Whitehead* and coeditor of *Finding a Way Home: A Critical Assessment of Walter Mosley's Fiction* and *Post-Soul Satire: Black Identity after Civil Rights*, all published by the University Press of Mississippi.

Danielle Fuentes Morgan is associate professor in the Departments of English and Ethnic Studies at Santa Clara University. She specializes in twentieth- and twenty-first-century African American literature and culture with emphasis on African American humor and popular culture. She is author of *Laughing to Keep from Dying: African American Satire in the Twenty-First Century*. Her writing has appeared in *Biography: An Interdisciplinary Quarterly*, *Pre/Text: A Journal of Rhetorical Theory*, *Journal of Science Fiction*, *Humanities*, and *College Literature*, as well as in a variety of edited collections on African American literature and culture. She has also contributed to *Vulture*, *Racialicious*, and *Al Jazeera*.

ABOUT THE CONTRIBUTORS

Derek Conrad Murray is professor of history of art and visual culture at the University of California, Santa Cruz. He is an interdisciplinary theorist specializing in the history, theory, and criticism of contemporary art and visual culture. He is associate editor of *Nka: Journal of Contemporary African Art* and is a member of the editorial advisory boards of *Third Text* and *Visual Studies*. He is the author of the edited volume *Visual Culture Approaches to the Selfie* as well as the monographs *Mapplethorpe and the Flower: Radical Sexuality and the Limits of Control* and *Queering Post-Black Art: Artists Transforming African-American Identity after Civil Rights*.

Kinohi Nishikawa is associate professor of English and African American studies at Princeton University. He is the author of *Street Players: Black Pulp Fiction and the Making of a Literary Underground* and a contributor to *Post-Soul Satire: Black Identity after Civil Rights*. Nishikawa's essays on Black print and popular culture have been published in *PMLA*, *American Literary History*, *MELUS*, *Chicago Review*, and other journals.

Sarah O'Brien is an academic editor living in Atlanta. Her work has appeared in *Cinema Journal*, *Screen*, *Framework*, and *Atlanta Studies*. She is author of *Bits and Pieces: Screening Animal Life in Film and Television*.

Keyana Parks is assistant professor of English at the University of Massachusetts Boston. Her research and teaching interests include twentieth- and twenty-first-century African American literature, humor, satire, and Black women's writing and feminism. She has published in *Post45* and has an article forthcoming in *Approaches to Teaching the Works of Ralph Ellison*.

Emily Ruth Rutter is associate dean of the Honors College and associate professor of English at Ball State University. Rutter is the author of four scholarly monographs: *Invisible Ball of Dreams: Literary Representations of Baseball behind the Color Line*; *The Blues Muse: Race, Gender, and Musical Celebrity in American Poetry*; *Black Celebrity: Contemporary Representations of Postbellum Athletes and Artists*; and *White Lies and Allies in Contemporary Black Media*. She is coeditor of *Revisiting the Elegy in the Black Lives Matter Era*. Her scholarship also appears in *African American Review*, *MELUS*, and *Tulsa Studies in Women's Literature*.

INDEX

2Chainz, 14
30 Rock (television series), 5
50 Cent, 230

Abbott Elementary (television series), 15n3
Adjei-Brenyah, Nana Kwame, 15n3; *Chain-Gang All-Stars*, 15n3; *Friday Black*, 15n3
affect theory, 200–210
Afropessimism, 23–24, 53
Allen, Reniqua, 65
Amen (television series), 77n5
Amos 'n' Andy Show, The (television series), 157
André 3000, 253, 257
Appiah, Kwame Anthony, 25
Aristotle, 246, 252; *Ethics*, 246
Asianness, 15, 74, 99, 177, 191, 261–74, 275n2, 275n9
Askaripour, Mateo, 15n3, 198n1; *Black Buck*, 15n3, 198n1
ATL (film), 69
Atlanta (city), 12–15, 38, 44, 69, 71, 77n7, 139–41, 143–44, 146, 150, 168n1, 173, 183n3, 184n4, 194, 247–48, 253
Atlanta (television series), 5, 9–15, 20–23, 26–29, 32, 33, 34, 35–37, 38, 39, 40, 44, 45, 46, 46n2, 47n3, 47nn11–12, 49, 51–62, 62n4, 64–73, 76, 77n4, 77n8, 77n11, 81–82, 85–92, 92n1, 93n4, 93n7, 93nn9–10, 94–102, 104, 106, 107n1, 108–9, 111, 115–20, 120n1, 125–38, 138n1, 138n3, 138n7, 139–50, 151n2, 151n10, 155–68, 169n7, 169nn14–15, 169n17, 169n19, 171–83, 183nn1–3, 184n4, 184n6, 184nn8–9, 185–98, 198n2, 198n4, 198nn6–9, 199–211, 211n3, 211nn6–7, 212–21, 221n2, 222nn5–6, 222nn10–11, 223nn12–15, 223n17, 229, 234–41, 241n2, 241n7, 242n8, 243–46, 248–57, 257n1, 258n2, 258n5, 258n11, 258n14, 261–70, 274, 275nn8–9
—characters: Ahmad White, 145, 146–47; Alex, 175, 177; Alexander Skarsgård, 198n9; Alfred/Paper Boi, 5, 8–9, 11, 14, 15, 27–29, 33, 35–37, 47n3, 51–54, 56, 60–62, 69, 72, 77n4, 77n11, 81–82, 87–90, 93nn7–8, 97–100, 116–20, 128–31, 138n3, 140–41, 145–50, 151n2, 155, 160, 168, 169n19, 174–78, 185–94, 196, 198n2, 198n7, 199, 201–10, 214, 220, 234–37, 240, 241n7, 244–46, 248–57, 257n1, 258n2, 258n11, 264–65, 267–68, 270, 275n9; Amber, 91, 93n10; Antoine Smalls/Harrison Booth, 97–99, 169n19, 262, 264–66; Benny Hope, 57, 100–101, 131, 182–83, 237–39, 266; Blueblood, 11, 146; Candice, 223n14; Chris, 174–75, 177, 211n3; Christina, 195, 198n8, 210; Ciara, 147, 150, 235–36; Clark County, 52, 191, 193, 250–52, 254–56; Craig, 86–87, 99, 118, 163–65, 190–91, 196; Darius, 5, 12, 27, 28, 47nn11–12, 54–62, 62n4, 69, 77n4, 93n8, 100–101, 118, 125, 127–37, 138n1, 138n7, 140, 142, 144–45, 147, 150, 155, 169nn14–15, 171, 173, 179–83, 189, 191, 214–15, 218–19, 222n10, 223n15, 237–39, 248, 250, 253–54, 265–66, 268–70, 275n9; Dave, 28, 72–73, 87–90,

295

296

INDEX

92, 93n8, 189–90; Dr. Deborah Holt, 97, 169n19, 265; Demarcus, 11–12; Devin, 174–78, 257; Duncan, 88–89; Earn, 5, 11, 14, 15, 21, 26–29, 33, 35–37, 44, 45, 47n11, 51–54, 56, 57–62, 62n13, 69, 71–73, 77n4, 86–92, 93n8, 99, 109, 115–20, 128–33, 138n3, 139–40, 143, 144–45, 147, 155–57, 158–60, 162–68, 169n7, 169n15, 169n20, 171, 173–79, 181, 183n1, 185–97, 198n4, 198nn6–8, 207–10, 214, 217, 220, 222n6, 222nn10–11, 234, 238, 240, 241n7, 244–46, 248–57, 267–70, 275nn8–9; Gayle, 91, 93n10; Jayde, 159–60, 162, 166, 207–10, 216; Johnny, 29, 35, 37, 40, 44; Johnny Lee, 175, 177; Justin Bieber, 14, 52, 99, 100, 201–6, 211, 211n7, 234–35, 253; Khalil, 47n11; Kirkwood Chocolate, 11, 14, 166–67; Lisa, 29, 35, 37, 40, 44; Loquareeous, 91, 93n10; Lorraine (Alfred's mother), 147, 150, 151n10, 178; Lorraine (in "New Jazz"), 47n3, 47n11, 52, 150, 151n10; Lottie, 11, 27, 86, 117, 119, 160, 165, 166–68, 169n20, 195, 197, 208–9, 214, 222n10, 244, 251, 253; Lucas, 15, 73, 191, 250–51, 256; Mark, 174–75, 177; Monique, 86–87, 99, 118, 162–66, 196; Myra, 115, 117, 173–74, 178–79; Nadine, 218–19, 223n15; Prescott, 88–90, 93n9; Raleigh, 116–17, 191; Socks, 92, 191; Teddy Perkins, 56, 57, 100–101, 131, 171, 174, 179–83, 184n9, 237–40, 262, 266; Thomas Washington, 11, 145, 184n8; Tobias Walner, 161–62, 163, 167, 189, 217, 221; Tracy, 56–62, 62n13, 69, 87–90, 93n8, 129–30, 255; Uncle Willy, 139, 145, 146, 256, 258n15; Valencia Joyner, 193–94, 202–3, 235, 253; Van, 5, 11, 14, 27, 69, 100, 118, 119–20, 150, 155–57, 158–68, 169n7, 169nn14–15, 169n17, 187, 189, 194–97, 198n4, 198nn8–9, 199, 201, 207–10, 213–21, 222n6, 222nn10–11, 223nn12–14, 244, 251, 252, 275n9; Wally, 146–48, 236, 239, 242n8; Zan, 99–100, 104, 131–32, 141, 219, 251, 262, 267–70, 274

—episodes: "Alligator Man," 10, 49, 127, 139–40, 143, 144, 145–46, 253–54, 256; "Andrew Wyeth: Alfred's World," 9, 29, 132, 140, 146, 189–90, 258n2; "B.A.N.," 49, 77n11, 97–99, 143, 145, 169n19, 193, 251, 264–67; "The Big Bang," 13, 14, 15, 20, 28, 35, 51, 69, 71, 77n8, 116–18, 125, 143, 145, 147, 159, 160, 185–93, 198n7, 215, 248–49, 251–52, 254; "The Big Payback," 92, 101; "Born 2 Die," 62n4, 92, 191, 222n11, 258n11; "Cancer Attack," 92, 191, 258n14; "Champagne Papi," 127, 191, 212–21, 222n11, 223nn12–14, 223n17, 254, 258n5; "The Club," 127, 128, 148–49, 220, 252, 253; "Crabs in a Barrel," 10, 15, 73, 119, 127, 252, 256; "Crank Dat Killer," 47n11, 183n2, 258n2; "FUBU," 14, 71, 115–16, 171–79, 181, 183, 183n4, 256–57; "Go for Broke," 169n15, 252, 258n5; "The Goof Who Sat by the Door," 11, 15n4, 34n6, 101, 135, 140, 144, 145, 151n2, 184n8; "Helen," 27, 140, 158, 166–68, 183n3, 194–97, 198n4, 198n8, 209–10, 211n3, 222n6; "The Homeliest Little Horse," 15, 34n2, 51, 62n13, 73, 92, 109, 116, 151n2, 168, 198n6, 251; "It Was All a Dream," 11–12, 62n4, 125, 127–28, 211n3, 222n10, 275n9; "The Jacket," 132, 252–53, 257; "Juneteenth," 73, 77n15, 86–87, 118, 158–59, 162–66, 190–91, 193, 196–97, 251; "Light-Skinned-ed," 14, 101; "Money Bag Shawty," 51–53, 56, 117–18, 138n7, 250–51, 254, 256; "The Most Atlanta," 11, 143, 146, 222n6; "New Jazz," 34n6, 47n3, 47n11, 52, 135, 144, 150, 151n2, 151n10, 255, 257n1, 258n14; "Nobody Beats the Biebs," 52, 57–58, 93n8, 99, 100, 127, 133–37, 142, 193–94, 201–6, 211, 234–35, 238–39, 241n7, 252, 253; "North of the Border," 60–61, 87–90, 93nn8–9, 180, 183n3, 245, 252, 255; "The Old Man and the Tree," 53–54, 92, 191; "Rich Wigga, Poor Wigga," 92, 101, 183n2, 184n6; "Sinterklaas Is Coming to Town," 51, 92, 169n14, 257n1; "Snipe Hunt," 132, 140, 166–68, 222n6; "Sportin' Waves," 52, 57–59, 118, 129, 145, 191, 193, 205–6, 252, 254, 275n8; "Streets on Lock," 28–29, 35–37, 40, 44, 45, 46, 47n3, 49, 145, 191, 249–51, 253, 254–55; "The Streisand Effect," 52, 57, 99–100, 104,

128–29, 131–33, 137, 145, 155, 191, 219, 251, 267–70, 274; "Tarrare," 27, 169n17, 198n9, 222n6, 223n14; "Teddy Perkins," 54–56, 57, 92n1, 100–101, 127, 131, 140, 171–74, 179–83, 184n9, 189, 214, 220–21, 236–40, 254, 265–66; "Three Slaps," 10, 13, 90–92, 93n10, 107n1, 136, 140, 144, 151n2; "Trini 2 De Bone," 92; "Value," 100, 158–62, 189, 207–10, 216–17, 221, 222n6; "White Fashion," 34n6, 47n11, 53, 92, 128, 183n2, 198n2, 258n14; "Woods," 28, 81–82, 90, 93n7, 140–41, 146–50, 151n10, 189, 214, 220–21, 235–36, 238, 242n8, 254–55; "Work Ethic!," 11, 14, 34n6, 166–67, 211n3, 222n6
Austen, Jake, 211n2
Awkwafina, 263, 275n2
Awkward, Michael, 96

Bailey, Moya, 168n4
Bakhtin, Mikhail, 187, 189
Baldwin, James, 7, 73, 104
Bastién, Angelica Jade, 15n2, 29–30, 186, 193
Beatty, Paul, 13, 36, 38–46, 47n12, 69, 156, 158, 263, 275n1; *Hokum*, 156; *The Sellout*, 13, 36, 38–46, 47nn4–6, 47n10, 69, 158; *Tuff*, 263; *The White Boy Shuffle*, 46, 69, 275n1
Beetz, Zazie, 5, 69, 100, 150, 155, 158, 187, 198n4, 199, 213, 221n1
Bell, W. Kamau, 15n3
Bennett, Joshua, 140, 148, 150
Bennett, Michael, 132
Beyoncé, 65, 73, 77n16
Bhabha, Homi K., 21, 26
Bieber, Justin, 52, 201, 206, 211nn6–7, 234
Big Tymers, 255–56; "#1 Stunna," 255–56; "Still Fly," 256
Biz Markie, 213; "Nobody Beats the Biz," 213
Black-ish (television series), 15n3, 142
Black Lady Sketch Show, A (television series), 15n3
Black Lives Matter, 22, 64, 93n10
Blackness, 9, 10–12, 19–34, 35, 38, 40, 45, 46, 51–52, 53, 62, 63–76, 96, 99–106, 108–20, 126, 140–42, 148–50, 155–68, 171–83, 183n2, 186, 189, 194–95, 198n4, 200, 206, 211n7, 213–21, 230, 235, 237–38, 261–74, 275n9; and authenticity, 27, 30–32, 33, 34n5, 98–100, 101, 106, 108–9, 117–20, 121n8, 162, 171, 175–79, 184n8, 190, 192, 236, 249; and fetishization, 23, 25, 26, 82–90, 92, 93n5, 102, 105, 271, 275n2; and masculinity, 68, 117–18, 141, 146, 148, 155–58, 162–65, 168, 169n19, 174–78, 188, 194, 215–16, 220, 228–30, 232, 236–40, 251, 253, 271; and respectability, 14, 64, 109–20, 155–56, 158–65, 168, 168n2, 178–79, 196; and trauma, 12, 19, 23–26, 29–34, 66, 93n6, 100–101, 105, 171–72, 179–83, 237–39, 266; and women, 14, 30, 67–68, 71, 155–62, 164–68, 168n2, 168n4, 172, 194–95, 201, 207–10, 212–21, 222n6, 223n13
Black Wall Street Massacre, 13
Blank, Radha, 13, 29, 30, 77n13; *The Forty-Year-Old Version*, 13, 20, 29, 30–32, 33, 34, 77n13
Blaxploitation films, 21, 148
Blount, Tommye, 148
Bogle, Donald, 148
Boisseron, Bénédicte, 126, 131, 136, 138n2, 138n4, 138n10, 140, 142, 144, 146
Bordwell, David, 247
Bostrom, Nick, 218
Bradley, Regina M., 12
Bradley, Stefan M., 110, 112
Bravo, Janicza, 15n3; *Lemon*, 15n3; *Zola*, 15n3
Brewer, Craig, 243; *Hustle & Flow*, 14, 243–44, 246–49, 251, 254
Brown, James, 100
Brown, Michael, 5, 65
Brown, Robert A., 4
Broyard, Anatole, 104
Bunyasi, Tehama Lopez, 83
Burke, Kenneth, 204–5
Bush, Gerard, 29; *Antebellum*, 20, 29–30
Butler, Judith, 33–34
Butler, Octavia, 222n4

Cam'ron, 56
Carmichael Show, The (television series), 15n3

Carpenter, Faedra Chatard, 161
Carpio, Glenda R., 96, 146
Cassin, Barbara, 189
Chamberlain, Wilt, 268
Chan, Jackie, 256
Chappelle, Dave, 6, 64, 77n2; *Chappelle's Show*, 263
Charity, Justin, 15n2, 19
Charles, Julia, 95, 97, 101–2, 107n3
Childish Gambino, 5, 14, 67, 163, 192, 227–32, 234, 240, 241n1, 272; "3005," 227–32, 238, 241n1, 241n3; *Because the Internet*, 14, 227, 229–30; *Camp*, 67; *Clapping for the Wrong Reasons*, 230; "Outside," 67; *Redbone*, 163; "Telegraph Ave.," 230–32; "This Is America," 5, 241n2, 272
Chin, Frank, 263; *The Chickencoop Chinaman*, 263
Cho, Margaret, 263
Claborn, John, 138n2
Clinton, Bill, 238
Coates, Ta-Nehisi, 65
Coel, Michaela, 221n2; *I May Destroy You*, 221n2
Cole, Bob, 262
Coleman, Robin R. Means, 241n6
Collins, Patricia Hill, 156–57
Community (television series), 5, 69, 143, 151n7
Confederate flag, 12, 54–55, 60–61, 62n11, 88–89, 93n8, 180
Conway, Kellyanne, 9
Cosby Show, The (television series), 104, 142
Coscarelli, Joe, 21
Cousins, Linwood, 108
COVID-19 pandemic, 3, 5, 9
Crenshaw, Kimberlé Williams, 4, 62n3
Crime Mob, 149; "Knuck If You Buck," 149
criminal justice system, 28–29, 35–37, 46n2, 49, 85, 87, 182, 249–50, 258n7, 273–74
Curb Your Enthusiasm (television series), 65

D4L, 61, 89, 180; "Laffy Taffy," 61, 89, 180
DaCosta, Nia, *Candyman*, 20
D'Angelo, 222n11
David, Larry, 66

Davis, Miles, 275n10
Davis, Shardé M., 230
Deep Space Nine (television series), 121n8
de la Bruyère, Jean, 245–46, 253; *The Characters of Theophrastus*, 245, 253
Delfonics, 146; "Hey Love," 146
Diallo, Mariama, *Master*, 20
Dickson-Carr, Darryl, 7, 8, 20, 22, 95–96, 127–28, 157–58, 169n10
Different World, A (television series), 67–69, 77n6
Diff'rent Strokes (television series), 77n5
Dixon, Ivan, 15n4; *The Spook Who Sat by the Door* (film), 15n4
dogs, 14, 57–58, 125–38, 138n1, 139–40, 141–42, 145, 146, 151n2, 151n5, 241n1, 269–70
Dolezal, Rachel, 96–97, 107n2, 266
Donahue, James J., 121n13
Drake, 127, 213–19, 221, 222n11, 223n17, 258n5
Du Bois, W. E. B., 62n3, 73, 110, 141–42, 150
Ducotey, Yvelin, 13
Durant, Kevin, 68
Dylan, Jesse, 121n5; *How High*, 121n5

Earl Sweatshirt, 230
ecocriticism, 125–27, 130–38, 138n2
Edmond, Maura, 241n4
Edmonds, Brittney M., 15n1
educational system, 13, 38–39, 51, 67–68, 74–76, 108–20, 121n5, 161–62, 174–79, 183, 199, 209
Elam, Michelle, 107n6
Ellis, Trey, 64, 108, 115, 120
Ellison, Ralph, 242n8; *Invisible Man*, 242n8
empathy, 23, 26, 34, 85, 99, 131, 181–82, 199–200, 204–5, 207, 210
Empire (television series), 143
Evans, Danielle, 15n3; *The Office of Historical Corrections*, 15n3
Everett, Percival, 15n3, 39, 54–55, 187; "The Appropriation of Cultures," 54–55; *Dr. No*, 15n3; *Erasure*, 39; *The Trees*, 15n3

Fairey, Shepard, 3
Family Matters (television series), 77n6, 142

Family Ties (television series), 142
Fanon, Frantz, 26
Fauset, Jessie Redmon, 266; *Plum Bun*, 266
Finley, Jessyka, 67, 76, 87
Fisher, Rudolph, 7
Flack, Roberta, 220; "Compared to What," 220
Fleabag (television series), 213
Fleetwood, Nicole R., 158
Francis, Terri S., 157
Fresh Prince of Bel-Air, The (television series), 68, 142
Friends (television series), 142
Frye, Northrop, 49–51, 53, 62n1, 187
Full House (television series), 71
Fumodoh, Ziwe, 77n1
Future, 243; *F.B.G: The Movie*, 243; "See It to Believe It," 243

Gaines, Kevin, 110
Garner, Eric, 5
Gates, Henry Louis, Jr., 101, 102, 104, 113, 188–90, 192
Gaye, Marvin, 237
Gillespie, Carmen, 94
Gillota, David, 76
Gilmore, John T., 245
Giltner, Scott, 138n5
Girls (television series), 213
Glover, Donald, 5, 9–10, 12, 14, 20, 26, 35, 36, 38, 44, 45, 47n12, 51, 53, 64, 66–70, 77n2, 77n7, 82, 85, 92, 96, 99, 100, 115, 128, 140, 149, 151n7, 155, 158, 166, 169n13, 182, 185, 199, 211n6, 214, 218–19, 228–29, 231, 234–41, 241n2, 244, 248, 250, 262; as Childish Gambino, 5, 14, 67, 163, 192, 227–32, 234, 240, 241n1, 248, 272
Glover, Stephen, 5, 10, 14, 235
Godfrey, Mollie, 266–67
Good Times (television series), 77n4
Goofy Movie, A (film), 11, 101, 184n8, 211n3
Gould, Gaylene, 65–66, 77n2
Gray, Herman, 142
Green, Misha, 222n4; *Lovecraft Country* (television series), 93n2, 222n4
Greenberg, Jonathan, 95, 100, 142, 143

Greenidge, Kaitlyn, 7, 158; *We Love You, Charlie Freeman*, 7
Greenlee, Sam, 15n4; *The Spook Who Sat by the Door* (novel), 15n4
Griffin, Dustin, 187
Griffith, D. W., 148; *Birth of a Nation*, 148
Gucci Mane, 250
Guerrero, Lisa A., 5–6, 8, 9, 96, 101, 171–73, 178, 180–82, 186
Gunna, 250, 258n7

Haggins, Bambi, 142
Hall, Stuart, 26, 108
Haney-López, Ian F., 112
Hansberry, Lorraine, 209; *A Raisin in the Sun*, 209
Harris, Cheryl I., 264
Harris, Jeremy O., 15n3, 39, 47n7, 77n10; *Slave Play*, 15n3, 39, 47n7, 77n10
Harrison, Sheri, 190
Harrison-Kahan, Lori, 95
Harris-Perry, Melissa V., 169n6, 172–73, 179, 182–83, 207–8
Hartman, Saidiya, 23, 53
Hatcher, Carlene Polite, 158
Hayes, Terrance, 15n3, 148; *American Sonnet for My Past and Future Assassin*, 15n3
Hegel, Georg Wilhelm Friedrich, 33–34
Henry, Brian Tyree, 5, 27, 35, 52, 69, 97, 116, 128, 140, 150, 155, 185, 199, 214, 234, 244
Hicks, Scott, 138n2
Higginbotham, Evelyn B., 168n2
hip hop, 14, 32, 56, 60–61, 69, 81–82, 87–89, 92, 119, 149, 173, 183n2, 185, 192–94, 202, 204–6, 228–30, 243–57, 265, 267–68
Ho, Jennifer Ann, 274
Hobson, Maurice J., 141
Hobson, Mellody, 110
Hoggart, Richard, 111, 120n4
Holland, Sharon Patricia, 25–26
hooks, bell, 39, 82, 84, 86–87, 88, 89, 90, 92, 137, 157
horror (genre), 82, 84–86, 92, 229, 231, 233–38, 241n6; and comic tone, 82, 84–86, 92, 93n2, 190, 212–13, 232, 235
Houston, Whitney, 104

Hughes, Akilah, 20
Hughes, Langston, 7, 257; "Mother to Son," 257
Hurricane Katrina, 65
Hutcheon, Linda, 51, 54, 201, 204–5, 211n4
Hwang, David Henry, 263; *Yellowface*, 263

Irby, Samantha, 15n3

Jackson, Austin, 176
Jackson, Leigh-Ann, 178
Jackson, Michael, 100, 182, 214, 232–34, 237–38, 240, 241n6, 266; "Thriller," 232–34
Jackson, Ronald L., II, 201–2, 204, 211n1
Jacobs-Jenkins, Branden, 15n3, 39; *Gloria*, 15n3; *An Octoroon*, 39
James, Darius, 39; *Negrophobia*, 39
James, LeBron, 68, 211n7
James, Marlon, 194
Jay-Z, 230
Jeezy, 243, 249; *Let's Get It: Thug Motivation 101*, 243; "Streets on Lock," 249; "Thug Motivation 101," 243
Jeffersons, The (television series), 77n5
Jemisin, N. K., 222n4; *Broken Earth* (series of novels), 222n4
Jenkins, Barry, 181; *Moonlight*, 181
Jenner, Caitlyn, 97, 264–65
Jerng, Mark C., 172, 182
Jewell, K. S., 169n6
Johnson, Lindgren, 138n2, 138n5, 138n10, 140
Johnson, Mat, 15n3; *Invisible Things*, 15n3; *Loving Day*, 15n3
Johnson, T. Geronimo, 15n3; *Welcome to Braggsville*, 15n3
Jordan, Michael, 211n7
Juvenal, 106; *Satires*, 106

Kaufman, Burton I., 4, 6
Keith Ape, 269; "It G Ma," 269
Kemp, Jerome, 246
Key, Keegan-Michael, 76
Key & Peele (television series), 189
Kincaid, Jamaica, 33
King, Martin Luther, Jr., 73, 118, 188
King, Rodney, 65
King, Stephen, 241n6

Kingston, Maxine Hong, 263; *Tripmaster Monkey*, 263
Kirkland, David E., 176
Kiwanuka, Michael, 132, 270; "Home Again," 132, 270
Knievel, Evel, 256
Knight, Charles A., 126
Knutson, Harold C., 246
Kopp, Luvena, 199
Kravitz, Lenny, 263
Kubrick, Stanley, 163; *Eyes Wide Shut*, 163

Landis, John, 232–34, 238; *An American Werewolf in London*, 232, 233; *Michael Jackson's Thriller*, 232–34, 238, 240, 241n6
Larsen, Nella, 266; *Passing*, 266
Last O.G., The (television series), 15n3
Lee, Spike, 15n3, 64, 77n2, 157, 163, 189, 199, 211n3; *Bamboozled*, 39, 157–58, 163, 199–200; *BlacKkKlansman*, 15n3, 189; *Chi-Raq*, 15n3
Leverette, Tru, 106, 194
Levinas, Emmanuel, 25
Ligon, Glenn, 200
Little Marvin, 29
Little Richard, 100
Living Single (television series), 67–69, 142
Locke, John, 244–45
Lott, Eric, 82, 93n5
Love (television series), 213
Lubiano, Wahneema, 156
Ludacris, 14, 211n7, 251
Lupe Fiasco, 230
Lynch, David, 149; *Twin Peaks* (television series), 149

Mack, Maynard, 186
Malcolm X, 59, 86, 118, 164, 175, 188
Manning, Brandon J., 13, 15n1, 36, 47n13, 63–64, 67, 68, 77n1
Mansbach, Adam, 6; *Angry White Black Boy*, 6
Mapplethorpe, Robert, 26
Markley, Scott N., 143
Marriott, David, 26
Martin, Trayvon, 5

Maslow, Abraham, 215
Masschelein, Anneleen, 215
Master of None (television series), 263
Maus, Derek C., 6, 108, 121n6, 125–26, 187
McAllister, Marvin, 263
McCormick, Joseph P., II, 4
McGehee, Molly, 184n5
McKittrick, Katherine, 265
McQueen, Steve (actor), 268–69
McQueen, Steve (film director), 128, 275n6; *Hunger*, 275n6; *Shame*, 275n6; *Twelve Years a Slave*, 275n6
Memento (film), 255
Mercer, Kobena, 233–34, 237, 241n5
Meyer, John C., 95
MF Doom, 11
Migos, 258n5
Mills, Charles W., 50
minstrelsy, 14, 32, 93n5, 199–211, 211nn1–3, 211n7
mixed-race identity, 13, 27, 67, 94–96, 99–100, 102–6, 114, 194–95, 274; and transracialism, 95–102, 106, 107n1, 169n19, 262, 264–66
Mohai, Paul, 138n9
Monáe, Janelle, 30
Morgan, Danielle Fuentes, 6, 8, 9, 12, 13, 38, 63–65, 98, 101, 108–9, 114, 120, 162, 172, 178, 181, 199–200; and kaleidoscopic Blackness, 9, 63, 69, 70, 109, 114, 120, 172, 178
Morris, Wesley, 92
Moten, Fred, 262, 265–66, 274
Moynihan Report, 159
Muñoz, José Esteban, 200
Murai, Hiro, 5, 14, 229–32, 234–38, 240–41, 272
Murfin, Ross C., 200–201
Murphy, Eddie, 98
Murray, Derek Conrad, 199
music industry, 28, 52, 56, 62n6, 69, 72–73, 86, 89–90, 92, 100–101, 164, 169n20, 187–88, 192–94, 199, 203–6, 234–36, 245, 248, 250–57, 258n11

Nabers, Janine, 166
Nakamura, Lisa, 23, 26
Nakkula, Michael, 121n7
Napper, George, 112
Neal, Mark Anthony, 64–65, 169n20
New Girl (television series), 65
Nigeria, 127–29, 269
Nishikawa, Kinohi, 192, 228
Notorious B.I.G., 243; "Juicy," 243; *Ready to Die*, 243

Obama, Barack, 3, 7, 64, 73, 83, 98, 113, 189; presidency of, 4–5, 7, 65, 110, 112, 143
Obama, Michelle (Robinson), 110–11
Office, The (television series), 65
O'Reilly, Bill, 56
Oscarville, 13
Outkast, 12, 14, 15, 252–53, 257; "Elevators (Me & You)," 253, 257; *Southernplayalisticadillacmuzik*, 12; "Welcome to Atlanta," 12, 14

Painter, Nell Irwin, 94
Pareles, Jon, 249
Parker, Kim, 274
Parker, Morgan, 15n3; *Magical Negro*, 15n3
Parks, Keyana, 66
Parks, Suzan-Lori, 39; *The Red Letter Plays*, 39
Parks and Recreation (television series), 143
Parry, Tyler D., 126, 130
pastoral, 126, 130, 132–33, 144
Peele, Jordan, 13, 29, 76, 82–85, 87, 89, 148, 222n4, 223n16; *Get Out*, 13, 19–20, 222n4; *Nope*, 222n4; *Us*, 20, 82–87, 89, 90, 92, 92n11, 93n6, 148, 150, 222n4, 223n16
Penny, Prentice, 70–71
Perry, Imani, 85
Perry, Tyler, 11, 166, 211n3
Pickens, Theri, 170n22, 179
police violence, 5, 12, 22, 28, 49, 57, 65, 87, 139, 264, 273
Post Malone, 89

Queen Sugar (television series), 143
queerness, 13, 29, 31, 35–38, 40, 42–46, 46n2, 47n3, 47n7, 47nn10–11, 47n13, 97, 114–15, 169n7, 169n19, 233, 264–65

race, 4–5, 22, 94–106, 107n1, 127, 133–36, 171–83, 201, 229, 251, 261–74; and language, 7, 14, 68, 180, 185–98, 206; and postracialism, 3, 4, 45, 65, 94, 96, 103, 106, 112–13, 130–31, 142–43, 213–14; and representation, 22–26, 29–34, 59, 67, 140–41, 156–58, 160, 166–67, 171–72, 176–83, 183n2, 184n6, 199–211, 271–74; and segregation, 38–44, 64–65; and socioeconomics, 27–29, 31–32, 38, 51–52, 66, 68, 75–76, 104–5, 108–16, 118–20, 129–33, 136–38, 143–44, 146, 156, 162–66, 175–77, 179, 182, 191–92, 195–97, 203, 205, 208, 213–14, 251, 270

racism, 6–9, 21–26, 28–29, 38–44, 45, 46, 49–62, 65–67, 97, 101, 105–6, 108, 110, 112–17, 125–26, 130–31, 132–33, 135–37, 146, 157–58, 163, 168n2, 198n2, 199–202, 204, 206, 211n3, 215, 265, 272–74

Rae, Issa, 13, 64, 65–70, 72, 74, 75, 77n2, 77n7, 213; *Insecure*, 64, 65–71, 73–76, 77n4, 77n16, 143, 158, 213, 222n3, 263; *The Misadventures of Awkward Black Girl*, 65–66, 67, 70

Raleigh, Elizabeth, 96

Rankine, Claudia, 169n5; *Citizen: An American Lyric*, 169n5

Ray, Sarah Jaquette, 133

Ray, Supryia M., 200–201

Reed, Ishmael, 157–58, 169n9, 263; *Flight to Canada*, 157–58, 169n8; *Japanese by Spring*, 263

Reid, Kiley, 15n3; *Such a Fun Age*, 15n3

Renz, Christopher, 29; *Antebellum*, 20, 29–30

Riley, Boots, 15n3, 189; *Sorry to Bother You*, 15n3, 189, 191

Robinson, Craig, 69

Robinson, Stefani, 236

Rock, Chris, 6, 64, 77n2, 98

Root, Maria P. P., 102

Roots (television miniseries), 104

Roseanne (television series), 71

Ross, Fran, 158, 187, 194; *Oreo*, 187, 194–95

Ross, Janelle, 4

Rowe, Kathleen, 216

Ruff, Matt, 222n4; *Lovecraft Country* (novel), 222n4

Ruffin, Kimberly N., 130

Ruffin, Maurice Carlos, 15n3; *We Cast a Shadow*, 15n3

Russell, Damon, 243; *Snow on tha Bluff*, 14, 243–44, 247–48, 253, 258nn3–4

Russell, Margaret M., 120

Rutheiser, Charles, 144

Saadiq, Raphael, 230

satire, 5–10, 13–15, 20–22, 27–34, 35–41, 43, 45–46, 47n11, 49–62, 63–76, 82–92, 95–106, 108–9, 112–20, 125–38, 140–44, 146–50, 155–68, 169n10, 171–73, 179–83, 185–97, 198n1, 212–21, 228–29, 234–36, 240–41, 241n6, 243–45, 261–73; contemporary characteristics of, 5–9, 12, 13, 36, 47n13, 63–69, 125–26, 142–44, 182, 186, 213–14; degenerative/subversive definition of, 51, 54–62, 68–69, 157–58, 169n10, 186–87; Horatian variety of, 108, 126; and hyperrealism, 156–58, 161, 166–68, 172–73; and irony, 6, 14, 27–28, 36, 44, 46, 74, 98–99, 103, 117, 119–20, 126, 133, 158–60, 165, 188–89, 197, 199–211, 211n4, 215, 218, 250, 257, 261, 272; Juvenalian variety of, 108, 126–27; Menippean variety of, 186–87; normative definition of, 49–51, 52, 54, 55–62, 186; and parody, 11, 16n4, 39–40, 46, 51, 54–55, 57–58, 62n4, 67, 70–71, 77n16, 93n10, 98, 166, 182, 192, 205, 211n3, 228, 233; and the post-soul aesthetic, 6–7, 64–65, 109; and surrealism, 156–58, 160–68, 169n19, 171, 198n4, 212–14, 216–21, 223n17; and the uncanny, 144, 194, 198n4, 212–21, 238, 240

Saturday Night Live, 6, 98

Schuyler, George S., 7, 102; *Black No More*, 102

Scott, Rion Amilcar, 15n3; *The World Doesn't Require You*, 15n3

Scrubs (television series), 143

Seinfeld (television series), 65

Seinfeld, Jerry, 66

Senna, Danzy, 13, 94, 96, 102–3, 106, 198n1; *Caucasia*, 102–3; "Mulatto Millennium," 102; *New People*, 13, 94–96, 102–6, 198n1

INDEX

Serling, Rod, 231; *The Twilight Zone*, 14, 212, 214–21, 222nn7–8, 223n16, 223n18
Seymour, Nicole, 126–27, 134–36
Shakur, Tupac, 249
Shange, Ntozake, 165; *for colored girls who have considered suicide when the rainbow is enuf*, 165–66, 170n21
Shaw, Todd C., 4
Simien, Justin, 13, 47n13, 93n3, 111; *Bad Hair*, 93n2; *Dear White People* (film), 13, 108–9, 111–17, 120, 120n1, 121n5, 121n8, 121n10; *Dear White People* (television series), 47n13, 120n1
Simpson, Tyrone, 66–67
Singleton, John, 121n5; *Higher Learning*, 121n5
situation comedy, 20, 65–66, 67–69, 142–45, 149
slavery, 23, 39–44, 50, 60–61, 70, 77n10, 85, 89–91, 92, 94, 127, 130, 132, 157, 163, 207, 255
Smith, Candis Watts, 83
Smith, Jeanne Rosier, 128
Smith, Kimberly K., 138n2
Sollors, Werner, 102
Sosa, Sammy, 237
Soulja Boy, 258n2
speculative fiction, 213–14, 218, 221, 222n4
Stanfield, LaKeith, 5, 27, 54, 69, 87, 100, 118, 125, 140, 155, 173, 189, 214, 238, 248, 265
Star Trek, 113, 121n8
Stephens, Vincent L., 94
stereotypes, 14, 21–22, 26, 31–32, 38, 41, 46, 47n11, 69–70, 94, 98–99, 101–2, 108–20, 125–27, 132–34, 136–37, 141, 148, 155–68, 169n6, 169n20, 172, 199–210, 211n1, 228–29, 253, 262, 269, 273
Stewart, Anthony, 94
Sykes, Wanda, 64, 77n2
Syms, Martine, 15n3

Tan, Andrew, 263
Tatum, Beverly Daniel, 112, 115, 121n7
Tay-K, 254
Taylor, Brandon, 15n3; *Real Life*, 15n3
Taylor, Yuval, 211n2

Terry, Chris L., 15n3; *Black Card*, 15n3
Terry, Sierriana, 143, 149
Them (television series), 13, 20, 29, 30, 32–33
Them Two, 90; "Am I a Good Man?," 90
Theophrastus, 245–46
Thomas, Mickalene, 15n3
Thompson-Spires, Nafissa, 15n3; *Heads of the Colored People*, 15n3
Thurman, Wallace, 7
Thurston, Baratunde, 15n3
Tillet, Salamishah, 8, 47n9, 53, 70
transgender identity, 35, 37, 47n3, 264–65
trickster, 126–31, 133, 137, 138n3, 146
Trump, Donald, 4–5, 6, 55, 64
Tucker, Terrence T., 5, 7, 8, 180, 183
Turner, Ike, 275n10
Turner, Tina, 170n23
Twenties (television series), 15n3
Tyler, Tom, 141

Underground Railroad, The (television series), 20
Usher, 230

Van Peebles, Melvin, 33, 262–63; *A Bear for the FBI (Un Ours Pour le FBI)*, 33; *Watermelon Man*, 263
Verhoeven, Monique, 121n7
Verschelden, Cia, 115, 117
Vick, Michael, 138n7
Vollmer, Laura J., 121n5

Wade, Ashleigh, 218
Waldau, Paul, 135
Walker, Kara, 15n3
Walkowitz, Rebecca, 189–91
Wanzo, Rebecca, 66, 70
Warner, Kristen J., 170n22
Washington, Booker T., 73, 110
Wayans, Keenen Ivory, 263; *White Chicks*, 263
Weems, Carrie Mae, 15n3
Weheliye, Alexander, 26
Weinbrot, Howard D., 186
Weisenburger, Steven, 51, 169n10
Wells-Barnett, Ida B., 112, 121n6

West, Cornel, 27
Westbrook, Russell, 68
Whale, James, 238; *The Invisible Man*, 238
What's Happening!! (television series), 77n5
What's Love Got to Do with It? (film), 166, 170n23
White, E. Francis, 168n2
Whitehead, Colson, 198n1, 222n4; *Apex Hides the Hurt*, 198n1; *The Intuitionist*, 222n4; *Sag Harbor*, 198n1; *Zone One*, 222n4
whiteness, 6, 7, 8, 9, 10, 13–14, 24, 31–32, 43, 44, 47n10, 52, 53, 55–56, 59–61, 70–76, 81–92, 97, 98, 100–101, 103–5, 108–11, 118, 135–36, 156, 161, 167, 168, 169n19, 175, 178, 179–83, 183n2, 189, 190–91, 194–95, 197, 198n4, 200, 206–7, 235, 250–51, 258n11, 261–66, 270–74, 275n6; and liberalism, 6–8, 19, 23, 31–32, 50–62, 71–76, 83–87, 90–92, 110–13, 164, 206, 273; and white supremacy, 3, 8, 9, 30, 55–56, 59–61, 66, 82–83, 86, 88–92, 102, 131, 137, 158, 173, 179–80, 199, 207, 272, 274
Wilder, Craig Steven, 121n10

Wilderson, Frank B., III, 23–24
Will & Grace (television series), 71
Williams, Katt, 139, 256, 258n15
Williams, Raymond, 145
Williams, Serena, 169n5, 198n8, 237
Williamson, Terrion L., 160
Wilmore, Larry, 4–5, 76
Winters, Joseph R., 197
Wire, The (television series), 22
Wonder, Stevie, 173; "Sweet Little Girl," 173
Woods, Tiger, 263
Wu-Tang Clan, 263

Yamashita, Karen Tei, 263
Yang, Bowen, 263
Yingling, Charlton W., 126, 130
Young, Harvey, 265
Young, Vershawn Ashanti, 266–67
Young Thug, 250, 258n7; "Paid the Fine," 250
Yu, Charles, 15, 261, 263–64, 270; *Interior Chinatown*, 15, 261–64, 270–74

Ziwe (television series), 15n3, 275n10